WOODWORKERS' ESSENTIAL

Facts, Formulas & Short-Cuts

WOODWORKERS' ESSENTIAL

Facts, Formulas & Short-Cuts

FIGURE IT OUT, WITH OR WITHOUT MATH

Ken Horner

CAMBIUM PRESS
Bethel, CT

WOODWORKERS' ESSENTIAL
Facts, Formulas & Short-Cuts

ISBN 1-892836-15-7
First printing: April 2003
Printed in the United States of America

Published by
    Cambium Press
    PO Box 909
    57 Stony Hill Road
    Bethel, CT 06801

    Library of Congress Cataloging-in-Publication Data

    Horner, Ken 1936-
      Woodworkers' essential facts, formulas & short-cuts : figure it out,
    with or without math / Ken Horner. -- 1st ed.
        p.cm
    Includes index.
     ISBN 1-892836-15-7
    1. Woodwork.   I Title.
    TT180.H665 2003
    684'.08--dc21

                              2003005981

Dedication

This book is dedicated to all you woodworkers who, like me, go into your shop alone in the evening or on weekends and try to fashion wood into furniture. We luxuriate in the smell of sawdust and resin and love the feel of a freshly planed piece of wood. The formulas and the discussions and the problems in this book are for you. When you're making a little patio wheelbarrow and can't figure out how to divide that circle of redwood for seven spokes, find the soluton here. When you have no inkling how to draw an ellipse for the top of a butler's tray table, I hope you use this book.

In Mendocino, California September 8, 2001, James Krenov announced his retirement from the College of the Redwoods Fine Woodworking Program. He spoke of his love for woodworking and said "The nicest thing about hand tools is that when you're sure of your hand and of your tool and of your edge—while you work, your mind can wander and you can reminisce. You can move back and become an observer and watch yourself as you work."

To loosely quote David Pye, "The difference between a piece of furniture that sings and a piece that is forever silent is sometimes very small. Only a whisper apart."

So, after solving the math problem, sharpen your plane blade, put a piece of walnut in your bench vise, and begin to work. You can reminisce and observe yourself as you begin to make a piece of furniture that will sing.

Contents

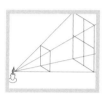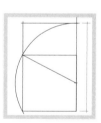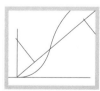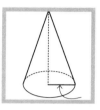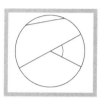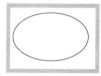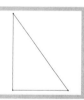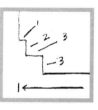

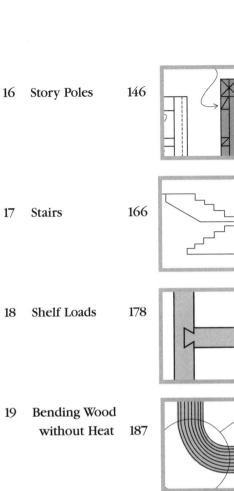
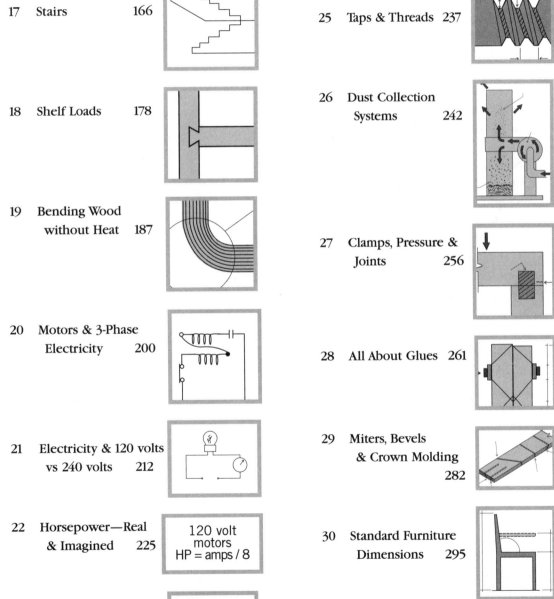

120 volt
motors
HP = amps / 8

Preface

This book started as a vague collection of math formulas, figures, and charts tossed into a shoe box that I kept in my wood shop. As the scraps and calculations grew, I gathered them into a loose-leaf notebook that I stored on a shelf near my workbench. The title on the spine said "Shop Math". I delved into the notebook often, its purpose was to remind me how to solve specific woodworking problems. Over the years, as I encountered and solved new problems, the collection grew until it was finally necessary to arrange the information into some semblance of order. At this point it became apparent there was enough data for a book.

There are very few jigs mentioned in this book—on purpose. First and foremost, the book would have grown by hundreds, if not thousands, of pages if I had tried to include jigs as solutions to woodworking problems. And, besides, there are plenty of books on jigs. The infrequent jigs that are included are present because they are directly derived from the math solution. It seemed ridiculous, for example, to explain how to calculate the radii and points along the arc of an ellipse and then to not show how to draw that figure with a simple jig. We don't go into our shops just to do math. While the math may be interesting, we all want a practical solution to whatever problem we are trying to resolve. With the widespread use of the hand calculator, I have dispensed with trigonometry tables and have instead included, when appropriate, the step-by-step use of a calculator to solve a problem.

Then there is the math vs. rule-of-thumb dilemma. Early on, my publisher, John Kelsey, was adamant that woodworkers would not buy a woodshop problem-solving book if it had only math solutions. He was insistent that each problem had to be solved, if at all possible, by a seat-of-the-pants method in addition to the math solution. Sometimes the rule-of-thumb answer is right on, sometimes it is a close approximation—but it is there if you want to use it.

Acknowledgements

The thirty chapters in this book cover a wide range of subjects—each deemed necessary to discuss and solve a different woodshop problem. In trying to cover each subject in a concise yet thorough manner, I continually relied on friends and colleagues from my South Bay Woodworkers Association. Fred Sotcher, an electrical engineer, read and added to the three chapters on Electricity, Motors and Horsepower. I also borrowed heavily from his monograph "Sotcher on Safety" for the safety section of Electricity. Dr. Chris Atwood, an aeronautical engineer, read and criticized the Dust Collection section. Bob Bennett, an electrical engineer, gave helpful suggestions for the Miters and Bevels chapter and Tom Kenyon, a mechanical engineer, helped with the Wood Bending section. Thanks guys and I'll see you all at the next meeting. Thanks also to Terry O'Donnell and John Lavine for help on the Proportions chapter.

My son Douglas Horner and my brother Byron Horner, between them, read and commented on nearly every chapter. Byron, a mechanical engineer and math whiz, checked and often corrected my formulas and calculations. Douglas, an architect and woodworker, was especially helpful in modifying the plans and drawings throughout the book and making them more readable. Bran Chapman converted my pencil sketches into clean drawings for publication. Theirs was an enormous task and I extend many thanks.

Ken Horner, Sunnyvale, Ca. 2003.

CHAPTER 1

Drawing Plans from Pictures

Many of your woodworking project ideas probably come from measured drawings and plans that have dimensions. But what if you want to reproduce a piece of furniture from a photo? Magazines, catalogs, and daily newspapers all provide good ideas. Once you find a picture of a piece you'd like to build, you can figure the dimensions using the following procedures, and thus you can create your own plans.

Finding a Photo

By carefully measuring the height, width, and depth of the piece of furniture in a photo, and knowing the overall dimensions, you can calculate the ratio between photo-size and actual-size. These overall ratios can then be used to find the dimensions of the sub-parts. For example, the height ratio of a chest can be used to find the heights of the individual drawers.

Obtain the largest possible photo or drawing of the piece you want to reproduce. Enlarge small magazine photos on a copy machine; the larger the photo, the more accurate your dimensioning will be. Calculating an object's dimensions is easiest when you work from an angled view of the piece.

Figure 1

39 1/2 "

CLIP THE PICTURE OR USE A HIGH-QUALITY PHOTOCOPY OF THE ITEM YOU WANT TO DRAW. A THREE-QUARTER VIEW WORKS BEST. HEIGHT AND WIDTH DIMENSIONS CAN BE FOUND BY MEASURING THE CHEST AND USING THE RATIO METHOD.

Fig. 2. Chest of Drawers

This perspective is also called a three-quarter view, because it shows three faces. If you can, choose a view with as much long dimension as possible. Most illustrations in catalogs and magazines are accompanied by the piece's length, width (or depth), and height, which will help you get started on drawing your plans. Most furniture made in the US is fairly standard in size, so for photos without dimensions you will be able to estimate as needed. For example, most coffee tables are about 19 inches high, 18 inches wide, and 36 to 48 inches long. **Chapter 30** includes furniture standards that will help make estimates. See also **Chapter 4**, Proportions, to find eye-appealing dimensions.

Charting Dimensions

To practice making plans from pictures, pick a project from a woodworking book or magazine that shows both a photo and a dimensioned line drawing. Make your own line drawing from the photo, calculate the dimensions, and then compare your numbers with the published dimensions. In this way you will be able to assess your efforts.

The following example uses a chest of drawers (**Figure 2**) made by Richard Jones and published in *Woodwork Magazine* (p.40, April 2001).

FROM THE PHOTO, TRACE THE OUTLINE AND MAIN DETAILS.
DON'T INCLUDE A LOT OF DETAIL THAT WOULD CLUTTER THE DRAWING.

Fig. 3. Line Drawing of Chest of Drawers

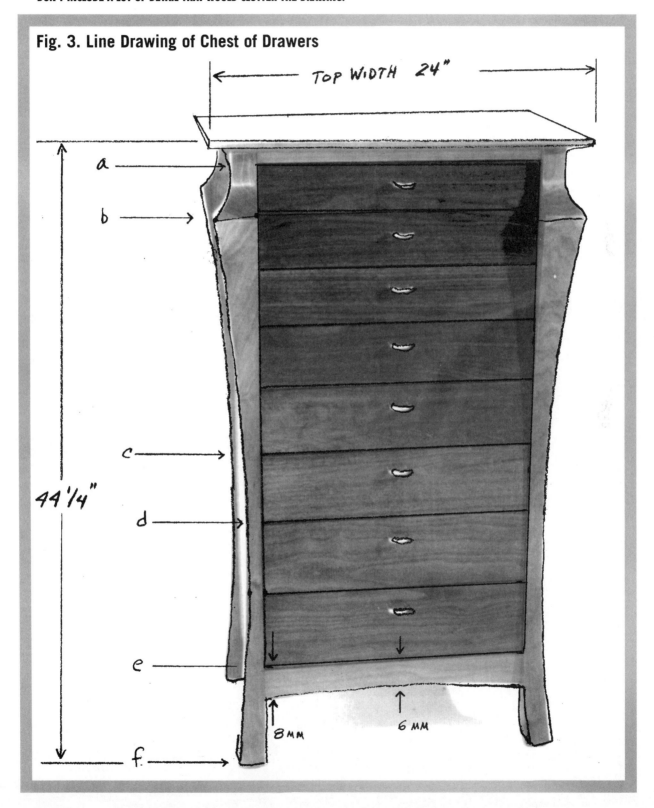

USE A CHART SUCH AS THIS FOR RECORDING RATIOS OF YOUR PHOTO-TO-PLANS PROJECT

Fig. 4. Ratio Chart (Blank)

	Length	Width	Height
INCHES (Actual)			
MM (Measured)			
RATIO (in ÷ mm)			

THE GIVEN DIMENSIONS IN INCHES ARE COMPARED TO THE MEASURED DIMENSIONS IN MILLIMETERS (MM). A RATIO FOR EACH DIMENSION IS FOUND BY DIVIDING INCHES BY MILIMETERS.

Fig. 5. Ratio Chart for Chest of Drawers (Filled In)

	Height	Width
INCHES (Actual)	$44\frac{1}{4}$	24
MM (Measured on photo	165	100
RATIO (in ÷ mm)	0.270	0.240

MEASURE THE INDIVIDUAL DIMENSIONS IN MILLIMETERS (MM) AND MULTIPLY BY THE RATIO, TO FIND CALCULATED VALUES IN INCHES.

Fig. 6. Dimension Chart for Chest of Drawers

	Measurement mm	Ratio	Calc. Decimal Inches	Calc. Fraction Inches	Actual Inches
Height					
Drawer-1	12	0.270	3.24	3 ¼	3 ⅛
Drawer-2	14	0.270	3.78	3 ¾	3 ½
Drawer-3	15	0.270	4.05	4	3 ⅞
Drawer-4	16	0.270	4.32	4 ¼	4 ¼
Drawer-5	17	0.270	4.59	4 ⅝	4 ⅝
Drawer-6	18	0.270	4.86	4 ⅞	5
Drawer-7	19	0.270	5.13	5 ⅛	5 ⅜
Drawer-8	20	0.270	5.40	5 ⅜	5 ¾
Bottom of Leg	16	0.270	4.32	4 ¼	4 ⅜
Bottom Rail Left	8	0.270	2.16	2 ⅛	2 ⅛
Bottom Rail Ctr	6	0.270	1.62	1 ⅝	1 ¾
Width					
Leg @ a	6	0.240	1.44	1 ½	1 $\frac{9}{16}$
Leg @ b	11	0.240	2.64	2 ⅝	2 ¾
Leg @ d	4	0.240	0.96	1	1 ⅛
Leg @ f	7	0.240	1.68	1 ¾	1 $\frac{13}{16}$
Drawer @ a	74	0.240	17.76	17 ¾	18 ⅛
Drawer @ c	71	0.240	17.04	17	18 ⅛
Drawer @ e	67	0.240	16.08	16	18 ⅛

1. For the clearest lines and for ease of use, cut out the picture. Otherwise make a high-quality photocopy (**Figure 2**).

2. Place a sheet of thin white paper over the picture and tape both papers to a window. With a black fine-line pen and ruler, trace the furniture piece. Trace carefully and be sure to mark drawers, rails, stiles, muntins, moldings, and other essential parts. Don't copy detail such as hardware, beading, and molding outlines that will clutter up the drawing (**Figure 3**).

3. From the photo description, copy the length, width, and height onto your drawing. Now you are ready to calculate dimensions for the rest of the project.

4. Make a ratio chart, as shown in **Figures 4** and **5**. You'll need to enter data here for the given height ($44\frac{1}{4}$ in.) and width (24 in.). There's not enough of the depth showing to chart.

5. Using a clear plastic ruler calibrated in millimeters, measure the outside height and width from the drawing. I use a millimeter rule rather than one calibrated in inches because of ease—it's easier to read 100 mm or 165 mm than $4\frac{1}{16}$ in or $6\frac{1}{2}$ in.— and it's easier to use the millimeter figures in formulas. Measure from the point nearest you—in our example this is the top left corner. Measure to the right for width, down for height. From the picture, the chest height measures 165 mm. and the width measures 100 mm. Plug these values into the ratio chart. Now divide each given value by your measured value and enter the ratio where indicated.

6. Construct a dimension chart as shown in **Figure 6.** Measure each dimension and place it in the chart, until all the numbers are entered. To compute inches, multiply the ratio for each dimension by the length in millimeters. In the example, I have converted the calculated decimal values to their nearest fraction. The last column shows the given or actual values for the drawing in the magazine.

The calculated values and the actual values correspond nicely for height because all pieces are measured close to the vertical center line. Note the width of drawers is different when the measurement is taken at drawer 1, drawer 4, and at drawer 8. This is because the bottom of the picture is further away from the camera than the top, and things appear smaller as they get further away. Because the width ratio was figured using the measurement at the top of the chest, the dimension of drawer 1 is more accurate.

Fig. 7 Cottage Armoire (Example 2)

IN THE CATALOG, THIS ARMOIRE'S DIMENSIONS ARE: 72 IN. H X 39-1/2 IN. W X 20 IN. D. THE ONLY OTHER DESCRIPTION GIVEN INDICATES THE PIECE CAN HOLD A 31-INCH TV AND VCR. PHOTO COURTESY COLDWATER CREEK.

Knowing this, you can compensate if width measurements have to be taken from the bottom of the picture.

Example 2

Shown above (**Figure 7**) is an armoire featured in a popular catalog. Only its main dimensions are given. The shawl over the door and the

COMPARE THE GIVEN DIMENSIONS IN INCHES TO THE MEASURED DIMENSIONS IN MILLIMETERS (MM). A RATIO FOR EACH DIMENSION IS FOUND BY DIVIDING INCHES BY MILLIMETERS.

Figure 8 Ratio Chart for Armoire

	Depth	Width	Height
INCHES (Actual)	20	39.5	72
MM (Measured)		66	136
RATIO (in. ÷ mm)		0.6	0.53

MEASURE THE INDIVIDUAL DIMENSIONS IN MILLIMETERS AND MULTIPLY BY THE RATIO TO FIND THE CALCULATED VALUES.

Figure 9 Dimension Chart for Armoire

	mm	Ratio	Calc. Decimal Inches	Calc. Fractional Inches
Height				
Door	65	0.53	34.45	34 1/2
Leg	8	0.53	4.24	4 1/4
Bottom Drawer	12	0.53	6.36	6 3/8
Middle Drawer	12	0.53	6.36	6 3/8
Top Drawer	12	0.53	6.36	6 3/8
Small Drawer	10	0.53	5.3	5 1/4
Door Rail	5	0.53	2.65	2 5/8
Door Panel	55	0.53	29.15	29 1/8
Width				
Door	32	0.6	19.2	19 1/4
Small Drawer	31.5	0.6	18.9	19
Large Drawer	61.5	0.6	36.9	37
Door Stile	5	0.6	3	3
Door Panel	22	0.6	13.2	13 1/4
Depth	Not Used			

quilt on the adjoining chair partially obscures the piece. The line drawing omits the open left door but we can assume it's symmetrical to the right door. The bottom right part of the armoire is drawn by extending the lines above and from the left.

After developing the charts (**Figures 8** and **9**) we can see whether the sum of the parts equals the whole. The combined heights of the door, leg, and four drawers adds up to $63\frac{1}{8}$ inches, which is $8\frac{7}{8}$ inches shorter than the total height given in the catalog. This difference can be apportioned between the drawer dividers, the top and bottom molding, and other chest dividers.

Rule of Thumb

In addition to using mathematics and ratios, accurate dimensions can also be obtained by making a simple graph to scale the drawing. We will use another catalog photo (**Figure 10**, next page) to illustrate this technique.

Scaling Dimensions

1. The sideboard shown in **Figure 10** is pretty simple in construction. For our purposes, the most important measurements are those of the drawer and the doors. This time we will measure directly from the photo.

2. Place one corner (marked 0) of a piece of white paper or light cardboard at the closest point on the top of the sideboard photo and lay the edge along the longest given dimension (**Figure 11**). Mark the paper edge where the far corner falls, working right to left. Mark this point: width 35 inches. Working downward, use a second edge of the paper to mark the height, and label this edge: height 36 inches. If our photo required depth dimensions, we would use a third edge of the scaling card for depth.

3. Use a piece of graph paper to establish the scale subdivisions (**Figure 12**); the smaller the squares, the more accurate you'll be. I used paper with four squares to the inch. Draw a horizontal line 5 inches long on the bottom of the graph paper and lay out a scale where one square equals 2 inches. Draw vertical lines upward from points 35 and 36.

Figure 10 Country Pine Sideboard
THE LISTED DIMENSIONS OF THIS SIDEBOARD ARE: 36 IN. H X 35 IN. W X 18 IN. D. PHOTO COURTESY OF SUNDANCE CATALOG.

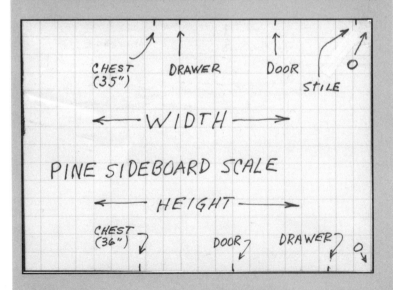

Figure 11 Scale for Pine Sideboard
USE THE SIDES OF A PIECE OF PAPER OR LIGHT CARDBOARD TO MEASURE THE WIDTH AND HEIGHT OF THE SIDEBOARD. ON THE APPROPRIATE SCALE, MARK OFF ALL WIDTH AND HEIGHT DIMENSIONS.

Fig. 12 Graph for Pine Sideboard
MARK DISTANCES FROM THE PINE SIDEBOARD SCALE ONTO THE CORRE-SPONDIONG LINE AND READ THE DIMENSIONS (IN INCHES) AT THE BOTTOM.

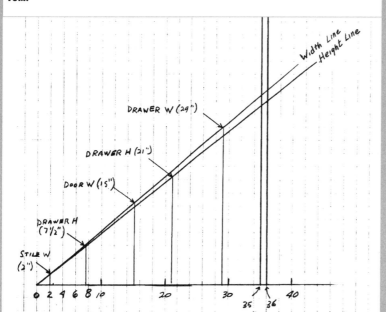

Fig. 13 Sketch of the Pine Sideboard
READ DIMENSIONS OFF THE SIDEBOARD GRAPH AND ENTER THEM ONTO THE SKETCH.

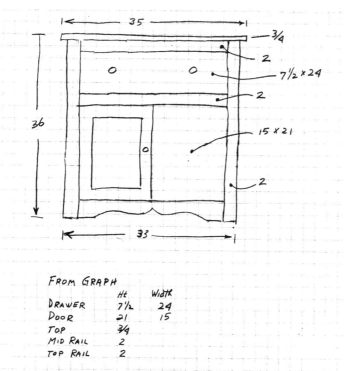

FROM GRAPH	Ht	Width
DRAWER	7½	24
DOOR	21	15
TOP	¾	
MID RAIL	2	
TOP RAIL	2	

4. Lay the pine sideboard scale on the graph so the corner marked 0 is on the graph paper 0, and the 35-in.-width mark is on the graph's 35 vertical line. Draw a line along this slant. Do the same for the 36-in. height on the 36 vertical line.

5. Use the edge of the pine sideboard scale to pick distances off the drawing. Mark height distances onto the graph's height line, and width distances onto the width line. By following the grid to the bottom, you can read inches. Don't get confused by odd fractional sizes—the nearest inch or half-inch often will do.

6. If a part is too small to determine its size accurately, just estimate.

7. Add up all the dimensions and see if the sum of the pieces fits the dimension of the whole. Adjust until they do.

Sketch Plan
Take a look at the sideboard sketch and the preliminary dimensions (**Figure 13**). When the top, the two rails, the drawer and door heights are added, we get $33\frac{1}{4}$ inches versus the 36 inches given. This $2\frac{3}{4}$-inches difference is the width of the bottom rail, which appears about right when compared with the stiles and other rails.

Add up the width of two stiles plus the two doors. This equals 33 inches, which is the proper width. Note: the given 35 inches included one inch on each side for the table top.

References

1. Richard Jones. "*Woodwork Magazine*", April 2001, p.40.

2. Sundance Catalog, Salt Lake City, Utah

3. Coldwater Creek Catalog, Sandpoint, Idaho

CHAPTER 2

Enlargement & Reduction

Once you've found **plans**, or drawn them yourself, you may decide the cabinet or sideboard is just a tad too wide for the space you've planned for it. You could just reduce the width 4 inches but what if you like the height to width proportions? How can you redimension the sideboard, that is, proportionately decrease the height, width and depth? To change the size of a piece and still keep the pleasing proportions, you must reduce all dimensions by the same ratio. This can be done with math, or a photocopier or light projector, or by using graphics.

Redimensioning

First let's look at the math of redimensioning. Imagine a square being projected onto a screen (**Figure 14**). As the screen is moved away from the projector, the image enlarges proportionally i.e. both the height and width double when the screen-to-projector distance doubles. Likewise, the height and width triple when the distance triples and so forth. This being the case, the sideboard can be redimensioned proportionally in both height and width by multiplying both dimensions by the same ratio.

THE IMAGE ENLARGEMENT IS PROPORTIONAL TO THE DISTANCE AND WIDTH AND HEIGHT MAGNIFY EQUALLY.

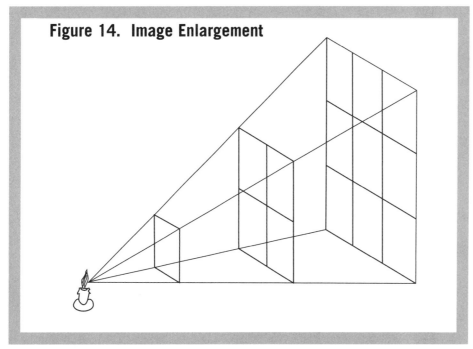

Figure 14. Image Enlargement

Proportional Ratio

The country pine sideboard we sketched in Chapter 1 (**Figure 15**) is 35 inches wide, 36 inches high and 18 inches deep. Perhaps the area you've chosen for this project will only accommodate a sideboard 32 inches wide. What are the steps to ratio redimensioning?

1. Determine the redimensioning ratio.

New width ÷ original width = redimensioning ratio

$32 \div 35 = .914$

x 100 = 91.4%

This means all the new dimensions will be about 9% smaller than they originally were.

2. Use the redimensioning ratio obtained from the width to find the new height and depth.

New height

= old height x 91.4%

= 36 x 0.914

= 32.91 ≈ $32\frac{7}{8}$"

New depth

= old depth x 91.4%

= 18 x 0.914

= 16.46 ≈ $16\frac{1}{2}$"

The new dimensions are

32" W x $32\frac{7}{8}$" H x $16\frac{1}{2}$" D.

3. Use the same ratio to reduce all other dimensions (**Figure 16**).

REDIMENSIONING BY 91.4% WILL REDUCE THE SIZE PROPORTIONATELY.

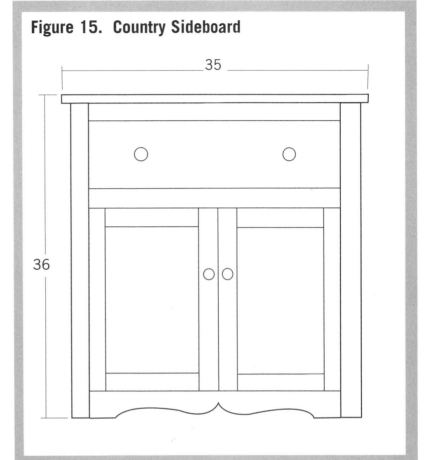

Figure 15. Country Sideboard

MULTIPLY ORIGINAL DIMENSIONS BY THE RATIO 0.914 TO FIND THE NEW DIMENSIONS FOR ALL PARTS.

Figure 16 Redimensioning Chart for Country Sideboard

		Old	x 0.914	New Decimal	New Fraction
Cabinet	Width	35		31.99 in.	32 in.
	Height	36		32.90 in.	32 ⅞ in.
	Depth	18		16.45 in.	16 ½ in.
Drawer	Height	7.5		6.86 in.	6 ⅞ in.
	Width	29		26.51 in.	26 ½ in.
Door	Height	21		19.19 in.	19 ¼ in.
	Width	15		13.71 in.	13 ¾ in.
Rail	Width	2		1.83 in.	1 ⅞ in.
Top	Width	35		31.99 in.	32 in.
	Depth	18		16.45 in.	16 ½ in.

Non-Linear Proportions
Area

Not all redimensions are linear. Note that the top of the original sideboard had an area of 630 sq. in. (35 x 18) while the area of the redimensioned top is 528 sq. in. (32 x 16.5). The length and depth of the top decreased by 9% while the area of the top decreased by 16% (630 - 528 ÷ 630 = 0.16). This is because length and width increase and decrease linerally while area changes by the ratio squared. If the length of a side of a square is doubled, the area of the square is quadrupled and this is something to consider if area is a factor in your project. This also can work in your favor.

You have a 3" x 3" x 6" high wooden box on your stove top for storing cooking utensils. After making a few new wooden spoons and a pasta fork, you find they won't all fit anymore and you decide to make a larger holder. After measuring the space, you find a 4" x 4" x 6" high box will fit nicely. Using these dimensions, how much area will you gain?

Area (footprint) of original box
= 3 x 3 = 9 sq. in.
Area (footprint) of new box
= 4 x 4 = 16 sq. in.

The area increase was 78% (16 ÷ 9 = 1.78) while the linear increase was only 33% (4 ÷ 3 = 1.33).

Volume

Volume, like area, also increases in a non-linear fashion. If the length of the side of a cube is doubled, the volume of the cube is increased by a factor of eight. The stove top box increased in volume from 54 cu. in. (3 x 3 x 6) to 96 cu. in. (4 x 4 x 6) or 78%.

$$96 - 54 = 42$$
$$42 ÷ 54 \times 100 = 78\%$$

Figure 17 shows the relationship between lines, squares and cubes as the sides are lengthened. The following rules apply when enlarging or reducing plans:

When comparing one-dimensional objects, use length.

When comparing two-dimensional objects, use area.

When comparing three-dimensional objects, use volume.

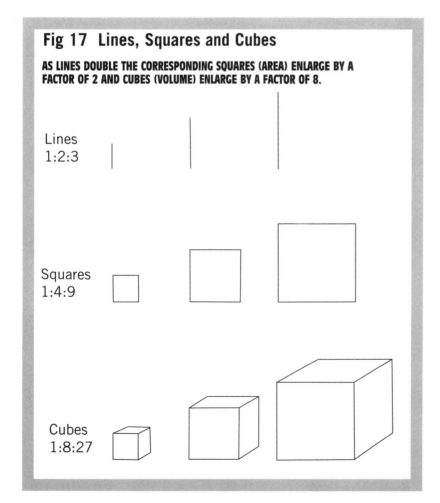

Fig 17 Lines, Squares and Cubes

AS LINES DOUBLE THE CORRESPONDING SQUARES (AREA) ENLARGE BY A FACTOR OF 2 AND CUBES (VOLUME) ENLARGE BY A FACTOR OF 8.

Lines
1:2:3

Squares
1:4:9

Cubes
1:8:27

Photocopier Enlargement

You may want to enlarge a picture or drawing to use as a pattern eg a flower or a bird for a marquetry project. For this project a photocopy machine can be used. To find the amount of reduction or enlargement use the following rules:

Percent enlargement = larger size ÷ smaller size x 100

Percent reduction = smaller size ÷ larger size x 100

An original picture of a flower is $2\frac{1}{2}$ inches and you need a $3\frac{1}{2}$ inch pattern. At what percentage should you set the enlargement?
Percent enlargement = larger size ÷ smaller size x 100
Percent enlargement
$$= 3.5 ÷ 2.5 \text{ x } 100$$
$$= 1.40 \text{ x } 100 = 140\%$$

Photocopy machines have maximum settings and if the redimensioning needed exceeds these limits, the change must proceed in steps.

For example, a rose pattern is 2 inches wide and we need to enlarge it to $9\frac{1}{2}$ inches. The maximum enlargement on the photocopy machine is 142%. Proceed as follows:

1) 2" x 1.42 = 2.84"
2) 2.84" x 1.42 = 4.03"

3) 4.03" x 1.42 = 5.73"
4) 5.73" x 1.42 = 8.13"
5) 8.13" x 1.42 = 11.55"

The first 4 enlargements at 142% brings the size to 8.13 inches however, the next enlargement at 142% makes the flower 11.5 inches wide, larger than the size we want, $9\frac{1}{2}$ ". We can calculate the correct last setting.
Percent enlargement = larger size ÷ smaller size x 100
$$9.5 ÷ 8.13 \text{ x } 100$$
$$= 1.17 \text{ x } 100 = 117\%$$

Now for the last enlargement use 117% instead of 142%.
5) 8.13" x 1.17 = 9.51"

At the photocopy center we would enlarge the original four times with a setting of 142% and then with a setting of 117% for the last setting.

Photocopier Reduction

Reduce a 10 inch shamrock to 2 inches using a photocopier having a maximum reduction of 50%.

1) 10" x 0.5 = 5"
2) 5" x 0.5 = 2.5"
3) 2.5" x 0.5 = 1.25"

The first two reductions at 50% bring the size to 2.5 inches. The next reduction makes a picture 1.25 inches, smaller than we want, 2". We can calculate the correct last setting.

Percent reduction = smaller size ÷ larger size x 100

Percent reduction = 2 ÷ 2.5 x
$$100 = 0.20 \text{ x } 100 = 20\%$$
3) 2.5" x 0.80 = 2"
Make the last setting 20% instead of 50%.

Rule of Thumb

Estimating the percentage setting on a photocopier to redimension a project is easy with a 'best estimate' method. Let's say we want to reduce a 5 inch relief-carving pattern to $3\frac{1}{4}$ inch. How can we estimate the percent reduction for the photocopier? Our thought process might go thus:

5 inches times 50% is $2\frac{1}{2}$ inches, too small.

5 inches times 60% is 3 inches, still too small.

5 inches times 70% is $3\frac{1}{2}$ inches, too large, but close.

$3\frac{1}{4}$ inch is halfway between 3 and $3\frac{1}{2}$ and 65% is halfway between 60% and 70%. Use the 65% setting and your 10-cent copy will be redimensioned correctly.

Figure 18 Triangular Proportioning

TRIANGLES CDE AND CFG HAVE THE SAME PROPORTIONS AS ABC.
RECTANGLE AB HAS THE SAME PROPORTIONS AS RECTANGLE ab.

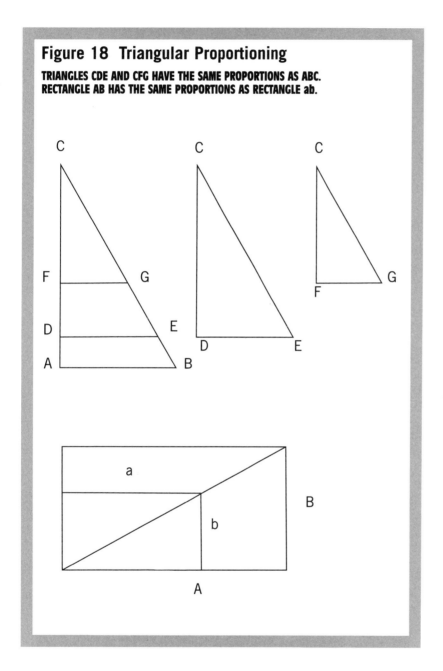

Magnifying Projector

Another way to enlarge a drawing or picture is to use a magnifying projector which can be purchased at low cost from most art supply stores. This simple light projector allows you to enlarge pictures and plans up to ten times. Small, flat three-dimensional objects such as coins, jewelry and plaques can also be magnified then traced.

Graphic Proportions

Any line drawn parallel to the base of a triangle (eg in **Figure. 18,** ABC) will form another triangle of similar angles and similar shape (eg triangles CDE and CFG).

This reproportioning method can be used on other shapes. To reduce or enlarge a rectangle, draw a diagonal and create two triangles in which the smaller rectangle (ab) is in strict proportion to the larger rectangle (AB).

If a series of lines are drawn from points on the base of a triangle to the apex they will cut any other parallel line in exactly the same proportion **(Figure 19)**. The divisions at the base of triangle ABC are in the same proportion as the divisions at the base of triangles CDE and CFG.

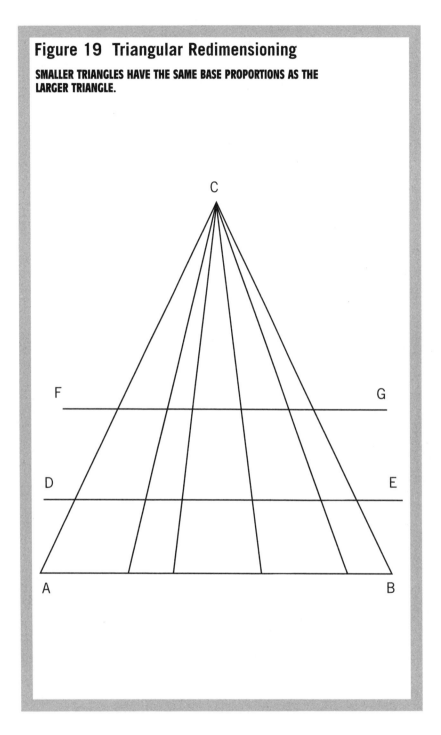

Figure 19 Triangular Redimensioning

SMALLER TRIANGLES HAVE THE SAME BASE PROPORTIONS AS THE LARGER TRIANGLE.

USING THE TRIANGULAR-APEX METHOD, A 41 INCH CHEST CAN BE REDUCED IN SIZE TO 29 INCHES. DRAWER DIMENSIONS CAN BE READ OFF THE SMALL SCALE DRAWING USING THE SAME SCALE THAT WAS USED TO MAKE THE ORIGINAL DRAWING.

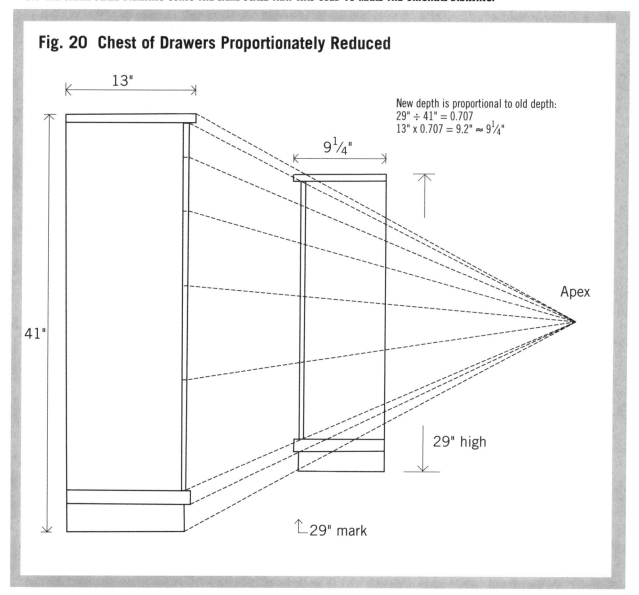

Fig. 20 Chest of Drawers Proportionately Reduced

New depth is proportional to old depth:
$29" \div 41" = 0.707$
$13" \times 0.707 = 9.2" \approx 9\frac{1}{4}"$

Apex

29" high

29" mark

Chest of Drawers

In **Figure 20** a 41 inch chest of drawers is reduced to 29 inches. These are the steps.

1. Draw the original chest to scale eg $\frac{1}{8}" = 1"$.

2. At mid-height and some distance away mark an apex.

3. Draw lines from the original chest to the apex, making all lines originate from the same vertical line.

4. With the $\frac{1}{8}" = 1"$ scale find the vertical line, parallel to the originating line, where the top and bottom lines are 29 inches apart.

5. Draw the 29 inch chest at this point.

6. The same scale, $\frac{1}{8}" = 1"$, can be used to find small dimensions from the reduced size chest, eg drawer and molding heights.

A COMPLEX MOLDING PROFILE IS REDUCED IN SIZE WITH THE TRIANGULAR-APEX METHOD.

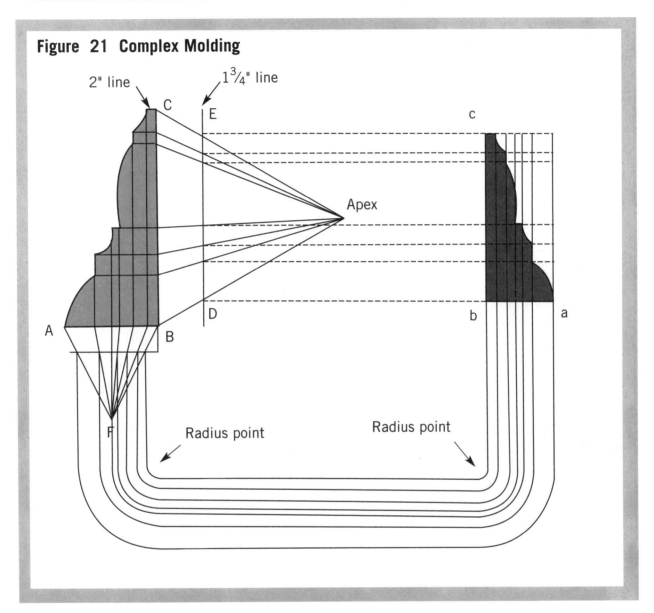

Figure 21 Complex Molding

Redimensioning a Molding

We can use this triangular proportioning to reduce or enlarge complex figures such as a piece of molding (**Figure 21**).

1. Draw the molding full size, ABC.

2. Draw the height DE of the reduced piece at a distance.

3. Draw an equilateral triangle with sides equal to the full size height of the molding, Apex BC.

4. Draw points of the molding from the profile to the front edge (line BC) and then to points cutting DE in exactly the same proportion.

5. The thickness of AB can also be enclosed in an equilateral triangle ABF and points stepped off on thickness ab.

CHAPTER 3

Drawing to Scale

Woodworkers often need to draw objects that at full size are too large to fit on a regular sheet of paper. In these cases, we need to reduce the diagram size in some regular proportion, so the representation will accurately portray the object, but will fit on the paper. This is "drawing to scale."

Half-Size Scale

The first choice of reduction, because of its simplicity, is half-size, where $\frac{1}{2}$ inch on the paper equals 1 inch on the object (**Figure 22**). You can figure these reductions in your head and draw them to scale with any ruler. This elementary scale can only be used if the object is slightly larger than the paper.

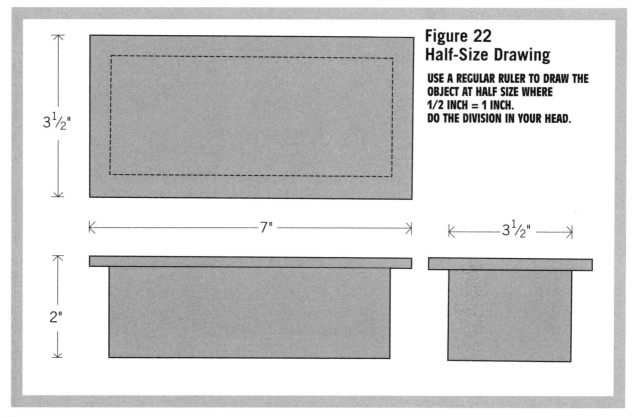

Figure 22
Half-Size Drawing

USE A REGULAR RULER TO DRAW THE
OBJECT AT HALF SIZE WHERE
1/2 INCH = 1 INCH.
DO THE DIVISION IN YOUR HEAD.

$3\frac{1}{2}$"

7"

$3\frac{1}{2}$"

2"

Because our woodworking projects usually are too large for the half-size scale, we turn to a tool regularly used by draftsmen and architects.

Architect's Scale

The architect's scale (**Figure 23**) is a triangular ruler; each face has two working edges. It has ten reduction scales and choosing one depends largely on the sizes of the object and the paper you're drawing on. With any of the scales, you can measure directly from ruler to paper without making any mathematical calculations.

The scales are: $\frac{3}{32}$, $\frac{1}{8}$, $\frac{3}{16}$, $\frac{1}{4}$, $\frac{3}{8}$, $\frac{1}{2}$, $\frac{3}{4}$, 1, $1\frac{1}{2}$, and 3 inches. The scale numbers represent how many inches on the drawing equal 1 foot of the object. With this range of scales you can dimension most projects to fit on an ordinary sheet of paper. For example, a drawing using the $\frac{3}{32}$-in. scale will have $\frac{3}{32}$ of an inch represent 1 foot. This ratio of 1:128 is the greatest reduction on the rule, and with it you could draw a 128-ft. building onto a 12-in. piece of paper.

Likewise, the 3-in. scale means 3 inches on the blueprint or drawing represents 1 foot of the object. With this 1:4 ratio, joinery and other small components could be detailed.

You can calculate the size of

Figure 23 Architect's Scale
THE THREE SIDES OF THE ARCHITECT'S RULER HAVE 10 SCALES THAT CAN BE USED TO PROPORTION DRAWINGS.

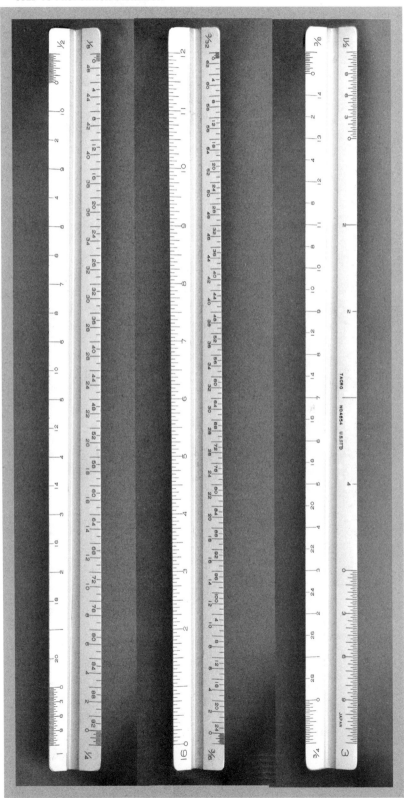

USE THE FRACTIONAL SCALE TO SHOW 1-5/8 INCH, AND USE THE LARGE OPEN SCALE TO SHOW 1 FOOT.

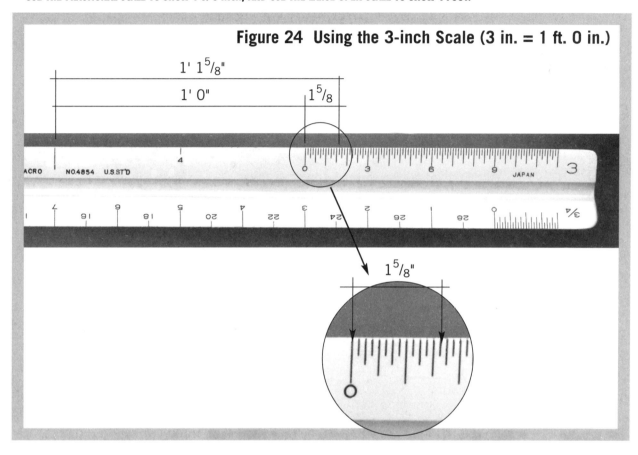

Figure 24 Using the 3-inch Scale (3 in. = 1 ft. 0 in.)

the drawing using any scale with the following formula:

Object size x scale fraction = drawing size

A 125-ft. building will need what size paper at $\frac{3}{32}$-in. scale?

Multiply the object size times the scale fraction to obtain the reduced size.

125 ft. x $\frac{3}{32}$
= 125 x 0.0938 = 11.7 in.

The 125 ft. building will be just under 12-in. at $\frac{3}{32}$-in. scale.

Scaling Feet

Architects work in feet and inches, so our first examples will follow this convention and we will measure in feet. Later, we'll discuss how to use the architect's scale when the dimensions are given in inches only.

Each of the scales on the rule ($\frac{3}{32}$ in. = 1 ft. 0 in. to 3 in. = 1 ft. 0 in.) has the first foot subdivided into inches. By using the subdivision plus the open part of the scale, you can mark a drawing with extreme accuracy. The larger the scale,

the more accurate the drawing, and the easier to represent details of construction.

To illustrate the use of the architect's scale, look at **Figure 24** (above) where the 3-in. scale is used to measure 1 ft. $1\frac{5}{8}$ in.

Here 1 ft. $1\frac{5}{8}$ in. is measured on the 3-in. scale by marking the fractional $1\frac{5}{8}$ in. to the right, and marking the 1-ft. position to the left in the open scales. Be careful to read the correct set of numbers, as each edge of the ruler has two scales

USE THE FRACTIONAL SCALE TO SHOW 5-1/2 INCH, AND USE THE LARGE OPEN SCALE TO SHOW 3 FEET.

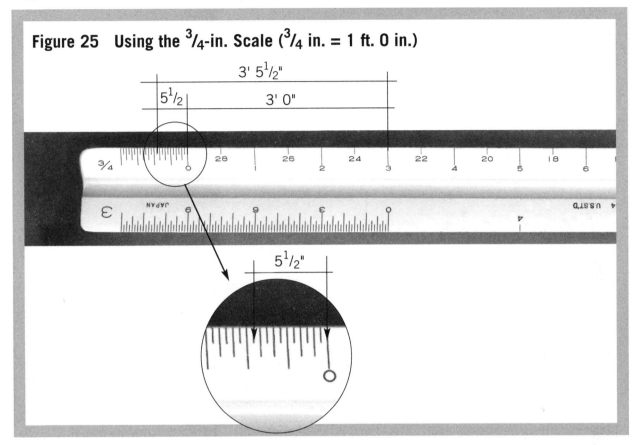

Figure 25 Using the $\frac{3}{4}$-in. Scale ($\frac{3}{4}$ in. = 1 ft. 0 in.)

running in opposite directions with numbers interspersed. The different scales are distinguished by their position and the type size of the numbers. This seems complicated until you pick up a scale and examine it for a couple of minutes.

Figure 25 (above) shows the $\frac{3}{4}$ in. scale and a measurement of 3 ft. $5\frac{1}{2}$ in. Hold the $5\frac{1}{2}$-in. mark on the small fractional scale to the mark and then make another mark at the 3-ft. point to the right.

One last illustration should suffice (**Figure 26,** next page). To measure 23 ft. 8 in., use the $\frac{1}{8}$-in. scale. Place the zero mark to the right of the first tick mark by four divisions (8 inches) and then make a mark at 23. This scales 8 inches plus 23 feet, or 23 ft. 8 in.

Once you've chosen a scale, note it on the drawing. In the example (next page) we would write $\frac{1}{8}$ in. = 1' 0" in. By writing it down you remind yourself and others that $\frac{1}{8}$ inch on this drawing is equal to 1 foot on the object.

USE THE FRACTIONAL SCALE TO SHOW 8 INCHES (4/6 OF 12 INCHES), AND USE THE LARGE SCALE TO SHOW 23 FEET.

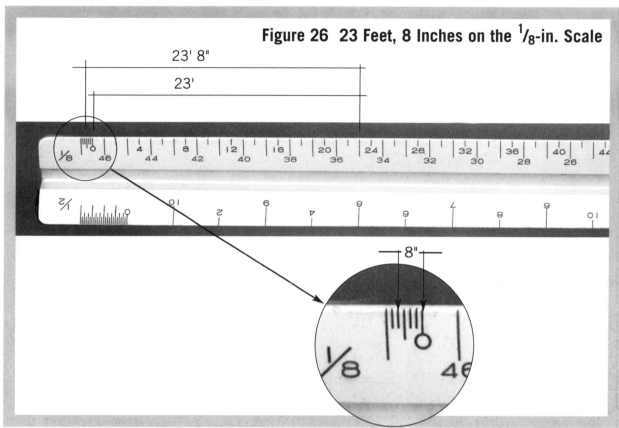

Figure 26 23 Feet, 8 Inches on the $^1/_8$-in. Scale

Construction details such as joinery, beading, molding, and other particulars are often done at full or half-size on another sheet of paper, or off to one side on the main sheet. Scale sizes can be mixed on the same blueprint as long as each scale is plainly noted.

Architects and engineers mark distances with a sharp pencil, then connect the marks with a flat ruler. I've never found it a problem to measure with the scale and also use it as a straight edge for drawing lines.

Of course, this method works less well if I'm using a T-square or parallel rule and drafting triangles. In layout work where extreme accuracy is required, you can use a needle or pin point set into a soft wood handle to prick a small hole into the paper instead of using a pencil mark.

Scaling Inches

Architects measure work in feet and inches, but most woodworkers measure in inches only. To a woodworker, a buffet is 58-inches long rather than 4 ft. 10 in. To use the architect's scale for inches we have to adopt a slightly different approach.

In the discussions concerning feet and inches, the fractional divisions on a scale represent fractions of a foot. When all measurements are in inches, the fractional divisions represent fractions of an inch, i.e., $^5/_8$, $^3/_8$ or $^1/_2$. See **Figure 27**.

WHEN DIMENSIONS ARE IN INCHES ONLY, THE SUBDIVISIONS MEASURE FRACTIONS OF AN INCH.

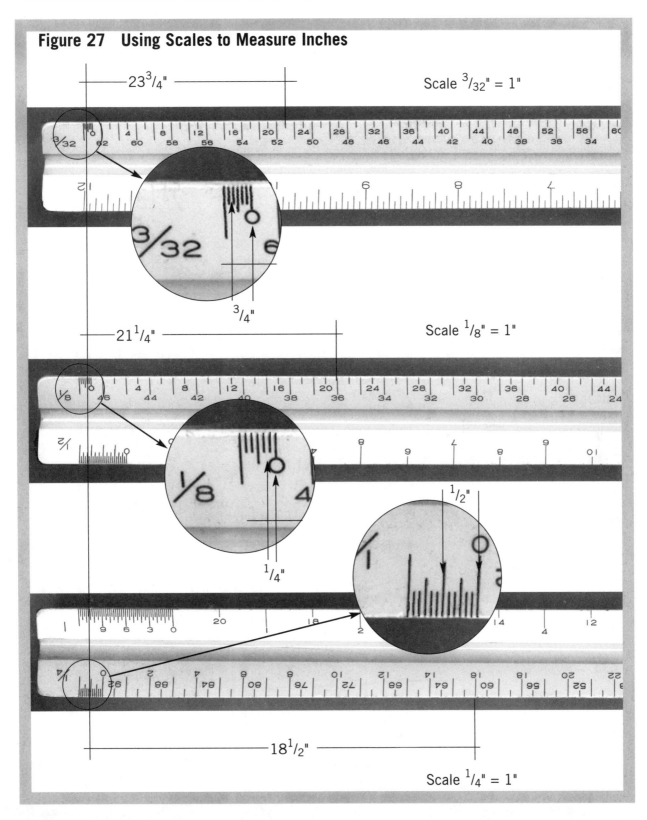

Figure 27   Using Scales to Measure Inches

With the following formula you can calculate the size of the blueprint drawing using any scale:

Ratio = Scale fraction x
　　object size (inch)
　　= drawing size (inch)

Ratio = project size (inch)
　　÷ drawing size (inch)

A grandfather clock is 82-inches tall. What scale should we use to get a drawing 6-inches tall?

Ratio = 82 ÷ 6 = 13+. Therefore we need a ratio of about 1 to 13. From the chart below we see the ratio of the $\frac{3}{32}$-in. scale is 1 to 11. The actual size of the drawing can be calculated thus:

Scale fraction x object size (inch)
　　= drawing size (inch)

$\frac{3}{32}$ x 82 = 7.7 in.
0.094 x 82 = 7.7 in.

Choosing a Scale

Architects and draftsmen quickly choose a scale, because they've been doing this for years. They know from experience what the optimum size a detail or drawing should be in order to clearly and fully represent all of its parts. When you encounter a new project, proceed along these lines:

Roll and Pick

1. Note the size of the desired drawing, for example: 6 inches.

2. Note the size of the object to be drawn, 7 ft. 6 in.

3. Start rolling the scale over and over, watching the 8-ft. mark on each scale. When you see an 8-ft. mark that is about 6 inches from the zero point, you have found the scale. In the present problem, this is the $\frac{3}{4}$ in. scale.

Multiply and Divide

Another way to choose a scale is to determine the ratio between the project size and the drawing size, and to find the appropriate scale in **Figure 28** below. Note the ratios are different for inches and feet.

Example: Draw a cabinet 12-ft. long onto a 9-in. piece of paper.
Scale ratio
　　= drawing size ÷ object size
Ratio = 9/12 ft. ÷ 12 ft.
　　= 0.0625
　　1 ÷ 0.0625 = 16
Ratio = 1 to 16 ft.. This would be the $\frac{3}{4}$ scale in feet.

To draw the 12-ft. cabinet in inches:
Scale ratio
　　= drawing size ÷ object size
Ratio = 9 in. ÷ 12 = 0.75
　　1 ÷ 0.75 = 1.3

Ratio = 1 to 1.3 in.
Chose the $\frac{3}{4}$ scale in inches.

Figure 28 Ratio Scale
ONCE YOU'VE DETERMINED THE RATIO BETWEEN THE PROJECT SIZE AND THE DRAWING SIZE, YOU CAN CHOOSE THE APROPRIATE SCALE.
Scale ratio = drawing size ÷ object size

	Inches	Feet
$\frac{3}{32}$ in. = 1 in.	= ratio 1 to 11	= 1 to 128
$\frac{1}{8}$ in. = 1 in.	= ratio 1 to 8	= 1 to 96
$\frac{3}{16}$ in. = 1 in.	= ratio 1 to 5	= 1 to 64
$\frac{1}{4}$ in. = 1 in.	= ratio 1 to 4	= 1 to 48
$\frac{3}{8}$ in. = 1 in.	= ratio 1 to 2.5	= 1 to 32
$\frac{1}{2}$ in. = 1 in.	= ratio 1 to 2	= 1 to 24
$\frac{3}{4}$ in. = 1 in.	= ratio 1 to 1.3	= 1 to 16
1 in. = 1 in.	= ratio 1 to 1	= 1 to 12
$1\frac{1}{2}$ in. = 1 in.	= ratio 1.5 to 1	= 1 to 8
3 in. = 1 in.	= ratio 3 to 1	= 1 to 4

Using the Architect's Scale

Use the following steps to draw a measured line using the architect's scale. Let's assume we are sketching a project $50\frac{1}{2}$ in. x $24\frac{3}{4}$ in., and want the longest dimension on the drawing to be about 6-inches.

1. Convert all measurements to feet and inches.
Length $50\frac{1}{2}$ in. = 4 ft. $2\frac{1}{2}$ in.
Width $24\frac{3}{4}$ in. = 2 ft. $\frac{3}{4}$ in.

2. Select the scale.
4 ft. x 12 = 48 in. ÷ 6 in. = 8 or 4 ft. ÷ 0.5 ft. = 8
Therefore we need a ratio of about 8:1. Scale $1\frac{1}{2}$ in. is 8:1.

3. Draw a horizontal line about 6-inches long to represent the long side of the box.

4. Position the scale so the $1\frac{1}{2}$-in. scale is on the line. Notice that feet are marked in the open scale to the right of zero, while inches are marked in the fractional divisions to the left.

5. Make a tick mark on the foot scale to the right of zero at the 4; this is 4 feet.

6. Make a tick mark on the inches scale to the left of the zero at $2\frac{1}{2}$; this is $2\frac{1}{2}$ inches.

7. Label this line 4 ft. $2\frac{1}{2}$ in.

8. Write: Scale $1\frac{1}{2}$ in. = 1 ft. 0 in.

CHOOSE A SCALE BY FINDING THE OBJECT SIZE IN THE FIRST COLUMN. THEN FIND THE SIZE OF THE DRAWING UNDER THE APPROPRIATE SCALE.

Figure 29 Choosing A Scale

Object Size (In)	Scale 3/32	Scale 1/8	Scale 3/16	Scale 1/4	Scale 3/8	Scale 1/2	Scale 3/4	Scale 1
12	1.1	1.5	2.3	3	4.5	6	9	12
24	2.3	3	4.5	6	9	12	18	24
36	3.4	4.5	6.8	9	13.5	18	27	36
48	4.5	6	9.0	12	18	24	36	48
60	5.6	7.5	11.3	15	22.5	30	45	60
72	6.8	9	13.5	18	27	36	54	72
84	7.9	10.5	15.8	21	31.5	42	63	84
96	9.0	12	18.0	24	36	48	72	96

Rule of Thumb

To find the right scale:

1. Find the size of your project in the first column of Fig. 29.

2. Follow that row to the right, to the size you want your drawing to be.

3. Follow the column up, to read the scale to use.

You want to draw a buffet that is 48-in. long. You'd like the drawing to be about 8-in. long. What scale should you use?

The number 48 is in the 4th row down. Follow that row to the right and find 6 in. under scale $\frac{1}{8}$, and 8 in. under scale $\frac{3}{16}$. Test both of these scales and use the one that fits your paper best.

CHAPTER 4

Proportions & the Golden Ratio

Pleasing proportions can be found by using the Golden Ratio for two-dimensional figures such as frames, trays and doors and for three-dimensional figures such as tables, chests and even lathe-turned bowls. Chest of drawer proportions are best done using a formula that increases each drawer size by a proportionate amount. Procedures for arriving at eye-pleasing designs are given in the following pages.

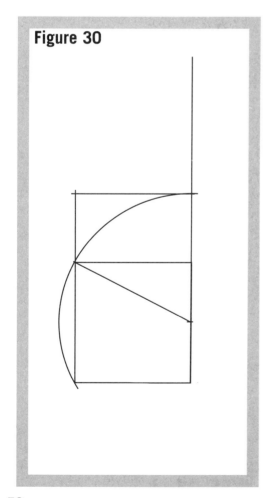

Figure 30

The Golden Ratio

Over the years woodworkers, among others, have used a sort of mythical, geometric proportioning system for designing beautiful objects. This 'golden ratio' was used to derive dimensions of classical Greek buildings and columns. The architects of the Parthenon used the ratio throughout, from the length, width and height of the structure itself to the columns whereby the height of a column determined its diameter and the size of the moldings. The Greeks referred to this proportioning system as both the 'golden rule' and 'the classical proportion'.

The Egyptians used the golden ratio to erect temples and tombs and they considered these correlations both religious and pleasing to the eye, calling them 'the sacred ratio'.

Furniture makers through the centuries have used similar proportions for their furniture designs; many designers and authors of the various pattern books, such as Thomas Chippendale, used these rules in their shops. In colonial America, cabinetmakers reinvented these 'golden proportions' by studying the three classic column types—Doric, Ionic and Corinthian—and in the mid-1800s Shaker craftsmen used the 'golden mean' extensively, finding great beauty and harmony in shapes derived from its principles. This system provides woodworkers with a way to relate height, width and length to each other proportionately so furniture may be artistically and mathematically joined.

And what is this magical proportion? For tables, cabinets and other square- or rectangle-like designs, any one dimension (height, width or length) is based on the other two. The golden ratio is expressed as follows:

The smaller part is to the larger as the larger is to the whole.

As a ratio, this can be stated thus:
'A' is to 'B' as 'B' is to 'A + B'
   or A/B = B/(A+B)

When we set A = 1 and solve this equation algebraically (see Math Box at right), we see that:
   B = 1.618

This means the first dimension multiplied by 1.618 equals the second dimension.

Practically, this ratio is:
first dimension x 1.618
   = second dimension

second dimension x 1.618
   = third dimension

The series of height, width and length combinations in **Figure 31** can be produced using this 1.618 ratio.

Here's the math

'A' is to 'B' as 'B' is to 'A + B'
Or A/B = B/(A+B)
$B^2 = A^2 + AB$
$B^2 - B - 1 = 0$

We can apply some numbers to this formula to help us see the basic relationship in more concrete terms. If we give A the value of 1 then we can use the Quadratic Equation to find the value of B.

$(-b \pm \sqrt{b^2 - 4ac})/2a$
$-b \pm \sqrt{b^2 - 4ac}/2a$
In this case, a=1, b= -1, c= -1
$B = (1 \pm \sqrt{1+4})/2$
The two answers are:
$B = (1 + \sqrt{5})/2$ and $B = (1 - \sqrt{5})/2$
We are only interested in the positive answer, so:
$B = (1 + \sqrt{5})/2 = (1 + 2.236)/2 = 3.236/2 = 1.1618$

So when we assume A=1 we see that B=1.618.

This means the first dimension multiplied by 1.618 equals the second dimension.

STARTING WITH 1, THE FIBONACCI SERIES CAN BE EXTENDED BY MULTIPLYING EACH NUMBER TIMES 1.618.

Figure 31 Golden Ratio Numbers (Fibonacci series)

Nominal dimensions

	First		Second		Third
1,2,3	1	x 1.618 =	1.62	x 1.618 =	2.62
3,5,8	3	x 1.618 =	4.85	x 1.618 =	7.85
5,18,13	5	x 1.618 =	8.09	x 1.618 =	13.08
8, 13, 21	8	x 1.618 =	12.94	x 1.618 =	20.94
13,21,34	13	x 1.618 =	21.03	x 1.618 =	34.03
21, 34, 55	21	x 1.618 =	33.97	x 1.618 =	54.98
34, 55, 89	34	x 1.618 =	55.01	x 1.618 =	89.01

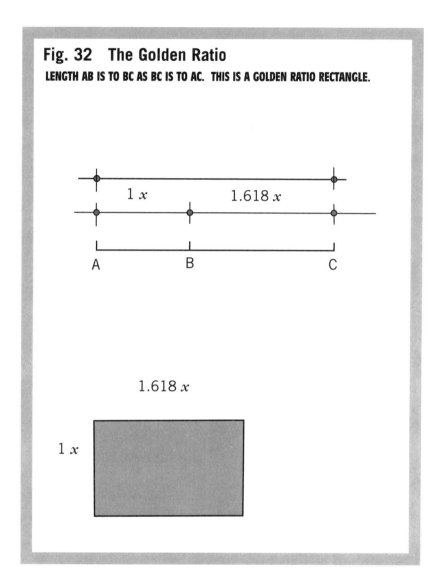

Fig. 32   The Golden Ratio

LENGTH AB IS TO BC AS BC IS TO AC. THIS IS A GOLDEN RATIO RECTANGLE.

$1\,x$ $1.618\,x$

A   B   C

$1.618\,x$

$1\,x$

The 1-2-3 and 3-5-8 series produce approximate whole numbers but after the third set of dimensions (5-8-13) the golden ratio number, 1.618, produces almost exact whole numbers for all successive combinations.

Using the closest whole number value, these numbers can be extended thus: 1, 2, 3, 5, 8, 13, 21, 34, 55, 89, 144, 233, 377, 610, 987... All numbers in the series fit the golden ratio criteria because every number is the product of multiplying the previous number by 1.618. This numerical progression is called the Fibonacci series, named after the Italian mathematician Leonardo Fibonacci (c. 1180-1228) who first discovered it. These numbers all also fit the golden ratio criteria in that every number after 8, when divided by the previous number, gives the ratio 1.618.

In **Figure 32** (left), the line ABC shows this ratio in one dimension and the rectangular box shows the golden ratio in two dimensions.

Thus, a small box for the coffee table measuring 5 in. H x 8 in. W x 13 in. L would fit the golden ratio. A coffee table measuring 21 in. H x 34 in. W x 55 in. L would also have classical proportions. Note that these numbers are in the series.

What if we want to use this ratio for a box 9 in. high? The number nine does not appear in the numerical series.

Mathematicians noted after the fifth number in the series, any number divided by the next lower one equals about 1.62 (13 ÷ 8 = 1.625). After eleven numbers the ratio is exactly 1.618 and continues thus for all successive numbers. This number 1.618 can be used to design furniture using any number whether it is in the series or not. Because the ratio of 1.618 only occurs after the fifth number, the ratio only applies with numbers five and higher.

There is also a convenient practical progression—every number in the series is the sum of the two previous numbers. Thus, in all cases when the golden ratio is applied in furniture design, the first dimension plus the second closely approximates, or exactly equals, the third dimension—a convenient progression.

For woodworking, use this rule:

**First dimension x 1.62
= second dimension
Second dimension
+ first dimension
= third dimension**

If height is known:
   H x 1.62 = W and H + W = L

THE HEIGHT X 1.62 = WIDTH. LENGTH = HEIGHT + WIDTH

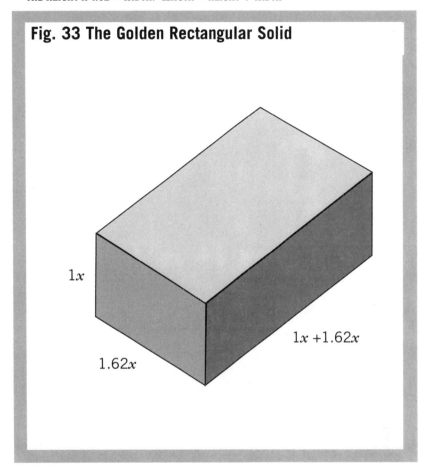

Fig. 33 The Golden Rectangular Solid

$1x$

$1.62x$

$1x + 1.62x$

If width is known:
   W ÷ 1.62 = H and H + W = L

If length is known:
   L ÷ 1.62 = W and W ÷ 1.62 = H

In practice, the shorter length of a design is multiplied by 1.62 to get the mid-distance. The longer distance is then derived by adding the other two. **Figure 33** above is an example of a golden rectangular solid where the smaller part is to the larger as the larger is to the whole, giving rise to the 1.618 factor.

Many wood workers derive the basic dimensions for furniture using this ratio. Some even base skirt width, leg diameter, width and height of carvings and the three dimensions of the cabriole leg on this ratio.

For example, if were designing a coffee table and decided the height should be 16 inches. What would the golden ratio proportion method suggest for width and length?

A GOLDEN RECTANGLE MAY BE DRAWN FROM A SQUARE USING A COMPASS.

Figure 34   Drawing a Golden Rectangle

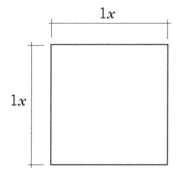

$1x$

$1x$

1. Start with a square whose sides equal the shorter dimension

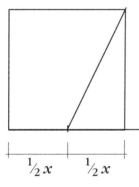

$\frac{1}{2}x$ $\frac{1}{2}x$

2. Find the midpoint of one side. Set a compass from the midpoint to the opposite corner of the square.

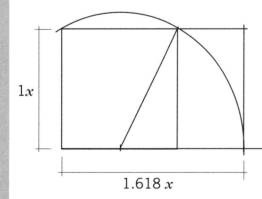

$1x$

$1.618\,x$

3. Swing that radius to find the corner of the Golden Rectangle.

Height x 1.62 = width
  16 x 1.62 = 25.92 or 26 in.
Height + width = length
  16 + 26 = 42 in.

We would then draw plans for a coffee table measuring 42 in. L x 26 in. W x 16 in. H.

The Greeks, who were adept at using geometry to visualize these relations, derived a method for constructing a series of rectangles based on these proportions. As shown in **Figure 34**, starting with a square with sides equal to the shorter dimension you want, find the midpoint along one side. Set the two points of a compass between that midpoint and one of the opposite corners of the square. Swinging that radius produces a new point that becomes the corner of a larger rectangle which is in 'golden proportions' to the original square.

Misperception

The dimensions derived from these mathematical formulae should never be thought of as absolute. Eye-pleasing proportions are sometimes surprising. In the previous discussions we considered mostly three dimensions. The golden ratio can also be used for two dimensional objects.

We want to design a wall mirror approximately 24"H to go above a vanity. Again, we

THE FIRST SKETCH SHOWS A GOLDEN RATIO RECTANGLE. THE MIDDLE SKETCH SHOWS THE SAME RECTANGLE WITH A 3-IN. FRAME. THE RIGHT FIGURE SHOWS THE GOLDEN RATIO INSIDE THE OUTER DIMENSIONS.

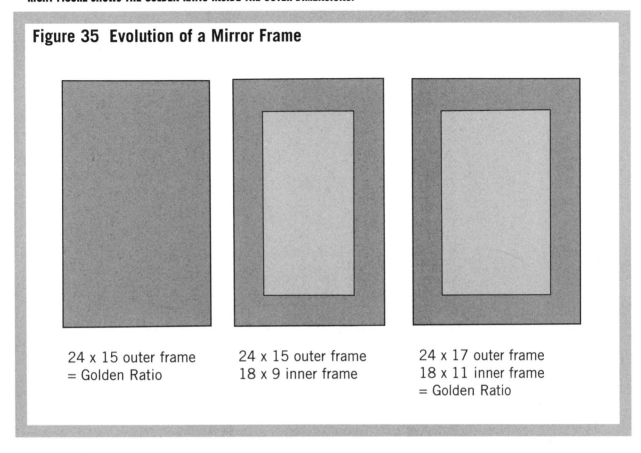

Figure 35 Evolution of a Mirror Frame

24 x 15 outer frame
= Golden Ratio

24 x 15 outer frame
18 x 9 inner frame

24 x 17 outer frame
18 x 11 inner frame
= Golden Ratio

want to use the golden ratio to home in on an eye-pleasing size. Our first inclination is to determine the proper width using the 24" height:

Height ÷ 1.62 = width
24" ÷ 1.62 = 14.8" ≈ 15"

When we draw this rectangle (see **Figure 35** above), the proportions look good. However, when we add a 3" frame (middle sketch) the dimensions no longer look right. The outside dimensions are the same, but adding the

frame makes the mirror look different and the figure is not as pleasing; somehow it seems too narrow. Apparently, the eye is drawn to the inner rectangle (9" x 18"), which is not a golden ratio. To be one, the inner rectangle should be 11" x 18" (18 ÷ 1.62 ≈ 11).

Changing the outer dimensions to 24" x 17", numbers that do not conform to the golden ratio, and drawing in the 3" frame, the picture looks better. The inner rectangle now is 18" x 11", numbers that do match

the golden ratio (right sketch). It seems the eye is drawn to the inside ratio dimensions rather than to the outside. Knowing the eye deceives the brain, we can use this to calculate dimensions of picture frames, mirrors, cabinets with prominent rails and stiles, and other furniture.

WITH THE SAME 10 X 6-1/4 X 3-3/4 PROPORTIONS, THREE DIFFERENT SHAPES ARE DRAWN.

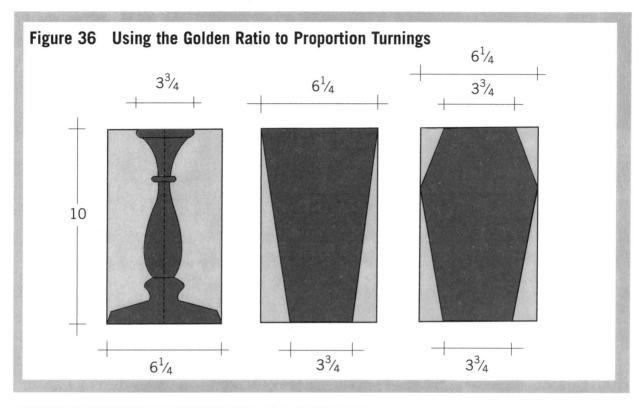

Figure 36   Using the Golden Ratio to Proportion Turnings

PLANNING THE DIMENSIONS FOR A BOWL GIVEN THE 3-1/2-IN. THICKNESS OF THE BLANK.

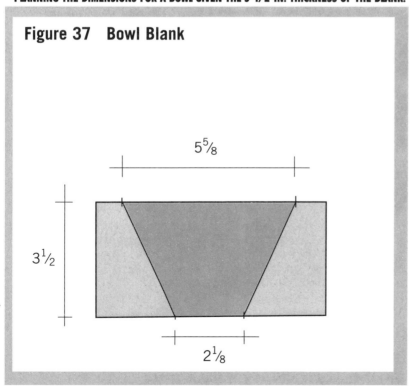

Figure 37   Bowl Blank

Wood Turning

Wood turners also use the golden ratio to plan proportions. **Figure 36** (above) shows shapes that conform to the golden ratio.

Figure 37 (left) shows the ratio being used to cut a bowl from a $3\frac{1}{2}$-in. blank. Using the golden ratio, we find dimensions of:

$3\frac{1}{2}$ in. H x $5\frac{5}{8}$-in. top dia.
   x $2\frac{1}{8}$-in. foot dia.
$3.5 \times 1.62 = 5.67 \approx 5\frac{5}{8}$
$3.5 \div 1.62 = 2.16 \approx 2\frac{1}{8}$

Spirals

A rather strange application of a logarithmic ratio (similar to the Golden Mean) is its use in drawing spirals. When the numbers 1, 1, 2, 3, 5, 8 and 13 are drawn as successive representative squares as seen in **Figure 38**, the diagonal points can be joined to produce a spiral. This type of spiral appears in nature eg the snail or Nautilus shell. Architectural carvers use this method to lay out complex designs of various sizes.

THE GOLDEN RATIO NUMBERS (1, 1, 2, 3, 5, 8, AND 13) ARE USED TO PRODUCE SUCCESSIVE SQUARES. WHEN ARCS ARE DRAWN FROM THE CORNERS OF EACH SQUARE, THE NAUTILUS SPIRAL IS PRODUCED

Rule of Thumb

Figure 38   The Nautilus Spiral

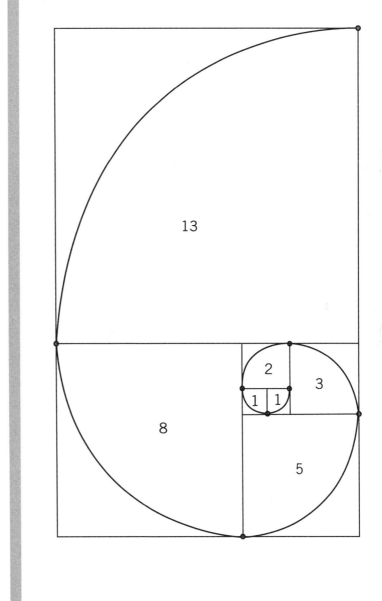

USE THIS TABLE TO PLAN SECTIONS OF A FENCE.

Figure 39 Fence Height to Section Length

Fence Height	Section Length
4	6 ½
4 ½	7 ¼
5	8
5 ½	9
6	9 ¾
6 ½	10 ½
7	11 ¼
7 ½	12
8	13

Design a Fence

You can use the golden ratio to plan a fence. The ratio 1:1.618 can be simplified to 5:8 (actual golden ratio is 5:8.09). If the fence is 5 ft. tall, plan on 8 ft. sections. In fact any length a little over 1½ times height will look good and 'feel right'.

Use the chart at left (**Figure 39**) to plan the length of fence sections according to the fence height.

Example: If you are building a $5\frac{1}{2}$-ft.-high fence, what would be the ideal section length? Using the fence height-to-length table (**Figure 39**), find $5\frac{1}{2}$ ft. The ideal section length is 9 ft.

Rule of Thumb
Use 6/10 for Estimating

To find pleasing shapes, use the 6/10 estimating method. The ratio 6:10 is close to the Golden Ratio (6:9.7).

1. Pick the middle dimension and multiply this by 6 and divide by 10 to get the smaller dimension.

2. Multiply the middle dimension by 10 and divide by 6 to get the larger dimension.

3. Round off all numbers.

In making a jewelry box that will be 7 in. long, how wide and how high should it be?

Length = 7 in.
Height: 7 x 6 = 42 ÷ 10
    = 4 plus
Width: 7 ÷ 10 = 70 ÷ 6
    = 11 plus

Therefore, draw up plans for a jewelry box measuring 4 in. H x 7 in. W x 11 in. L. These dimensions are very close to the Golden Ratio. ($4\frac{3}{8}$ x 7 x $11\frac{3}{8}$).

What would be the width of a picture frame that is 32 in. high?

Consider the 32 inches as both the large dimension and the small dimension:

32" x 10 = 320 "÷ 6 = 53"
32" x 6 = 192" ÷ 10 = 19"

Therefore draw a frame 32" x 53" or 32" x 19". Adjust the size for the most pleasing shape, including the picture, frame, and matting.

Other Pleasing Proportions

Figure 40 at right shows simple box shapes that are generally regarded as pleasing to the eye although they do not conform to the golden ratio. The cube is expanded to the double cube for more interest. The root-of-two cuboid still retains proportions that catch the eye, as does the 1:2:3 solid. A quick way to generate a root-of-two rectangle is to strike an arc from the diagonal of a square **(Figure 41)**.

Drawer Proportioning

In designing a chest of drawers, first resolve height and width dimensions. The golden ratio suggests that a 60-in.-high chest might be 37 in. wide (60 ÷ 1.62 = 37) for a pleasing appearance. The depth of a chest is often dictated by the intended use and where the piece will be positioned in the room—a bedroom chest might be 20 to 24 in. deep while a linen chest in a narrow hallway might be 15 to 18 in.

Choosing the number and height of the drawers presents more choices. Will the drawers all be the same height? Usually drawers of different heights are visually more interesting. Proportioning drawer heights is an interesting aspect of the project and is very practical

THESE PROPORTIONS CAN BE USED AS A GOOD STARTING POINT IN DESIGN.

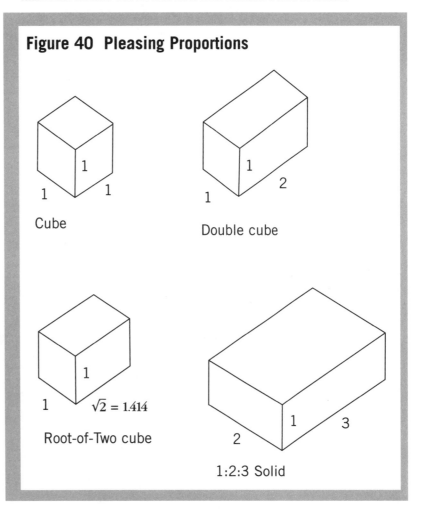

Figure 40 Pleasing Proportions

Cube

Double cube

Root-of-Two cube $\sqrt{2} = 1.414$

1:2:3 Solid

STRIKE AN ARC FROM THE DIAGONAL OF A SQUARE.

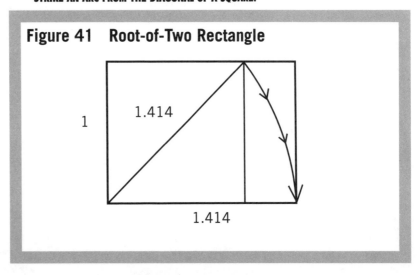

Figure 41   Root-of-Two Rectangle

1

1.414

1.414

BALANCE A COMPOSITION WITH INCREMENTAL PROPORTIONING SO EACH DRAWER IS LARGER THAN THE DRAWER JUST ABOVE. IN ALL CASES THE TOP DRAWER IS 5 IN.

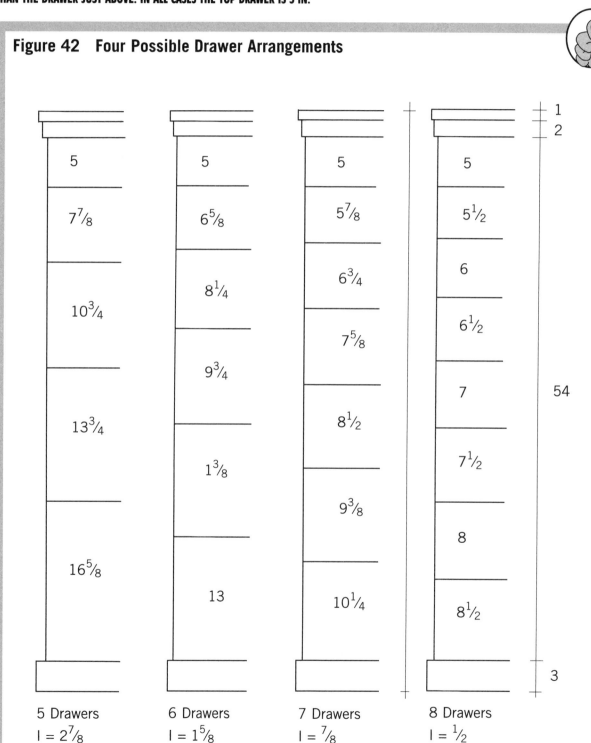

Figure 42 Four Possible Drawer Arrangements

5 Drawers
I = $2\frac{7}{8}$

6 Drawers
I = $1\frac{5}{8}$

7 Drawers
I = $\frac{7}{8}$

8 Drawers
I = $\frac{1}{2}$

—small items can be stored in small drawers at the top and bulky, perhaps heavy, items are stored in large drawers at the bottom. Drawers of different sizes seem also to balance the composition.

Woodworkers have long used a method of increasing drawer size by a given amount, say 1 in. If the top drawer is 4 in., then drawer 2 is 5 in., drawer 3 is 6 in., and so on. The problem here is that the height of the chest is not known until all the drawer heights have been added up.

Richard Jones in *Woodwork Magazine* presented an interesting method of figuring incremental drawer heights—after the size of the chest was chosen. Basically, imagine the total vertical opening in the chest filled with a certain number of equal sized drawers. The space left over is then divided incrementally between all the drawers. Here are the steps:

1. Set the chest height, e.g., 60 in.

2. Pick the number of drawers, e.g., 8.

3. Choose the top drawer height, e.g., 5 in.

4. Find the chest opening, e.g., 60 - 1 - 2 - 3 = 54 in. See **Fig. 42.**

5. Find the total height of all drawers by multiplying the number of drawers by the height of the top drawer: 5 in. x 8 = 40 in.

6. Subtract the total height of the drawers from the chest opening to give the height to be apportioned: 54 - 40 = 14 in.

7. Find the number of increments (I) in the stack of drawers.

1st drawer =	+0 x I
2nd drawer =	+1 x I
3rd drawer =	+2 x I
4th drawer =	+3 x I
5th drawer =	+4 x I
6th drawer =	+5 x I
7th drawer =	+6 x I
8th drawer =	+7 x I
Total increments (I) = 28	

8. Divide the 28 increments (I) into 14 in.

$$14 \div 28 = \tfrac{1}{2} \text{ in.}$$

Each drawer front will be $\tfrac{1}{2}$ in. taller than the one above, i.e., 5 in., $5\tfrac{1}{2}$ in., 6 in., etc.

In **Figure 42**, the four chests are all the same height, as are the chest openings. Also the top drawers are all the same height. The only difference is the number of drawers: 5, 6, 7, or 8. This method of determining drawer size simplifies consecutive additions when the chest height is already known.

IF THE CHEST HAS SIX DRAWERS, THE NUMBER OF INCREMENTS IS 15. USE THIS CONSTANT IN THE FORMULA.

Fig. 43 Increment Constants for Drawer Proportions

Drawers	Increments
2	1
3	3
4	6
5	10
6	15
7	21
8	28
9	36
10	45

EACH DRAWER IS PROPORTIONATELY LARGER THAN THE ONE ABOVE

Fig. 44 Drawer Sizes for Four Chests

5-drawer Chest	Top Drw	I = 2.9 Decimal	Fraction
1	5"	5.0"	5"
2		7.9	7 7/8
3		10.8	10 3/4
4		13.7	13 3/4
5		16.6	16 5/8

6-drawer Chest	Top Drawer	I = 1.6 Decimal	Fraction
1	5"	5.0"	5"
2		6.6	6 5/8
3		8.2	8 1/4
4		9.8	9 3/4
5		11.4	11 3/8
6		13.0	13

7-drawer Chest	Top Drawer	I = 0.9 Decimal	Fraction
1	5"	5.0"	5"
2		5.9	5 7/8
3		6.8	6 3/4
4		7.7	7 3/4
5		8.6	8 5/8
6		9.5	9 1/2
7		10.4	10 3/8

8-drawer Chest	Top Drawer	I = 0.5 Decimal	Fraction
1	5"	5.0"	5"
2		5.5	5 1/2
3		6.0	6
4		6.5	6 1/2
5		7.0	7
6		7.5	7 1/2
7		8.0	8
8		8.5	8 1/2

In **Figure 43**, the formula for finding the increment is:
Chest opening
= chest height - (top + top rail + base)

Total drawers height = number of drawers x top drawer height

Increment space = chest opening - total drawers' height
Increment = increment space ÷ drawer number constant

As an example, we can use a 66-in. chest with combined top, top rail, and base = $6\frac{1}{2}$ in. If we want to have seven drawers and have the top one be $4\frac{1}{2}$ in. high:

Chest opening = 66" - 6.5"
= 59.5"

Multiple drawers height
= 7 x 4.5 = 31.5 in.

Increment space
= 59.5 - 31.5 = 28 in.

Increment = 28 ÷ 21 (from **Fig**ure 43 chart) = 1.33 in.

We know the top drawer will be 4.5 in. and each succeeding drawer will be incrementally larger by 1.33 in. The total of all eight drawers is $59\frac{1}{2}$ in., the exact chest opening we determined earlier.

Drawer 1
= 4.5 + 0I = 4.50 = $4\frac{1}{2}$"

Drawer 2
= 4.5 + 1I = 5.83 = $5\frac{7}{8}$"

Drawer 3
= 4.5 + 2I = 7.16 = $7\frac{1}{8}$"

Drawer 4
= 4.5 + 3I = 8.49 = $8\frac{1}{2}$"

Drawer 5
= 4.5 + 4I = 9.82 = $9\frac{7}{8}$"

Drawer 6
= 4.5 + 5I = 11.15 = $11\frac{1}{8}$"

Drawer 7
= 4.5 + 6I = 12.48 = $12\frac{1}{2}$"

Decimal total = 59.43;
Fractional total = $59\frac{3}{8}$ in.

Figure 44 shows the measurements for similar chests, all with a top drawer height of 5 in., but with 5, 6, 7, or 8 drawers.

References:
Richard Jones, *Woodwork Magazine*, April 2001, p.41..

CHAPTER 5

Drawing Plans & Projections

Drawing is the graphic language used by woodworkers to express and record all of the ideas and information for building fine wooden objects. A woodworking or a technical drawing uses a precise, descriptive graphic language, whereas fine art drawing is primarily a means of aesthetic expression. Artists try to reproduce what they visualize in their minds. The draftsman precisely represents a three-dimensional object in a two-dimensional format.

Woodworkers have an exacting task because we are limited, usually, to line alone and cannot use color, gradation of tone, light, or shade. We can't make suggestions; we must impart precise and unambiguous information regarding every detail of a piece. Drawing, to a woodworker, is more than pictorial representation; it is a graphic language and the complete record of a work for analysis, construction, duplication, and repair.

By a logical system of "views", intricate and complicated shapes can be clearly shown. Exact and detailed sizes can be given without ambiguity. Individual parts can be identified for assembly and located in their correct position. In addition, descriptive notes and specifications identify materials, fasteners, finishes, and directions for construction and assembly.

In the artist's case, the result can be understood in greater or lesser degree by anyone and interpreted according to whim. The woodworker's drawing should not allow for interpretation. It must be unambiguous and exacting, and every woodworker should know how to make and read a drawing.

For planning and looking at a lot of options quickly, project sketches can't be beat. Developing your drawing skills will pay off big dividends, allowing more thoughtful detailing of your projects. The drawings don't have to be

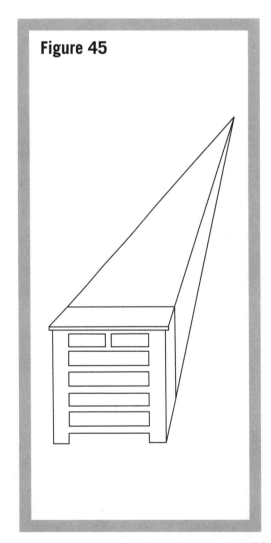

Figure 45

A PICTORIAL DRAWING DOES NOT REPRESENT THE TRUE SHAPE OF AN OBJECT. THE ORTHO-GRAPHIC VIEW SHOULD BE USED FOR DIMENSIONING. COMPARE THE DIMENSIONS OF THE DRAWER ON THE PICTORIAL DRAWING AND ON THE ORTHOGRAPHIC VIEWS.

Figure 46   Pictorial and Orthographic Drawing

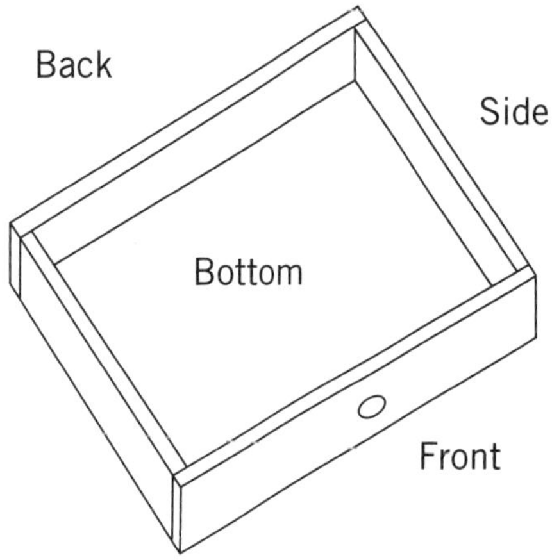

Back

Side

Bottom

Front

Pictorial Drawing

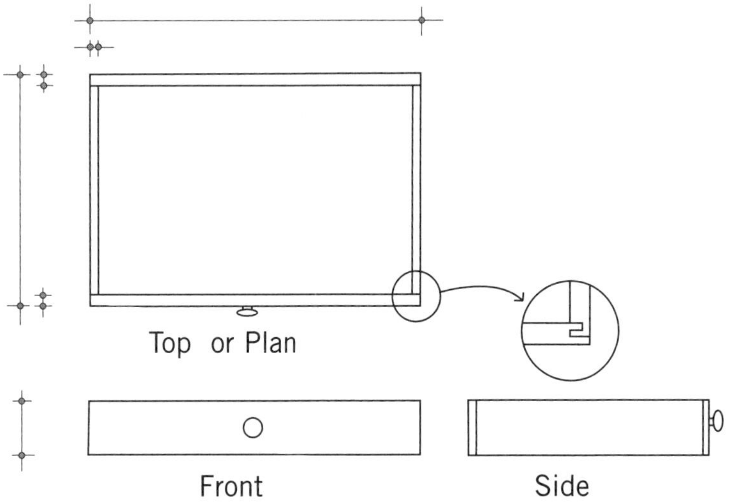

Top or Plan

Front

Side

Orthographic Drawing

pretty, just clear enough to accurately depict the object under study.

Rules for Drawing

To a skilled craftsman, a plan or working drawing is a detailed list of instructions for himself and others to follow. The drawing must contain all of the information necessary, set down in a form that is readily recognized. The information must follow a standard set of established rules that are universally interpreted by craftsmen to mean the same thing. Definite standards have been established so there can be no question in the interpretation, regardless of where the drawing is used.

To enumerate the rules, we will use a pictorial drawing and an orthographic drawing (**Figure 46**). A pictorial drawing is a representation of the appearance of the project, but does not represent the object in its true shape, for example: right angles are not square. An orthographic drawing represents the object in its true shape. Therefore, working drawings or blueprints are made from orthographic drawings.

Dimensions

Dimensioning is the most universal information found on any drawing, but dimension lines can be obtrusive. Because they follow the outline of the piece, they are as long as the part they are dimensioning and often come in sets of two or three. One line gives the overall dimension, while others give details about overall size.

The basic draftsman rule-of-thumb is: Say it once, say it correctly, and say it in the right place. To keep dimension lines from overpowering and interfering with the drawing, follow these guidelines:

1. Place dimension lines outside the view. Dimension lines inside the perimeter of the object have the effect of dividing either the form or the space, creating shapes that do not exist. One of the reasons for making a measured drawing is to show the proportion of the parts and their relationship to each other.

2. Dimension lines should be on the perimeter of the views, where they are less intrusive and produce a cleaner drawing. Vertical dimensions go outside the front and the end elevations, and horizontal dimensions outside the front elevations and the plan.

3. Dimensions should be applied to one view only, that is, the extension lines should be drawn from only one view, not from both. Dimensions should be placed on the view that shows the distance in its true length, not foreshortened.

4. Dimension lines should be spaced at least $\frac{1}{2}$ in. away from the outlines of the view; parallel dimension lines should be placed at least $\frac{3}{8}$ in. apart. The longer unbroken lines (overall dimensions) should be outside the shorter ones, in order to avoid crossing dimension lines with witness lines of other dimensions. An overall dimension showing the maximum size of the piece will be outside all other dimensions.

5. A line of any kind should never pass through a dimension figure. Dimension lines or witness lines should not cross. Hidden lines should not be used to dimension from.

When the drawing is viewed, the lines defining the structure and the parts should be distinct and clear. To this end, the dimension lines, cutting lines, center lines, etc., should be thinner and shouldn't interfere with the thicker lines depicting the object. In drafting, all lines should be black, but the thickness of the line varied.

IN THE ALIGNED SYSTEM (A), THE DIMENSIONS ARE ORIENTED PARALLEL WITH THE DIMENSION LINE. IN THE UNIDIRECTIONAL SYSTEM (B), ALL DIMENSONS ARE ORIENTED TO BE READ NORMALLY.

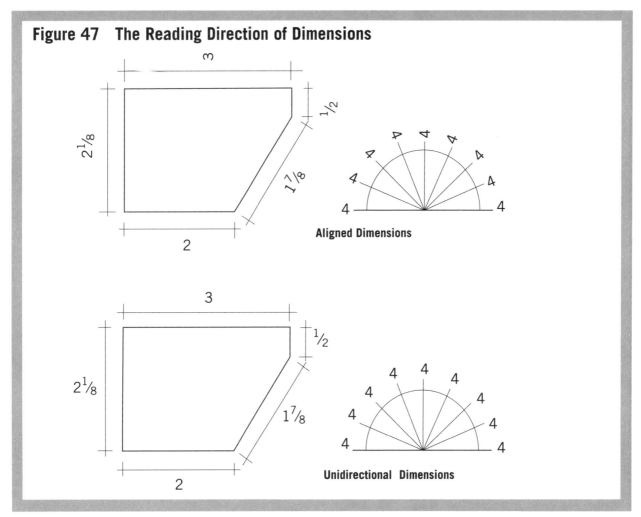

Figure 47   The Reading Direction of Dimensions

Aligned Dimensions

Unidirectional Dimensions

Feet and Inches

Feet and inches are indicated as 9'-6", not as 9'6" which, in haste, might be read as 96 in. When there are no inches, note this as 9'-0". When dimensions are all in inches, the inch mark is preferably omitted, thus 34 is used instead of 34". Some draftsmen omit all feet and inch marks, using the convention that numbers separated by a hyphen denote feet and inches, e.g., 3-4 equals 3 ft. and 4 in., whereas stand-alone numbers represent inches only, e.g., 40 equals 40 in.

The Reading Direction of Dimensions

Dimensions are arranged around an object in either the aligned system or the unidirectional system (**Figure** 47).

The aligned system is the older of the two methods. Here dimensions are oriented to be readable from a position parallel to the dimension line. The witness lines, as defined below, still must be perpendicular to the dimension line.

The unidirectional system is also called the horizontal system. All dimensions are oriented in one direction to be read from the bottom.

Witness Lines

In order to show where a dimension begins and ends, draw light lines perpendicular to the ends of the part. These are called witness lines. These are thin where they leave the object, then thicker where they intersect with the dimension line. Witness lines should be drawn so there is no ambiguity as to which part is being dimensioned.

Dimension Lines

In the past, dimension lines were depicted as a broken line, and the dimension figures were written in the break. Modern practice seems to prefer a continuous line with the dimension figure written off to one side. Use whichever you feel comfortable with but once you choose, stay with that convention throughout the drawing.

Arrowheads

Where a dimension line meets or crosses a witness line, some sort of mark is needed to clearly indicate where the dimension starts and ends. The traditional symbol was the arrowhead or a 45° slash, which was nestled tightly against a witness line. Again, modern blueprint drafters have changed. Instead of stopping at the witness lines, dimension lines now extend beyond, and tick marks or circles are used to show where the dimensions start and stop.

Tolerances

The amount of tolerance on a dimension is marked on a dimension line, for example, $\pm \frac{1}{32}$". This means the finished dimension on the part can vary $\frac{1}{32}$ in. above or $\frac{1}{32}$ in. below the basic size. The total tolerance is $\frac{1}{32}$ in. $+ \frac{1}{32}$ in. $= \frac{1}{16}$ in.

Hidden Lines and Broken Lines

A section of a drawing that is hidden by another part is shown by a series of short dashes. A broken line in any of the views indicates that only part of the piece is shown (**Figure 48**).

Sectional Views

If the project has a simple interior construction, hidden lines can be used to indicate interior parts. Often, however, when the interior is complicated or when several different pieces are assembled in place, an attempt to show the construction on an exterior view results in a confusing mass of dotted lines, annoying to draw and difficult, if not impossible, to read clearly. In such cases, one or more of the views is made "in section."

If part of the piece was cut, or broken away and removed, the

**A BROKEN LINE INDICATES THAT PART OF THE JOB IS HIDDEN FROM VIEW.
INSIDE DETAILS ARE SHOWN WITH SECTIONAL VIEWS.**

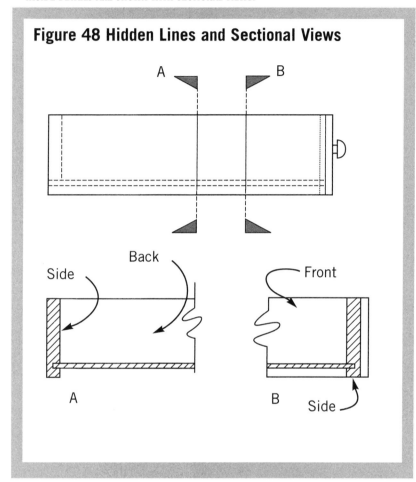

Figure 48 Hidden Lines and Sectional Views

interior construction or a section of the job would be shown. On a drawing, the same idea is conveyed by using cutting plane lines (one long line and two short dashes), arrows, and letters. The arrowheads show the direction of view of the cut—i.e., the direction you're looking at the section. The letters show where the cut is made. The cut surface is indicated by section lining, sometimes called "cross-hatching."

This view can be made larger to show detailed construction. Sometimes a circle is shown around part of the job and an enlarged view of that part shown at another place on the drawing. It must be emphasized that, in removing the nearer portion of the object to make the sectional view, this portion is not omitted when making other views.

Sectional Elevation

If what we are drawing is more complex than can be conveyed with a small section cut, we need to draw a large sectional elevation to get all the parts in context. Draw the whole object from the side or front, showing all the parts as seen from the cut in the direction of the arrowhead. Only the parts that were actually cut have cross-hatching. Plywood cuts are sometimes shown with multiple plies rather than cross-hatching.

On full-view sectionals, the long cutting line and the second arrowhead are usually omitted. A long line through the object would be unnecessarily obtrusive. If a drawing were made looking down on the piece after an imaginary horizontal cut was made, it would be called a sectional plan.

Alphabet of Lines

To read and use a blueprint, use these names and follow these methods of designating the various kinds of lines (**Figure 49**).

Methods of Drawing

Before starting a project, most woodworkers like to have a pretty good idea what it is they are building. Whether it is an original design or a copy of an old classic, adjustments are easier to make on paper than with wood. There are several drawing methods that allow the woodworker to see an exact representation of the project and work out all the details, before ever lifting a stick of wood heavier than a pencil. Three types of projections are commonly used to draw woodworking plans: orthographic, isometric, and oblique.

EVERY LINE ON A BLUEPRINT DENOTES SOMETHING. USE THESE TO CONVEY WHAT YOU MEAN

Figure 49 Alphabet of Lines

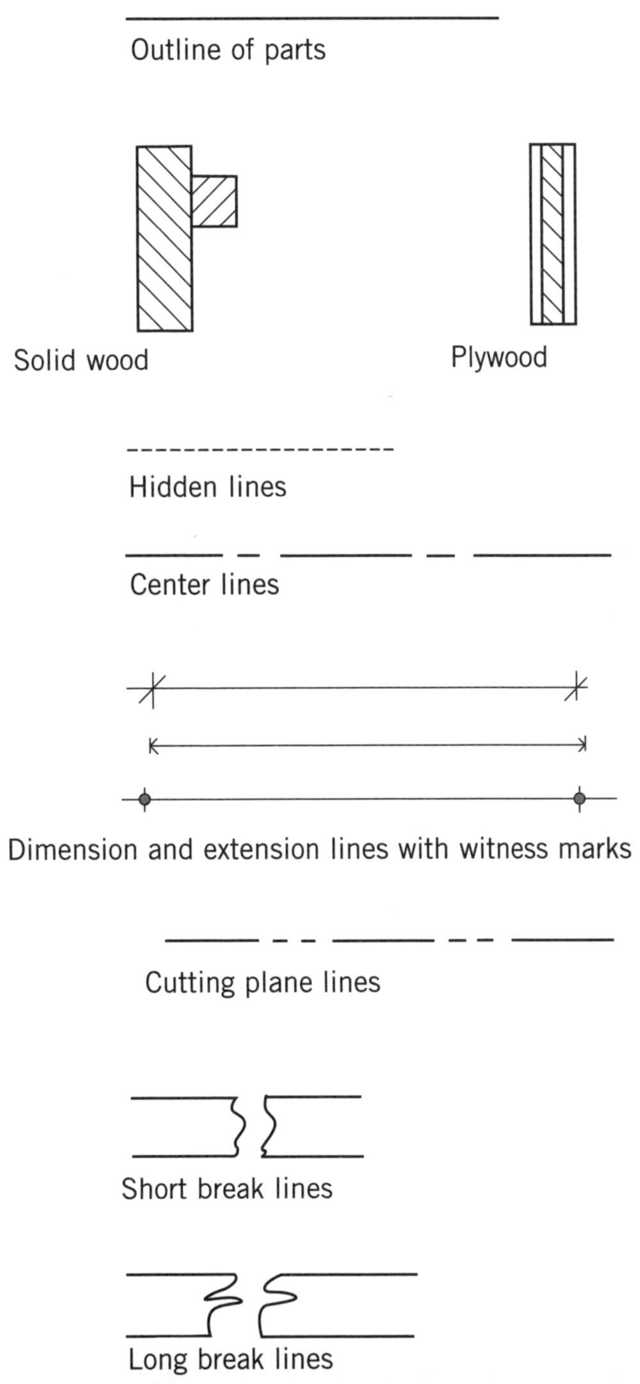

Outline of parts

Solid wood   Plywood

Hidden lines

Center lines

Dimension and extension lines with witness marks

Cutting plane lines

Short break lines

Long break lines

THIS IS THE FAMILIAR FRONT, TOP, AND END VIEW OFTEN USED BY WOODWORK-ERS. THE DETAILED SECTION GIVES A CLOSE-UP OF THE APRON-LEG JOINERY.

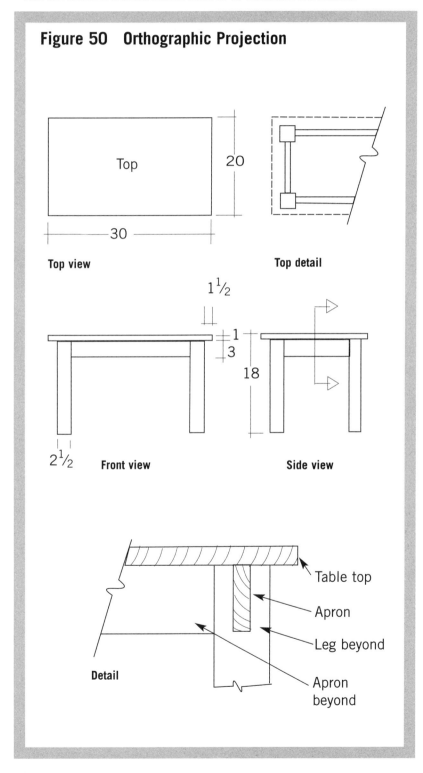

Figure 50   Orthographic Projection

Top view

Top detail

Front view

Side view

1½

1
3

18

2½

Detail

Table top

Apron

Leg beyond

Apron beyond

Orthographic Projection

An orthographic projection is the straight extension of all views of an object as if they are in the same plane, i.e., flat on the paper (**Figure 50**). This is the familiar two-view or three-view drawing seen on plans where the typical front view is projected upward for a top or plan view, and sometimes to the right for an end or side view. This projection is also called an elevation of the object, the same as the side view of a home on an architect's house plan.

To use the orthographic method, draw the longest horizontal and vertical dimensions of the front face of the object. Next, fill in details such as leg widths and apron heights. Above this front view, draw the top view. To the right, draw the end view. On these three views dimension the overall length, width, and depth of the piece. Next add the dimensions of the parts. The advantage of this approach is that it is easy to figure out joint design and construction methods. A disadvantage of an orthographic drawing is that it is unreal, an object is really never seen in this manner—although this violation of reality is mitigated by the ease with which dimensions can be added and parts can be measured.

IN A TRUE PERSPECTIVE DRAWING, ALL PARALLEL LINES CONVERGE AT A SINGLE SPOT CALLED THE VANISHING POINT.

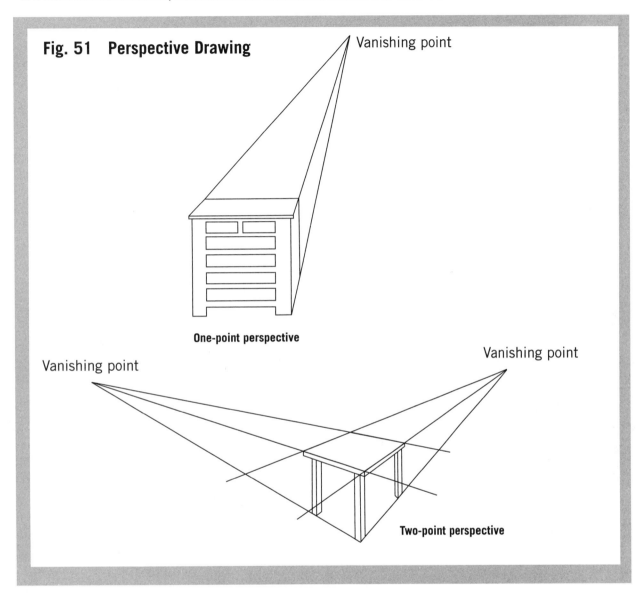

Fig. 51   Perspective Drawing

Vanishing point

One-point perspective

Vanishing point

Vanishing point

Two-point perspective

The detail magnifies a section of the drawing for a closer look. The arrows in the main drawing show where the cut through the object is made and the direction of the view.

Isometric Projections

This projection shows all three dimensions in one drawing but they are not true perspectives: there is no vanishing point (**Figure 51**).

In an isomeric projection (**Figure 52**) all parts are to scale and accurate measurements can be made from them. Isometric (equal measure) drawings are based on three axes inclined to the drawing surface. These are most often a 30°/60° drawing or a 60°/60° drawing.

To use the isometric method, first draw a vertical line representing the height of your object. Next, draw two base lines at 30° and 60° to the

IN THIS PROJECTION ALL PARTS ARE TO SCALE ALTHOUGH IT IS NOT TRUE PERSPECTIVE.

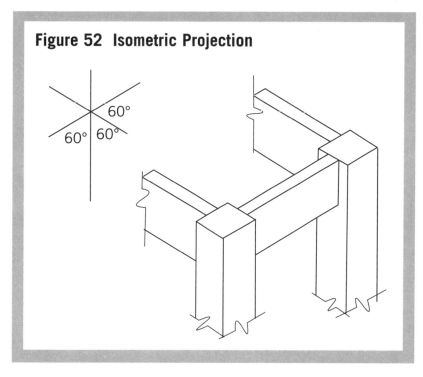

Figure 52 Isometric Projection

THIS PERSPECTIVE HAS TWO DIMENSIONS AT 90° AND THE THIRD AT 30° OR 45°. WHILE THIS PROJECTION DOESN'T GIVE A TRUE PERSPECTIVE, MEASUREMENTS CAN EASILY BE TAKEN FROM THIS TYPE OF DRAWING.

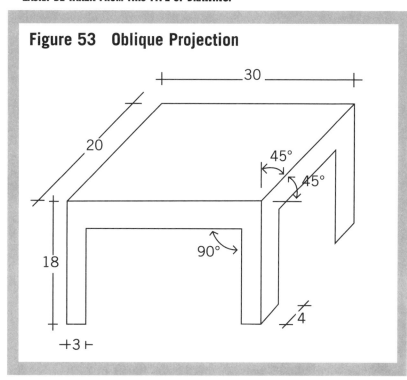

Figure 53   Oblique Projection

horizontal. These represent the length, height, and depth. On these three views, scale the length, width and depth of the object. A disadvantage of an isometric drawing is that it is not a true perspective. All parts are drawn the same length instead of shortening as they recede into the distance. The advantage is that it is a wonderful way to lay out joints and construction details in a project.

Oblique Projections

The oblique projection is the representation often used by woodworkers. This type of illustration is similar to an isometric projection in that it has three axes upon which measurements can be made. However, in the oblique or slanting illustration, two of these axes are at a right angle, while the third axis usually is at 30° or 45° (**Figure 53**).

To make an oblique drawing, start with a point representing a front corner and draw from it the three axes, one vertical, one horizontal, and one at an angle. On these three lines, scale the height, width, and depth of the object. A disadvantage of the oblique drawing is the distortion produced by the lack of convergence in receding lines. This violation of perspective is less noticeable if the longest dimension is drawn horizontal at the front, the next longest dimension drawn perpendicular at 90° either up or down, and the shortest dimension drawn receding into the paper at 30° or 45° Any face parallel to the picture plane will be projected without distortion, an advantage over an isometric projection in which all faces are distorted.

The oblique projection at **Figure 53** shows a table, 18 in. H x 20 in. W x 30 in. L. This was drawn using the $\frac{3}{32}$ scale ($\frac{3}{32}$" = 1") with an architect's rule. See Chapter 3 for more on using an architect's scale.

Practical Geometry

Every woodworking drawing is made up of straight lines, curved lines, or combinations of the two. The following examples of basic geometry show methods of drawing lines and figures useful to woodworkers.

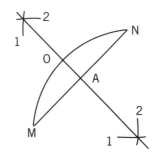

FIG. 54. TO BISECT A STRAIGHT LINE OR THE ARC OF A CIRCLE
Let line MN be the given line to be drawn into equal halves. With centers M and N and any radius greater than one-half of MN, draw the arcs 1 and 2. Through the points of intersection of these arcs draw a line. The intersection with the given line MN, and the arc MON, shown by OA will give the required points.

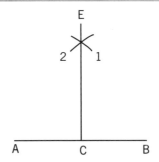

FIG. 55. TO ERECT A PERPENDICULAR FROM A GIVEN LINE
Locate point C at the middle of line AB. With the point of the compass on A and any radius greater than AB, describe an arc at 1. On B, with the same radius, describe the arc 2. Through the intersection of arcs 1 and 2, draw the line EC, which will be the required perpendicular.

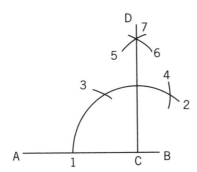

FIG. 56. TO ERECT A PERPENDICULAR NEAR THE END OF A GIVEN LINE
Locate point C, from which the perpendicular is to be erected, on line AB. With C as center and with any convenient radius, describe the arc 1-2. Using the same radius, step off this distance from 1 to 3 and 3 to 4. Using any radius with 3 and 4 as centers, describe arcs 5 and 6 intersecting each other at 7. Draw a line from C through 7, which will give the perpendicular at the given point C.

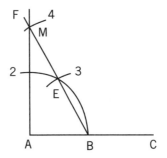

FIG. 57. TO ERECT A PERPENDICULAR AT THE END OF A GIVEN LINE
On line AC, set the point of the compass on A, and with any radius describe the arc B2. On B, with the same radius, describe the arc 3 intersecting arc B2 at E. Through E draw line BF indefinitely. From E with radius BE, describe arc 4, intersecting line BF at M. Connect MA, which will be the perpendicular required.

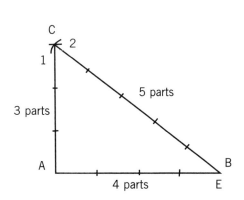

FIG. 58. TO ERECT A PERPENDICULAR AT THE END OF A GIVEN LINE
Draw AB making it equal to the length of four parts, by any scale. At point A and with a radius equal to three parts, scribe arc 1.
At point B and with a radius equal to five parts scribe arc 2 intersecting at C. Draw line AC, which is the required perpendicular. This is the 3-4-5 right triangle method.

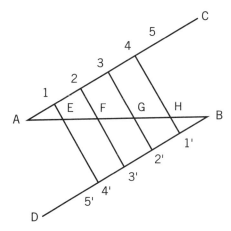

FIG. 59. TO DIVIDE A LINE INTO ANY NUMBER OF EQUAL PARTS
Let AB be the given line to be divided, in this case into five parts. Draw line AC at any angle to line AB, and line BD parallel to line AC. On lines AC and BD, set off five equal spaces as indicated from 1 to 5, and 1' to 5'. Connect points 1-4' and 2-3', etc., and the points of intersection at E, F, G, and H on line AB will divide the line into five equal parts.

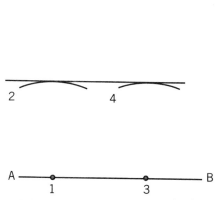

FIG. 60. TO DRAW A LINE PARALLEL TO A GIVEN LINE
Near the end of line AB at 1, set the point of the compass, and with any radius, describe arc 2. With the same radius on point 3, describe the arc 4. A line drawn touching the arcs 2 and 4 will be parallel to AB.

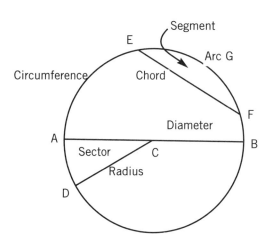

FIG. 61. TO DRAW A CIRCLE AND ITS PROPERTIES
Bisect line AB at C. With the point of a compass at C, and radius CA, describe the circumference of the circle. The diameter of a circle is any straight line drawn through the center to opposite points of the circumference, such as AB. The radius of a circle is any line, as CA and DC, drawn from the center to any point in the circumference; two or more such lines are radii, the plural of radius. An arc of a circle is any part of the circumference, as arc G. The sector of a circle is the part of a circle between the radii and the arc that they intercept, as ACD. A segment of a circle is a part cut off by a chord, as EFG. A chord of a circle is a straight line joining the extremities of an arc, but not passing through the center, as EF.

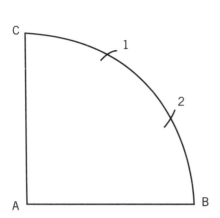

FIG. 62. TO TRISECT A 90° ANGLE
Construct a 90° angle CAB. With any radius, describe arc BC. With the same radius and B and C as centers, describe arcs B1 and C2, thus dividing the 90° angle into three equal parts. By using this method a variety of angles, such as 30°, 60°, or 120° may be obtained.

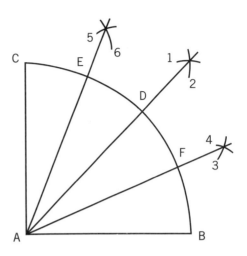

FIG. 63. TO BISECT A 90°, 45°, OR ANY ANGLE
Construct a 90° angle CAB. With any radius, describe arc BC. With any radius, describe arcs B1 and C2, thus dividing angle CAB into two 45° sections. By further bisections, angles DAB and CAD can be divided into 11-1/2° sections following the principles just explained. By using the principles of trisection and the principles of bisection, a great variety of angles can be obtained, such as 15°, 22-1/2°, 30°, 45°, 52-1/2°, 60°, 75°, and so forth.

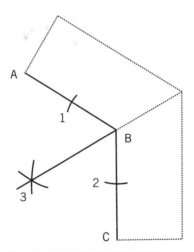

FIG. 64. TO BISECT A GIVEN ANGLE
Draw the given angle ABC. With any convenient radius and B as center, describe the arcs 1 and 2. With the same or a larger radius and 1 and 2 as centers, describe arcs intersecting at 3. Draw a line from 3 to B, which divides the angle ABC into two equal parts.

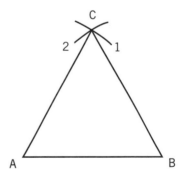

FIG. 65. TO DRAW AN EQUILATERAL TRIANGLE, ONE SIDE BEING GIVEN
Draw line AB and with A as center and AB as radius, describe arc 1. With B as center and the same radius, describe arc 2 intersecting the former arc at C. Draw the lines BC and AC, and ABC is the required equilateral triangle.

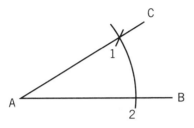

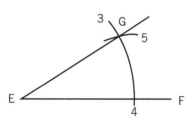

**FIG. 66. TO CONSTRUCT AN ANGLE
SIMILAR TO A GIVEN ANGLE**
Let CAB be the given angle. With A as center and with any radius,
describe arc 1-2, touching both sides of the angle. Draw line EF equal
to AB. With E as a center and radius A2 of the given angle, describe arc
3-4. With 4 as center and radius 1-2, describe arc 5 intersecting arc 3-
4 at G. A line drawn from E through point G completes the angle equal
to CAB.

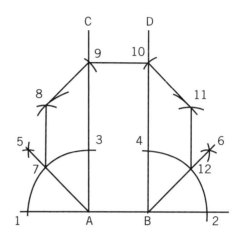

**FIG. 67. TO CONSTRUCT AN OCTAGON,
ONE SIDE BEING GIVEN**
Draw line AB, which is the length of the given side. Extend AB indefinitely, as shown by 1 and 2. From A and B, erect indefinite perpendiculars as AC and BD. With A and B as centers and using any radius, draw
the arcs 1-3 and 4-2. Bisect the angles 1-A-3 and 4-B-2 by 5-A and B-
6. On these two lines set off A-7 and B-12, equal to AB. From 7 and 12,
erect the perpendiculars 7-8 and 12-11, equal to AB. With 8 and 11 as
centers and AB as radius, describe arcs 9 and 10, intersecting perpendiculars AC and BD at 9 and 10. Connect 8-9, 9-10, and 10-11; this
completes the octagon.

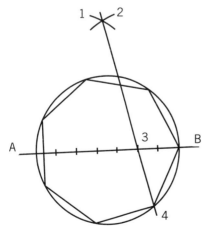

**FIG. 68. TO INSCRIBE ANY REGULAR POLYGON
IN A CIRCLE**
Divide the diameter AB of the circle into as many equal parts as the
polygon is to have sides, in this case seven. With A and B as centers
and a radius equal to AB, describe arcs A1 and B2. From the intersection of arcs 1 and 2 draw a line through the second point of the diameter divisions at 3, extending to the circumference of the circle at 4. A
line drawn from B to A is one of the sides of the polygon.

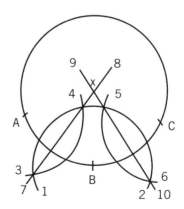

**FIG. 69. TO FIND THE CENTER OF A CIRCLE
WHEN THE CIRCUMFERENCE IS GIVEN**
Let ABC be the given circle. From any point on the circle as B, with any
radius, describe the arc 1-2. Then from the points A and C, with the
same radius, describe the intersecting arcs 3-4 and 5-6. Through the
points of intersection, draw the lines 7-8 and 9-10, which will meet in
x; this will be the center of the circle.

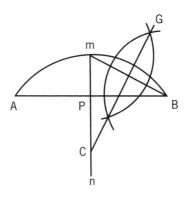

FIG. 70. TO DESCRIBE THE SEGMENT OF A CIRCLE OF ANY GIVEN CHORD AND HEIGHT
Draw the line AB, which will be the given chord. Draw the perpendicular mn indefinitely, and make Pm the given height. Connect mB and bisect Mb by the line CG, intersecting the perpendicular mn at C. The C will be the center from which to describe the segment AmB.

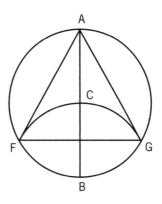

FIG. 71. TO INSCRIBE AN EQUILATERAL TRIANGLE IN A CIRCLE
Draw the line AB, which will be the diameter of the given circle. With B as center and BC (the radius of the circle) as radius, describe the arc FCG. To complete the inscribed triangle, connect by straight lines FA, AG, and GF.

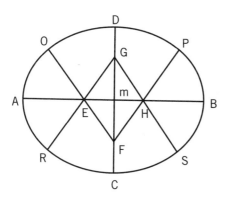

FIG. 72. TO DRAW AN APPROXIMATE ELLIPSE, GIVEN THE MAJOR AND MINOR AXES
Draw the major diameter AB and the minor diameter CD. On line CD, lay off mF and mG, equal to the difference between the major and minor diameters. On the line AB, lay off mE and mH equal to three-quarters of mG. Connect points FHGE and extend the lines. With center E and radius EA, describe arc RAO. With center F and radius FD, describe arc ODP. In a similar manner, describe arcs PBS and SCR from centers H and G. This is not a practical method when the major diameter is more than twice the minor.

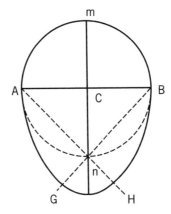

FIG. 73. TO DRAW AN EGG-SHAPED OVAL WITH ARCS OF CIRCLES
With C as the center, describe the circle AmBn. Through the center C, perpendicular to AB, draw the line mn. Through n draw Bn and An indefinitely. On A and B as centers, with AB as radius, describe the arcs BH and AG. With n as center, describe the arc GH to complete the figure.

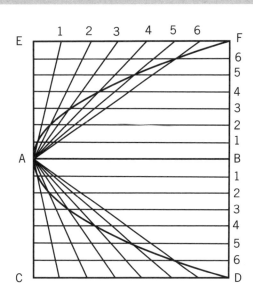

**FIG. 74. TO DRAW A PARABOLA,
GIVEN THE AXIS AB AND THE DOUBLE ORDINATE FD**

Draw AB and FD perpendicular to AB. Draw EF and CD parallel and equal to AB. Divide EF and BF into the same number of equal parts. From the divisions on BF, draw lines parallel to axis AB, and from the divisions on EF, draw lines to the vertex A. Similarly numbered lines intersect, through which the curve is traced. In like manner, obtain the opposite side.

CHAPTER 6

Converting Numbers

Most of us use calculators to do woodworking math and then use a carpenter's tape when we're ready to measure and cut. Calculators use decimals like 0.5, 0.25, 0.125, and 0.0625, while our tapes are divided into fractions like $\frac{1}{2}$, $\frac{1}{4}$, $\frac{1}{8}$, and $\frac{1}{16}$. In designing a dresser, suppose we come up with a drawer width of 19.21 in. How do we convert this decimal to a fraction when it's time to measure the wood?

The ability to convert numbers to decimals, decimals to fractions, fractions to millimeters, and millimeters to decimals is necessary for any woodworker. To do it quickly and accurately is a must. In this chapter you'll find formulas and charts to help you along.

Decimals to Fractions

In our example, 0.21 can be thought of as twenty-one one-hundredths or 21/100. This still doesn't get us any closer to measuring the distance on a piece of wood because our tapes aren't calibrated in 100ths. But you can convert decimals to usable fractions.

First decide how precise you want the answer to be, i.e., to the nearest 8th, the nearest 16th, or perhaps the nearest 32nd. Multiply the decimal by the denominator for the fraction you want and take the nearest whole number of the answer as the numerator of the fraction. It's actually easier to demonstrate than it is to tell. In the example above, we want to convert 0.21 to a fraction.

Nearest 8th:

$0.21 \times 8 = 1.68$

DUPLICATE THIS CHART AND HANG IT IN YOUR SHOP.

Figure 75 Inch Fractions - Decimal Equivalents

Inch Fraction	Decimal Inch	Inch Fraction	Decimal Inch
$\frac{1}{64}$	0.016	$\frac{33}{64}$	0.516
$\frac{1}{32}$	0.031	$\frac{17}{32}$	0.531
$\frac{3}{64}$	0.047	$\frac{35}{64}$	0.547
$\frac{1}{16}$	0.063	$\frac{9}{16}$	0.563
$\frac{5}{64}$	0.078	$\frac{37}{64}$	0.578
$\frac{3}{32}$	0.094	$\frac{19}{32}$	0.594
$\frac{7}{64}$	0.109	$\frac{39}{64}$	0.609
$\frac{1}{8}$	0.125	$\frac{5}{8}$	0.625
$\frac{9}{64}$	0.141	$\frac{41}{64}$	0.641
$\frac{5}{32}$	0.156	$\frac{21}{32}$	0.656
$\frac{11}{64}$	0.172	$\frac{43}{64}$	0.672
$\frac{3}{16}$	0.188	$\frac{11}{16}$	0.688
$\frac{13}{64}$	0.203	$\frac{45}{64}$	0.703
$\frac{7}{32}$	0.219	$\frac{23}{32}$	0.719
$\frac{15}{64}$	0.234	$\frac{47}{64}$	0.734
$\frac{1}{4}$	0.250	$\frac{3}{4}$	0.750
$\frac{17}{64}$	0.266	$\frac{49}{64}$	0.766
$\frac{9}{32}$	0.281	$\frac{25}{32}$	0.781
$\frac{19}{64}$	0.297	$\frac{51}{64}$	0.797
$\frac{5}{16}$	0.313	$\frac{13}{16}$	0.813
$\frac{21}{64}$	0.328	$\frac{53}{64}$	0.828
$\frac{11}{32}$	0.344	$\frac{27}{32}$	0.844
$\frac{23}{64}$	0.359	$\frac{55}{64}$	0.859
$\frac{3}{8}$	0.375	$\frac{7}{8}$	0.875
$\frac{25}{64}$	0.391	$\frac{57}{64}$	0.891
$\frac{13}{32}$	0.406	$\frac{29}{32}$	0.906
$\frac{27}{64}$	0.422	$\frac{59}{64}$	0.922
$\frac{7}{16}$	0.438	$\frac{15}{16}$	0.938
$\frac{29}{64}$	0.453	$\frac{61}{64}$	0.953
$\frac{15}{32}$	0.469	$\frac{31}{32}$	0.969
$\frac{31}{64}$	0.484	$\frac{63}{64}$	0.984
$\frac{1}{2}$	0.500	1	1.000

Rule of Thumb
Decimals to Fractions

When we divide or multiply with a calculator, we often come up with strange decimals, such as 6.395. What is 0.395 in fractions?

An easier way to convert decimals to fractions is to use a conversion chart.

Look up 0.395 in the conversion chart (**Figure 75**). The nearest fraction is $\frac{25}{64}$, so the measurement is $6\frac{25}{64}$. You can see on the chart that $\frac{3}{8}$ and $\frac{13}{32}$ are close. If you don't need the precision, use one of these fractions.

Rule of Thumb
Fractions to Decimals

To convert fractions to decimals, use the Fraction —Decimal Equivalents chart. What is the decimal equivalent of the fraction $\frac{17}{64}$? **Figure 75** shows 0.266.

The decimal 0.21 is the same as the fraction 1.68/8 or rounded up is $\frac{2}{8}$ or $\frac{1}{4}$. We can also calculate 0.21 to the nearest 16th, 32nd, and 64th.

Nearest 16th:
0.21 x 16 = 3.36/16, rounded to $\frac{3}{16}$ in.
Nearest 32nd:
0.21 x 32 = 6.72/32, rounded to $\frac{7}{32}$ in.
Nearest 64th:
0.21 x 64 = 13.44/64, rounded to $\frac{13}{64}$ in.

Decide how precisely you want to measure. In marquetry or inlay, you would choose much closer tolerances than in house framing.

Convert the decimal 0.81 to a fraction.

Nearest 4th:
0.81 x 4 = 3.24/4 ≈ $\frac{3}{4}$
Nearest 8th:
0.81 x 8 = 6.48/8 ≈ $\frac{6}{8}$ = $\frac{3}{4}$
Nearest 16th:
0.81 x 16 = 12.96/16 ≈ $\frac{13}{16}$
Nearest 32nd:
0.81 x 32 = 25.92/32 ≈ $\frac{26}{32}$ = $\frac{13}{16}$

Note when converting 0.81 to the nearest 32nd, the answer $\frac{13}{16}$ was the same as converting to the nearest 16th. When you get an answer like 12.96/16, which is very close to $\frac{13}{16}$, going to the next fraction usually will not result in greater accuracy.

Convert 0.46 to a fraction.
Nearest 4th:
0.46 x 4 = 1.84/4 ≈ $\frac{2}{4}$ = $\frac{1}{2}$
Nearest 8th:
0.46 x 8 = 3.68/8 ≈ $\frac{4}{8}$ = $\frac{1}{2}$
Nearest 16th:
0.46 x 16 = 7.36/16 ≈ $\frac{7}{16}$
Nearest 32nd:
0.46 x 32 = 14.72/32 ≈ $\frac{15}{32}$
Nearest 64th:
0.46 x 64 = 29.44/64 ≈ $\frac{29}{64}$.

Fractions to Decimals

This one is easy. To convert a fraction to a decimal, just divide the numerator by the denominator, that is, divide the top number by the bottom number.

Convert the fraction $\frac{7}{8}$ to its decimal equivalent.
7 divided by 8 is 0.875

Feet-Plus-Inches to Feet

Mixed numbers such as feet and inches present a problem when you're adding or subtracting them. You need to convert the mixed numbers to all feet or all inches. Let's do feet first.

What is 12 ft. 7 $\frac{3}{8}$ in. in feet?

1. Convert the fraction first:
$\frac{3}{8}$ in. = 0.375 in.
0.375 in. ÷ 12 in/ft. = 0.031 ft.

2. Convert inches to feet.
7 in. ÷ 12 in/ft. = 0.583 ft.

3. 12 ft. = 12 ft.

4. Now all parts of the measurement, 12 ft., 7 in., and $\frac{3}{8}$ in., are in the same units. Add all three.

    0.031 ft. ($\frac{3}{8}$ in.)
+ 0.583 ft. (7 in.)
+ 12.000 ft. (12 ft.)
= 12.614 ft.

This number can be converted to inches:

    12.614 ft. x 12 in/ft.
= 151.37 in.

Feet-Plus-Inches to Inches

Convert 6 ft. 3-3/16 in. to inches.

    3/16 in. = 0.188 in.
3 in. = 3 in.
6 ft. = 6 x 12 in/ft. = 72 in.

Add the three parts of the fraction:

    72 + 3 + 0.19 = 75.19 in.

This number can be converted to feet.

    75.19 in. ÷ 12 in/ft. = 6.27 ft.

Metric Equivalence

Woodworkers sometimes measure in centimeters and millimeters because greater precision is possible. For example, a small part might measure $\frac{17}{32}$ in. This is somewhat hard to draw and measure, while the metric equivalent 13.5 mm is fairly easy.

Inches to Metric

Inches x 2.54
    = centimeters (cm)

Inches x 25.4
    = millimeters (mm)

Six inches equal how many mm?
    6 x 25.4 = 152.4 mm

Metric to Inches

Millimeters (mm) ÷ 25.4
    = inches

Centimeters (cm) ÷ 2.54
    = inches

Many drill bits are sized in metric today. What is the nearest decimal fraction to 10 mm?
    10 mm ÷ 25.4 = 0.3937 in.

The fraction-to-decimal chart (**Figure 75**) shows that 0.3937 is between $\frac{25}{64}$ in. and $\frac{13}{32}$ in.

You also could use the chart of

Fig. 76 Inch Fractions - Metric Equivalents

Inch Fraction	Metric MM	Inch Fraction	Metric MM
1/64	0.397	33/64	13.097
1/32	0.794	17/32	13.494
3/64	1.191	35/64	13.891
1/16	1.588	9/16	14.288
5/64	1.984	37/64	14.684
3/32	2.381	19/32	15.081
7/64	2.778	39/64	15.478
1/8	3.175	5/8	15.875
9/64	3.572	41/64	16.272
5/32	3.969	21/32	16.669
11/64	4.366	43/64	17.066
3/16	4.763	11/16	17.463
13/64	5.159	45/64	17.859
7/32	5.556	23/32	18.256
15/64	5.953	47/64	18.653
1/4	6.350	3/4	19.050
17/64	6.747	49/64	19.447
9/32	7.144	25/32	19.844
19/64	7.541	51/64	20.241
5/16	7.938	13/16	20.638
21/64	8.334	53/64	21.034
11/32	8.731	27/32	21.431
23/64	9.128	55/64	21.828
3/8	9.525	7/8	22.225
25/64	9.922	57/64	22.622
13/32	10.319	29/32	23.019
27/64	10.716	59/64	23.416
7/16	11.113	15/16	23.813
29/64	11.509	61/64	24.209
15/32	11.906	31/32	24.606
31/64	12.303	63/64	25.003
1/2	12.700	1	25.400

fraction to metric equivalents (**Figure 76**), which shows $\frac{25}{64}$ is 9.92 mm and $\frac{13}{32}$ is 10.32 mm. Choose the drill a little over or under, depending on your need.

CHAPTER 7

Joining Lines, Curves & Planes

Good furniture design consists of integrating lines, planes, and curves into a pleasing composition. Most of us have used a quarter or a coffee can lid as a pattern to draw a curve between two planes. In this chapter, you will learn how to draw more complicated and eye-pleasing joinery.

THE CYMA CURVE CONNECTS TWO PARALLEL LINES. THE ARCS CAN BE EQUAL, AS IN THE TOP DRAWING, OR UNEQUAL, AS IN THE BOTTOM FIGURE.

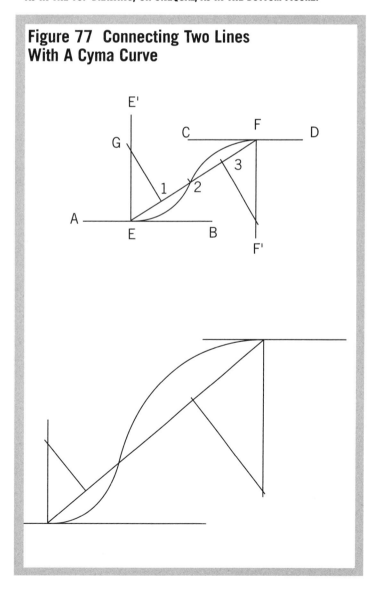

Figure 77 Connecting Two Lines With A Cyma Curve

The Ogee Curve

When building furniture, one often wants to join two lines with an eye-pleasing curve rather than a simple butt joint. This is especially true when working with molding and cabinet bases. The ogee curve serves this purpose. The ogee, which in architecture and math is called a cyma curve, is laid out as shown in **Figure 77** at left:

1. Draw the two parallel lines (that will be connected by the reverse curve) as AB and CD.

2. From the points on these lines where you want to connect with the cyma curve, draw a diagonal line (as EF) and divide it into four equal parts as points 1, 2, and 3.

3. From E draw a line perpendicular to AB as EE'. From Point 1 draw a line perpendicular to EF until it strikes EE' and establishes G.

4. With G as center, and EG as radius, strike the half of the curve from E to 2. Repeat the operation for the other half of the curve, as shown.

This curve can also be made using two arcs of different radii. Instead of dividing the diagonal EF into four equal parts, divide the diagonal into two spaces, according to the desired curve, as E2 and 2F.

Find the center of each space as Point 1 and 3, and proceed as before.

Joining Non-parallel Lines with Arcs

In the examples above, the lines to be joined were parallel. **Figure 78** at right shows two lines at right angles, two lines at less than 90°, and two lines at more than 90°, which are joined with smoothly flowing arcs.

The method is as follows:

1. Draw AB and AC, the two lines to be joined.

2. Choose points D and E, equidistant from A, as the points where the joining curve will begin and end.

3. Draw a line perpendicular to line AB at D, and a line perpendicular to line AC at E. These two lines intersect at point F.

4. Draw arc DE using point F as the center and FE as the radius (FE = FD).

By changing points D and E the curve can be larger or smaller.

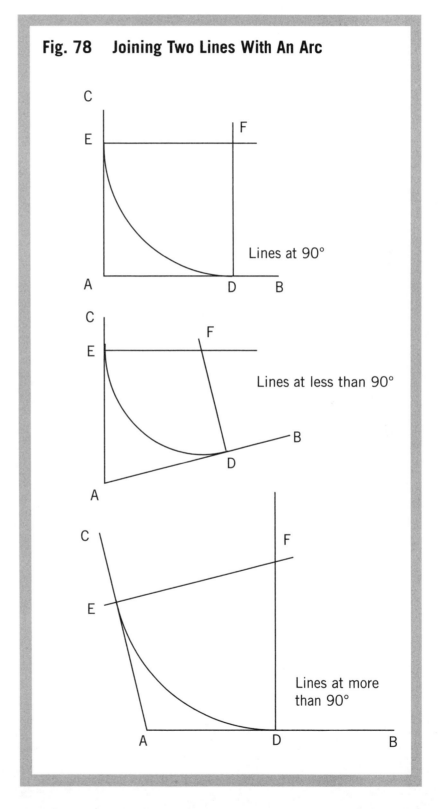

USE A COMPASS TO JOIN TWO LINES WITH A SMOOTHLY FLOWING ARC. THIS METHOD WORKS FOR ALL INTERSECTING LINES.

Fig. 78　Joining Two Lines With An Arc

Lines at 90°

Lines at less than 90°

Lines at more than 90°

THE ARC RADIUS CAN BE CHANGED TO MAKE A SMALL OR LARGE CURVE CONNECTING THE FOOT TO THE BASE.

Fig. 79 Joining Cabinet Base to Foot

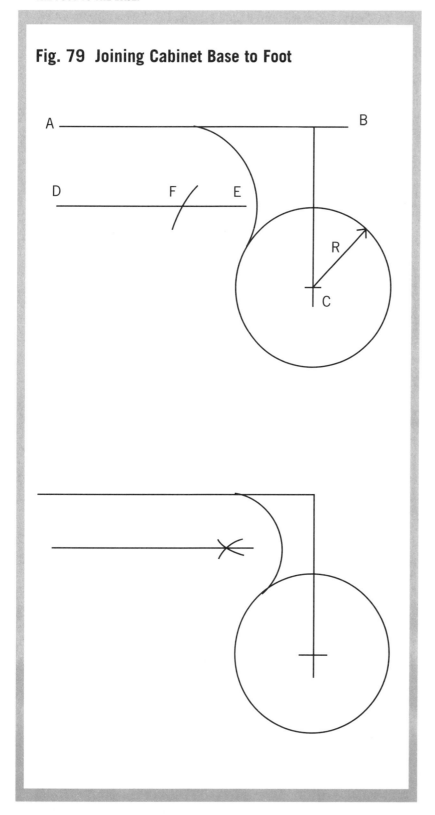

Joining Lines to Circles

In making bases for cabinets and chests we often have the circular foot size already in mind and need to join the cabinet base to the foot. This math problem involves joining a line to a circle.

In **Figure 79**, line AB represents the cabinet base and the circle is the foot pad. To connect the two with a smooth arc:

1. To draw an arc the same size as the foot, set the compass to distance R.

2. Draw line DE parallel to line AB at a distance R.

3. Construct an arc of radius 2R centered at C and crossing line DE at F.

4. Draw the joining arc of radius R using F as the center.

The second figure shows a different sized arc joining the line and circle. In this case, parallel lines AB and DE were less than R distance apart.

Joining Circles to Circles

To join two circles with a smooth arc (**Figure 80**):

1. Draw the two circles.

2. Decide the size of arc you want and increase the radius of each circle by that amount.

3. Using these new radii, draw intersecting arcs crossing at A.

4. Using point A as the center, draw the required tangent arc.

You can draw a different curve to connect the circles by choosing a larger arc, radius R. This produces a smoother arc, and in some cases a more pleasing transition.

Rule of Thumb
Joining Perpendicular Lines With Curve to Changing Radii

Earlier we joined two perpendicular lines with a smoothly flowing arc in which the radius remained the same.

In **Figure 81**, we show a way to join two right angle lines with a smoothly flowing curve with a changing radius. Use this formula to find the disk radius.

Radius = (BC - AB) / 0.43

VARY POINT 'A' TO GET ARCS OF DIFFERENT SIZES.

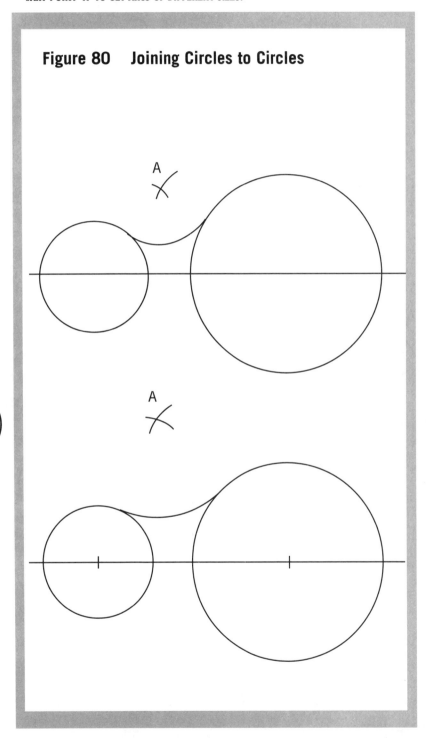

Figure 80   Joining Circles to Circles

Figure 81   Use Wooden Disk and String for Changing-Radius Curve

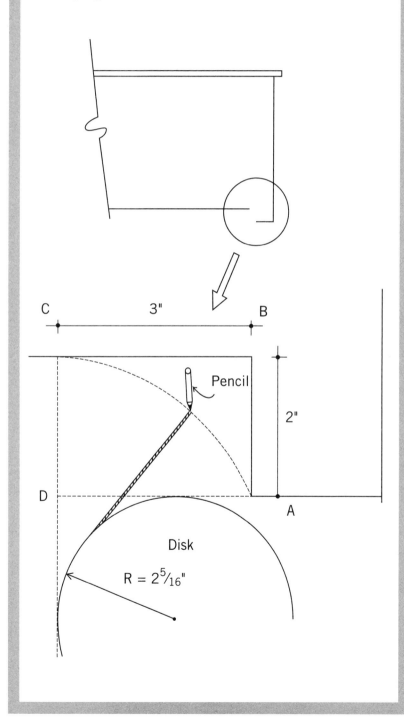

where BC is greater than AB. This formula gives the radius of the disk needed to draw the curve. As shown in the figure, first make the layout with perpendicular lines at the points where the curve will meet the straight lines. Measure the distances and call the longer 'BC', the shorter 'AB'.

The formula gives you the radius of the disk to be used.

In building a cabinet base we want a smooth curve between the foot and the cabinet bottom. The base bottom is 2 inches from the floor, therefore 'A-B' = 2 inches. We want Point 'C' on the raised portion of the base bottom to meet the foot at Point 'A', where line 'B-C is 3 inches. Draw a curve with changing radii between points 'A' and 'C'.

A-B = 2 in. and B-C = 3 in.
Radius = (3 - 2) ÷ 0.43
Radius = 1 ÷ 0.43 = 2.33 in.
     or $2\frac{5}{16}$ in.

Cut a plywood disk with radius $2\frac{5}{16}$ in. Place the disk against the extension of line C-D and baseline A-D. Tack a string to the edge of the disk and, using a pencil, scribe a curved line from A to C.

Note: You have just drawn one quadrant of an ellipse. These points also could have been joined using the methods described in Chapter 10, *Ellipses and Ovals.*

CHAPTER 8

Size & Measurement

Surface Area, Perimeter, Circumference, and Volume

In woodworking we think primarily in terms of height, width, and depth. But size can be measured in many ways, and sometimes we need to calculate area, perimeter/circumference, and volume. While using these formulas, you will get the best results if you first:

1. Sketch the problem to be solved, showing the dimensions in the same units as they appear in the problem. For example, when a formula uses the radius, sketch the radius, not the diameter.

2. From this chapter, select the figures similar to your sketch.

3. Replace the letters used in the figure with the measurements from your problem.

4. Select the formula in which the dimension to be found is shown to the left of the equal sign.

5. Substitute each letter in the formula with the corresponding dimension of your problem.

6. Perform the required operations.

Remember, multiplication signs are not always given in formulas. The formula: Area = $\frac{1}{2}$ bh, for calculating the area of a triangle, should be translated as: Area = $\frac{1}{2}$ times b times h. Unless otherwise stated, all dimensions must be measured by the same unit. For example, a measurement of feet and inches must be changed to either all feet or all inches.

The product of the measures of two dimensions, such as area, results in square units. The product of measures in three units, such as volume, results in cubic units.

Figure 82

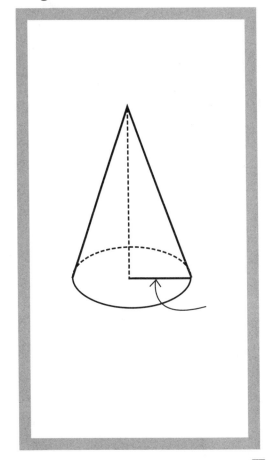

Figure 83

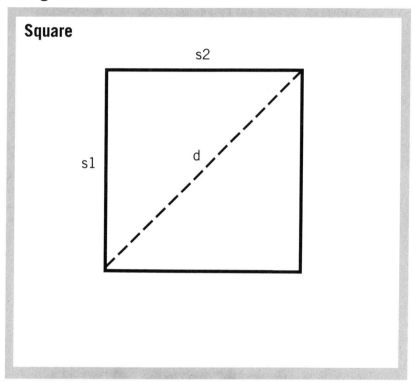

Square

Square

A = area, s = side, d = diagonal, c = circumference
A square is a four-sided figure where all sides are equal and all angles are right angles (90°).

Area

The area of a square is determined by multiplying the length by the width.
Example: s = 14 in.

Area: A = s x s
Area = 14 x 14 = 196 sq. in.

Circumference

The perimeter or circumference of a square is found by adding all four sides.

Circumference:
C = s1 + s2 + s3 + s4 = 4s
C = 14 + 14 + 14 + 14
$\quad$ = 4 x 14 = 56 in.

Diagonal

The diagonal of a square divides the square into two right triangles. The length of the diagonal can be thought of as the hypotenuse of a right triangle. According to the Pythagorean Theorem:

Diagonal Length:
$d^2 = s^2 + s^2$
$d = \sqrt{2s^2}$
d = 1.41 s
And where s = 14
Diagonal Length = 1.41 x 14
$\quad$ = 19.8 in.

Rectangle

A = area, b = base or length, h = height or width, d = diagonal

A rectangle is a four-sided figure having four right angles but whose sides are not equal in length. By definition, opposite sides must be equal in length.
Example: h = 12 in., b = 15 in.

Area

The area of a rectangle is length times width.

Area: A = bh
Area = 12 x 15 = 180 sq. in.

Circumference

The circumference of a rectangle is the sum of all sides.

Circumference: C = 2h + 2b
Circumference
=(2 x 12) + (2 x 15)
= 24 + 30 = 54 in.

Diagonal

According to the Pythagorean Theorem, the diagonal is:

Diagonal Length:
$dl = \sqrt{b^2 + c^2}$
$d = \sqrt{15^2 + 12^2}$
$= \sqrt{225 + 144} = \sqrt{369}$
= 19.2 in.

Figure 84

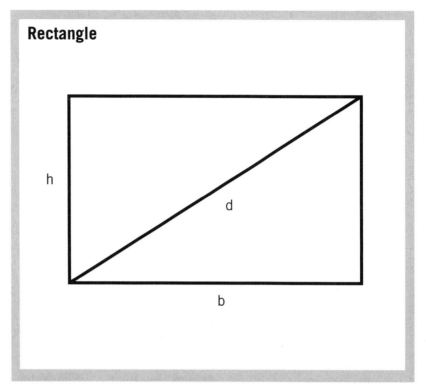

Rectangle

Right Triangle

A = area, a = hypotenuse,
b = height, c = base
Example: b = 12 in., c = 20 in.

Area

When any rectangle is cut in half by a diagonal, two right triangles are formed. The area of any triangle can be thought of as one-half of the rectangle it was formed from.

Area Right Triangle:
$A = \frac{1}{2} \ bc$
Area = $\frac{1}{2}$ x 12 x 20
     = 120 sq. in.

Diagonal

The diagonal or hypotenuse (side a) can be found:
Diagonal: $a = \sqrt{b^2 + c^2}$
$a = \sqrt{12^2 + 20^2}$
   $= \sqrt{144 + 400}$
   $= \sqrt{544} = 23.32$ in.

Using this equation, the length of any one side may be found if the other two sides are known.
$a = \sqrt{b^2 + c^2}$
$b = \sqrt{a^2 - c^2}$
$c = \sqrt{a^2 - b^2}$

Circumference

The circumference is the sum of the three sides.
Circumference: C = a + b + c
C = 23.32 + 12 + 20
  = 55.3 in.

Angle

To figure the angle of a right triangle, use the sine, tangent, or cosine formula.
sin = opposite ÷ hypotenuse
tan = opposite ÷ adjacent
cos = adjacent ÷ hypotenuse
For example to find Angle-1 when hypotenuse a = 23.32, b = 12 and c = 20:

sin = b ÷ a
sin = 12 ÷ 23.3
sin = 0.515
arcsin 0.515 = 31°
To solve this problem with a calculator, see **Figure 86** below.

Using the tan and cos formulas, we get the same answer:

tan = b ÷ c
tan = 12 ÷ 20 = 0.60
arctan 0.60 = 31°

cos = c ÷ a
cos = 20 ÷ 23.3 = 0.858
Arccos 0.858 = 31°

Angle-2 can also be calculated:
sin = c ÷ a
sin = 20 ÷ 23.3 = 0.858
arcsin 0.858 = 59°

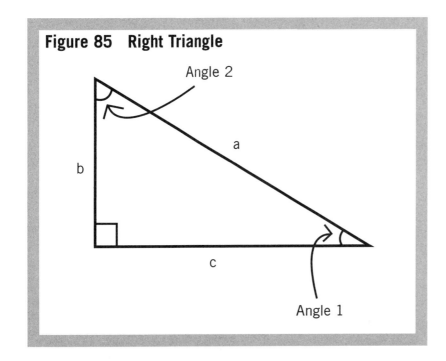

Figure 85   Right Triangle

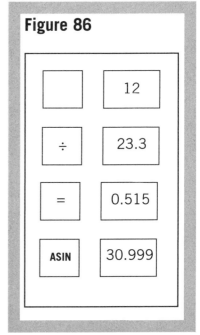

Figure 86

Acute Triangle

a, b, c = sides; h = height
An acute triangle is one in which all of the angles are acute, i.e., less than 90°.
Example: b = 17.5 in., h = 14 in.

Area

The area of any triangle is $\frac{1}{2}$ base times height.

Area: $A = \frac{1}{2}$ bh
Area = $\frac{1}{2}$ (17.5 x 14)
  = $\frac{1}{2}$ (245) = 122.5 sq. in.

Circumference

The circumference is the sum of all sides.
Circumference: C = a + b + c

Parallelogram

A = area, b = base,
h = height/altitude

A parallelogram is a four-sided figure with parallel opposite sides.

Example: b = 24 in., h = 10 in.

Area

The area of a parallelogram is base times height, where the height is always measured perpendicular to the base.
Note: this is NOT the base times side a.

Area: A = bh
Area = 24 x 10 = 240 sq. in.

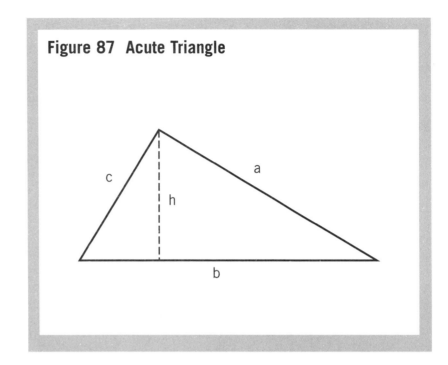

Figure 87 Acute Triangle

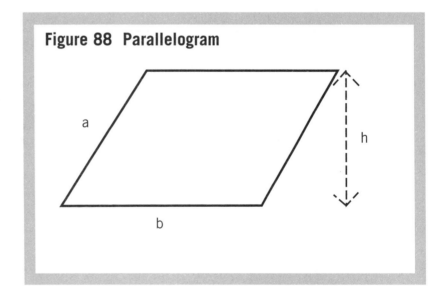

Figure 88 Parallelogram

Circumference

The circumference of a parallelogram is the sum of the four sides.
Circumference: C = 2a + 2b

Trapezoid

A = area, a = one base, b = other base, h = height/altitude

A trapezoid is a four-sided figure in which two sides are parallel.

Example: a = 20 in., b = 30 in., h = 12 in.

Area

The area of a trapezoid is found by adding the two bases together and dividing by two (to average) and multiplying by the height.

Area: $A = \frac{1}{2} (a + b) h$

Area = $\frac{1}{2} (20 + 30)$ x 12
    = 25 x 12 = 300 sq. in.

Circumference

The circumference of a trapezoid is the sum of the four sides.

Circumference: C = a + b + c + d

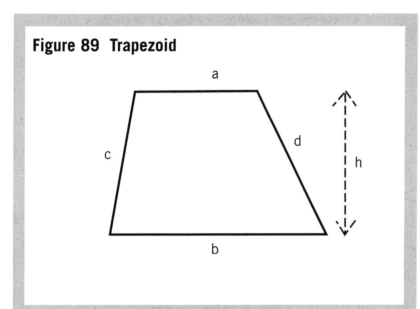

Figure 89 Trapezoid

Pentagon

A = area, s = side

A regular pentagon is a figure having five equal-length sides and five equal angles.

Example: s = 8.5 in.

Area

The area of a pentagon is the length of a side squared times the constant 1.72.

Area: $A = 1.72 \, s^2$
Area = 1.72×8.5^2
    = 1.72 x 72.25
    = 124.27 sq. in.

Circumference

The circumference of a pentagon is the length of one side times five.

Circumference: C = 5s
Circumference = 5 x 8.5
    = 42.5 in.

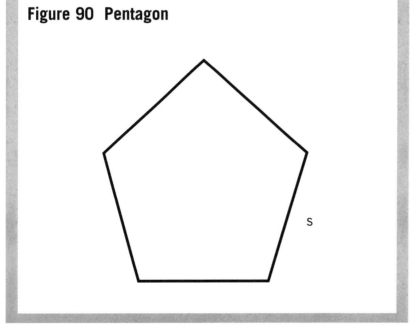

Figure 90 Pentagon

Hexagon

A = area, s = side

A regular hexagon is a figure having six equal-length sides and six equal angles.
Example: s = 6 in.

Area
The area of a hexagon is the length of a side squared times the constant 2.598.

Area: $A = 2.6 \, s^2$
Area $= 2.6 \times 6^2$
   $= 2.6 \times 36 = 93.6$ sq. in.

Circumference
The circumference of a hexagon is the length of one side times six.

Circumference: $c = 6s$
Circumference $= 6 \times 6 = 36$ in.

Octagon

A = area, s = side
A regular octagon is a figure having eight equal-length sides and eight equal angles.

Example: s = 4.5 in.

Area
The area of an octagon is the length of a side squared, times the constant 4.828.
Area: $A = 4.828 \, s^2$
Area $= 4.8 \times 4.5^2$
   $= 4.8 \times 20.25 = 97.2$ sq. in.

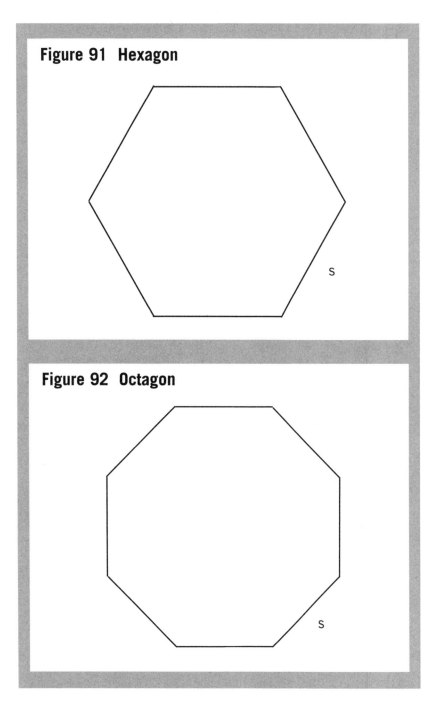

Figure 91   Hexagon

s

Figure 92   Octagon

s

Circumference
The circumference of an octagon is the length of one side times eight.

Circumference: C = 8s
Circumference $= 8 \times 4.5 = 36$ in.

USE THESE CONSTANTS TO FIND AREA AND RADII OF INNER AND OUTER CIRCLES OF VARIOUS REGULAR POLYGONS.

Figure 93 Regular Polygons

Name	Number Of Sides	Area Constant K	Radius Of Inner Circle	Radius Of Outer Circle
Triangle, equilateral	3	0.433	0.289	0.577
Square	4	1.000	0.500	0.707
Pentagon	5	1.721	0.688	0.851
Hexagon	6	2.598	0.866	1.000
Heptagon	7	3.634	1.038	1.152
Octagon	8	4.828	1.207	1.307
Nonagon	9	6.182	1.373	1.462
Decagon	10	7.694	1.539	1.618
Undecagon	11	9.366	1.703	1.775
Dodecagon	12	11.196	1.866	1.932

Regular Polygons

A = area, s = side, n = 1 to 12 or larger, K = constant

A regular polygon is a multi-sided figure having all sides and all angles equal. If the length of one side is known, the area can be determined by using the area constant (K) from the table in **Figure 93**.

Area

If the length of one side is known, the area can be determined by using the area constant (K) from the table.

Example:
n = 7 (heptagon),
s = 5 in.

The area of a polygon can be found by multiplying the appropriate constant times the length of a side squared.

$A = \text{area constant } s^2$
$\text{Area heptagon} = 3.634 \times s^2$
$\text{Area} = 3.634 \times 5^2$
$\quad = 3.634 \times 25 = 90.85 \text{ sq. in.}$

Side Length

Knowing the size of the polygon, we can determine the length of the sides by using the constant for the inner circle.

Problem: Given an octagonal wall clock that is 16-in. wide, what is the length of a side (**Figure 94**)? In this case, n = 8, radius of inner circle is $\frac{1}{2}$ x 16 = 8 in.

Length of Side: L = Radius
    ÷ Inner Radius Constant
    L = r ÷ K
    L = 8 ÷ 1.207 = 6.63 in.

Knowing the size of the polygon, we can also determine the length of the sides by using the constant for the outer circle.
Side Length = Radius
    ÷ Outer Radius Constant
Side = r ÷ K

Problem: What is the length of each side of an eight-sided figure, when the distance from point-to-point is 17 in. (**Figure 95**)? In this case, n = 8 and the radius of outer circle is
    $\frac{1}{2}$ x 17 = 8.5 in.

Side Length = Radius ÷ Outer Radius Constant
    Side Length: L = r ÷ 1.307
    L = 8.5 ÷ 1.307 = 6.5 in.

Figure 94 Problem: Find the side of the polygon

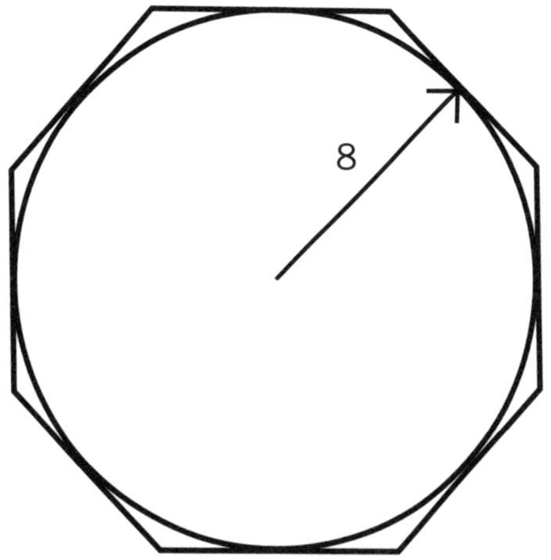

Figure 95 Problem: Find the side of the polygon

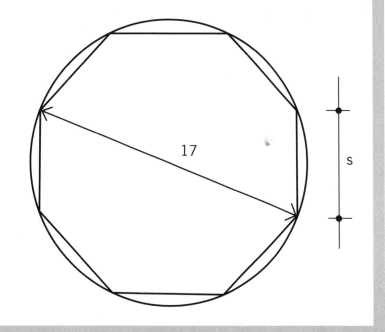

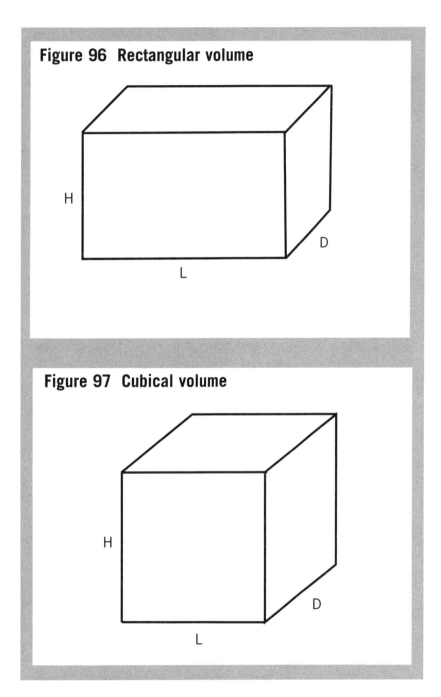

Figure 96 Rectangular volume

Figure 97 Cubical volume

Volume

Along with circumference/perimeter, and area, the third type of measurement that woodworkers need be concerned with is volume. A solid has three dimensions — length, height, and thickness; or length, height, and depth.

Rectangular Box

Example: Length = 35 in., height = 24 in., depth = 12 in.

A rectangular box is a solid bound by six rectangles.

The volume of a rectangular box is length times height times depth.

Volume: $V = L H D$

Volume = 35 x 24 x 12
 = 10,080 cu. in.

To convert to cubic feet: There are 12 x 12 x 12 cubic inches in one cubic foot.

12 x 12 x 12 = 1728 cu. in.
10,080 ÷ 1728 = 5.83 cu. ft.

Square Box (Cube)

Example: Length = height = depth = $6\frac{1}{2}$ inches.

A cube is a rectangular box with six, equal-length sides. All six sides are equal squares. The volume of a cube is length times height times depth, but because all sides are equal, the volume of a cube is one side cubed.

Volume: $V = L^3$
Volume = 6.5^3
   = 274.625 cu. in.

Cylinder

r = radius, d = diameter of
circular base, h = height
Example: h = 6 ft., d = 4.5 ft.

A cylinder is a solid with a
uniformly curved surface. Its
ends are equal parallel circles.

Volume: $V = \pi r^2 h$
Volume = 3.14 x 2.25^2 x 6
   = 3.14 x 5.063 x 6
   = 95.38 cu. ft.

The surface area of a cylinder is
the circumference of the
bottom or top circle times the
cylinder height.

Curved Surface Area:
CSA = circumference x height
Circumference = πd
Curved Surface Area = πdh
   = 3.14 x 4.5 x 6
   = 84.78 sq. ft.

Cone

r = radius, h = height, s = slant
length, d = diameter
Example:
s = 6 in., d = 3 in., h = 5.8 in.

A cone is a solid with a circular
base. The curved surface tapers
uniformly from the base to a
point, called the vertex.

Figure 98 Cylinder

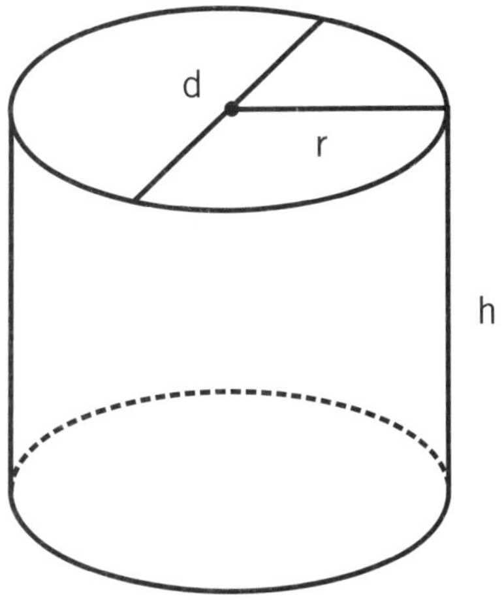

Figure 99 Cone

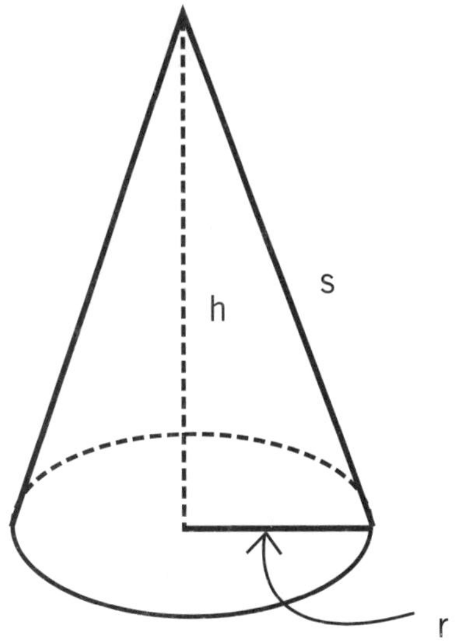

Volume of a Cone: $V = 1/3 \pi r^2 h$
$V = 0.333$ x 5.8 x 3.14 x 1.5^2
Volume = 13.67 cu. in.

The surface area of a cone is a
function of the slant length and

the circumference of the circle.
Surface Area: SA = πrs
Surface area = 3.14 x 1.5 x 6
   = 28.27 sq. in.

Special Shapes

Sometimes a problem can be solved by breaking it down into smaller sections.

Problem: We want to make an eight-sided frame. The frame must fit into a rectangle 18 in. wide by 45 in. high. What is the length of the six short sides, and what is the length of the two long sides (**Figure 100**)? The short sides should all be the same length.

Solution: Assume the rectangle contains two squares, one at the top and one at the bottom. Our problem now is to turn each square into an octagon.

1. Draw a circle inside the top square.

2. Use the formula and the constant in **Figure 93** to find the length of a side of a polygon.

Side length = inner circle radius ÷ octagon constant
L = 9 ÷ 1.207 = 7.46 in.

3. The length of side s is:
$$h^2 = s^2 + s^2$$
$$h = \sqrt{2s^2}$$
$$h = 1.414\,s$$
$$s = h \div 1.414$$
$$s = 7.46 \div 1.414 \approx 5\tfrac{1}{4} \text{ in.}$$

4. The length of the long side of the frame is the total length (45) minus two times the side s of the triangle.

$$2 \times 5\tfrac{1}{4} = 10\tfrac{1}{2}$$
$$L = 45 - 10\tfrac{1}{2} = 34\tfrac{1}{2} \text{ in.}$$

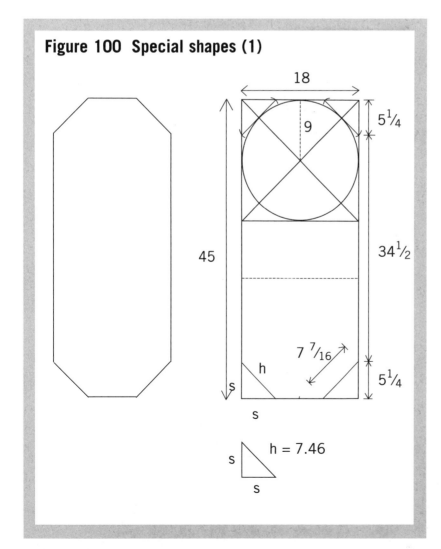

Figure 100 Special shapes (1)

Rule of Thumb

In the previlous problem, the eight-sided frame can be drawn without using any math—and the sides can be measured from the drawing. First construct the square abcd (**Figure 101**).

1. Draw diagonal ac and find the center e

2. Set dividers to length ae

3. From a swing arc f

4. From b swing arc g

5. From c swing arc h

6. From d swing arc i

7. Connect fh and gi

8. Treat the bottom square in a similar manner

Draw full size and use as a pattern, or measure the sizes from the pattern. This method only works for an octagon, but this approach can be adapted to any regular geometric figure.

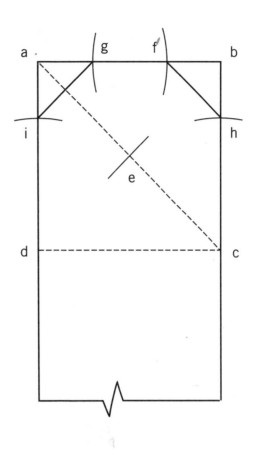

Figure 101 Special shapes (2)

CHAPTER 9

Circles

The circle is used constantly in woodworking. In the following pages you'll see how to construct circles inside and outside of polygons, how to divide the perimeter of a circle into multiple equal parts, and, in general, learn all the properties of a circle.

The **radius** of a circle is a straight line drawn from the center to the circumference.

The **diameter** of a circle is a straight line passing through the center of the circle with both ends ending at the circumference. The length of the diameter is twice that of the radius.

The **chord** of a circle is a straight line joining the extremities of an arc. A chord that passes through the center is a diameter.

The **sector** of a circle is a pie-shaped figure bounded by two radii and the included arc.

The ratio of the circumference to the diameter is expressed by the Greek letter π, 'p', pronounced 'pie', and approximately equal to 3.1416. The value of π may be computed to any number of decimal places but in woodworking is usually used as 3.14.

Example: d=8, r=4

Both the area of a circle and the distance around the circle (circumference) can be determined once the radius or diameter is known.

Area = πr^2 = 3.14 r^2

A = 3.14 x 4 x 4 = 50.24 sq. in.

Area = $\frac{1}{4} \pi d^2$ = 0.785 d^2

A = 0.7854 x 8 x 8 = 50.24 sq. in.

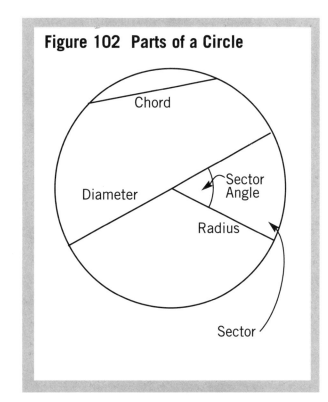

Figure 102 Parts of a Circle

Chord

Diameter

Sector Angle

Radius

Sector

The circumference of a circle is calculated from the formula:

Circumference = πd
C = 3.14 x 8 = 25.12 in.

The **sector of a circle** is the pie-shaped piece formed by an angle drawn from the center of the circle. Its area is proportional to the area of the whole circle, as the angle of the sector is to 360°. To find the area of the sector, multiply the area of the circle by the ratio of the angle to 360°. For example, for a sector with a 40° angle:

Sector area
  = angle/360 x circle area
Sector area = 40/360 x 50.25
  = 0.11 x 50.25 = 5.58 sq. in.

The sector area can also be calculated if the sector arc length is known.

Sector area
  = 0.5 x arc length
  x circle radius
Sector area = 0.5 x 2.78 x 4
  = 5.56 sq. in.

The length of the sector arc is also proportional to the total length of the circle (circumference).

Sector arc length
  = 40/360 x circumference
Sector arc length
  = 40/360 x 25.12
  = 0.111 x 25.12 = 2.79 in.

Rule of Thumb
The area of a circle is about 75% of the area of the surrounding square (78% to be exact).

Use this fact to estimate the area of a circle.

Problem: What is the area of a circle with a diameter of 2 ft.?

Solution: The area of the surrounding square is
  2 x 2 = 4 sq. ft.

  4 sq. ft. x 75% is 3 sq. ft. The exact figure is:

  4 x 0.78 = 3.12 sq. ft.

**MULTIPLY DIAMETER BY CONSTANT
TO FIND THE CHORD LENGTH**

Fig. 103
Circle Division Table

Spaces	Chord Length
3	0.866
4	0.707
5	0.588
6	0.500
7	0.434
8	0.383
9	0.342
10	0.309
11	0.282
12	0.259

**TO FIND THE CHORD LENGTH, USE THE CIRCLE DIVISION TABLE TO FIND THE
CONSTANT, AND MULTIPLY BY THE CIRCLE DIAMETER.**

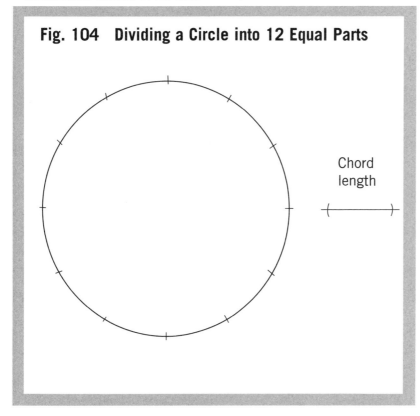

Fig. 104   Dividing a Circle into 12 Equal Parts

Chord length

The sector arc length can also be calculated thus:

Sector Arc Length
= 0.00873 x Sector Angle
x Circle Diameter
Sector Arc Length
= 0.00873 x 40 x 8 = 2.79 in.

Spacing Off the Circumference of Circles

When you need to lay out a certain number of spaces around a circle, use the circle division table (**Figure 103**). To do so, just pick the number of divisions you want from the spaces column. Multiply the selected chord length constant times the diameter of your circle, and set a divider to this reading. Then step the dividers around the circle, marking each point.

Problem 1: We have a 12-in. x 12-in. piece of walnut we want to use for a wall clock. How do we make 12 equal divisions for the numerals (**Figure 104**)?

First draw a 10-in. circle. Then use the 12 factor from the chart above. Multiply the diameter (10) times the factor (0.259).
10 in. x 0.259 = 2.59 in.

We can convert 0.59 to a fraction in this manner:
0.59 x 32 = 18.9/32 $\approx \frac{19}{32}$
0.59 x 16 = 9.44/16 $\approx \frac{9}{16}$
0.59 x 8 = 4.72/8 $\approx \frac{5}{8}$

This is the length of the chord

(2.59 in. or $2\frac{9}{16}$ in.) necessary to divide the circumference of the 10-in. circle into 12 equal parts. This can be accomplished either with a ruler or by setting dividers to $2\frac{9}{16}$ in. and stepping around the circle.

If measuring the 2.59 or $2\frac{9}{16}$ chord in inches proves too tedious, do the calculations in metric.
10-in. diameter x 25.4 mm/in
 = 254 mm diameter
254 x 0.259
 = 65.79 mm (chord length)

Problem 2: In the problem above, if the clock face circle had a diameter of 6 in., then the chord would have been:
6 in. x 0.259 = 1.55 in.

We can convert 0.55 to a fraction in this manner:
0.55 x 32 = 17.6/32
 $\approx \frac{18}{32} = \frac{9}{16}$
 0.55 x 16 = 8.8/16 $\approx \frac{9}{16}$
 0.55 x 8 = 4.4/8 $\approx \frac{4}{8} = \frac{1}{2}$

Again, set dividers to $1\frac{9}{16}$ in., and step around the 6-in. circle.

In metric this would be:
6 in. x 25.4 mm/in = 152.4 mm
152.4 x 0.259
 = 39.47 mm (chord length)

Problem 3: We're building a kitchen stool and we need to drill three holes in the bottom of the seat for the legs (**Figure 105**). The seat diameter is 15 in. and we want each leg to be inset $1\frac{1}{2}$ in.

The diameter of our working circle is:
15 in. – 3 in. = 12 in.

The chord length is figured using the circle division table.
12 in. x 0.866 = 10.4 in.

We can convert 0.4 to a fraction like this:
 0.4 x 32 = 12.8/32 $\approx \frac{13}{32}$
 0.4 x 16 = 6.4/16 $\approx \frac{6}{16} = \frac{3}{8}$
 0.4 x 8 = 3.2/8 $\approx \frac{3}{8}$

1. Draw a 12-in. circle (radius = 6 in.) on the 15-in. diameter seat and make a mark at any point (A).

2. From mark (A), measure $10\frac{3}{8}$-in. chords to (B) and to (C).

3. Draw lines from A, B, and C to the center. On each line, mark a point that is a distance sufficient to place the edge of the leg on the 12-in. circle. For example, if the stool leg is 2-in. diameter, drill the holes 1 in. from the 12-in. circle.

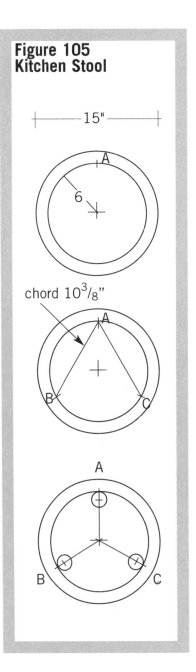

**Figure 105
Kitchen Stool**

15"

6

chord $10\frac{3}{8}$"

A

A
B   C

A
B   C

DIVIDE THE WHEEL INTO SEVEN SECTORS TO LOCATE THE POSITIONS FOR THE SPOKES.

Fig 106   Small Flower Cart

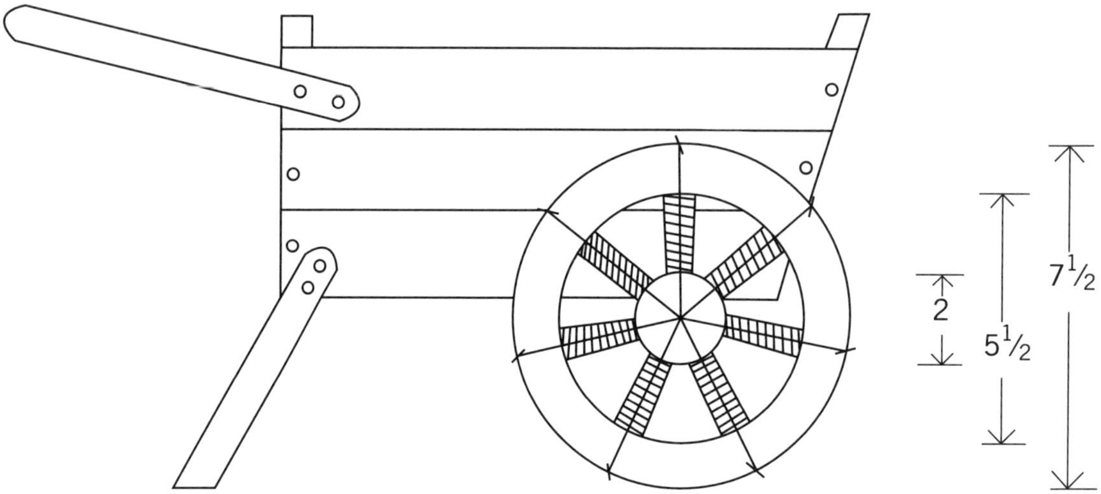

Problem 4: A small flower cart has $7\frac{1}{2}$ in. diameter wheels. We want to construct it with seven spokes.

Draw a circle with radius of $3\frac{3}{4}$ in. ($\frac{1}{2}$ x $7\frac{1}{2}$). Using the factor table for 7 we get:
7.5 in. x 0.434
= 3.26 in. or $3\frac{1}{4}$ in.

The chord length for stepping off the seven marks is $3\frac{1}{4}$ in. Use a ruler on the full-scale piece or step off the distance with a compass. You can divide the inside of the wheels, and the hub, in the same way (**Figure 106**).

The circle division table (**Figure 107**) gives chord constants for 3 to 100 sectors. Woodworkers seldom need more than 12 divisions, but two extreme examples come to mind. Gears for a wooden clock may need 30, 48, or 64 teeth. Fluting, with a router and a homemade jig or on a lathe, may require 8 to 15 indexing pins.

To calculate further chords use this formula:
Constant = sin (180 ÷ n) where n = number of divisions

Example: What is the constant (K) for a 12-sided figure?
K = sin (180 ÷ 12)
  = sin 15 = 0.2588

With a calculator (**Figure 108**):
1. Enter 180 ÷ 12 = 15
2. sin
3. 0.2588

Polygons from Circles

The circle division table can also be used to construct polygons inside circles. In the examples just given, the 12 chords for the clock can be joined to give a dodecagon, a regular 12-sided polygon. The three-legged stool example will give an equilateral triangle.

Example - What is the width of the staves for a six-sided bucket with a diameter of 12 in. (**Figure 109**) The bucket will be 14 in. high.

MULTIPLY DIAMETER BY CONSTANT TO FIND THE CHORD LENGTH

Fig.ure 107   Circle Division Table

Sides	Constant	Sides	Constant	Sides	Constant
1	n/a	21	0.149	41	0.077
2	n/a	22	0.142	42	0.075
3	0.866	23	0.136	43	0.073
4	0.707	24	0.131	44	0.071
5	0.588	25	0.125	45	0.070
6	0.500	26	0.121	46	0.068
7	0.434	27	0.116	47	0.067
8	0.383	28	0.112	48	0.065
9	0.342	29	0.108	49	0.064
10	0.309	30	0.105	50	0.063
11	0.282	31	0.101	51	0.062
12	0.259	32	0.098	52	0.060
13	0.239	33	0.095	53	0.059
14	0.223	34	0.092	54	0.058
15	0.208	35	0.090	55	0.057
16	0.195	36	0.087	56	0.056
17	0.184	37	0.085	57	0.055
18	0.174	38	0.083	58	0.054
19	0.165	39	0.080	59	0.053
20	0.156	40	0.078	60	0.052

Figure 108

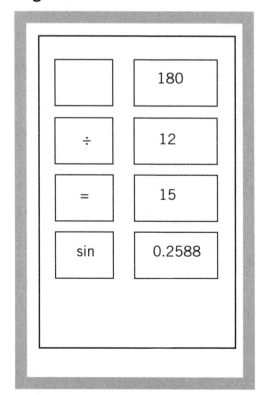

USE THE CONSTANT FROM THE CIRCLE DIVISION TABLE TO FIND THE CHORD LENGTH.

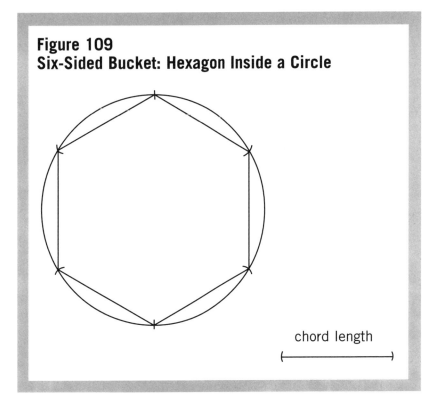

Figure 109
Six-Sided Bucket: Hexagon Inside a Circle

chord length

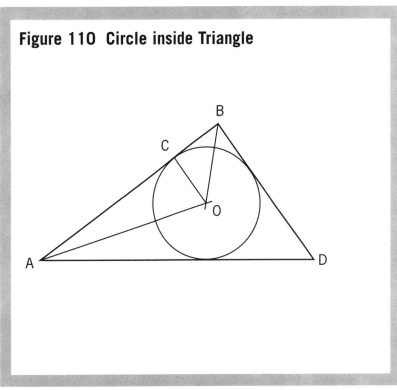

Figure 110 Circle inside Triangle

Using the constant from the circle division table
12 in. x 0.500
= 6 in. (chord length)

You could continue this problem assuming the bucket has a 10-in. bottom diameter.
10 in. x 0.500 = 5 in. (chord length)

Each of the six staves would be cut 14 in. long with top 6 in. wide and bottom 5 in. wide. Chapter 29, *Miters and Bevels,* explains how to find the miter on a six-sided figure.

See the section on regular polygons in Chapter 8, *Size and Measurement,* for more on constructing polygons inside and outside circles.

Drawing Special Figures Using Dividers/Compass
Certain figures useful to woodworkers can be drawn from a circle using a compass.

Circle in a Triangle
Starting with a triangle ABD:
1. Bisect any two angles and draw lines AO and BO.
2. Draw a line from O perpendicular to any side, e.g., OC.
3. Set dividers/compass to distance CO.
4. With O as the starting point, draw a circle inside the triangle.

Figure 111 Circle Outside Triangle

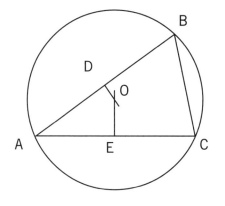

Figure 112 Circle Inside Square

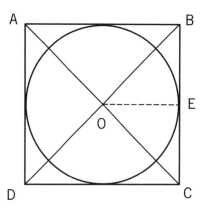

Circle Outside Triangle

Starting with a triangle:
1. Find the mid-point of any two sides, e.g., D and E.
2. Draw perpendicular lines from D and E, crossing at O.
3. Set compass to distance AO (or BO or CO).
4. Using O as center, draw circle outside triangle.

Circle Inside Square

Starting with a square:
1. Draw two diagonals: AC and BD.
2. Locate point E midway between points B and C.
3. Set compass to distance EO.
4. Using O as center, draw circle inside the square.

Figure 113 Circle Outside Square

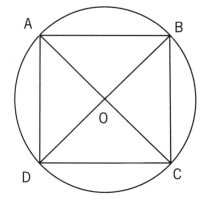

Figure 114 Hexagon Inside Circle

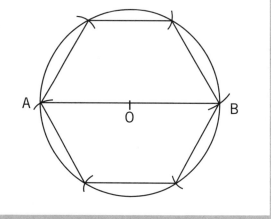

Circle Outside Square

Starting with a square:
1. Draw two diagonals: AC and BD.
2. Set compass to distance AO.
3. Using O as center, draw circle outside the square.

Hexagon Inside Circle

Starting with a circle:
1. Draw diameter AB with O as center.
2. Set compass to distance AO.
3. From A, step around circle.
4. Join points for six-sided figure in a circle.

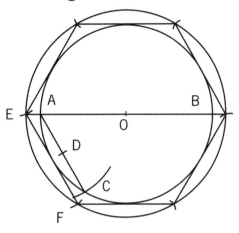

Figure 115 Hexagon Outside Circle

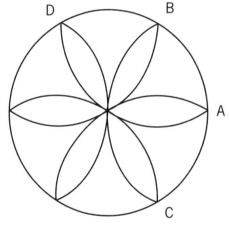

Figure 116 6-Petal Flower Inside Circle

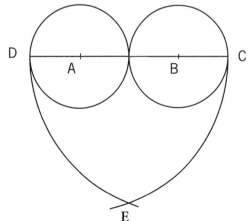

Figure 117   Heart from Circles

Hexagon Outside Circle

Starting with a circle:
1. Draw diagonal AB with O as center.
2. Set compass to distance AO.
3. Using A as staring point, mark C.
4. Draw line AC.
5. Draw line EF parallel to line AC, which just touches outside of circle.
6. Set compass to distance OE and draw outside circle.
7. Starting at E, step around circle.
8. Connect six points for six-sided figure outside circle.

6- Petal Flower Inside Circle

Starting with a circle:
1. Set compass to radius of circle.
2. Using A as starting point, scribe arc BC.
3. Using B as starting point, scribe arc AD.
4. Step around the circle for a six petal flower.

Heart from Circles

Starting with two circles:
1. With a compass draw two circles that touch.
2. Draw line through centers A and B, and mark C and D.
3. Set compass to distance AC.
4. Starting at A scribe arc CE.
5. Starting at C scribe arc DE.

Spheres

Spheres, or as we usually speak of them, balls, are the three dimensional extension of circles.

The **surface area** of a sphere, like the area of a circle, is a function of the radius and the constant pi.

Example: r = 1, d = 2
Surface area of sphere = $4\pi r^2$
$$= 4 \times 3.14 \times r^2 = 12.56 \ r^2$$
$$= 12.56 \times 1 \times 1$$
$$= 12.56 \ \text{sq. in}$$

The surface area of a sphere can also be expressed as a function of the diameter.

Surface area of sphere
$$= 4\pi \ (d/2)^2$$
$$= 4 \times 3.14 \times (d/2)^2$$
$$= 3.14 \ d^2$$
$$= 3.14 \times d \times d$$
$$= 3.14 \times 2 \times 2$$
$$= 12.56 \ \text{sq. in.}$$

The **volume** of a sphere, like the volume of a circle, is a function of radius and the constant pi.

Example: r = 1, d = 2
Volume of sphere = 1/3 ($4\pi r^3$)
$$= 4/3 \times 3.14 \times r^3 = 4.19 \ r^3$$
$$= 4.19 \times 1 \times 1 \times 1$$
$$= 4.19 \ \text{cu. in.}$$

The volume of a sphere can also be expressed as a function of the diameter.

Volume of sphere
$$= 4/3 \ \pi \ (d/2)^3$$
$$= 1.33 \times 3.14 \times (d/2)^3$$
$$= 0.522 \times d^3$$
$$= 0.522 \times d \times d \times d$$
$$= 0.52 \times 2 \times 2 \times 2$$
$$= 4.18 \ \text{cu. in.}$$

Figure 118 Spheres

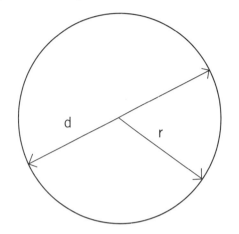

Rule of Thumb

The surface area of a sphere is four times the area of the corresponding circle.
Problem: What is the surface area of a billiard ball 2 in. in diameter?

Solution: A circle 2 in. in diameter has area = $3.14 \times r^2$. This is $3.14 \times 1 \times 1 = 3.14$. Multiply this by 4 to get the surface area of the billiard ball.
Surface area = $3.14 \times 4 \approx 12.5$ sq. in.

Rule of Thumb

The volume of a sphere is approximately $\frac{1}{2}$ the volume of the corresponding cube.
(Note: It's actually 52%)
Problem: What is the volume of a billiard ball 2 in. in diameter?

Solution: A cube 2 in. on a side has volume $2 \times 2 \times 2 = 8$ cu. in.
Volume cube ÷ 2 ≈ volume sphere
$8 \div 2 = 4$ cu. in.

CHAPTER 10

Ellipses & Ovals

Ellipses have an intriguing shape and are more interesting than a circle. They are used for mirror and picture frames, tabletops, inlays, and carved decorations. The shape is used in swimming pools, sink design, windows, dishes, throw rugs and furniture from foot stools to coffee tables. Part of the allure of the ellipse is the ever-changing shape, which challenges perception by the eye as it travels along a perimeter where the curvature constantly varies.

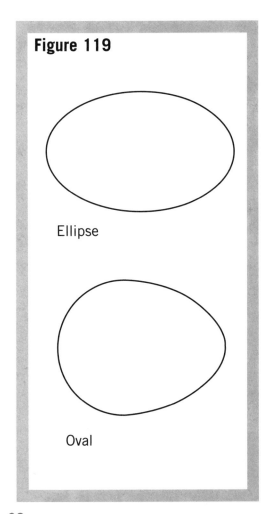

Figure 119

Ellipse

Oval

The elusive ellipse. Probably no other geometrical figure is written about as much. The woodworking literature has articles on drawing an ellipse with strings, paper, wooden sticks, triangles and squares. There are articles on how to cut a perfect ellipse with a router and how to construct the mechanical contrivances to do so. Under the math heading in one index of woodworking journals, 15 of the 68 entries concern the ellipse.

Perhaps this is a good place to discuss the difference between an 'oval' and an 'ellipse'. The dictionary defines oval thus:

Oval: (Latin ovum, egg) having the shape of an egg, with one end broader than the other; egg shaped.

The dictionary defines an ellipse thus:

Ellipse: a closed plane curve so constructed that the sum of the distances from any point on the curve to two fixed points within, called foci, is a fixed length.

Not a terribly informative definition, but now we know an ellipse is not egg shaped. Most of the pleasing shapes we woodworkers strive for are ellipses, not ovals—we don't try to make one end broader than the other. Go ahead and call them ovals, everyone knows what you mean. As

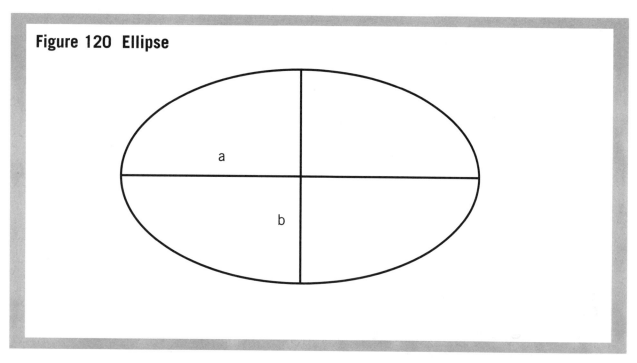

Figure 120 Ellipse

woodworkers, we are particularly intrigued by the ellipse because of our difficulties when trying to draw and construct one.

In an ellipse, the longest diameter is called the major axis and the shorter diameter is called the minor axis.

$a = \frac{1}{2}$ major axis,
  called major semiaxis
$b = \frac{1}{2}$ minor axis,
  called minor semiaxis

Example: major axis = 17, minor axis = 10

Ellipse Area = π ab
Area ellipse = π ab
  = 3.1416 ab
  = 3.14 x 8.5 x 5
  = 133.45 ≈ 133 29/64 sq. in.
  0.45 x 64 = 28.8/64 ≈ $^{29}/_{64}$

Ellipse Perimeter
  ≈ $\pi \sqrt{2[a^2 + b^2]}$ **(approx.)**

Ellipse Perimeter
  = $\pi \sqrt{2\,(a^2 + b^2)}$
  = $3.14 \sqrt{2\,(8.5^2 + 5^2)}$
  = $3.14 \sqrt{2 \times (72.25 + 25)}$
  = $3.14 \sqrt{2 \times 97.2}$
  = $3.14 \sqrt{194.5}$
  = 3.14 x 13.95 = 43.8 in.

A more exact approximation for the length of an ellipse perimeter is:
Ellipse Perimeter
= $\pi \sqrt{2(a^2 + b^2) - [(a - b)^2 / 2.2]}$
= 43.16 in.

Following are a few different methods for drawing this fascinating figure.

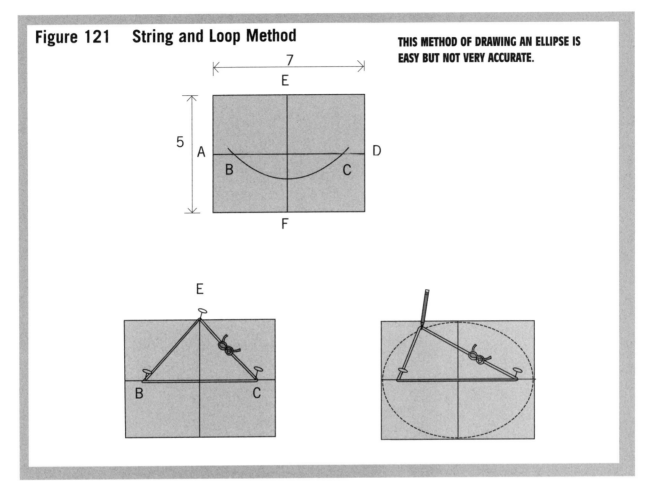

Figure 121   **String and Loop Method**

THIS METHOD OF DRAWING AN ELLIPSE IS EASY BUT NOT VERY ACCURATE.

String-Loop Method

This is probably the ellipse-drawing method (**Figure 121**) most discussed—and the method least likely to give satisfactory results.

1. Determine the length and width of the ellipse and draw a rectangle to these dimensions. In our example we will use 5 in. x 7 in. The ellipse will fit within this rectangle.

2. Draw the major axis AD and the minor axis EF, each crossing in the center.

3. Set a divider $\frac{1}{2}$ the length of AD ($3\frac{1}{2}$ in.), and swing an arc from E, crossing AD at points B and C. Points B and C are the focus points of the ellipse.

4. Place small nails at B, C, and E, and tie a loop of string around these points.

5. Remove the nail at point E. Now push a pencil against the string and draw the ellipse.

This well-known method is also called the "garden ellipse" because it is often used to lay out large garden plots using wooden stakes and rope or a garden hose. In the woodshop it leaves a lot to be desired. It is difficult to tie the string tight, the string stretches and slides up and down the pencil, and the pencil tends to wander. If you do use this method, draw only one quadrant then use it as a pattern for the other three sections.

Multiple Tangent Method

The multiple tangent method (**Figure 122**) is more precise than the string and loop procedure, but also takes more time.

1. Draw a rectangle on paper or directly on your workpiece, sized to the major and minor axes of the desired ellipse.

2. Divide the rectangle into four equal sections and work only on one quadrant.

3. Divide the longer line (the major axis) into equal units, e.g., 1-in. squares for a table top.

Divide the shorter line (the minor axis) in the quadrant into the same number of units as the longer line. Note: The length of these minor axis units will not be the same length as the major axis units.

4. Label points along the two axes. Let's use A-J, A'-J'. Note that the distance between A & B along the long axis is NOT the same as the distance between A' & B' along the short axis.

5. With a sharp pencil or pen, draw a line connecting A' of the short line to A on the long line. Connect successive points to draw the ellipse.

Example: The rectangle is 5 x 7. The minor and major axes of the quadrant are $2\frac{1}{2}$ in. and $3\frac{1}{2}$ in. Divide the 2.5-in. axis into ten 1/4-in. units, and label the points A'-J'. Divide the 3.5-in. axis into 10 units also by dividing 3.5 by 10:

$$3.5 \div 10 = 0.35 \approx \frac{11}{32} \text{ in.}$$

If it is easier to measure in millimeters, convert 3.5 in. to metric.
3.5 in. x 25.4 mm/in = 88.9 mm.
89 mm ÷ 10 = 8.9 mm

Using either 8.9 mm or $\frac{11}{32}$ in., mark 10 units on the major axis and label them J through A. Connect A-A', B-B', C-C', and so on to J-J'.

THIS METHOD IS VERY PRECISE BUT TIME CONSUMING.

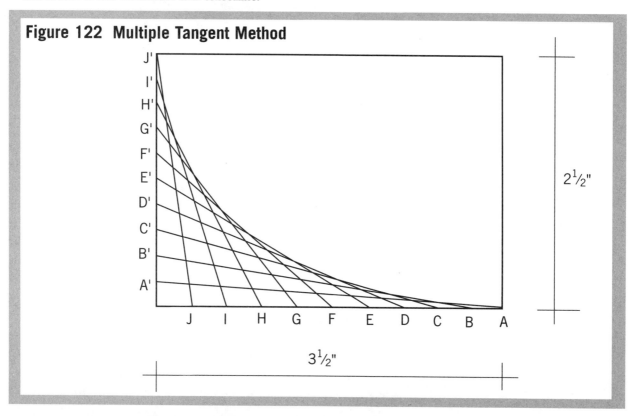

Figure 122 Multiple Tangent Method

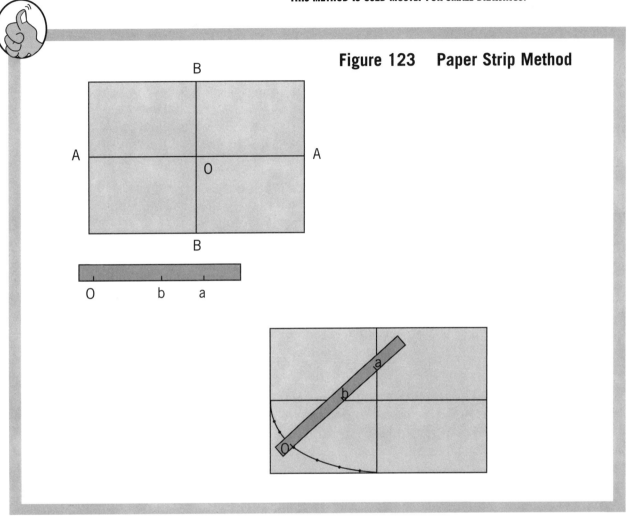

Figure 123   Paper Strip Method

Paper Strip Method

This method is used mostly for small drawings because of the difficulty of maneuvering the strip of paper over long distances. It is quick and easy.

1. Draw a rectangle with the same dimensions as the desired ellipse and mark points A to the left and right of center point O. Mark points B above and below.

2. On a separate strip of paper, mark point O along the edge near one end. Also mark point a at distance a-O, and point b at distance b-O.

3. Place this edge so that a falls on the vertical axis and b falls on the horizontal axis. O is a point on the ellipse.

4. Slide the paper marker along the axes and mark as many points as necessary. Connect the dots to form the ellipse.

T-Square Jig Method

This method uses the same theory as the paper strip method above, but uses wood instead of paper. This is the method of choice for wood-workers (**Figure 124**).

1. As in the previous methods, draw a rectangle with x and y axes the lengths of the ellipse diagonals. Draw on your workpiece or a paper. Use only one quadrant.

2. Construct a T-square as in Figure 124, where AB is about $\frac{1}{2}$ in. shorter than the major semiaxis of the ellipse, and the vertical CD is a little longer than twice the minor axis. The T-square must be flat so the scriber bar can pass over it.

3. Clamp or tack the T-square to the workpiece along major and minor axes.

4. Make a scriber of light-weight wood and drill holes at points E, F, & G, with EF equal to the minor semiaxis of the ellipse, and EG equal to the major semiaxis.

5. Drive finishing nails through points G & F. Place a pen or pencil at point E.

6. G is held firmly against CD and F firmly against AB while moving the marking stick, so that E scribes one-quarter of the ellipse.

PROBABLY THE BEST METHOD FOR WOODWORKERS.

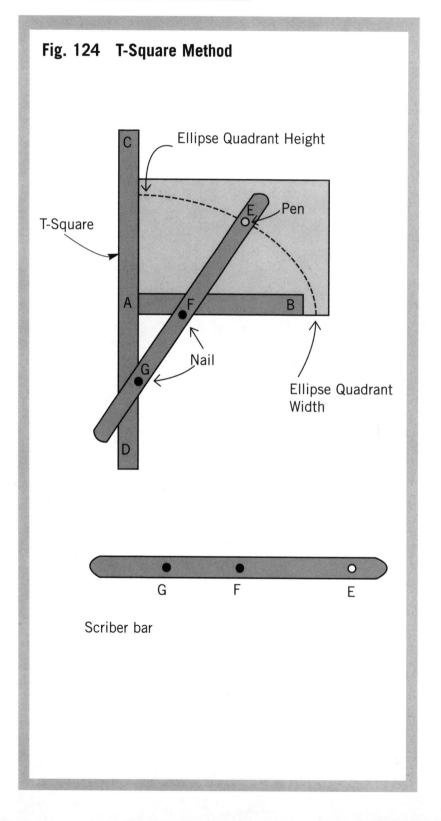

Fig. 124   T-Square Method

Scriber bar

THIS METHOD IS FAST AND ACCURATE FOR SMALL ELLIPSES.

Framer's Square Method

This method is fast to set up and easy to use and every woodworker should be familiar with it (**Figure 125**). Because of the size of a framer's square, this method cannot be used if one axis in the quadrant is more than 16 in.

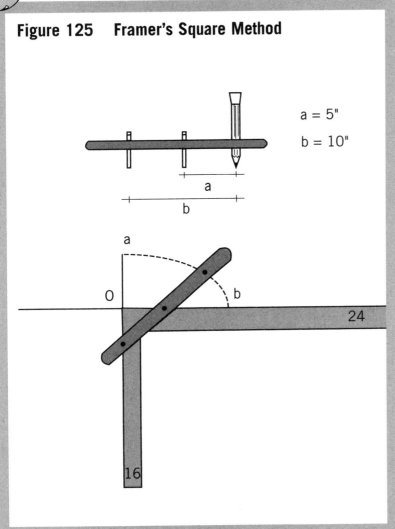

Figure 125   Framer's Square Method

a = 5"

b = 10"

1. Construct and use the same wood scriber as described in the T-square Jig Method.

2. Draw perpendicular lines representing the length and height of the quadrant.

3. Hold the framer's square tightly to the drawing along the major and minor axes as shown.

4. Hold the scriber firmly against the square and move the stick so that E scribes one quadrant of the ellipse.

Modified T-Square Method

This is a simple, fast and accurate way to draw an ellipse (**Figure 126**).

1. Start with a piece of plywood or heavy cardboard and mark $\frac{1}{2}$ the major (AC) and minor axes (AB), working with only one quadrant. Mark AC along the bottom of the board. Mark line AB vertically a few inches in from the left side. Make sure AB and AC are at right angles.

2. Clamp or temporarily attach with screws, a 1-in.-high x $\frac{3}{4}$-in.-wide fence board vertically along the minor axis AB.

3. Make a scribing slat of $\frac{1}{4}$-in. material about 2 in. longer than AC. Drill a hole at distance AC from one end and insert a pencil. Drill another hole at distance AB from the pencil and insert a finishing nail.

4. To use, place the slat flat against the vertical board. Slide the nail to the right along the bottom of the piece while you slide the end of the slat along the upright fence upward toward A.

5. The pencil scribes the elliptic quadrant.

THIS METHOD IS SIMPLE, FAST, AND ACCURATE.

Figure 126   Modified T-Square Method

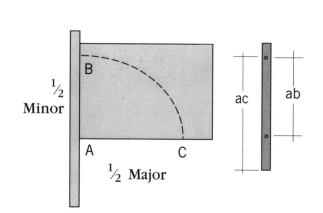

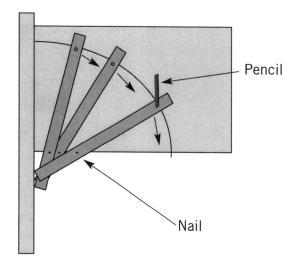

End View

$\frac{1}{2}$ Minor

B

A   C

$\frac{1}{2}$ Major

ac   ab

Pencil

Nail

THIS METHOD IS EASY TO USE ONCE THE JIG HAS BEEN MADE.

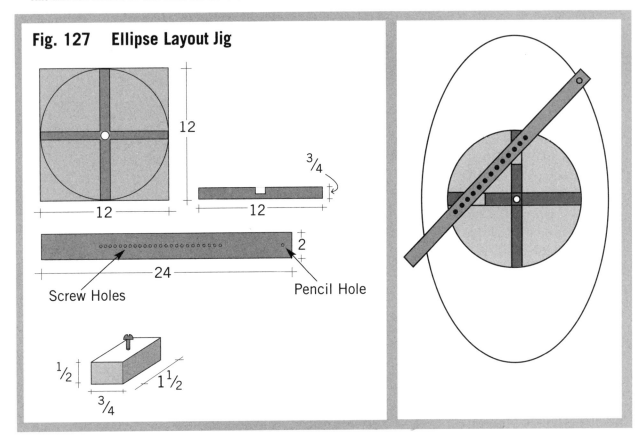

Fig. 127   Ellipse Layout Jig

Ellipse Layout Jig

This last method (**Figure 127**) uses a jig constructed with a fair amount of time, materials and labor. Unless you intend to do a lot of ellipse work, skip this one.

1. Start with a piece of $\frac{3}{4}$-in. ply or MDF about 12 in. x 12 in. Cut a dado $\frac{3}{4}$ in. wide x $\frac{3}{8}$ in. deep across the middle and up-and-down to form a cross.

2. Cut this piece into a 12-in. diameter circle and drill a $\frac{1}{2}$-in. peep-hole in the center.

3. Construct a beam of $\frac{1}{2}$-in. material 2 in. x 24 in., and drill a hole at one end for a pencil. Drill a series of $\frac{1}{8}$-in. holes every $\frac{1}{2}$ in., starting about 8 in. from the pencil hole. These holes should allow a #4 RH screw shank to rotate freely.

4. Make two sliding pieces of $\frac{3}{4}$-in. material $\frac{1}{2}$ in. H x $1\frac{1}{2}$ in. L and attach to the beam with 1-in. #4 round-head screws. Position the sliders so one screw is $\frac{1}{2}$ the major axis distance from the pencil, and the other is $\frac{1}{2}$ the minor axis distance. Make sure the sliders rotate freely on the beam.

5. To use, mark a center point on the project or pattern on which the ellipse is to be drawn and use the peep-hole to center the jig. A rubber pad under the jig or rubber feet will give sufficient traction to hold it in place.

6. Grasp the pencil and move it to draw the ellipse. If the slides don't glide smoothly in the grooves, it may be necessary to sand and wax the grooves and the sliders. A more elegant jig can be made using sliding dovetails instead of dados.

Ellipses with Special Dimensions

Drawing an ellipse around the rectangular top of a butler's tray table involves more than just drawing the figure. The table design is such that the ellipse must touch all four outside corners and the four wings must have equal width. Mathematically, every ellipse can have an infinite number of rectangles drawn inside it. But there is only one ellipse that fits around a specific rectangle, touching all four corners. This is our problem.

Butler's Tray Table

The rectangular top of a butler's tray table is 20.5 in. W x 31.75 in. L. An ellipse is to be drawn around this table, touching each corner, and each wing is to be the same width, about 5 in. (**Figure 128**). The special butler's tray hinges require a $\frac{1}{4}$-in. gap between the table and each wing—but this can be factored in later.

1. Draw a quarter ellipse 10.25 in. x 15.875 in. (one half of the top's total width and length) on a piece of poster board or thin plywood. Use the T-square method to draw the ellipse.

This ellipse touches the center point of one long side of the top and the center point of one short side. It must be enlarged so it is transcribed outside the table top and touches each of the four corners. The first inclination is merely to lengthen the distance on the T-square scribing slat so the pencil reaches the outside corners of the frame. But that doesn't work. To get a true concentric ellipse - one that has the same shape as the small one but bigger - we have to enlarge the original major and minor axes.

2. To enlarge the ellipse, find the shortest distance between one outside corner of the tray (F) to the ellipse (E). This distance turned out to be 5.375 in. ($5\frac{3}{8}$ in.). Mark new positions for all four points (A', B', C', and D') 5.375 in. out from their original positions (A, B, C, and D).

3. To find the new major semiaxis length, measure from the center (O) to (A'). This is 21.25 in. (5.375 in. + 15.875 in.). Find the new minor semiaxis length, (O) to (C'), 10.25 in. + 5.375 in. = 15.625 in. Make a new scribing slat using these dimensions.

4. Draw a new ellipse that touches each outside corner of the frame and the final test—the maximum width of each wing is 5.375 in.

The leaves can now be cut from the pattern material and used to trace the outline on the table stock. Remember the hinges! Reduce the width (on the long, straight side) of each wing by $\frac{1}{4}$ in., leaving the outer curves alone.

DRAW AN ELLIPSE TO FIT A SPECIFIC RECTANGLE.

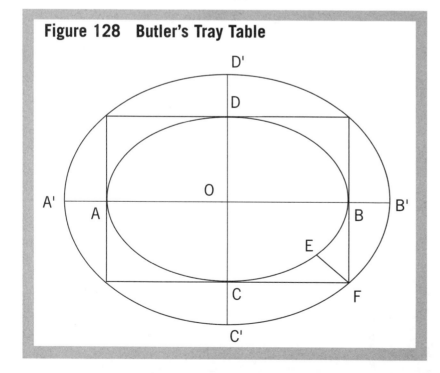

Figure 128 Butler's Tray Table

WHEN THE PROPOSED ELLIPTICAL SHAPE WAS ENLARGED TO FALL OUTSIDE THE LEGS, IT BECAME A CIRCLE.

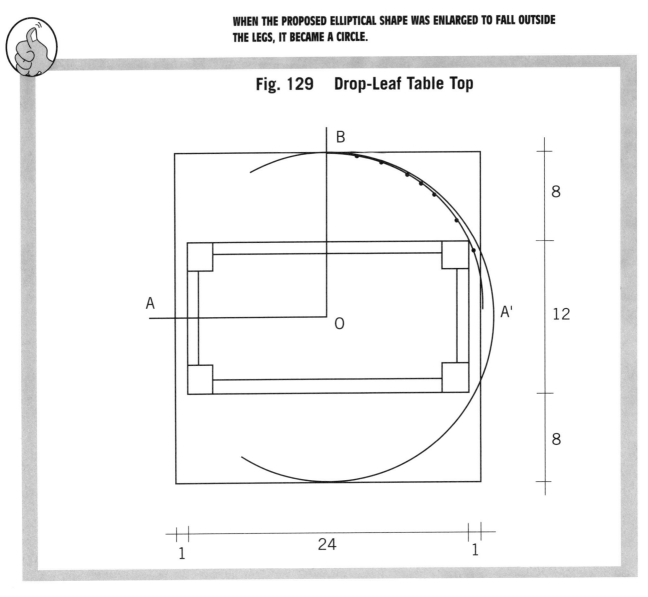

Fig. 129   Drop-Leaf Table Top

Drop-Leaf Table

A drop-leaf table (**Figure 129**) must have pleasing lines when the leaves are down as well as when the table is in use and the leaves are up. The base of our table is 12 in. x 24 in. We want the leaves to be about 8 in. wide, and the top must be outside the legs by at least 1 in.

1. Draw the base to scale. Draw a rectangle showing the proposed top: 26 in. x 28 in.

2. Divide the top into one quadrant (O-A = 13 in. x O-B = 14 in.) and sketch the appropriate ellipse. For a small model like this, use the Paper Strip Method explained earlier in this chapter.

3. The resulting ellipse is too close to the leg, so make the minor axis (O-A) 1 in. larger, 13 + 1 = 14 in.

4. Now the major axis is 14 in. and the minor axis is 14 in. Our ellipse has become a circle.

5. With a compass set to 14 in., from O draw a 28-in. circle around the table base.

CHAPTER 11

Arcs & Arches

In woodworking, the terms arc and arch are used interchangeably. But in the strictest sense, an arc is a portion of a circle while an arch is a structural device used for spanning an opening (**Figure 130**).

In this chapter you'll learn all about arcs and arches, including how to calculate the radii of arcs to build eye-pleasing arched cabinet doors, windows, and entryways. Use formulas or the easy-to-use Arc Rise Chart for the pirate's chest toy box with rounded lid. We also cover decorative arches with multiple spring points, and parabolas, those elusive curves that confer grace and beauty to projects.

AN ARC IS A PORTION OF A CIRCLE; AN ARCH SPANS AN OPENING.

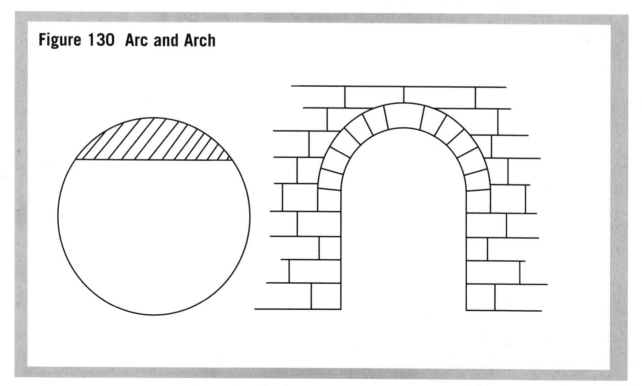

Figure 130 Arc and Arch

THE ARC IS DEFINED BY CHORD AC AND HEIGHT 'H'.

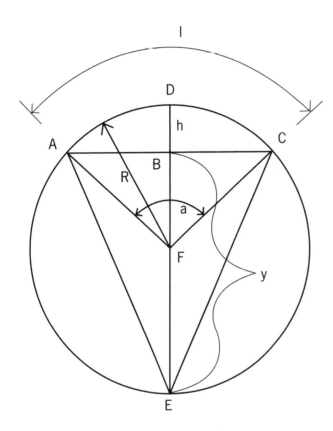

Figure 131   The Arc

AC	Arc Chord
h	Arc Height
R	Circle/Arc Radius
a	Arc Angle
DE	Circle Diameter
l	Arc Length
y	Circle Diameter minus h
F	Circle Center

Arc Radius $R = [(\tfrac{1}{2}AC)^2 + h^2] \div 2h$

Arc Length $l = \pi Ra \div 180$

Arc Height $h = R - \tfrac{1}{2}\sqrt{4R^2 - (AC)^2}$

Arc Angle (in degrees) $a = 2\sin^{-1}(AC \div 2R)$

ARCS

The arc is used in woodworking to reduce the apparent size of a horizontal span and to make otherwise awkward expanses appear narrower and more pleasing to the eye.

Radius of an Arc

In woodworking, we need to know the radius of an arc to set router trammels or to draw a curved line for cutting. **Figure 131** shows the parts of an arc and formulas for calculating radius, length, height, and angle. An arc is defined by the span AC and the rise 'h'.

For example, when making a pirate's chest toy box with a curved lid (**Figure 132**), we need to cut curved lid supports. To draw and cut the arcs, we need to know the arc radius. The end of the support is $1\tfrac{1}{2}$ in. and the center is $3\tfrac{1}{2}$ in. Therefore, the rise (h) is 3.5 - 1.5 = 2.0 in. over the 18-in. span AC.

h = 2, y = unknown, AC = 18
The formula for calculating the arc radius is:

Arc Radius R
$$= [(\tfrac{1}{2}AC)^2 + h^2] \div 2h$$
$$= [(\tfrac{1}{2} \times 18)^2 + 2^2] \div 2 \times 2]$$
$$= (81 + 4) \div 4$$
$$= 85 \div 4$$
R = 21.25 in.

USE THE ARC RADIUS FORMULA TO FIND THE LENGTH OF THE CURVED LID.

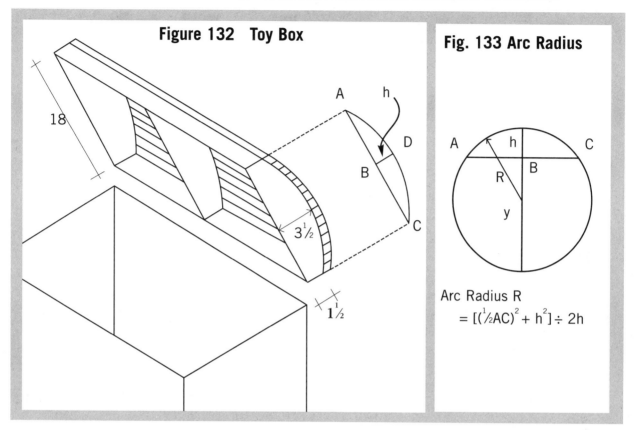

Figure 132   Toy Box

18

$3\frac{1}{2}$

$1\frac{1}{2}$

Fig. 133 Arc Radius

A   h   D
B
C

Arc Radius R
$= [(\tfrac{1}{2}AC)^2 + h^2] \div 2h$

With a $21\frac{1}{4}$-in. radius, draw the arc on a pattern and use it to cut the three lid supports.

Another formula for calculating arc radius is, perhaps, simpler to understand but requires three steps. In **Figure 133** above, the arc is defined by chord AC and height 'h'. In geometry, when a circle diameter crosses a chord (a chord is a straight line joining two points on a curve) at right angles (B), the products of the created pieces are equal. Therefore in **Figure 133**:
Find y:
AB x BC = h x y

and h = 2, AB = 9, BC = 9
    9 x 9 = y x 2
    81 = 2y
    y = 81 ÷ 2 = 40.5 in.

Find diameter of circle:
Diameter = y + h
    = 40.5 + 2
    = 42.5 in.

Find radius:
Radius = diameter ÷ 2
    R = 42.5 ÷ 2
    R = 21.25 in.

THIS METHOD IS USED OFTEN TO LAY OUT LARGE ARCHES AND ARCHED MOLDING IN RESTORING OLD BUILDINGS. BUILDERS MAKE THEIR OWN LONG TRAMMELS. AN ARCHED WINDOW IS LAID OUT USING THIS METHOD.

Figure 134 Laying Out the Radius of an Arc

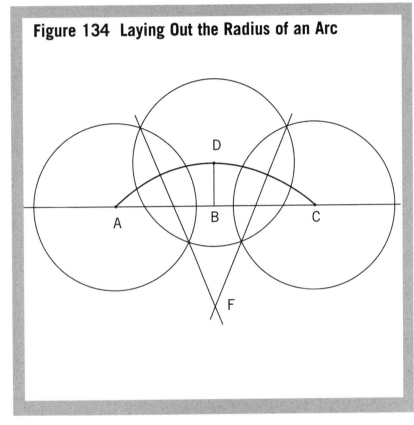

Rule of Thumb

If you want to draw an arc but don't care what the numerical value of the arc radius is, use trammel points and a large piece of plywood (**Figure 134**).

1. Draw a line the width of the chord AC.

2. At the center of this line mark the rise D.

3. With a trammel or dividers, draw a circle around the rise mark   (D).

4. Without changing the trammel setting, draw similar circles around A and C.

5. Draw lines through the points where the circles intersect to give F.

6. Set the trammel to distance DF (the arc radius) and starting from center (F), draw the arc ADC.

In **Figure 134,** the purpose of the three intersecting circles is to determine the centers of a line drawn from A to D and a line drawn from C to D. Another method of finding the centers of these lines is shown in **Figure 135**:

1. Draw a line the width of the chord AC.

2. At the center of this line mark the rise D.

3. Draw lines from A to D and from C to D.

4. Mark the center of line AD at E, and the center of line CD at F.

5. With a framer's square (or large T-square) draw perpendiculars from E and F to point G.

6. Set the trammel to distance DG (the arc radius) and draw the arc ADC.

Rule of Thumb

Here's another way (**Figure 136**) to draw an arc without all of the math. This is the method of choice for drawing full-sized arcs on the job.

1. On a piece of plywood, drive nails at the end points of the arc (AC) and at the highest point (D).

2. Lay two slats across points AD and CD as shown and tack them together.

THIS METHOD WILL WORK FOR VERY LARGE ARCHES

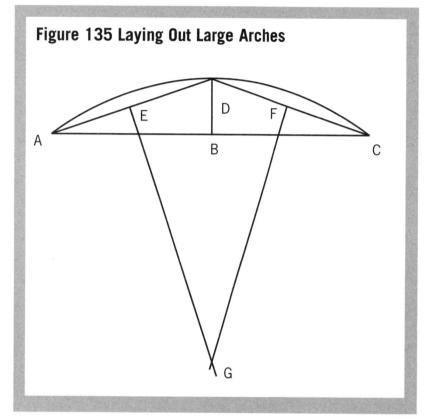

Figure 135 Laying Out Large Arches

3. Remove the nail at D.

4. Hold a pen in the interior joint and slide the "compass" from the middle to each end, allowing the pen to trace the arc.

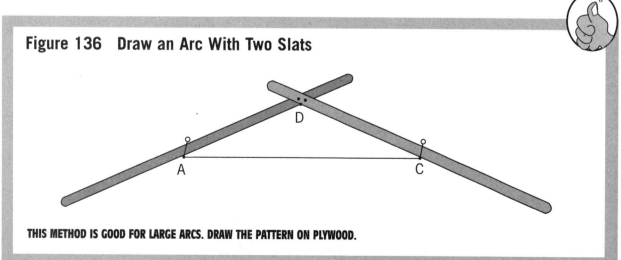

Figure 136   Draw an Arc With Two Slats

THIS METHOD IS GOOD FOR LARGE ARCS. DRAW THE PATTERN ON PLYWOOD.

HOOK CARPENTER'S TAPES AT EACH END AND AT THE TOP. PULL UNTIL THE THREE TAPES ALL READ THE SAME NUMBER.

Rule of Thumb

This method can be used on the job and gives a full-sized arc. It is fairly accurate but requires three tape measures and a lot of dexterity.

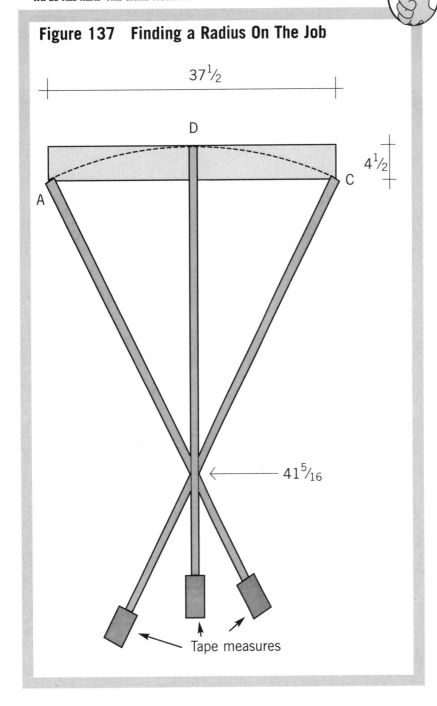

Figure 137   Finding a Radius On The Job

$37\frac{1}{2}$

$4\frac{1}{2}$

D

A

C

$41\frac{5}{16}$

Tape measures

1. Draw a rectangle the size of the arc you want to build, or mark the width and height on a piece of plywood.

2. Drive nails at points A, C and D.

3. Use three measuring tapes and hook one onto point A, one onto C, and one onto D.

4. Pull the tapes down and cross them.

5. Keep pulling until all tapes read the same at the cross. This is the radius.

CABINET DOORS SHOULD ALL LOOK UNIFORM.

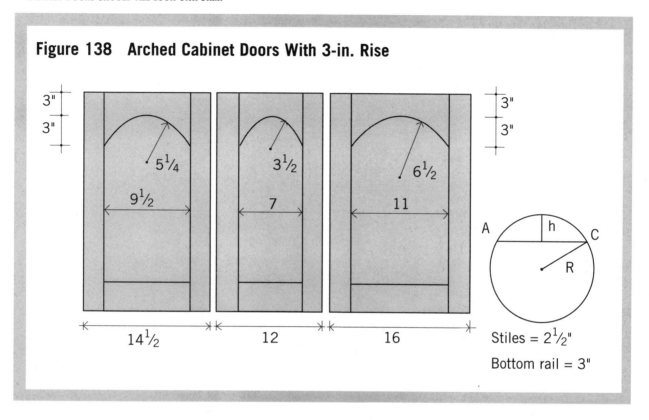

Figure 138   Arched Cabinet Doors With 3-in. Rise

Stiles = 2½"

Bottom rail = 3"

Arched Top Doors

Cabinet doors with arched tops can be constructed by cutting both the panel and the top rail with a router on a beam compass. The trammel length (radius) can be figured once the panel width and the arc rise are known.

In cabinets set in a row, it is important that the height of the door arches be uniform. In **Figure 138** three doors on the same cabinet have different widths. The arches at the top, however, have the same rise, in this case, 3 inches. To find the radius, use the formula:

Arc Radius
$$= [(½ \, AC)^2 \div 2h] + (h^2 \div 2h)$$

Door 1 AC = 9.5, h = 3
$$R = [(½ \times 9.5)^2 \div 2 \times 3]$$
$$+ (3^2 \div 2 \times 3)$$
$$= (22.56 \div 6) + (9 \div 6)$$
$$= 3.76 + 1.5$$
$$= 5.26 \approx 5¼ \text{ in.}$$

In the same manner, the other radii for doors (2) and (3) can be found.

Door 2 AC = 7, h = 3
$$R = [(½ \times 7)^2 \div 2 \times 3]$$
$$+ (3^2 \div 2 \times 3)$$
$$= (12.25 \div 6) + (9 \div 6)$$
$$= 2.04 + 1.5$$
$$= 3.54 \approx 3½ \text{ in.}$$

Door 3 AC = 11, h = 3
$$R = [(½ \times 11)^2 \div 2 \times 3]$$
$$+ (3^2 \div 2 \times 3)$$
$$= (30.25 \div 6) + (9 \div 6)$$
$$= 5.04 + 1.5$$
$$= 6.54 \approx 6½ \text{ in.}$$

The three door arches should be cut using radii of 5¼ in., 3½ in., and 6½ in. This way the height of all three arches will be the same.

AIM FOR A UNIFORM APPEARANCE OF ALL CABINET DOORS.

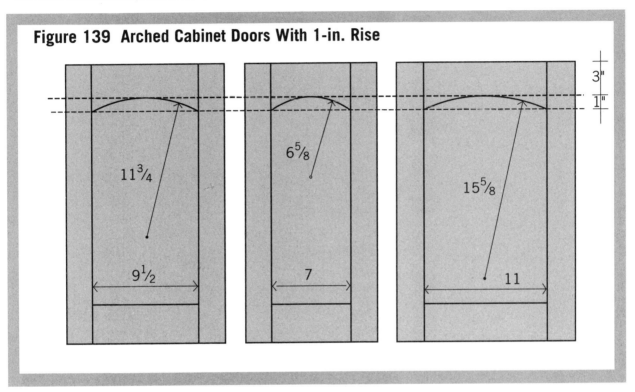

Figure 139 Arched Cabinet Doors With 1-in. Rise

Figure 139 shows the same cabinet doors with arc rises of 1 in.

The radius is calculated as before:
$$R = [(\tfrac{1}{2} AC)^2 \div 2h] + (h^2 \div 2h)$$

Door 1 AC = 9.5, h = 1
$$= [(\tfrac{1}{2} \times 9.5)^2 \div 2 \times 1]$$
$$+ (1^2 \div 2 \times 1)$$
$$= (22.56 \div 2) + (1 \div 2)$$
$$= 11.28 + 0.5$$
$$= 11.78 \approx 11\tfrac{3}{4} \text{ in.}$$

In the same manner the other radii for doors (2) and (3) can be found.

Door 2 AC = 7, h = 1
$$= [(\tfrac{1}{2} \times 7)^2 \div 2 \times 1]$$
$$+ (1^2 \div 2 \times 1)$$
$$= (12.25 \div 2) + (1 \div 2)$$
$$= 6.125 + 0.5$$
$$= 6.625 = 6\tfrac{5}{8} \text{ in.}$$

Door 3 AC = 11, h = 1
$$= [(\tfrac{1}{2} \times 11)^2 \div 2 \times 1]$$
$$+ (1^2 \div 2 \times 1)$$
$$= (30.25 \div 2) + (1 \div 2)$$
$$= 15.12 + 0.5$$
$$= 15.625 = 15\tfrac{5}{8} \text{ in.}$$

Finding Arc Radius With A Calculator

To find the arc radii of the cabinet door panels with a calculator, use the following steps:

1. Enter the panel width (AC)
2. Divide by 2
3. Squared
4. Divide by arc rise (h)
5. Add arc rise (h)
6. Divide by 2
7. Equals Radius

Example: Panel width (AC) = 11, arc rise (h) = 3, radius = 6.54.

Rule of Thumb

The chart in **Figure 140** gives the radii for rail lengths from 5 to 24 in. for arc rises of 1, 2, and 3 in.

For example (**Figure 141**), find the arc radius for a $10\frac{1}{2}$-in. door panel with a 2-in. rise.

Using the Arc Rise Chart, find rail length $10\frac{1}{2}$ in column 1. To the right in the column under h = 2 (2-in. rise), read $7\frac{7}{8}$ in.

Because the radii are linear, you can extrapolate between numbers for fractional rail lengths.

Find radius 'R' for rail length $11\frac{1}{4}$, h = 3

Rail length $11\frac{1}{2}$, h = 3, R = 7
Rail Length 11, h = 3, R = $6\frac{1}{2}$

Therefore:
Rail Length: $11\frac{1}{4}$ = 7.0 + 6.5
    = 13.5 ÷ 2 = 6.75.
Radius 'R' for rail length
    $11\frac{1}{4}$ = $6\frac{3}{4}$ in.

FIND THE RAIL LENGTH AND THE DESIRED ARC RISE (1, 2 OR 3) AND READ THE ARC RADIUS.

Figure 140
Arc Rise Chart

Rail Length	Arc Radius h = 1	Arc Radius h = 2	Arc Radius h = 3
5	3 5/8	2 1/2	2 1/2
5 1/2	4 1/4	2 7/8	2 3/4
6	5	3 1/4	3
6 1/2	5 3/4	3 5/8	3 1/4
7	6 5/8	4	3 1/2
7 1/2	7 1/2	4 1/2	3 7/8
8	8 1/2	5	4 1/8
8 1/2	9 1/2	5 1/2	4 1/2
9	10 5/8	6	4 7/8
9 1/2	11 3/4	6 5/8	5 1/4
10	13	7 1/4	5 5/8
10 1/2	14 1/4	7 7/8	6
11	15 5/8	8 1/2	6 1/2
11 1/2	17	9 1/4	7
12	18 1/2	10	7 1/2
12 1/2	20	10 3/4	8
13	21 5/8	11 1/2	8 1/2
13 1/2	23 1/4	12 3/8	9
14	25	13 1/4	9 5/8
14 1/2	26 3/4	14 1/8	10 1/4
15	28 5/8	15	10 7/8
15 1/2	30 1/2	16	11 1/2
16	32 1/2	17	12 1/8
16 1/2	34 1/2	18	12 7/8
17	36 5/8	19	13 1/2
17 1/2	38 3/4	20	14 1/4
18	41	21 1/4	15
18 1/2	43 1/4	22 3/8	15 3/4
19	45 5/8	23 1/2	16 1/2
19 1/2	48	24 3/4	17 3/8
20	50 1/2	26	18 1/8
20 1/2	53	27 1/4	19
21	55 5/8	28 1/2	19 7/8
21 1/2	58 1/4	29 7/8	20 3/4
22	61	31 1/4	21 5/8
22 1/2	63 3/4	32 5/8	22 1/2
23	66 5/8	34	23 1/2
23 1/2	69 1/2	35 1/2	24 1/2
24	72 1/2	37	25 1/2

FIND THE ARC RADIUS IN THE ARC RADIUS CHART.

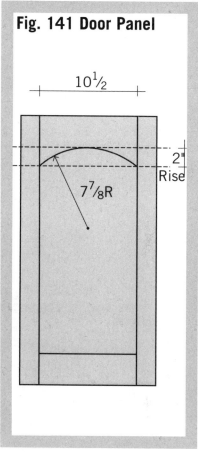

Fig. 141 Door Panel

$10\frac{1}{2}$

2" Rise

$7\frac{7}{8}$R

Find Arc Length

Earlier in this chapter we calculated the radius of an arc while building a pirate's chest toy box with a curved lid. Now we need to know the length of the arc across the top of the lid in order to cut the proper number of slats. And, we need to cut them at the proper angle to insure a tight fit.

Before arc length (l) can be calculated, we need arc height (h) and arc angle (a).

Known: chord AC = 18, AB = 9, radius R = $21\frac{1}{4}$

Unknown: height 'h', arc length 'l', and angle 'a'.

Find Arc Height

$h = R - \frac{1}{2}\sqrt{4R^2 - (AC)^2}$

$= 21.25 - \frac{1}{2}\sqrt{[4 \times 21.25^2 - 18^2]}$

$= 21.25 - \frac{1}{2}\sqrt{1806 - 324}$

$= 21.25 - \frac{1}{2}\sqrt{1482}$

$= 21.25 - 19.25$

$h = 2$ in.

Find Arc Angle

Before we can calculate arc length 'l', we have to know angle 'a'. We know from trigonometry that the sine of an angle of a right triangle is the opposite side divided by the hypotenuse. In our case, this is AB ÷ radius (R). This will give us angle 'a1' which is $\frac{1}{2}$ of angle 'a'.

sin a1 =

= opposite side ÷ hypotenuse

sin a1 = 9 ÷ 21.25 = 0.4235

In a table of trigonometric functions, find 0.4235 under the sin column. With a scientific calculator use the sin-1 or ASIN button.

The angle whose sine is 0.4235 is 25°

The total angle of the arc is:

a = 2 x a1

= 2 x 25

a = 50°

THE LENGTH OF AN ARC 'L' DEPENDS ON THE CHORD LENGTH (AC) AND THE ARC RISE (H).

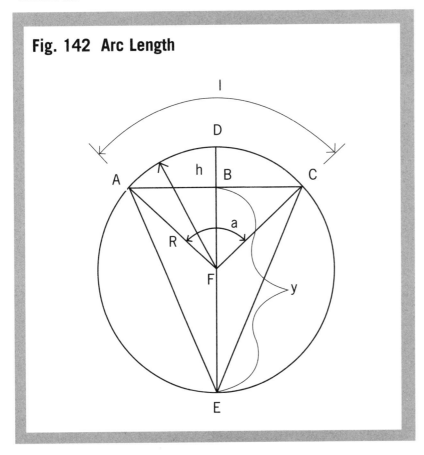

Fig. 142 Arc Length

FIND ARC LENGTH:

Proportion Method

The ratio of the angle of the arc to 360° is the same ratio that the length of the arc is to the length (circumference) of the whole circle.

Circumference = πd
$$= 3.14 \times 42.5 = 133.5 \text{ in.}$$

Known: c = 133.5
    circle angle = 360°
    arc angle = 50°

Unknown: Arc length l

Arc length is to 50° as circle circumference is to 360°

Arc length L
   = (circumference x angle
      of the arc) ÷ 360
   L = (c x arc angle)
      ÷ circle angle
   L = (133.5 x 50) ÷ 360
   L = 18.54 ≈ $18\frac{1}{2}$ in.

Geometry Method

   L = (πRa) ÷ 180, where R = 21.25, a = 50°
   = (3.14 x 21.25 x 50) ÷ 180
   L = 18.54 ≈ $18\frac{1}{2}$ in.

Finally, we know the length of the arc across the top of the chest is $18\frac{1}{2}$ in. Now we can calculate the number of slats needed.

Assuming we use slats of 1.0 in. width, how many will we need?

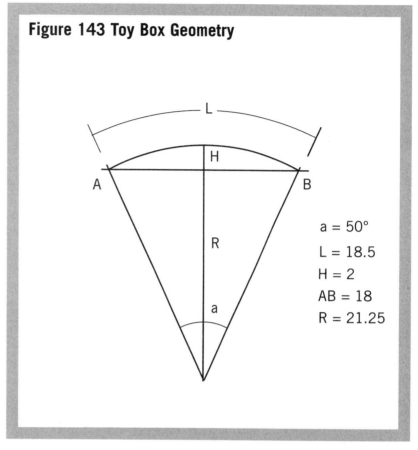

Figure 143 Toy Box Geometry

a = 50°
L = 18.5
H = 2
AB = 18
R = 21.25

And at what angle should the table saw blade be set?
18.5 ÷ 1.0 = 18.5 slats
We can use 18 slats of 1 in. and 1 slat of $\frac{1}{2}$-in. width. To figure the saw blade angle, we divide the arc degrees by the number of segments (slats).

   50° ÷ 18.5 = 2.7°
Blade angle = $\frac{1}{2}$ x 2.7° = 1.35°

But when a 1-in. slat was cut and laid on the arc, it rocked. The slats should be narrower.

Redo calculations with $\frac{3}{4}$-in. slats.
   18.5 in. arc length

÷ 0.75 in. slat width = 24.67
≈ 25 slats $\frac{3}{4}$ in. wide
In a trial, a $\frac{3}{4}$-in. slat laid flat on the arc did not rock.

   50° ÷ 24.67 ≈ 2.0°
blade angle = $\frac{1}{2}$ x 2.0 = 1.0°

Finally! We should cut 23 slats, $\frac{3}{4}$ in. wide and 2 slats 5/8 in. wide with a blade tilt of 1°.

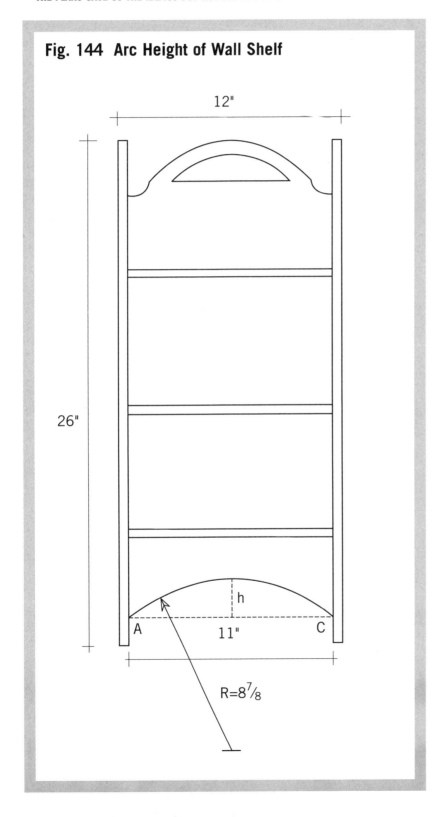

Fig. 144 Arc Height of Wall Shelf

Arc Height

In building a New England wall shelf, the plans gave dimensions for the bottom arc, for example, chord length (AC = 11") and radius (R = $8\frac{7}{8}$"). However, I wanted to know the height (h) of the arc because I planned to redimension and make the wall shelf proportionately smaller.

$$h = R - \tfrac{1}{2} \sqrt{[4R^2 - (AC)^2]}$$
$$= 8.9 - \tfrac{1}{2} \sqrt{[\,4 \times 8.9^2 - 11^2]}$$
$$= 8.9 - \tfrac{1}{2} \sqrt{[\,316.8 - 121]}$$
$$= 8.9 - \tfrac{1}{2} \sqrt{195.8}$$
$$= 8.9 - \tfrac{1}{2} (14)$$
$$= 8.9 - 7 = 1.9 \approx 1\tfrac{7}{8} \text{ in.}$$

Knowing the arc height, (h) = $1\frac{7}{8}$ in., we can proceed with redimensioning and construction.

ARCHES

In construction and architecture, an arch is a structural form made up of a series of wedge-shaped stones arranged over a void. An arch supports the weight of the structure above.

Woodworkers seldom use the arch as support. We use an arc to simulate an arch mainly to lead the eye gracefully across a span and to lessen the apparent size of a cross piece.

Roman Arch

Archaeologists have unearthed forms of pointed arches in buildings dating to 2000 B.C. Mesopotamians and Greeks expanded the use of the arch for aqueducts, monumental gates, and bridges. The arch is aesthetically appealing to the eye and necessary when the spanned opening is too wide to permit the use of a lintel. The Romans introduced the round arch, believing it more appealing than the pointed arch. However, it still required an iron rod cross tie, or some solid mass to keep the arch from spreading laterally. Typically, a stone wall supported either side of a span, or an adjoining arch provided stability. Or, when an arch spanned a river, the ravine wall buttressed the arch. In cathedrals and buildings these counter forces were added

THE ROMAN ARCH NEEDS A BUTTRESS TO TRANSMIT OUTWARD FORCE DOWNWARD.

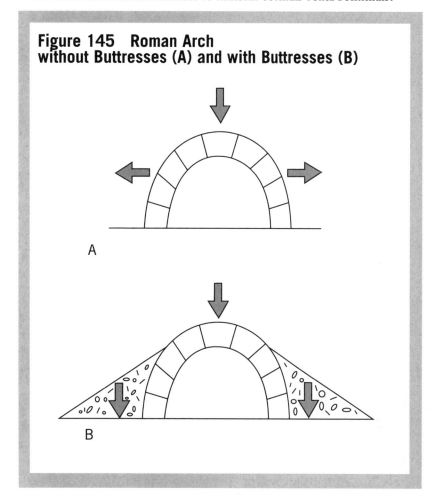

Figure 145   Roman Arch without Buttresses (A) and with Buttresses (B)

outside and were called "flying buttresses." They effectively countered the outward thrust and transmitted the forces downward (**Figure 145**).

THE CATENARY ARCH (B) IS MODELED AFTER A HANGING CHAIN (A).

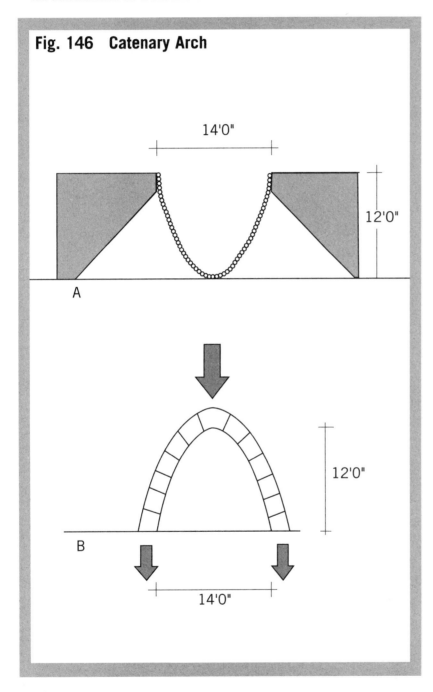

Fig. 146 Catenary Arch

Catenary Arch

The dictionary defines the word "catenary" as pertaining to or resembling a chain. In math it is the curve of a perfectly flexible, non-elastic cord or chain hanging freely from two points.

Because a catenary arch follows the same path as a hanging chain, all force upon the top is transmitted downward and a buttress is unnecessary. An example of this is Eero Saarinen's St. Louis arch. When planning an arch that has support on both sides, use any curve that fits the plan and is pleasing to the eye. When planning an arch that must carry weight and essentially stands alone, plan the arch by suspending a chain between the sides of the span and use the resulting curve as a pattern for the catenary arch (**Figure 146**).

Special Arches

Various forms of arches are shown in **Figure 147**. These are arches drawn with circular curves that have multiple spring lines, i.e., points from which the arcs spring.

DIFFERENT ARCHES ARE SHOWN WITH THEIR GEOMETRIC CONSTRUCTION: (A) SEMICIRCULAR, (B) SEGMENTAL, (C) LANCET, (D) EQUILATERAL, (E) 2-CENTERED, (F) 4-CENTERED, (G) TREFOIL, (H) OGEE-CYMA.

Figure 147 Decorative Arches

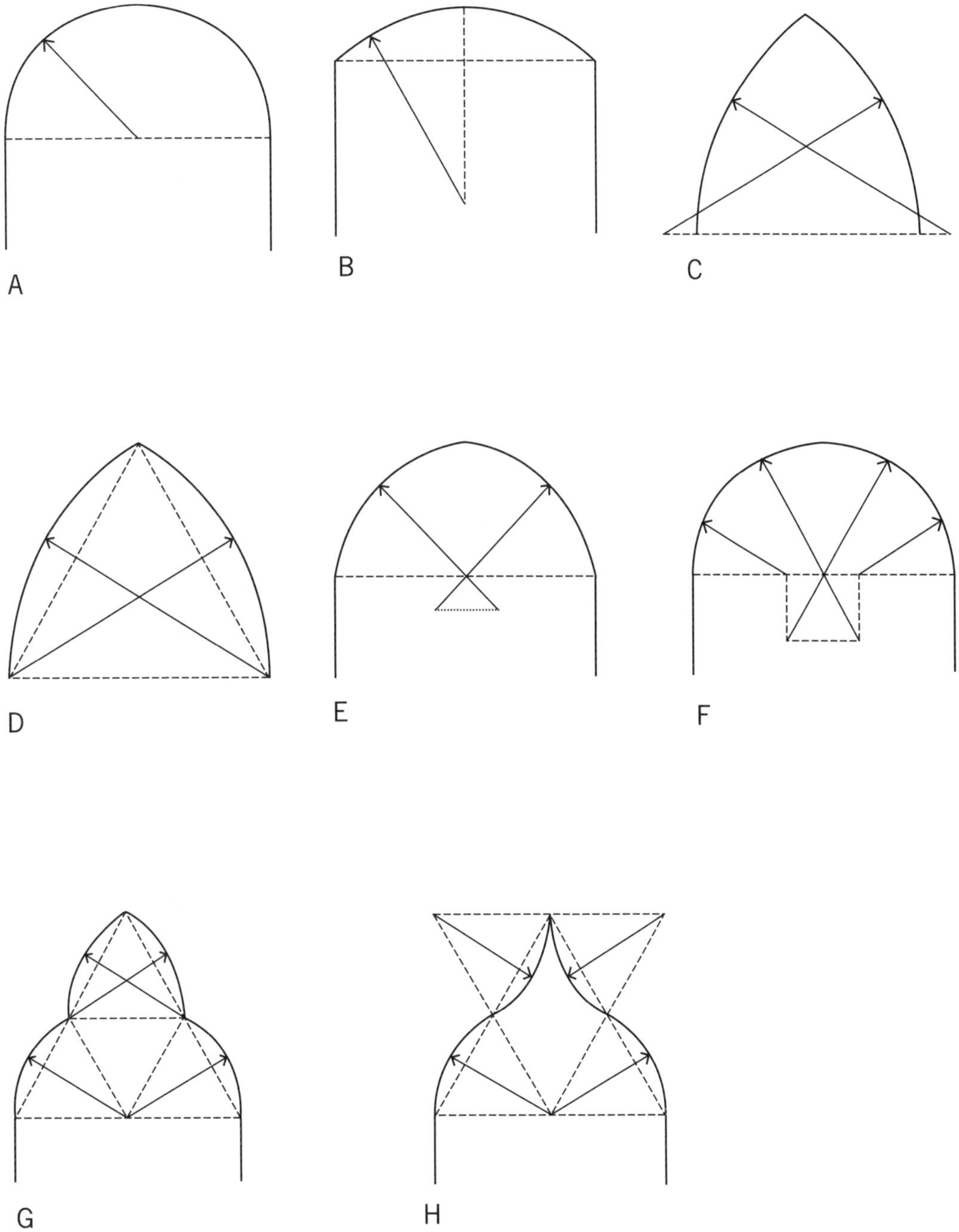

PARABOLIC ARCHES

The parabola is a plane curve generated by a moving point, so that its distance from a fixed point, called the focus (F), is always equal to its distance from a straight line, called the directrix (A-B). Among its practical applications are: searchlights, parabolic reflectors, loud speakers, highway sections, and bridge arches. When the focus (F) and the directrix (AB) are given, as in **Figure 148**, draw the axis through F perpendicular to AB. Through any point D on the axis, draw a line parallel to AB. With the distance DO as radius and F as a center, draw an arc intersecting the line, thus locating a point P on the curve. Repeat the operation as many times as needed.

A PARABOLA CAN BE CONSTRUCTED WHEN THE FOCUS (F) AND DIRECTRIX (A-B) ARE GIVEN.

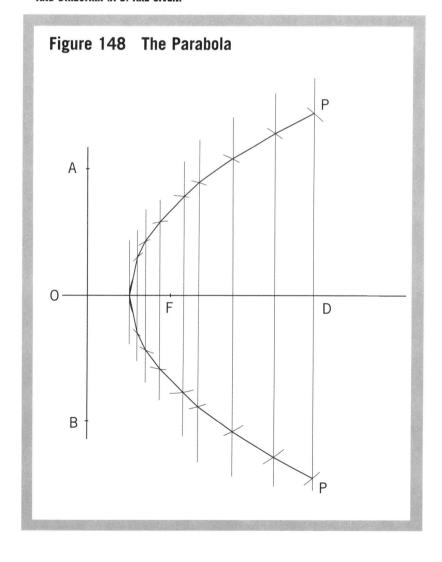

Figure 148   The Parabola

Parallelogram Method

When constructing a parabola (**Figure 149** top), the dimensions of the enclosing rectangle —the width and height of the parabola—usually are known.

The method is thus:
1. Draw the rectangle with span AO and rise AB of the required parabola.

2. Divide AO and AB into the same number of equal parts and label them from O to A and from A to B.

3. From divisions on AB draw lines to O.

4. From divisions on AO draw lines parallel to AB.

5. The intersections of the lines from AB, and the corresponding lines from AO, are points on the curve (dotted line).

Offset Method

Again given the enclosing rectangle, a parabolic arch may be drawn by plotting the offsets from line AO (**Figure 149** bottom). The offsets vary in length as the square of the distance from O. If AO is divided into four parts then distance 3 to 3' will be $1 \div 4 \times 4$ or $\frac{1}{16}$ AB. Because 2 is twice as far from O than 3 is, then distance 2 to 2' will be $2^2 \times \frac{1}{16}$ AB. Likewise because 1 is three times as far from O than point 3, the distance 1 to 1' will be 3^2 x $\frac{1}{16}$ AB.

For example if AB = 50 mm then:

3 to 3' = 50 x $\frac{1}{16}$
    = 50 x 0.063 = 3.1 mm
2 to 2' = 50 x $\frac{4}{16}$
    = 50 x 0.250 = 12.5 mm
1 to 1' = 50 x $\frac{9}{16}$
    = 50 x 0.563 = 28.1 mm

If AO had been divided into five parts, the relations would be 1/25, 4/25, 9/25, 16/25. The denominator in each case is the square of the number of divisions. Traditionally, this was the method used by civil engineers in drawing parabolic arches for bridges and road section curves.

THE METHOD USED TO CONSTRUCT THE PARABOLIC ARCHES ARE: (A) PARALLELOGRAM, (B) OFFSET.

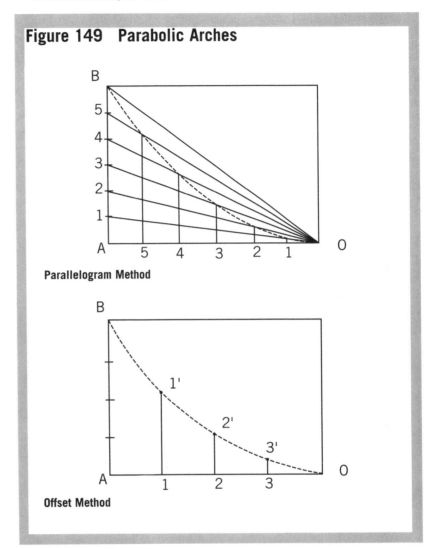

Figure 149   Parabolic Arches

Parallelogram Method

Offset Method

CHAPTER 12

3-4-5 Equals 90 Degrees

A triangle with sides measuring 3, 4, and 5, will always contain a perfect 90° angle at the intersection of sides 3 and 4. Without getting Pythagorean about it, the 3-4-5 system is a simple way to lay out square corners—corners that are 90°. This is done by measuring a distance of three units (3 inches, 3 feet, or 3 yards) along one side. The adjoining side is laid out with four units, again using inches, feet, or yards. When the diagonal measures 5 units, the corner will be square; or, if you prefer, when the corner is square, the diagonal will measure 5 units.

BASED ON THE PYTHAGOREAN THEOREM, THIS SYSTEM IS USED TO LAY OUT 90° CORNERS.

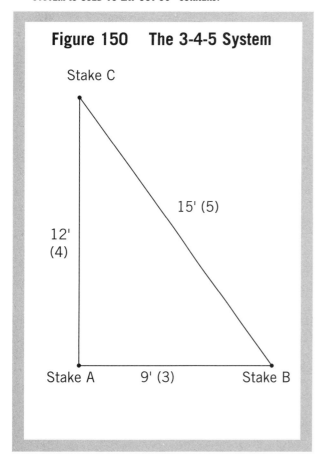

Figure 150   The 3-4-5 System

Stake C

15' (5)

12' (4)

Stake A   9' (3)   Stake B

The 3-4-5 method is as convenient for squaring-up small boxes as it is for laying out a softball diamond. Once you know the length of the sides of the square, you can find the diagonal distance by using a formula. You can also find the diagonal number in an easy-to-use chart.

Playhouse

To lay out the corners of a backyard playhouse, or any size foundation (**Figure 150**), use the 3-4-5 system to ensure that the first three posts are at 90° and, therefore, that these two sides are square.

Locate one corner of the new playhouse foundation and drive in stake A. From this point, measure 9 ft. (three times 3 ft.) and drive in stake B. Using a 25-ft. tape measure or a rope marked appropriately along its length, locate the third stake, C, 12 ft. (four times 3 ft.) from stake A and 15 ft. (five times 3 ft.) on a diagonal from stake B.

The same method can be used to square up a cabinet carcass or other projects in the shop. The theory behind the 3-4-5 system is that, in a

THE SUM OF THE SQUARES OF TWO SIDES EQUALS THE SQUARE OF THE HYPOTENUSE.

WHEN THE THREE SIDES OF THE TRIANGLE EQUAL ANY OF THESE COMBINATIONS, THE ANGLE IS 90 DEGREES.

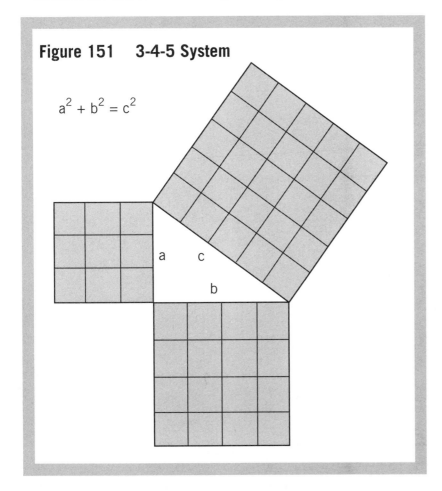

Figure 151   3-4-5 System

$$a^2 + b^2 = c^2$$

a   c

b

Fig 152 Pythagorean Triples

3	4	5	*
5	12	13	
6	8	10	*
7	24	25	
8	15	17	
9	12	15	*
9	40	41	
10	24	26	
12	16	20	*
12	35	37	
14	48	50	
15	20	25	*
15	36	39	
16	30	34	
18	24	30	*
20	21	29	
21	28	35	*
24	32	40	*
27	36	45	*
30	40	50	*

* = Based on 3-4-5

right triangle (**Figure 151**), the sum of the squares of the two adjacent sides equals the square of the hypotenuse (diagonal).

Pythagorean Sets

The table in **Figure 152** shows Pythagorean sets or triples, which are those whole numbers that satisfy the formula:

$$a^2 + b^2 = c^2$$

Use any three numbers in a row to lay out a 90° corner.

Building Foundation

Use the 3-4-5 system to lay out a square building foundation, for example, for a deck or a room addition (**Figure 154**).

1. Mark the approximate position of the foundation and drive a stake at the first corner. Put a nail in the top.

2. Measure the correct distance and drive a stake for the second corner; drive a nail in the top.

Rule of Thumb

Large Layouts

Large dimensional material, such as 4 x 8 sheets of plywood, has factory-squared corners and can be used as large squares. When a project requires a larger square corner, use the 3-4-5 string method. To lay out square corners of the backyard playhouse:

1. Cut a string or cord 12 ft. long (3 + 4 + 5 = 12).

2. Make marks with tape or a marker at 3 ft. and 8 ft., effectively dividing the cord

Figure 153   Laying Out a Large Area
USE THE 3-4-5 METHOD TO LAY OUT A FOUNDATION.

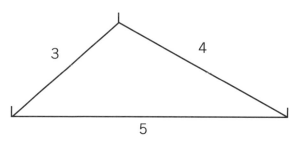

into 3-ft., 4-ft., and 5-ft. lengths.

3. Drive in a stake for the first corner, and attach both ends of the 12-ft. cord with a nail.

4. Pull the cord taut and

drive another stake at the 3-ft. mark.

5. Loop the cord around the 3-ft. stake (or the nail in the top) and again pull the cord tight. Drive a third stake at the 8-ft. mark. This is a 3-4-5 triangle and a 90° right angle.

3. Erect batter boards at all corners. Batter boards are horizontal boards fastened to short 2 x 4 posts. Leave 3 ft. between the boards and the approximate foundation line.

4. Pull string lines over two batter boards and adjust until they cross over the two corner stakes; a plumb bob is useful here.

5. Cut a saw kerf or drive a small nail into the edge of one batter board and fasten the string. The kerf or nail marks the exact spot in case the

string breaks. It's a good idea to use spring clamps here to hold the twine to the batter boards - clamps make adjustments very easy. Once you have everything perfect, set the string permanently.

6. Pull the twine taut and fasten it to corner 2 batter board, making sure the string is directly over the stake.

7. Temporarily fasten the twine to corner 3 batter board. Use the 3-4-5 system to get the corner square. Saw a kerf and fasten the strings at corner 3. Drive a stake at this corner.

USE THE 3-4-5 SYSTEM TO GET FOUNDATION CORNERS SQUARE.

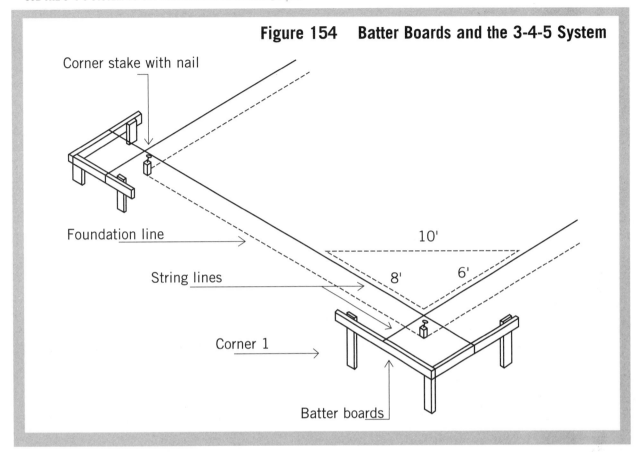

Figure 154   Batter Boards and the 3-4-5 System

8. Continue around the foundation until all corners are square. As a final check, measure the diagonals. If the layout is square, they should be equal in length.

Softball Field

The 3-4-5 method can also be used for large layouts, such as a softball diamond where the bases are the four corners of a 60-ft. square (**Figure 155**). The diagonal of a square is 1.414 times the length of a side, therefore the distance from home to second base is 60 x

1.414 or about 85 ft. (84.85 ft., actually).

$$a^2 + b^2 = c^2$$
$$c = \sqrt{[a^2 + b^2]}$$
$$c = \sqrt{[60^2 + 60^2]}$$
$$c = \sqrt{[3600 + 3600]}$$
$$c = 84.85$$
$$84.85 \div 60 = 1.414$$

1. Get a light rope and knot or mark the rope at the following distances from one end: 60 ft., 85 ft., and 120 ft.

2. Drive a stake for home plate and attach the cord end.

3. Pull the cord taut, and mark 2nd base at 85 ft.

4. Next, attach the 120-ft. mark at 2nd base. Again, pull the cord tightly and mark 1st base at the 60-ft. mark.

5. With the cord still attached to home and 2nd base, grasp the 60-ft. mark and walk across the diamond (square) opposite of first base. Pull the cord tight and mark 3rd base at the 60-ft. mark.

This method can be used with any size square if you have a string or cord as long as the sum of two sides (home to first and first to second), and can figure the diagonal (home to second base). Remember, the diagonal of a square is 1.414 times the length of one side.

Diagonal Chart

Use the chart in **Figure 156** to find the length of the diagonal for any square with a side length from $\frac{1}{32}$ (0.03125)

through 100. The units are immaterial - use millimeters, inches, feet, yards or miles.

Find the length of the diagonal of a square with sides measuring $\frac{3}{4}$ in. long.

Locate $\frac{3}{4}$ (or 0.750) in the chart. Read that the diagonal equals 1.061 in.
A value that isn't in the chart can be found by adding two or more smaller values.

Find the length of the diagonal of a square with one side measuring $3\frac{15}{16}$ in.

The number $3\frac{15}{16}$ in. is not in the chart; 3 is and so is $\frac{15}{16}$ in.

Locate 3 on the chart and read diagonal length equals 4.243. Find $\frac{15}{16}$ on the chart and read 1.326. Add these two values: $4.243 + 1.326 = 5.569 \approx 5\frac{9}{16}$ in.

Therefore, the diagonal of a $3\frac{15}{16}$-in. square is $5\frac{9}{16}$ in.

Hardball Field

What is the distance from home plate to second base in a big league baseball park?

Home to first base is 90 ft. From the chart we see the diagonal of 90 is 127.278. To convert 0.278 feet to inches multiply by 12.

$0.278 \times 12 = 3.336$ in.

THE DIAGONAL OF A SQUARE IS 1.414 TIMES THE LENGTH OF ONE SIDE.

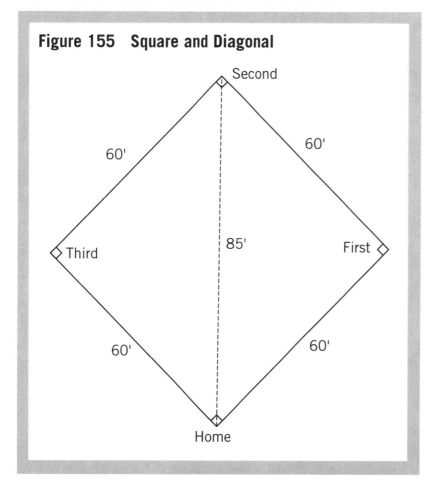

Figure 155   Square and Diagonal

Second

60'   60'

85'

Third   First

60'   60'

Home

FIND THE LENGTH OF THE SIDES OF THE SQUARE AND READ THE LENGTH OF THE DIAGONAL.

Figure 156 Diagonal Chart

Side Length Fraction	Side Length Decimal	Diagonal	Side Length	Diagonal	Side Length	Diagonal	Side Length	Diagonal	Side Length	Diagonal
1/32	0.031	0.044	1	1.414	31	43.840	61	86.266	91	128.692
1/16	0.063	0.088	2	2.828	32	45.254	62	87.680	92	130.106
3/32	0.094	0.133	3	4.243	33	46.669	63	89.095	93	131.521
1/8	0.125	0.177	4	5.657	34	48.083	64	90.509	94	132.935
5/32	0.156	0.221	5	7.071	35	49.497	65	91.923	95	134.349
3/16	0.188	0.265	6	8.485	36	50.911	66	93.337	96	135.763
7/32	0.219	0.309	7	9.899	37	52.325	67	94.751	97	137.177
1/4	0.250	0.354	8	11.314	38	53.740	68	96.166	98	138.592
9/32	0.281	0.398	9	12.728	39	55.154	69	97.580	99	140.006
5/16	0.313	0.442	10	14.142	40	56.568	70	98.994	100	141.420
11/32	0.344	0.486	11	15.556	41	57.982	71	100.408		
3/8	0.375	0.530	12	16.970	42	59.396	72	101.822		
13/32	0.406	0.575	13	18.385	43	60.811	73	103.237		
7/16	0.438	0.619	14	19.799	44	62.225	74	104.651		
15/32	0.469	0.663	15	21.213	45	63.639	75	106.065		
17/32	0.531	0.751	16	22.627	46	65.053	76	107.479		
9/16	0.563	0.795	17	24.041	47	66.467	77	108.893		
19/32	0.594	0.840	18	25.456	48	67.882	78	110.308		
5/8	0.625	0.884	19	26.870	49	69.296	79	111.722		
21/32	0.656	0.928	20	28.284	50	70.710	80	113.136		
11/16	0.688	0.972	21	29.698	51	72.124	81	114.550		
23/32	0.719	1.016	22	31.112	52	73.538	82	115.964		
3/4	0.750	1.061	23	32.527	53	74.953	83	117.379		
25/32	0.781	1.105	24	33.941	54	76.367	84	118.793		
13/16	0.813	1.149	25	35.355	55	77.781	85	120.207		
27/32	0.844	1.193	26	36.769	56	79.195	86	121.621		
7/8	0.875	1.237	27	38.183	57	80.609	87	123.035		
29/32	0.906	1.282	28	39.598	58	82.024	88	124.450		
15/16	0.938	1.326	29	41.012	59	83.438	89	125.864		
31/32	0.969	1.370	30	42.426	60	84.852	90	127.278		

To convert the decimal 0.336 to a fraction, multiply by 32 to get 32nds, 16 to get 16ths, 8 to get 8ths, and 4 to get 4ths.

$0.336 \times 32 = 10.75/32 \approx {}^{11}\!/_{32}$ in.

$0.336 \times 16 = 5.37/16 \approx {}^{5}\!/_{16}$ in.

$0.336 \times 8 = 2.68/8 \approx {}^{3}\!/_{8}$ in.

$0.336 \times 4 = 1.34/4 \approx {}^{1}\!/_{4}$ in.

In this case, because we don't need more accuracy, we probably would place second base 127 ft. $3\frac{1}{4}$ in. from home plate.

CHAPTER 13

Measuring Wood

Wood is measured and sold many different ways: by the sheet, by the piece, by the board foot, by the lineal foot and, incredibly, by weight.

Cheaper woods are sold by the piece, while expensive hardwoods are sold by the board foot and lineal foot. Board feet are calculated by using width, thickness, and length in inches or in feet. Two charts make it easy to find the board feet in a piece of standard width and thickness lumber.

Figure 157

1 board foot

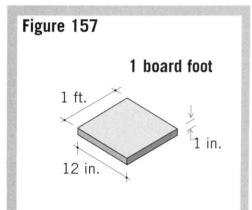

1 ft.

1 in.

12 in.

'Quarters'

1/4 = $\frac{1}{4}$ in. thick
2/4 = $\frac{1}{2}$ in. thick
3/4 = $\frac{3}{4}$ in. thick
4/4 = 1 in. thick
5/4 = 1$\frac{1}{4}$ in. thick
6/4 = 1$\frac{1}{2}$ in. thick
7/4 = 1$\frac{3}{4}$ in. thick
8/4 = 2 in. thick

Sheet

Sheet goods, which include plywood, fiberboards, wood paneling, and door skins are measured and sold by the sheet. Paneling and plywood normally come as 4-ft. x 8-ft. sheets, although both can be found as 4-ft. x 10-ft. sheets in specialty shops. Door skins are usually 40 in. x 80 in., which will adequately cover a standard residential 3-ft. x 6-ft.8-in. door. At lumberyards, the price listed is the price per sheet.

Piece

Less expensive lumber such as 2 x 4 x 92$\frac{1}{2}$ in. wall studs, 1 x 6 x 6 ft. fence boards, 4 x 4 posts, and most dimensioned stock found at home improvement stores and lumber yards are sold by the piece.

Weight

Some tropical, exotic hardwoods—cocobolo, other rosewoods, pink ivory and ebony—are scarce. They are sometimes sold by weight.

Board Foot and Lineal Foot

Expensive hardwoods are sold by the board foot. This is sometimes converted into a price per lineal foot by the lumber yards. Dealers measure stock thickness in fours or quarters (fourth of an inch)—5/4 is spoken as "five-quarters."

Lineal Feet

Lumber sold by the lineal foot can be 1 x 2, 1 x 6, 1 x 8—any size. A bin marked $1.50 LF means whatever size the board in this bin is, you are paying by the foot. For instance, a 6-ft. piece costs $9. and a 4-ft. board, $6.

Board Feet

Flooring, siding, and better cabinet-grade woods are usually measured and sold by the board foot (**Figure 158**). Cabinetry and furniture plans often list the board feet needed for the project. So, what is a board foot?

A board foot is a measure of volume and equals 144 cubic inches. This can be a piece of lumber 1 in. thick by 12-in. wide by 1 ft. long; or 2 in. thick by 3 in. wide by 2 ft. long. Both equal one board foot.

CALCULATING BOARD FEET

To determine the number of board feet in a piece of lumber, the following formula is used:

• **Inches x inches x feet / 12**

Example: Find the number of board feet (BF) in a piece of black walnut 2 in. thick, 10 in. wide and 5 ft. long.

Thickness (inches) x width (inches) x length (feet)/12

$$BF = 2 \times 10 \times 5/12$$
$$= 100 \div 12 = 8\tfrac{1}{3} \text{ BF}$$

Example: Find the number of board feet in 10 pieces of red oak 2 in. thick, 10 in. wide and 6 ft. long.

ONE BOARD FOOT = THICKNESS (IN.) X WIDTH (IN.) X LENGTH (FT.) DIVIDED BY 12.

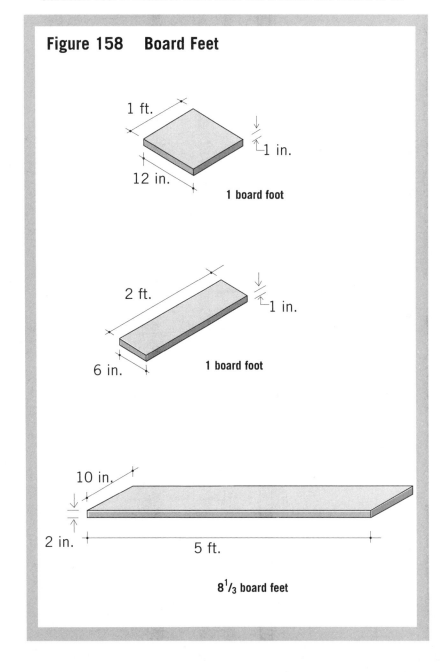

Figure 158   Board Feet

1 ft.
12 in.
1 in.
1 board foot

2 ft.
6 in.
1 in.
1 board foot

10 in.
2 in.
5 ft.
$8\tfrac{1}{3}$ board feet

FIND THE LUMBER SIZE AND MULTIPLY THE LENGTH IN FEET TIMES THE VALUE IN COLUMN 4 TO ESTIMATE BOARD FEET.

Figure 159
Board Feet Estimation

Nominal Size	Thickness	Width	BF Est.*
1 x 2	1	2	1/6
1 x 4	1	4	1/3
1 x 6	1	6	1/2
1 x 8	1	8	2/3
1 x 10	1	10	5/6
1 x 12	1	12	1
2 x 2	2	2	1/3
2 x 4	2	4	2/3
2 x 6	2	6	1
2 x 8	2	8	1 1/3
2 x 10	2	10	1 2/3
2 x 12	2	12	2
3 x 3	3	3	3/4
3 x 4	3	4	1
3 x 6	3	6	1 1/2
3 x 8	3	8	2
3 x 10	3	10	2 1/2
3 x 12	3	12	3
4 x 4	4	4	1 1/3
4 x 6	4	6	2
4 x 8	4	8	2 2/3
4 x 10	4	10	3 1/3
4 x 12	4	12	4

* Multiply this figure times Length in feet to get BF.

$10 \times 2 \times 10 \times 6/12 = 100$ BF

- **Inches x inches x inches/144**

For short boards, where it's more convenient to measure length in inches, use this formula to calculate board feet:

**Pieces x thickness (inches)
x width (inches)
x length (inches/144)**

Example: Find the number of board feet in a piece of 8/4 maple 6-in. wide x 18-in. long.

When all dimensions are in inches, divide by 144 instead of 12.

$BF = 1 \times 2 \times 6 \times 18/144$
$= 216 \div 144$
$= 1.5 = 1\frac{1}{2}$

This same example could be calculated by converting the 18-in. length to 1.5 ft.:

$BF = 1 \text{ piece} \times 2 \times 6 \times 1.5/12$
$= 18/12 = 1\frac{1}{2}$

Board Feet to Lineal Feet

The plan calls for 35 BF of 2/4 maple. The lumber yard sells $\frac{1}{2}$ in. (2/4) stock in 6-in. widths by the lineal foot. How many lineal feet do we need?

First, find the number of board feet in 1 lineal foot of the $\frac{1}{2}$-in. x 6-in. stock at the lumber yard:

1 BF = thickness inches x width inches x length inches/144

$BF = 2/4 \times 6 \times 12/144$
$= 36/144$
$= \frac{1}{4}$

Therefore, each lineal foot equals $\frac{1}{4}$ board foot, or 4 lineal feet equals 1 board foot.

Find how many lineal feet there are in the 35 board feet the plan calls for:

1 BF = 4 LF
35 BF x 4 = 140 LF

We need 140 lineal feet of the lumberyard stock. If the boards in the bin are 8 ft. long then:

140/8 = 17.5 boards needed.

Use **Figure 159** to find the board feet, knowing the size of the lumber.

Example: Using the estimation chart, how many board feet are there in a 2 x 4 board 20 ft. long?

From the chart find 2 x 4 and the estimate factor is 2/3.

$2/3 \times 20 = 40/3 = 13\frac{1}{3}$ BF.

Example: We need 10 pieces of 1 x 6 stock 7 ft. long. How many board feet is this?

In **Figure 159** we find 1 x 6 and the factor of $\frac{1}{2}$.

$\frac{1}{2} \times 7 \times 10 \text{ pieces} = 35$ BF

Rule of Thumb

Use **Figure 160** to find board feet from 1 x 2 to 4 x 12 lumber.

Example: How many board feet are in a 3 x 10 that is 16 ft. long?

The chart shows 40 BF.

Figure 160   Table for Converting Linear Feet to Board Feet
LOCATE THE LUMBER SIZE AND LENGTH AND READ BOARD FEET.

Nominal Size	Actual Size	8	10	12	14	16	18	20
1 x 2	3/4 x 1-1/2	1.33	1.67	2.00	2.33	2.67	3.00	3.33
1 x 4	3/4 x 3-1/2	2.67	3.33	4.00	4.67	5.33	6.00	6.67
1 x 6	3/4 x 5-1/2	4.00	5.00	6.00	7.00	8.00	9.00	10.00
1 x 8	3.4 x 7-1/4	5.33	6.67	8.00	9.33	10.67	12.00	13.33
1 x 10	3/4 x 9-1/4	6.67	8.33	10.00	11.67	13.33	15.00	16.67
1 x 12	3/4 x 11-1/4	8.00	10.00	12.00	14.00	16.00	18.00	20.00
2 x 2	1-1/2 x 1-1/2	2.67	3.33	4.00	4.67	5.33	6.00	6.67
2 x 4	1-1/2 x 3-1/2	5.33	6.67	8.00	9.33	10.67	12.00	13.33
2 x 6	1-1/2 x 5-1/2	8.00	10.00	12.00	14.00	16.00	18.00	20.00
2 x 8	1-1/2 x 7-1/4	10.67	13.33	16.00	18.67	21.33	24.00	26.67
2 x 10	1-1/2 x 9-1/4	13.33	16.67	20.00	23.33	26.67	30.00	33.33
2 x 12	1-1/2 x 11-1/4	16.00	20.00	24.00	28.00	32.00	36.00	40.00
3 x 3	2-1/2 x 2-1/2	6.00	7.50	9.00	10.50	12.00	13.50	15.00
3 x 4	2-1/2 x 3-1/2	8.00	10.00	12.00	14.00	16.00	18.00	20.00
3 x 6	2-1/2 x 5-1/2	12.00	15.00	18.00	21.00	24.00	27.00	30.00
3 x 8	2-1/2 x 7-1/4	16.00	20.00	24.00	28.00	32.00	36.00	40.00
3 x 10	2-1/2 x 9-1/4	20.00	25.00	30.00	35.00	40.00	45.00	50.00
3 x 12	2-1/2 x 11-1/4	24.00	30.00	36.00	42.00	48.00	54.00	60.00
4 x 4	3-1/2 x 3-1/2	10.67	13.33	16.00	18.67	21.33	24.00	26.67
4 x 6	3-1/2 x 5-1/2	16.00	20.00	24.00	28.00	32.00	36.00	40.00
4 x 8	3-1/2 x 7-1/4	21.33	26.67	32.00	37.33	42.67	48.00	53.33
4 x 10	3-1/2 x 9-1/4	26.67	33.33	40.00	46.67	53.33	60.00	66.67
4 x 12	3-1/2 x 11-1/4	32.00	40.00	48.00	56.00	64.00	72.00	80.00

CHAPTER 14

Room Perimeter & Area

A woodworker must be able to find the total length around a room (perimeter) in order to purchase molding. He must also be able to figure the square footage (area) of a room or house, and odd shapes pose special problems. A little thought and use of the 'jig-jog' method will make the tasks easier.

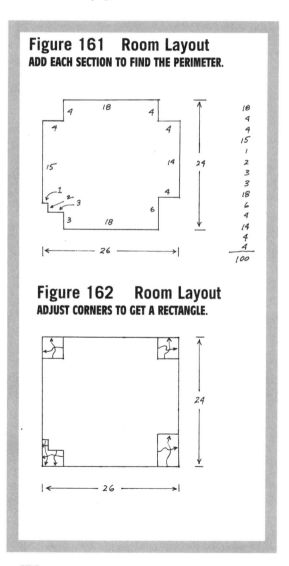

Figure 161   Room Layout
ADD EACH SECTION TO FIND THE PERIMETER.

Figure 162   Room Layout
ADJUST CORNERS TO GET A RECTANGLE.

ROOM PERIMETER

In woodworking and construction work, it's often necessary to figure the distance around an irregular rectangular figure. Typical jobs include installing baseboard, cove molding around a ceiling, forming a concrete footing for a building, or adding a perimeter inlay around a table top.

Figure 161 shows a possible room layout. To determine the baseboard needed, one could add up the individual distances. This lengthy, longhand calculation will give the correct answer, but there is a better way.

Figure 162 shows how each inward 'jig' and 'jog' can be equated to a similar external 'jog' and 'jig.' The result is a rectangular figure better suited for perimeter calculations. Once these have been mentally moved so that we have a rectangle, we use the simple rule:

Perimeter = (length x 2) + (width x 2) . . . . or,
Perimeter = (length + width) x 2

The calculation becomes:

Perimeter = (24 + 26) x 2
= 50 x 2
= 100 ft.

This method of calculating length of perimeter can

only be used when the 'jigs' and 'jogs' occur at corners.

Figure 163 shows the same room as before but with a fireplace in the center of one wall - not in a corner. This is how you could figure this layout:

Perimeter = square perimeter + insets
Perimeter = (24 + 26) x 2 + 2 + 2
= 104 ft.

ROOM AREA

The previous methods will help determine a perimeter length, but figuring an area requires a different approach. While a jig in or a jog out requires the same amount of molding, the area is not the same.

Calculations of square footage of complicated areas can be simplified by breaking the area into rectangles. Because of the complexity of most floor plans, it is easier to break irregularly shaped spaces into two or more rectangles.

Figure 164: The floor plan shown can be broken into two areas: a 9-ft. by 14-ft. rectangle and a 4-ft. by 5-ft. rectangle.

9 x 14 = 126
4 x 5 = 20
126 + 20 = 146 sq. ft.

We also could look at the room as a 13-ft. x 14-ft. rectangle

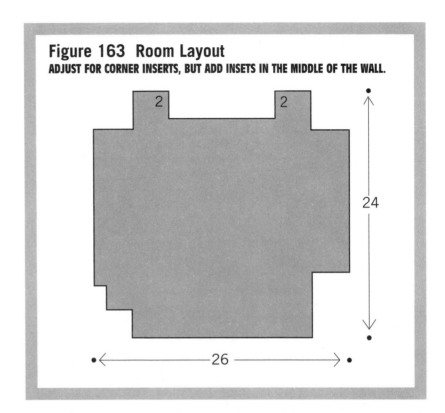

Figure 163 Room Layout
ADJUST FOR CORNER INSERTS, BUT ADD INSETS IN THE MIDDLE OF THE WALL.

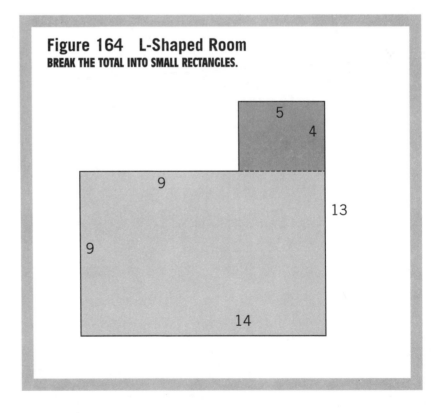

Figure 164   L-Shaped Room
BREAK THE TOTAL INTO SMALL RECTANGLES.

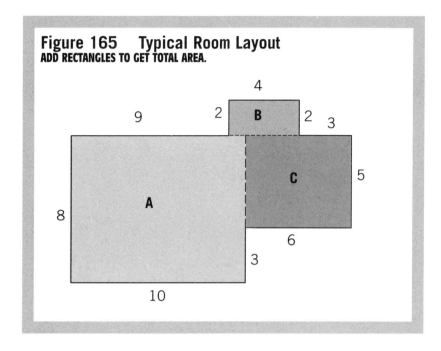

Figure 165 Typical Room Layout
ADD RECTANGLES TO GET TOTAL AREA.

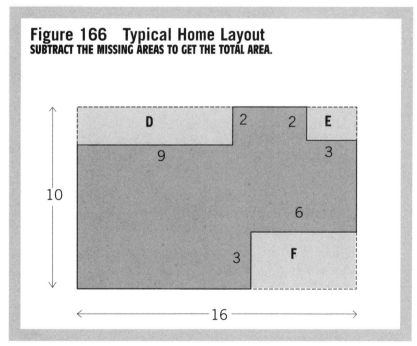

Figure 166 Typical Home Layout
SUBTRACT THE MISSING AREAS TO GET THE TOTAL AREA.

minus a 4-ft. x 9-ft. section. Using this method, the area would be:

$$(13 \times 14) = 182 - (4 \times 9)$$
$$= 146 \text{ sq. ft.}$$

Figure 165: A more complicated space is shown here. The square footage can be figured thus:

Adding rectangles:

Area A = 8 x 10 = 80 sq. ft.
Area B = 2 x 4 = 8
Area C = 5 x 6 = 30
Total = 118 sq. ft.

Figure 166: Total area minus pieces:

Total Area = 10 x 16 = 160 sq. ft.
Area D = 2 x 9 = 18
Area E = 2 x 3 = 6
Area F = 3 x 6 = 18
Total = 42
160 - 42 = 118 sq. ft.

CHAPTER 15

Slats & Spaces

Equal spacing is a problem found in many woodworking projects. In this chapter you will learn how to calculate baluster and slat spacing down to the nearest $\frac{1}{16}$ inch. You'll also find five seat-of-the-pants methods to accomplish the same thing—but without the math.

Equal spacing is a problem we often encounter when constructing bed headboards, porch railings, fences, gates—anything where a long void is to be filled by multiple slats. These solids, usually wood, should be spaced evenly to present a balanced appearance. How do we space these spindles, balusters, pickets, or slats equally?

Simply put, there is a total distance (width) to be filled with a combination of solids and spaces. A simple formula illustrates the problem:

Width to fill = solids + spaces

or

Width to fill = slats + voids

The solids = slat width x number of slats

Solids = Sw x Sn

and the voids = void width x number of voids

Voids = Vw x Vn

Post-To-Post

We are not interested in the width of the end posts. We are only interested in the inner distance, whether it is between bed posts, gate stiles, or something else. We will call the width the post-to-post distance (PP)

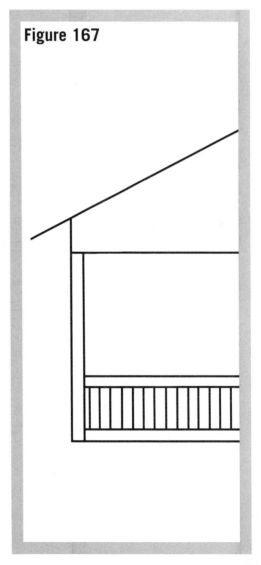

Figure 167

Bed

We're building a bed (**Figure 168**), and the headboard and footboard will have slats between the end posts. The distance between the posts is 52.5 in. We want to use 2.5-in. wide slats. We also want approximately 2.0-in. voids between the slats. How many slats will we need and what is the exact spacing? Assume there is a void next to each post; therefore the voids will number one greater than slats.

The post-to-post distance is equal to the slat width times the number of slats plus the void width times the number of voids.

The main formula is:
Post-to-post distance
    = (no. of slats x slat width)
    + (no. of voids x void width)

$$PP = Sw \times Sn + Vw \times Vn$$
Where Sw = slat width; Sn = number of slats; Vw = void width; and Vn = number of voids.

Remember the voids number one more than slats. Therefore:
    Sn+1 = number of voids
    Post-to-post Distance
    = (Sn x Sw) + (Vn x Vw)

Substitute Sn+1 for Vn
Post-to-post distance
    = (Sn x Sw) + (Sn+1 x Vw)
52.5 = (Sn x 2.5) + [(Sn+1) x 2]
52.5 = 2.5 Sn + 2 Sn + 2
52.5 - 2 = 4.5 Sn
Sn = 50.5 ÷ 4.5 = 11.22 slats

With a post-to-post distance of 52.5 in., slats of 2.5 in., and with voids of 2.0 in., we need 11.22 slats. We can now plug 11 slats into the formula and calculate

the exact spacing:
    PP = (Sn x Sw) + (Vn x Vw)
    Vw = [PP - (Sn x Sw)] ÷ Vn
    Vw = [52.5 - (11 x 2.5)] ÷ 12
    Vw = (52.5 - 27.5) ÷ 12
    Vw = 25 ÷ 12 = 2.08 in.
Convert 0.08 to a fraction:
    0.08 x 16 = 1.28/16 or $\frac{1}{16}$
    0.08 x 32 = 2.56/32 or $\frac{3}{32}$
    0.08 x 64 = 5.12/64 or $\frac{5}{64}$
Therefore 2.08 in. = ≈ $2\frac{5}{64}$ in.

If the $2\frac{5}{64}$-in. voids seem too hard to lay out, other options are:

1. Change the post-to-post distance to accommodate 11 slats and 12 voids thus:
11 slats x 2.5 in. + 12 voids x 2.0 in.
    = 27.5 in. + 24.0 in. = 51.5 in.

This new post-to-post distance of 51.5 in. instead of 52.5 in. uses 2.5-in. slats and 2.0-in. voids.

2. Keep the post-to-post distance at 52.5 in., but make the first and last void $\frac{1}{2}$-in. larger, i.e., 2.5 in. each.

Post-to-post distance = 2.5 + (11 x 2.5) + (10 x 2) + 2.5 = 52.5 in.

3. Keep the post-to-post distance at 52.5 in. but make the middle slat 3.5 in. instead of 2.5 in., and the other slats 2.5 in. and the voids 2.0 in.
Post-to-post distance = (12 x 2) + 3.5 + (10 x 2.5) = 52.5 in.

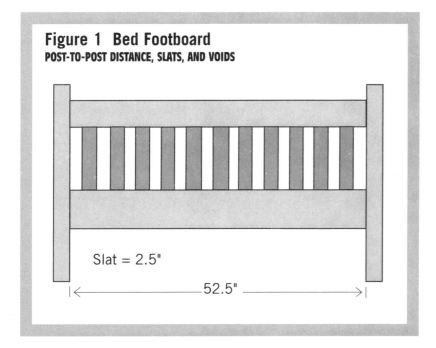

Figure 1 Bed Footboard
POST-TO-POST DISTANCE, SLATS, AND VOIDS

Slat = 2.5"

|←——————— 52.5" ———————→|

Gate

A woodworking magazine published plans for a gate (**Figure 169**) with nine $\frac{3}{4}$-in. spindles and included all dimensions except the spacing of the spindles (slats). The solution is thus:

The spindles are $\frac{3}{4}$-in. diameter. The post-to-post distance is the overall gate width, $35\frac{7}{8}$ in., minus the post widths (3 in. each) or $29\frac{7}{8}$ in. The number of spindles = 9, the number of voids (spaces) = 10. Again, the formula is:

Post-to-post distance = (no. of slats x slat width) + (no. of voids x void width)

PP = Sw x Sn + Vw x Vn
$Vw = [PP - Sn \times Sw] \div Vn$
$Vw = [(35\frac{7}{8} - 6) - (9 \times \frac{3}{4})] / 10$
$Vw = [(35.875 - 6.0) - (9 \times 0.75)]/10$
$Vw = [29.875 - 6.75] \div 10$
$Vw = 23.125 \div 10 = 2.31$ in.

Convert 0.31 to a fraction:
$0.31 \times 8 = 2.48/8 = 2/8 = \frac{1}{4}$
$0.31 \times 16 = 4.96/16 = \frac{5}{16}$
$0.31 \times 32 = 9.92/32 = 10/32 = \frac{5}{16}$

Therefore, $2.31 \approx 2\frac{5}{16}$ in. We can check the answer like this:

Post-to-post distance
$= (9 \times 0.75) + (10 \times 2.31)$
$= 6.75 + 23.1 = 29.85$ in.

Convert 0.85 to fractions:
$0.85 \times 8 = 6.8/8 = \frac{7}{8}$

Figure 169   Gate With Spindles
THE PLANS OMITTED THE SPINDLE SPACING.

3"

$35\frac{7}{8}$"

$29.85 = 29\frac{7}{8}$ in.
With round spindles, we need to drill holes. Therefore, we are concerned with the distance to the center of the slat, rather than the distance to the edge of the slat. The first and last holes are marked the width of the void (Vw) plus one-half of the spindle diameter from the face of the post, 2,685 in. or $2\frac{11}{16}$. All subsequent holes are VW + Sw apart, or $3\frac{1}{16}$ in. apart.

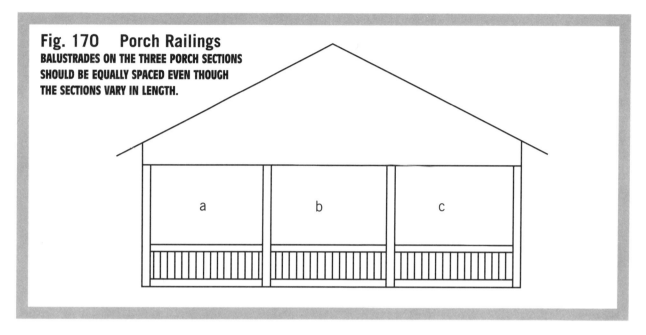

Fig. 170   Porch Railings
BALUSTRADES ON THE THREE PORCH SECTIONS
SHOULD BE EQUALLY SPACED EVEN THOUGH
THE SECTIONS VARY IN LENGTH.

a   b   c

Porch Railings

A porch railing reaching from one side of the house to the other presents another type of problem when the porch posts aren't the same distance apart (**Figure 170**). The balusters should all be the same size and the voids between the balusters should all appear to be evenly spaced along the whole porch length.

Porch section (a) post-to-post
   = 9 ft. 8 in. = 116 in.
Porch section (b) post-to-post
   = 9 ft. 5 in. = 113 in.
Porch section (c) post-to-post
   = 10 ft. $7\frac{1}{2}$ in. = $127\frac{1}{2}$ in.
The balusters are uniformly $1\frac{3}{4}$ in. square

What is the spacing in the three sections of porch railing?

Many city building codes require that balusters be no further than 4 inches apart. Therefore, we will use this as the initial void width.

PP = Sw x Sn + Vw x Vn
Let the number of slats = Sn and the number of voids = Sn+1 remembering voids number one more than slats.

Porch railing (a) 116 in.:
116 = (1.75 x Sn) + (4 x Sn+1)
116 = 1.75 x Sn + 4 x Sn + 4
116 - 4 = 5.75 x Sn
Sn = 112 ÷ 5.75
Sn = 19.5 (the number of slats) rounded to 20
Vn = 20 + 1 = 21 (the number of voids)

If we choose to put 19 slats into this section, the spacing will be larger than the 4-in. limit, so we will use 20 slats. Now we can plug 20 slats into the formula and get the exact spacing.

116 = (1.75 x 20) + (Vw x 21)
116 = 35 + 21 x Vw
Vw = (116 - 35) ÷ 21
    = 81 ÷ 21 = 3.85 in.
Changing 0.85 to a fraction:
0.85 x 8 = 6.8/8 = $\frac{7}{8}$

Therefore, the spacing on porch railing (a) is $3\frac{7}{8}$-in.

Porch Railing (b) 113 in.:
113 = (1.75 x Sn) + (4 x Sn+1)
113 = 1.75 x Sn + 4 x Sn + 4
5.75 x Sn = 113 - 4
Sn = 109 ÷ 5.75
Sn = 18.96 ≈ 19
Sn = 19 (the number of slats)
Vn = 19 + 1 = 20 (the number of voids)

The spacing on porch section (b) with these 19 slats will be 4 in. The difference from the 3-7/8-in. spacing on porch area (b) will not be noticeable.

Porch Area (c) $127\frac{1}{2}$ in.:

$127.5 = (1.75 \times Sn) + (4 \times Sn+1)$
$127.5 = 1.75 \times Sn + 4 \times Sn + 4$
$5.75 \times Sn = 127.5 - 4$
$Sn = 123.5 \div 5.75$
    $= 21.5$ rounded to 22
$Sn = 22$ (the number of slats)
$Vn = 22 + 1 = 23$ (the number of voids)
$Vw = (127.5 - 38.5) \div 23 = 3.87$

We can put 22 slats on this section of porch at $3\frac{7}{8}$ in. spacing.

To summarize:
Porch railing (a) 116 in., 20 slats with $3\frac{7}{8}$-in. voids between.
Porch railing (b) 113 in., 19 slats with 4-in. voids between.
Porch railing (c) $127\frac{1}{2}$ in., 22 slats with $3\frac{7}{8}$-in. voids between.

Unit Spacing

A different way of solving the equal spacing problem is by units. Because one slat and one void always occur together we can consider the two as a unit. And because there is always one extra void in an equal proportion post-to-post problem, the width of one void is subtracted from the total width first:

(Post-to-post distance - 1 void) ÷ unit length = units in span

A garden swing has a back with vertical slats (**Figure 171**).

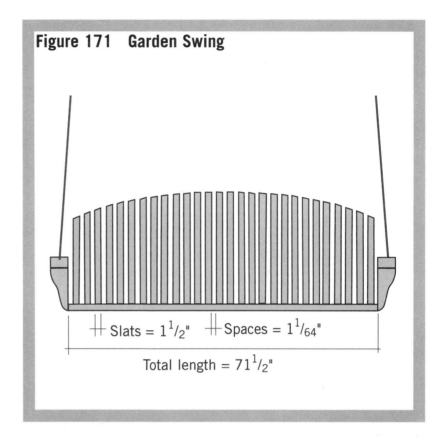

Figure 171   Garden Swing

Slats = $1\frac{1}{2}$"   Spaces = $1\frac{1}{64}$"

Total length = $71\frac{1}{2}$"

The post-to-post distance is 71.5 in. The slats are 1.5-in. wide and we want voids of about 1 in. **(Post-to-post distance - 1 void) ÷ unit length = units in span**

Post-to-post distance - 1 void
    $= 71.5 - 1 = 70.5$
Unit length $= 1.5 + 1 = 2.5$
$70.5 \div 2.5 = 28.2$ units

Therefore, we use 28 slats (1.5 in.) and 29 voids (1 in.)
$(28 \times 1.5) + (29 \times 1)$
    $= 42 + 29 = 71$ in.

The post-to-post distance is 71.5 in. How do we gain the extra $\frac{1}{2}$ inch?

a) Make the first and last void $1\frac{1}{4}$ in. instead of 1 in; this would be a nice balance.

b) Make each void $1\frac{1}{64}$ in. This is the exact width.
$71.5 - 42 = 29.5$ in. (space for the voids)
$29.5 \div 29 = 1.017$ in. $= 1\frac{1}{64}$ in.

c) Make the middle two slats or the first and last slats 1.75 in. each instead of 1.5 in. Either would be a nice balance.

d) Fudge eight slats by $\frac{1}{16}$ in. (4 on each end) or 16 slats by $\frac{1}{32}$ in. (8 on each end). Neither would be noticeable.

Figure 172 Picket Fence

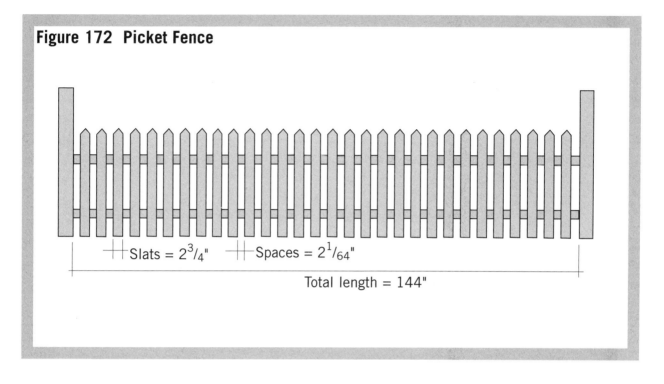

Slats = $2^3/_4$"   Spaces = $2^1/_{64}$"

Total length = 144"

Picket Fence

A picket fence is 12-ft. long post-to-post (**Figure 172**), each picket is $2^3/_4$-in. wide, and we want voids about 2-in. wide. What is exact spacing between pickets?

12 ft. x 12 in/ft = 144 in.
(post-to-post distance - 1 void) ÷ unit length = units in span
PP = 144 - 2 = 142
142 ÷ (2.75 + 2)
    = 142 ÷ 4.75 = 29.9 units

Therefore, we use 30 pickets (2.75 in.) and 30 voids (2 in.)

(30 x 2.75) + (30 x 2)
    = 82.5 + 60 = 142.5 in.
142.5 in. + 2 in. (1 void)
    = 144.5 in.

And the extra $^1/_2$ inch? Don't worry about it. You can easily lose it over the 12-ft. distance.

Slats Outnumber Voids
Patio Trellis

In all the previous problems, the situations were post-to-post and the voids numbered one more than the slats. The situation might be reversed (**Figure 173**).

A patio trellis structure is 14 ft. long. We want to cover it with redwood 2x4s ($1\frac{1}{2}$ in. x $3\frac{1}{2}$ in.) laid on the flat with approximately 3-in. voids. What is the spacing?

Let Vn = number of voids,
    Vw = void width
Let Sn = number of slats,
    Sw = slat width

Remember that the slats number one more than the voids so:
Sn = Vn+1
Overall length
    = 14 ft. x 12 in/ft = 168 in.
Total length
    = (Sw x Sn) + (Vw x Vn)
168 = 3.5 x Vn+1 + 3 x Vn
168 = 3.5 x Vn + 3.5 + 3 x Vn
6.5 x Vn = 168 - 3.5
Vn = 164.5 ÷ 6.5
Vn = 25.3 (the number of voids)

Now set number of voids at 25 and recalculate:
168 = 3.5 (25 + 1) + (Vw x 25)
168 = 91 + (25 x Vw)
Vw = (168 - 91) ÷ 25
Vw = 77 ÷ 25 = 3.08
0.08 x 16 = 1.28/16 = $\frac{1}{16}$

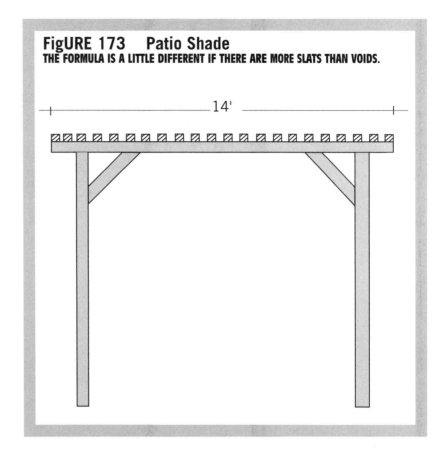

FigURE 173   Patio Shade
THE FORMULA IS A LITTLE DIFFERENT IF THERE ARE MORE SLATS THAN VOIDS.

14'

Set the 2x4 slats with $3\frac{1}{16}$-in. spacing.

Rules of Thumb

In some cases when woodworkers build a porch or deck they try to lay out the railing balusters with equal spaces between them and really don't care what the spacing is. These five empirical methods get the job done.

1. Proportioning Tool

Woodworking catalogs sell a proportioning tool (**Figure 174**). This is an accordion-like device that can be pulled to any length up to 24 in., and equal distances marked at the apexes of the folds. In a similar manner an expandable kiddy gate or a wall-mounted hat rack of a similar design can be used to lay out equal units on longer projects.

The distance between a-b-c-d-e-f-g are equal and will remain equal as the ends are moved outward or inward. If the rack doesn't expand far enough,

divide your length into equal sections—halves, thirds, fourths—and proportion each section separately.

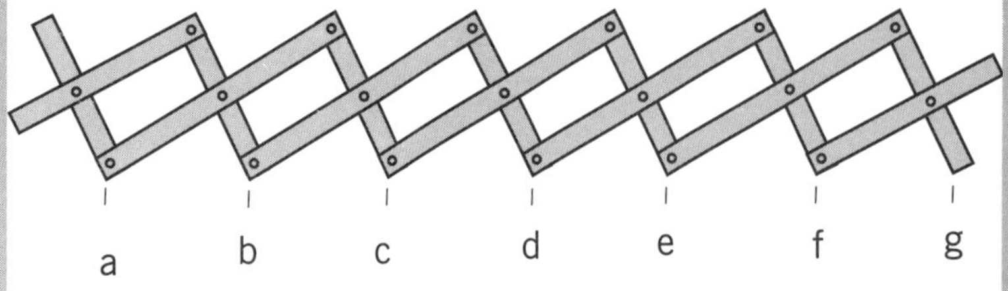

2. Multiple Centers

Find the center of the space and place a slat there. Find the centers on both sides and place slates there. Continue dividing the remaining spaces until all the spaces are filled in and all the slats are a uniform distance apart.

3. String Method

Stretch a cord to the length of the space and cut it. Fold the cord in half, then into fourths, then into eights and so forth until you've found some small distance that is the proper spacing. Cut a piece of wood to this length and use it as a spacing jig.

4. Story Pole

To illlustrate this method, imagine we want to put railing balusters between two posts that are 9 ft. 8$\frac{1}{2}$ in. apart, though the actual distance doesn't really matter (**Figure 175**). The balusters are 2 in. wide and we want them to be about 4 in apart.

Cut a length of 1x2 pine a little longer than the post-to-post distance, say 11 ft. Make marks on this story pole, then use it to space the slats. To figure where to make the marks use this formula:

Figure 174   Kiddy Gate
USE THIS DEVICE TO PROPORTION SPACES.

a   b   c   d   e   f   g

Marks = $\frac{1}{2}$ Slat Width + Space Width + $\frac{1}{2}$ Slat Width

In our example this will be:
(0.5 x 2) + 4 + (0.5 x 2) = 6 in.

Start at one end of the story pole and make a mark every six inches. Do this the entire length. Also make marks 1 in. from the left end and 1 in. from the last mark on the right end. This is one-half the width of one slat. Drive a small nail near the left end of the story pole and attach it to the left-hand post at the 1-in. mark. Tilt the pole up and nail it to the other post so the 1-in. mark is even with the inside edge of the right-hand post, as in **Figure 175**.

Use a framer's square to transfer the marks on the pole down to the porch floor. For more on *Story Poles*, see Chapter 17.

5. Split the Difference

Finally, perhaps the simplest method is to space the slats with a spacer block of eyeballed size. Accumulate the "extra" space at the center, or else in the two spaces at either edge, whichever you prefer (**Figure 176**).

To split the difference to either side, center the middle slat, then use the block to space the remaining slats to either side. You'll end up with non-matching but equal-sized

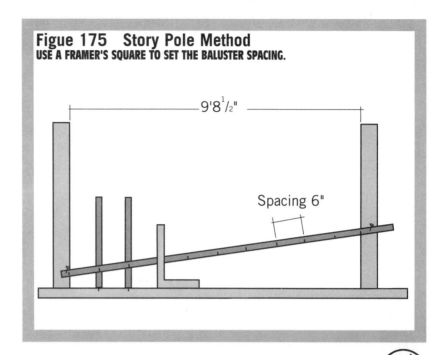

Figue 175   Story Pole Method
USE A FRAMER'S SQUARE TO SET THE BALUSTER SPACING.

9'8$\frac{1}{2}$"

Spacing 6"

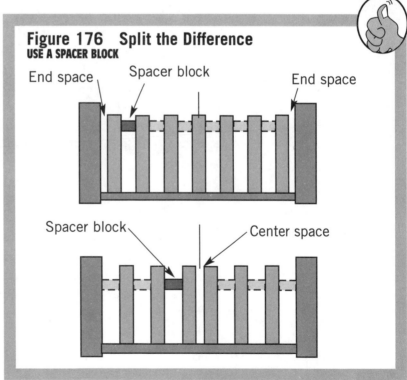

Figure 176   Split the Difference
USE A SPACER BLOCK

End space   Spacer block   End space

Spacer block   Center space

spaces at either end. If you want to accumulate the extra space in the middle, work toward it from both sides simultaneously. The center space will either be larger than the block, or smaller, and it will look OK to you, or not. If not, adjust the size of the block and try again.

CHAPTER 16

Story Poles

One of the first tools a woodworker buys is a good, retractable, steel measuring tape. They come in a variety of lengths and widths, and through the years we've used them, abused them, cursed them, and lost them. We constantly use them to make cut-off marks, to lay out dados and joinery positions, or to just find the length of a piece of wood. It's hard to imagine woodworking without a tape measure, so how did cabinetmakers construct beautiful furniture with accuracy and precision, hundreds of years ago, long before tape measures came into general use?

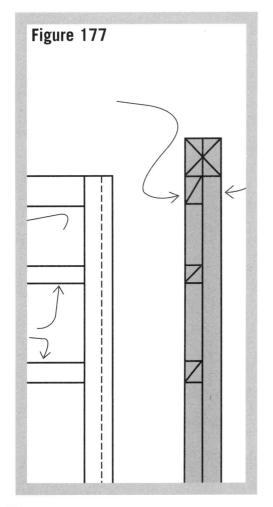

Figure 177

Everyone has heard some version of the story. One day, the old timer shows up at the job site. He wanders around for a while, looks things over with a practiced eye, then tells the foreman that he's the cabinetmaker and he's there to measure the kitchen. All the other workers have their 'bags'—heavy leather belt pouches, weighted down with a dozen or so tools - hammer, pliers, screwdrivers, tri-squares, wire cutters, crayon markers, pencils, and two or three tape measures. The old timer unpacks his 'tools,' which consist, in their entirety, of a pencil and three long, slender sticks.

A half-hour later as he's leaving, someone notices the sticks are now covered with lines and written notations. When questioned, he says he's measured the kitchen and is headed back to his shop to build the cabinets—apparently without having once pulled out a tape measure or committing a single line to a piece of paper. When pressed, the old timer will probably grin and explain a little about story poles. After all, he explains, as he carefully packs his sticks into his truck, marking lengths and widths on a stick is a lot easier than measuring and writing down the figures on a scrap of paper. And back in the shop those figures have to be reinterpreted and transferred to pieces of wood. He contends that all this writing and transferring leads to mistakes. He prefers to take full-size, direct measurements on story poles back with him.

A story pole, sometimes called a story stick, is a clean, light-colored piece of wood that is laid out with all the full-size dimensions and details needed. A story pole can be a full-size layout of the cross section of a wall, all the joinery of a cabinet, or the spacing for roof shingles. Think of a story pole as your personal ruler showing only the marks you need.

A story pole eliminates mathematical errors in measuring and calculating. How many times a day can you calculate one-half of $13\frac{7}{8}$ or $8\frac{1}{4}$ minus $\frac{5}{16}$ without making a mistake? In fact, the use of a story pole dates back to the time when cabinetmakers were illiterate and couldn't do those mathematical calculations. It makes measuring almost foolproof and gives a standard against which to double check all dimensions. Today there are a few joiners, chairmakers, and framers who still use story poles, but with laser measurements and computer-generated blueprints, it is becoming a lost art.

A story pole is either set out full size from a working drawing or marked directly from the project, or a combination of both. It could represent a kitchen wall where cabinets are to be installed or a piece of furniture you want to duplicate. The wonderful thing about a story pole is that the whole system works without the need for measurements or calculators. If you want to copy a chiffenrobe, first sketch the piece for reference. Next, hold a stick next to the cabinet and pencil off the various widths and heights directly onto the story pole. Record any and all unusual joinery or fancy details. Back at the shop, lay the story pole alongside the wood chosen and copy the measurements directly onto the wood without ever using a tape measure.

Because story poles are used in so many different ways, the rest of this chapter is organized as if we were building a house and using story poles from the ground up.

Rules of Thumb

1. Lay out the story pole during a quiet time. A mistake here will be mass-produced later with disastrous results.

2. Be very accurate. The importance of accuracy in stick layout cannot be emphasized too strongly. If you are transferring data from a drawing to the story pole, do it twice to check your measurements.

3. Mark the 'zero' end prominently. More than one project has been derailed by a craftsman scaling from the wrong end of the pole.

4. Use a sharp pencil for stick layout. It will help you make accurate marks and if you don't, the line will be easy to erase. Afterwards, you might want to cut small, sharp notches for important marks, like the top and bottom of a leg or the outer limits of a door or window.

5. Don't crowd too much data on one stick. Ideally, you need three poles - one for vertical height, one for width across the front, and one for depth. You could grab one 2x2 and use a different side for each dimension but this can become confusing. Having separate sticks for different dimensions also means you can lay them side by side for comparison or even tack one to the wall later and use it as a template for cabinet installation.

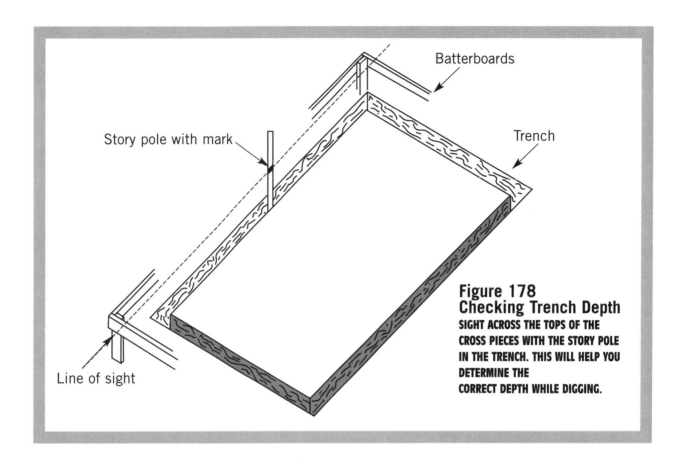

Story pole with mark

Batterboards

Trench

Line of sight

Figure 178
Checking Trench Depth
SIGHT ACROSS THE TOPS OF THE
CROSS PIECES WITH THE STORY POLE
IN THE TRENCH. THIS WILL HELP YOU
DETERMINE THE
CORRECT DEPTH WHILE DIGGING.

Site Layout

Usually a story pole is thought of as a marked stick used to record intricate data such as rails and stiles or room dimensions. Builders also use simple story poles to check the depth of foundation trenches. In areas with a frost-line, building inspectors will often bring a story pole to the site and use it to measure the minimum required depth of trenched footings before giving their okay.

Batterboards and string give a quick vertical reference for determining how deeply to trench. However, the string is removed during excavation and wound around the batter boards. Enter the story pole. A 2x2 board is cut about four feet longer than the required depth of the trench, e.g., 42 in. in Southeastern Michigan to 18 in. in non-frost areas of California. The story pole is marked with a piece of yellow tape at the required trench depth plus the height of the batter boards. One person sights from the top of one batterboard to another, while a helper walks the story pole along the trench. The mark on the story pole will line up with the tops of the batterboards when the trench is the correct depth. As an example, if the footing is to be 24 in. deep and the batter boards are 18 in. high, the yellow mark is placed 42 in. from the bottom end (24 in. + 18 in.).

Bolt Holes in Sills

Anchor bolts are used to secure the sill plate of a wall to the house foundation. The bolts are embedded in the concrete footing, then holes are drilled into the 2x4 sill plate before it is attached with nuts. A story pole, of sorts, will speed the location of these holes. Use a piece of $\frac{1}{8}$-in. x 1-in. metal about 20 in. long. Notch one end to fit around the anchor bolt. For a 2x4 sill plate, drill a hole $3\frac{1}{2}$ in. from the notch and put in a small machine screw.

To use the anchor bolt marker, snap a line the width of the sill plate from the edge of the foundation. Place the sill plate on the foundation with the edge opposite the side of the chalk line where it normally would go. Make sure the sill is placed directly on the line and that the end of the plate is in the right spot. Hold the notch of the marker against the bolt and at right angles to the plate. With a hammer, tap the screw to leave an indentation in the sill, marking the location to be drilled. Drill the holes and drop the sill plate over the bolts.

The marker can also be made from a piece of $\frac{3}{4}$ x 2-in. pine or plywood. Drill a hole the size of the anchor bolt at one end and 3?-in. distance from the hole drive in a hanger nail.

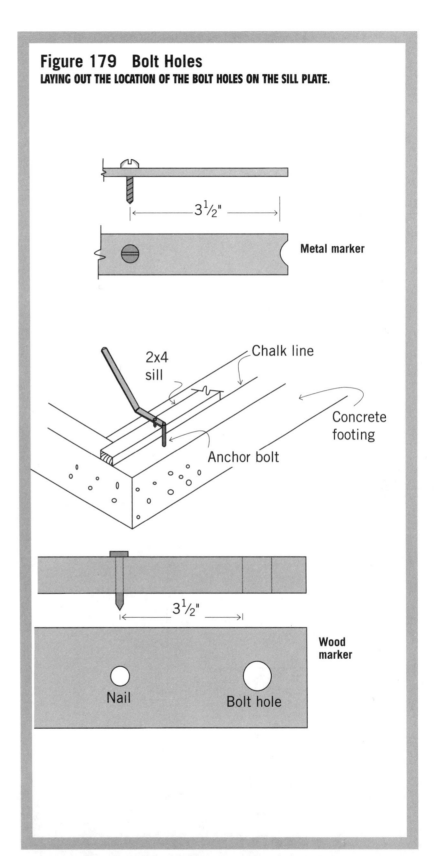

Figure 179   Bolt Holes
LAYING OUT THE LOCATION OF THE BOLT HOLES ON THE SILL PLATE.

3½"

Metal marker

2x4 sill

Chalk line

Concrete footing

Anchor bolt

3½"

Wood marker

Nail

Bolt hole

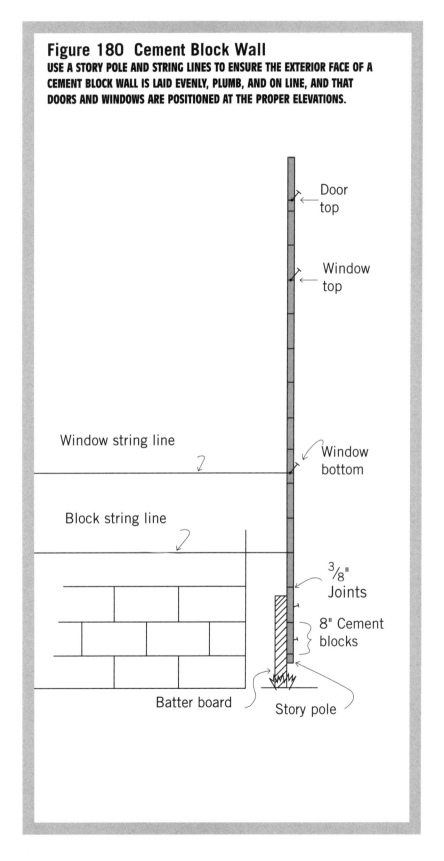

Figure 180 Cement Block Wall
USE A STORY POLE AND STRING LINES TO ENSURE THE EXTERIOR FACE OF A CEMENT BLOCK WALL IS LAID EVENLY, PLUMB, AND ON LINE, AND THAT DOORS AND WINDOWS ARE POSITIONED AT THE PROPER ELEVATIONS.

Door top

Window top

Window string line

Window bottom

Block string line

$\frac{3}{8}$" Joints

8" Cement blocks

Batter board

Story pole

Cement Block and Stone Exterior Walls

A story pole or course pole is simply a board with markings a certain distance apart to provide an accurate method of positioning the top of the masonry for each course. If the mortar joints are $\frac{3}{8}$ in. thick, don't worry, you just need to mark the top of each course of masonry. This is the point where the line is stretched and the level at which each course is laid.

For a stone wall, make story poles of 2x4's and nail them at each end of the wall to the batterboards. Check to make sure they are plumb and that the outboard edges line up with the building lines. Stretch a pair of string lines between the poles and visually align the face of each stone with the strings. To locate horizontal features such as window sills and door headers, drive nails along the edges of the story poles at the proper elevations and stretch string between the nails.

Framing Gable Roof Ends

Gabled roof end studs should be aligned with wall studs if the roof is to be sheathed with plywood or siding. A story pole can be used to note the pitch-cut locations on these studs for a gable (**Figure 181**). Begin by selecting a straight stud that is long enough to extend above the top of the rafter at the highest stud. This story pole will eventually have the height of the notches for all the gable studs marked on it. Draw a big "L" on one face to indicate the left side of the gable, and an arrow to show which way is up. A general rule in making a story pole is to leave nothing to chance by making all kinds of notes. Once back at the shop or down off the ladder, those little marks and ticks should all mean something.

Begin marking at the high end of the gable by putting the bottom of the story pole directly over the stud nearest the peak. As in the drawing, **Figure 181**, the story pole is held against the rafter at the top, and plumbed with a level. Next, make a mark on the rafter to show the uphill side of the gable stud for future nailing; a slanting line on the edge of the story pole records the bottom of the rafter. With these marks made, pull the story pole away from the rafter and draw an "X"

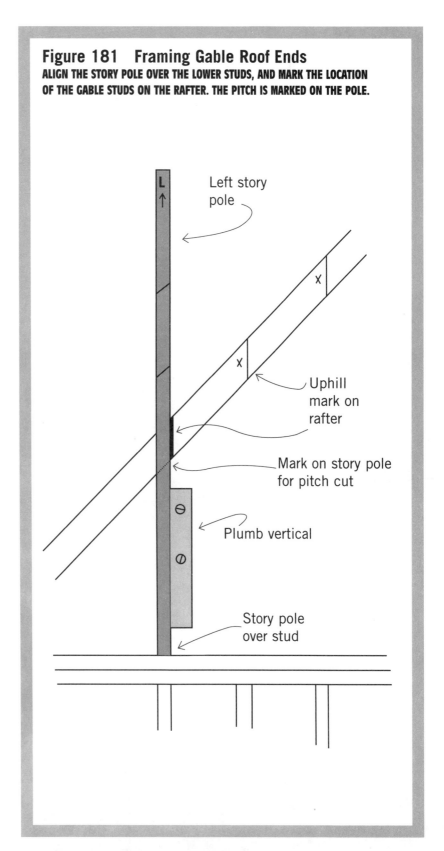

Figure 181   Framing Gable Roof Ends
ALIGN THE STORY POLE OVER THE LOWER STUDS, AND MARK THE LOCATION OF THE GABLE STUDS ON THE RAFTER. THE PITCH IS MARKED ON THE POLE.

Figure 182 Transfer Data
From the Story Pole to the Studs
THE MARKS ON THE STORY POLE INDICATE THE LENGTH OF EACH STUD. THE DIAGONAL MARKS SHOW THE RAFTER PITCH FOR NOTCHING AND THE CUT-OFF LENGTHS.

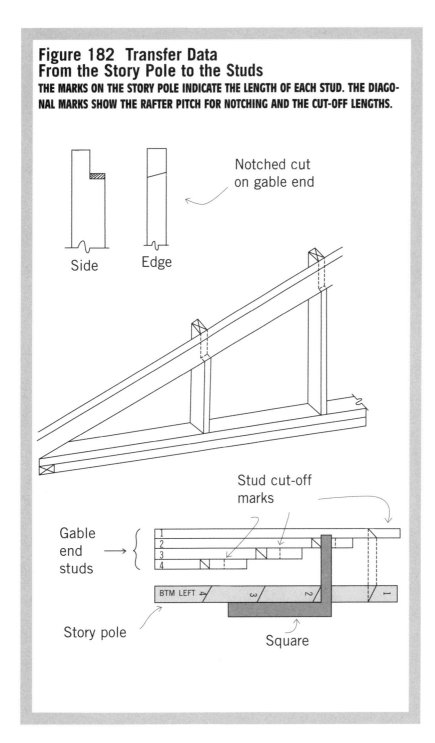

Notched cut on gable end

Side

Edge

Stud cut-off marks

Gable end studs

BTM LEFT

Story pole

Square

on the rafter on the downhill side of the line to show on which side of the line the stud will go.

Repeat this procedure for all studs on the left side of the gable. Use a different story pole and do the same for the studs along the right side. Using different studs for left and right doesn't waste lumber because the story poles, once used, can be cut and used anywhere on the job. Trying to record too much info on one story pole can be confusing and if the wrong side is used, the wrong size studs will be cut . . . these are also known as kindling.

The story poles can now be used to mark the studs for length and to indicate the pitch for cutting. Transfer the marks from the story pole to the ganged studs with a framer's square (**Figure 182**).

Timber Framing

A timber frame house can be laid out with a long measuring stick i.e., a full-size story pole. On it, mark all of the lengths and locations needed to lay out the frames and beams. The advantage is that all the necessary layout data is written on the story pole, which can be laid directly on the beam. The timber framer can then position joints away from defects in the lumber because all points are clearly marked on the stick. The story pole also minimizes careless errors committed during repeated measurements. It also eliminates the need to memorize increments or constantly refer to plans for them.

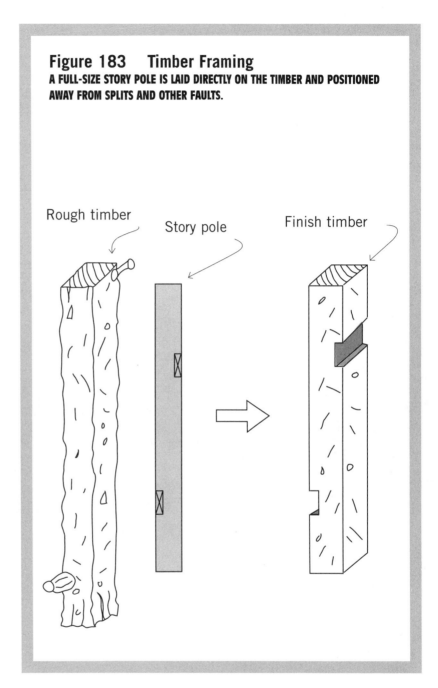

Figure 183   Timber Framing

A FULL-SIZE STORY POLE IS LAID DIRECTLY ON THE TIMBER AND POSITIONED AWAY FROM SPLITS AND OTHER FAULTS.

Rough timber

Story pole

Finish timber

Siding

To install siding, two types of story poles are used: a layout pole to determine the courses for all walls, and a story pole for each wall to record items such as window and door casings **(Figure 184)**.

The layout pole has saw kerfs along its length that mark the distance between each course of siding. Find this distance by measuring a few boards and determining the average width. Factor in the gap between boards and mark this distance on the layout pole as guide marks for chalk lines. Use a water level to transfer marks from one end of the wall to the opposite and then around the corner and down the next wall. This level datum line is used to register the story pole on all sides of the house.

Lay out a story pole for each wall to show where the window trim and door trim will be, and where the siding starts and stops. Make the story pole of 1x material. Using a line 1 in. below the sill as a reference, mark the windows and doors. To find the best layout for the siding, place the layout pole alongside the story pole and adjust them up and down to see where the siding will break on the trim of the windows and doors. Fit the courses as evenly as possible between the tops and bottoms of the windows and between the bottoms of the windows and the first course, which should be at least 1 in. below the sill. The goal is to avoid narrow strips of siding above or below a window or door. Transfer marks from the story pole to the walls' snap lines between marks. Use these lines as guides to nail the siding. Rarely will you discover a perfect layout, but you can find significant problems before the nailing starts.

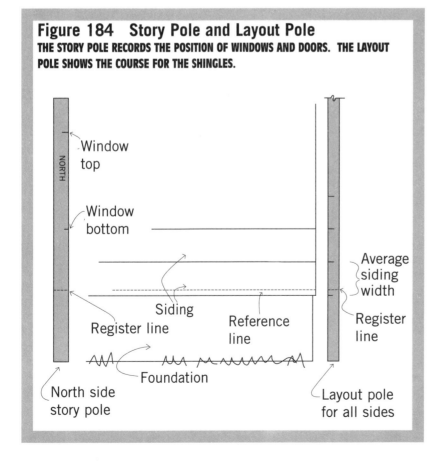

Figure 184   Story Pole and Layout Pole
THE STORY POLE RECORDS THE POSITION OF WINDOWS AND DOORS. THE LAYOUT POLE SHOWS THE COURSE FOR THE SHINGLES.

NORTH

Window top

Window bottom

Siding

Register line

Reference line

Average siding width

Register line

Foundation

North side story pole

Layout pole for all sides

Sidewall Shingling

Before putting on sidewall shingles, try to calculate the exposure so that the butt edge of the nearest course of shingles lines up with the bottom edge of the window sill. This not only makes the job look nice, but also saves the trouble of cutting shingles to fit around a casing. If the window sills on all four sides of the house aren't on the same level, some cutting to fit is inevitable. You'll have to choose which casings to align; usually I pick those in the front of the house. For example, if the bottom of the window sill is 30 in. up on the wall, with 6 in. of exposure, your fifth course will line up right on the casing edge. If you want a 7 in. exposure, four courses will bring you 2 in. short of the casing height. Your best bet in this situation is to make up the difference by adding $\frac{1}{2}$-in. extra exposure to each of the lower courses. Try a mock-up to determine if a $\frac{1}{2}$-in. variation in the exposures is objectionable.

To map the course layout, vertically hold a story pole with the course lines marked on it. Use this guide to transfer course lines from corner to corner. You can pull a string, or tack horizontal guide boards across the wall sections, to align each course as it is nailed up.

The story pole and guide board arrangement works best on broad expanses of wall unbroken by casings. For small sections (e.g., between windows), it is troublesome to cut and nail up guide boards. Work will go faster with chalk lines snapped from the story poles to line up the courses.

If you are shingling an old house, there is a good chance that some settling has occurred and the house isn't level. Rather than shingling on these skewed lines, register a line around the house with a water level. Use the story pole and snap a level chalk line several courses up but below window sills, so your line is uninterrupted. Nail down the bottom course following the existing contour of the house. For the second and all successive courses up to your reference line, compensate in small increments so that by the time you reach the line, you'll have a level course all the way around the house. For example, if one corner is 1 in. lower than its neighbor and your line is five courses up, compensate $\frac{3}{16}$ in. on each course.

$$1 \div 5 = 0.2 \approx \frac{3}{16} \text{ in.}$$

It's difficult for the eye to detect such small adjustments.

Clapboard Siding

The two most important parts of layout for siding are setting the first course and varying subsequent courses so they line up with the horizontal sections of the trim. Use a water level to align the first course around the house, then use story poles to align the rest of the courses.

By aligning siding courses to the top and bottom of window sills, tops of header casings, and the underside of frieze boards, you can save a lot of cutting and still have a good looking job. Achieve these alignments by increasing or decreasing the amount of exposure of individual siding courses. There are limits, but usually $\frac{1}{4}$- to $\frac{3}{8}$-in. differences won't be noticeable.

To make sure the courses are evenly spaced, make a "swing stick" out of a piece of 1x2 at least 6 ft. long **(Figure 185)**. Starting at the top and extending to the bottom, make a series of marks along one edge, each equal to the siding's maximum allowable exposure (e.g., every $4\frac{1}{2}$ in. for 6-in. wide stock). Mark an arrow at the top of the stick to indicate "Up".

Using a level, chalk a line on the wall even with the window sill's bottom edge. Stand the swing stick upright anywhere between the window and a corner board with the arrow pointing up. Tip the swing stick so one mark near the bottom aligns with the bottom of the first level course, and another higher mark aligns with the chalk line indicating the bottom of the window sill. Now transfer all marks from the stick to a story pole and use this story pole to mark each end of the wall for snap lines.

Use this same procedure to evenly space courses between the top of the window and the frieze and to align courses from the top of the window down to the bottom of the window sill.

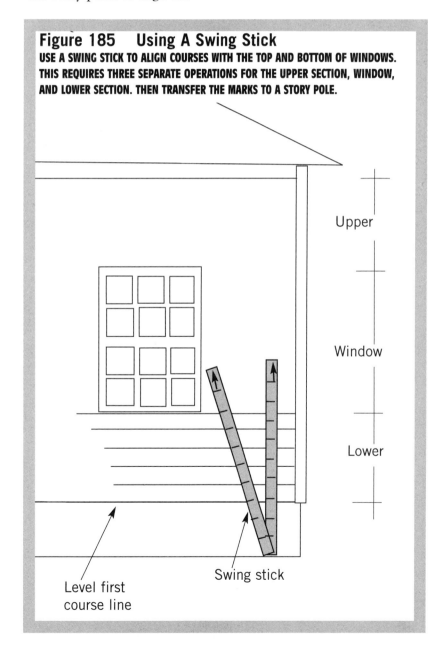

Figure 185   Using A Swing Stick
USE A SWING STICK TO ALIGN COURSES WITH THE TOP AND BOTTOM OF WINDOWS. THIS REQUIRES THREE SEPARATE OPERATIONS FOR THE UPPER SECTION, WINDOW, AND LOWER SECTION. THEN TRANSFER THE MARKS TO A STORY POLE.

Upper

Window

Lower

Swing stick

Level first
course line

Setting Counter Tiles

Layout for tile means establishing order and geometry where there were none because surfaces are never perfectly flat or absolutely plumb. Layout then, is a series of reasonable approximations, and a story pole can make the job easier.

Start with a 1x2 pole marked to represent the width of a tile plus one grout joint. Using this story pole you can quickly see how many tiles will fit in a given area and where partial tiles will be placed.

First, draw an alignment axis line on the counter top to indicate the grout joint of the front bullnose or edge trim. Lay the story pole on the counter next to the long axis line to see how many tiles you will need and if you'll have to cut any at the ends. If the counter will have a sink, cook top, or other cutout, use the story pole to position tiles symmetrically on each side. Move the pole left to right until unit marks are equidistant from each side of the sink's rough opening, then transfer those two marks onto the layout axis running along the front of the counter. With a framing square perpendicular to the front axis, transfer these marks to the back of the counter.

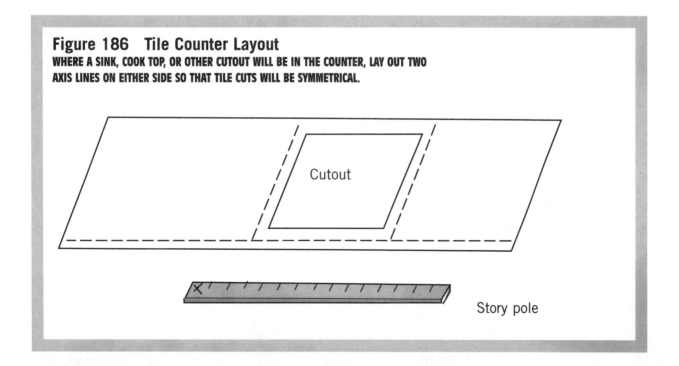

Figure 186   Tile Counter Layout

WHERE A SINK, COOK TOP, OR OTHER CUTOUT WILL BE IN THE COUNTER, LAY OUT TWO AXIS LINES ON EITHER SIDE SO THAT TILE CUTS WILL BE SYMMETRICAL.

Cutout

Story pole

Roofing

Shingles are laid on a roof so that a part of each shingle's length is covered by the courses above. Because of this overlap, the roof is often three layers thick. Shingles are available in different lengths (18, 24, and 32 in.) and the length establishes the weather exposure of the courses on the roof. Longer shingles can have more exposure: $5\frac{1}{2}$ in. for an 18-in. shingle, $7\frac{1}{2}$ in. for a 24-in. shingle, and 10 in. for a 32-in. shingle. The course can vary by $\frac{3}{4}$ in. short or $\frac{1}{4}$ in. long. For example, to ensure a course meets at the bottom of a sky light you could run 18-in. shakes in courses from $6\frac{3}{4}$ in. to $7\frac{3}{4}$ in.

A roof may require 30 squares of shingles of 3000 sq. ft. At a 6-in. exposure this is about 13,000 shingles. If you can save 10 seconds per shingle by using story poles, that would be 36 hours less spent on a boiling hot roof.

On a roof, use story poles made of lightweight sheet metal and lay out all courses before nailing starts (**Figure 187**) Tack both story poles to the ridge side by side, then lay out each course with a broad felt tip pen or wax pencil. For an obstruction like an air conditioner or skylight, alter the courses to accommodate the feature. Mark both strips and once the courses are set, tack one story pole at each end of the roof. Snap lines, usually six courses at a time, then roll the sheet metal story poles up to the ridge where they are out of the way, and nail the shingles.

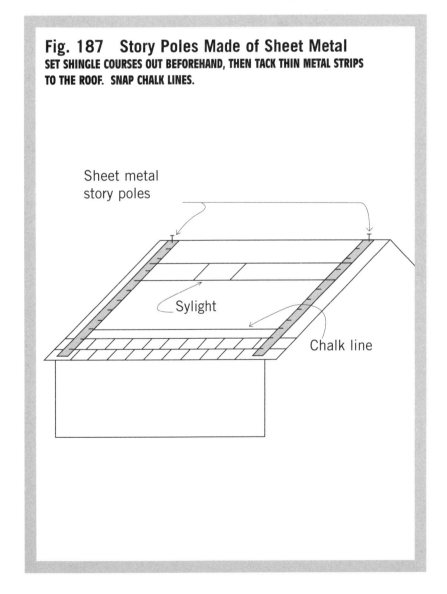

Fig. 187 Story Poles Made of Sheet Metal
SET SHINGLE COURSES OUT BEFOREHAND, THEN TACK THIN METAL STRIPS TO THE ROOF. SNAP CHALK LINES.

Sheet metal story poles

Sylight

Chalk line

French Doors

You could make a full-size drawing and then transfer the dimensions to story poles - one for height and one for width. Perhaps a better way would be to draw the full-size door with all dimensions directly on the story poles (**Figure 188**). These now become the supreme reference throughout construction and allow you to avoid using a measuring tape. Transfer the layout from the story pole to boards and cut.

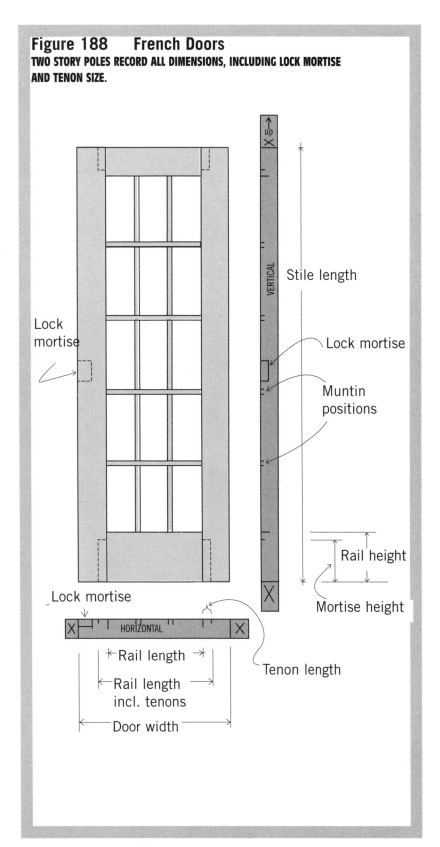

Figure 188   French Doors
TWO STORY POLES RECORD ALL DIMENSIONS, INCLUDING LOCK MORTISE AND TENON SIZE.

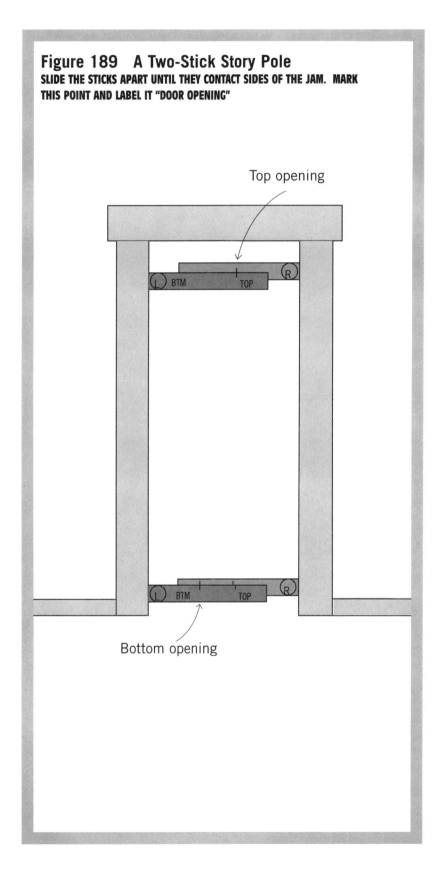

Figure 189   A Two-Stick Story Pole
SLIDE THE STICKS APART UNTIL THEY CONTACT SIDES OF THE JAM. MARK THIS POINT AND LABEL IT "DOOR OPENING"

Top opening

L   BTM   TOP   R

L   BTM   TOP   R

Bottom opening

Windows and Door Openings

In heaven and in theory, square is square. But on earth, walls, casements, and door jambs seldom are. In trim carpentry, a tape measure is not very useful, but a two-stick story pole is (**Figure 189**). Use a thin strip ripped from a jointed 2x4, and saw the ends square. To use, hold the two together and slide apart. When they make contact with opposite sides of jambs, clamp them together and mark a line across from one to the other. Label this mark "top opening width". If top and bottom of jamb are not the same width, record: "bottom opening width".

Back in the shop, use the story poles to determine the door width by subtracting the clearance, for example, $\frac{5}{32}$ in. Make another mark and label it: "door width". If the top and bottom clearances are different, you will also need to know which jamb, if either, is plumb. Construct the door to the wider dimension. Then, using the story pole, plane one edge to fit the opening.

Figure 190 Record Room Dimensions With Three Story Poles
USE VERTICAL, HORIZONTAL AND DEPTH STORY POLES TO LOCATE DOORS, WINDOWS, ELECTRIC LIGHTS, AND OUTLETS. THIS IS MORE ACCURATE THAN BY USING A TAPE MEASURE.

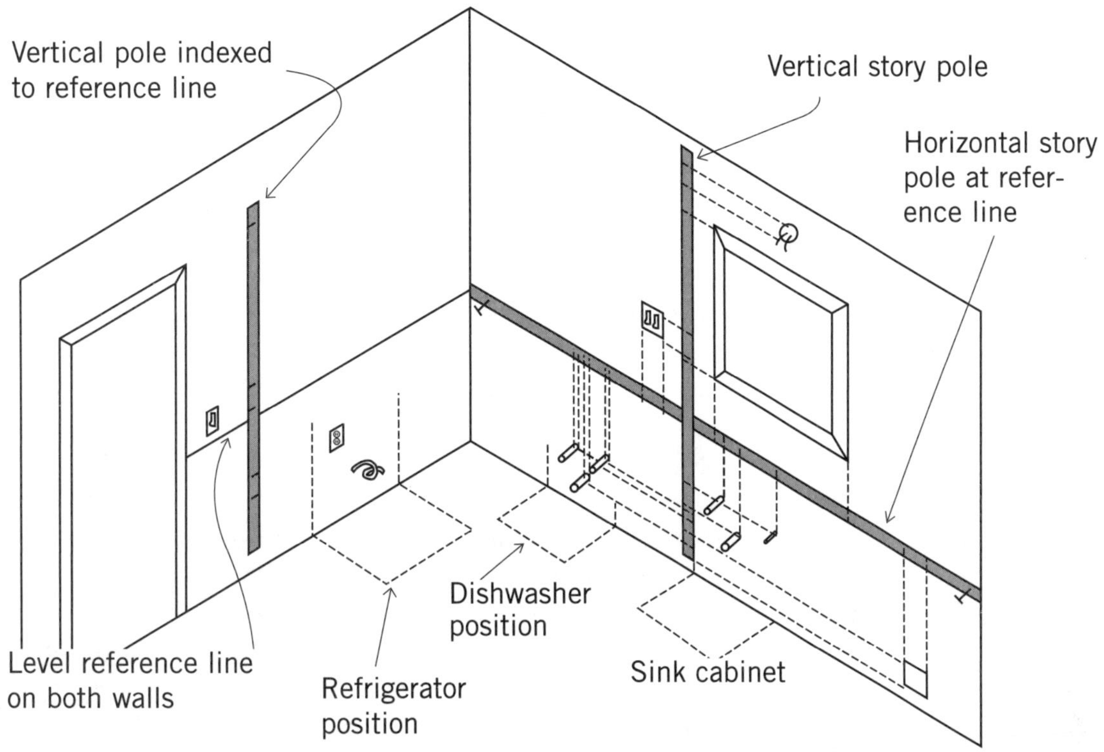

Vertical pole indexed to reference line

Vertical story pole

Horizontal story pole at reference line

Level reference line on both walls

Refrigerator position

Dishwasher position

Sink cabinet

Kitchens

Professional carpenters no longer use story poles to lay out a kitchen like they did 20 or 30 years ago. My dad used story poles and they were one of his most valuable tools. The room dimensions were transferred to story poles along with the locations of doors, windows, electrical and plumbing services, and other details (**Figure 190**). Today, professionals use laser levels to draw a horizontal reference line around the room, then record the positions of pipes and windows. Back at the office they enter all the data into a PC: the location of all the fixtures, the size and location of each cabinet and fixed appliance. In short order, a $10,000 software program will churn out a diagram of the wall with locations of all appliances and cabinet units; a drawing of each cabinet with complete dimensions; and finally, a cutting list and blueprints of whatever is needed.

The average "Joe Woodworker"

doesn't have laser levels, sophisticated computer programs or a printer big enough to generate an 18 in. x 24-in. set of blue prints. But we do have something pretty good - the old story pole.

Story poles may seem awkward to use and confusing at first, but you will begin to rely heavily on them once you've seen how much help they can be. For example, once you have all the room details on the sticks you can determine exactly how the cabinets should be placed within the kitchen. A sink cabinet can be laid out so that the faucet is centered beneath a window. An upper unit can be made and positioned on the stick and later on the wall so that it won't interfere with an existing electrical switch or an air conditioning grill.

Make the story poles from $3/4$-in. sticks $1\frac{1}{2}$ in. wide. Light-colored woods are best because pencil marks show up better. You'll need three sticks for each wall—one each for horizontal, vertical, and depth dimensions.

Horizontal Wall Story Pole
Let's put cabinets into a kitchen. Start by cutting a story pole the length of the sink wall. Label it: "Kitchen, Sink Wall, Horiz". At the ends write "Left" and "Right". Draw two lines lengthwise to divide

the stick into three long divisions. The upper division will be for upper cabinetry, the middle for wall items, and the bottom division for lower cabinets.

In the kitchen, draw a horizontal reference line along each wall, about 50 in. from the floor. Use a spirit level to make sure it is absolutely horizontal. Because base cabinets are generally 36-in. high and the bottom of wall cabinets 18 in. higher, 50 in. is a good height to use. The line will not be obscured and can be used later to level the cabinets by measuring down for the base units and up for the uppers. Use a framer's square or a level to transfer the location of windows, doors, pipes, drains, electrical lamps, and outlets to the reference line. Tack the horizontal story pole against the wall next to the line and mark each item in the middle division. Label each mark on the story pole so it will make sense back in the shop later. All wall dimensions are now marked on the wall and on the horizontal story pole (**Figure 191**).

Vertical Wall Story Pole
Make a vertical wall story pole about 6 in. shorter than the full floor-to-ceiling height. With a level or plumb-bob, draw a vertical line on the wall. Find the highest point on the floor

and hold the vertical story pole against the line at this position. Make a mark on the pole at the horizontal reference line. Floor slope and imperfections are negated by indexing the vertical pole to the horizontal line. Record the same items on this pole, i.e., windows, outlets, etc.

Depth Story Pole
If necessary, record data on a wall depth story pole.

Back in the shop, lay the horizontal story pole on the floor and mark the locations of the fixed appliances (refrigerator, dishwasher, stove) in the middle division. Locate the overall parameters of the upper and lower cabinets on this story pole. Mark upper cabinet units on the upper side of the face and lower cabinet units on the lower side of the face. Use colored pencils if it helps to keep them straight. On the lower part of the story pole, sketch in the future sink base cabinet under the window and near the water pipes. On the upper part of the story pole, mark the upper cabinets on either side of the window. On these long, narrow pieces of wood, an entire kitchen full of cabinets can be laid out full-size, and at the same time fitted to the fixed appliances.

For example, locate the sink base cabinet, then mark 24 in. to the right to locate the dishwasher. Mark this on the lower part of the story pole. Locate the refrigerator at the end. The space between the dishwasher and the fridge will determine the width of the drawer cabinet, and the rails can be cut using the marks on the story pole. Measure from the sink to the left to get the dimensions of that cabinet, or lay the story pole on the wood and mark directly.

Cabinets

Once you've decided where the cabinets are to be positioned, make separate story poles for the construction of each unit (**Figure 192**). Draw a line down the middle of a story pole. Put internal components on one side and external on the other. This keeps dimension lines apart, and also shows how components relate to one another.

To transcribe the outside lines of the cabinet from the site pole to the cabinet story pole, hold the cabinet story pole firmly against the site pole and make sure the cabinet story pole is longer than the site pole. Transfer the marks showing the outside dimensions of the cabinet. Square the tick marks across the cabinet story pole. Make it a habit to hold the pencil point on the tick mark; bring the square up snug to it. Now use a flat 12-in. steel ruler to draw in the widths of stock that make up the carcass, the clearances for hinges, locks, etc. Don't depend on a carpenter's measuring tape for these exacting dimensions. Now you can arrive at the

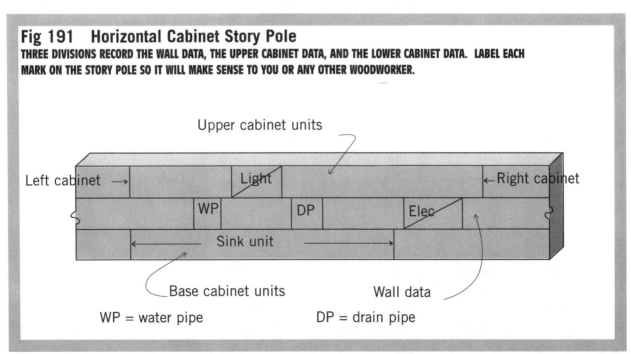

Fig 191   Horizontal Cabinet Story Pole
THREE DIVISIONS RECORD THE WALL DATA, THE UPPER CABINET DATA, AND THE LOWER CABINET DATA. LABEL EACH MARK ON THE STORY POLE SO IT WILL MAKE SENSE TO YOU OR ANY OTHER WOODWORKER.

Upper cabinet units

Left cabinet →

Light

← Right cabinet

WP

DP

Elec

Sink unit

Base cabinet units

Wall data

WP = water pipe

DP = drain pipe

length of the case's components. For example, the length of a door rail is the result of subtracting the widths of the stiles at either end and then adding in the length of the tenons. Because all the cabinet parts and joints are marked out full-size, it is easier and more accurate to build from story poles than from scaled-down drawings.

Use a cabinet vertical story pole and the height of the cabinet side piece to lay out the location of dados for shelves and cross supports under drawers. The sticks will serve as guides when building the cabinets. Lengths, widths, and positions of the joints can all be marked on the material directly from the story stick - no measurements are necessary, so fewer errors are made. And, if you add to the kitchen later, the sticks are a detailed record of the existing cabinets. Use the measurements taken from the sticks, to write up cutting lists for tops, bottoms, sides, and partitions. The story pole will show the depth and width of every component of the cabinet.

When it is time to cut the pieces for the cabinets you could use a tape measure to transfer dimensions from the cabinet story pole onto the stock. To avoid errors, lay the pole onto the stock and mark

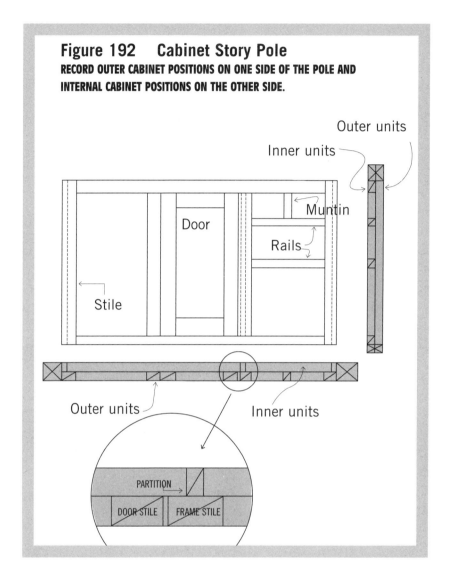

Figure 192   Cabinet Story Pole
RECORD OUTER CABINET POSITIONS ON ONE SIDE OF THE POLE AND
INTERNAL CABINET POSITIONS ON THE OTHER SIDE.

Outer units
Inner units
Muntin
Door
Rails
Stile
Outer units
Inner units
PARTITION
DOOR STILE   FRAME STILE

directly. Old timers used to say: "A tape measure will get you close, but a story pole will put you right on the dot." You can also use the story pole to put stops on the miter gauge of the table saw before making cuts.

Finally, use the room story poles for installing cabinet components on site. To position the "boxes" for fastening a cabinet base unit, tack a horizontal stretcher across the

top of the partitions before installing the face frame. To position the free-floating inner partition at the required distance from the cabinet ends, tack the cabinet story pole across the front of the cabinets. Line up the partition with the marks indicating its position, and fix it in place.

Stairs

There is no other home project fraught with so much danger as a poorly designed staircase. Imagine walking down the stairs carrying a laundry basket or with a baby in your arms. Once into the rhythm, you find each step without looking until . . . one step isn't there. Your foot feels for a surface, you falter, and fall.

In a situation like this, the usual culprit is either the top or bottom step. If all risers are cut the same height and then finish flooring is installed, the adjacent step will differ from the others by the thickness of the flooring. Steps next to a landing will also require special treatment if the landing has flooring that makes the unit rise here different from the other steps.

It almost goes without saying that with a set of stairs, every step must be the same height. If the sub-floors and finish flooring aren't figured in right from the planning stage, the unit rise of the top and bottom steps will be different from the others. With a story pole you can factor in all these dimensions and "construct" the stairs on the stick before you begin to build (**Figure 193,** next page).

Use a full-size story pole and start at the bottom. Either set the pole onto the finish flooring or set it on the rough floor. Mark the thickness of the finish flooring on bottom of the pole. Find the total rise of the stairs, that is, the vertical distance from the top of the finished bottom floor to the top of the finished second floor. Mark the total rise on the story pole. From the total rise, calculate the unit rise (see Chapter 17, *Stairs*) and using dividers, walk off the tread intervals on the story pole. Draw in the sub-flooring, the finish flooring, and carpeting, while keeping to the same unit rise for every step. With this method, every step will be the same height (have the same unit rise) even though all risers cut in the stair stringer will not be the same height.

Note: Story poles are also used in Chapter 15, *Slats and Spaces*, and in Chapter 1, *Drawing Plans from Pictures*, Chapter 2, *Enlaregement and Reduction*, Chapter 12, *3-4-5- Equals 90 Degrees,* CHapter 15, *Slats and Spaces*, and Chapter 17, *Stairs*.

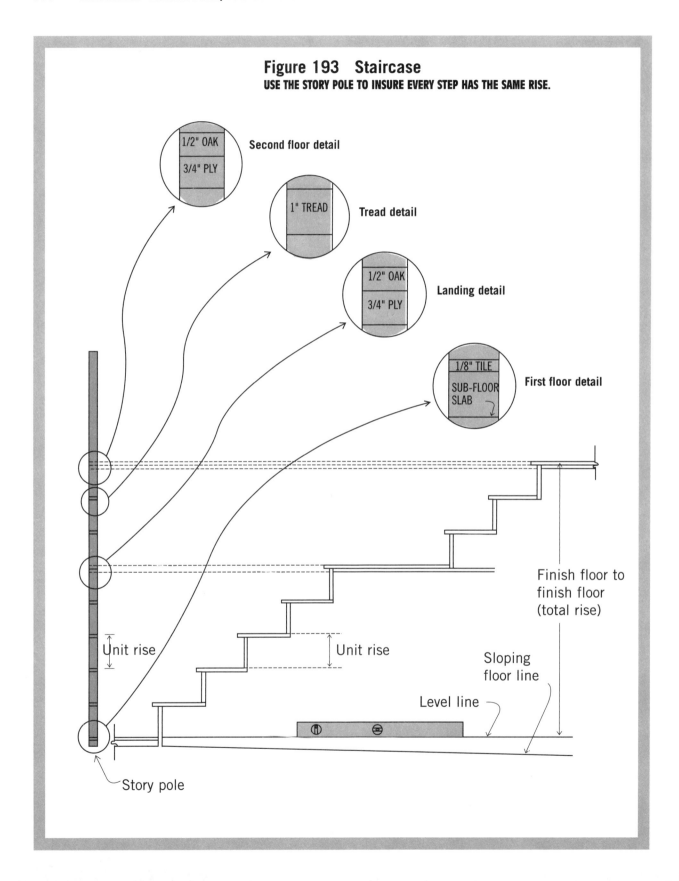

Figure 193   Staircase
USE THE STORY POLE TO INSURE EVERY STEP HAS THE SAME RISE.

1/2" OAK
3/4" PLY
Second floor detail

1" TREAD
Tread detail

1/2" OAK
3/4" PLY
Landing detail

1/8" TILE
SUB-FLOOR
SLAB
First floor detail

Finish floor to
finish floor
(total rise)

Unit rise

Unit rise

Sloping
floor line

Level line

Story pole

CHAPTER 17

Stairs

Typically, stairs are designed according to their intended use. Exterior steps leading from the sidewalk to the front porch are wide, made of durable material such as concrete or stone, and slope forward to drain melting snow and ice. Stairs that are used daily to move traffic from one floor in a house to another are wide and comfortable to use. Service stairs to the basement or the attic, which get only occasional use, can be narrower and steeper.

This chapter will show you how to design safe stairs for outside, inside, basement/attic, and deck placement. Also, see *Chapter 16* for a discussion on using story poles for setting out stairways.

The most important considerations in designing stairways are safety and ease of travel. Towards these ends, consider the importance of riser height, tread depth, stairway width, headroom, and an appropriate handrail. Every step must be the same size; all risers must be identical in height and all treads be the same depth. This includes steps to a landing and steps from the landing to the next floor. Variations in riser height as small as $\frac{1}{4}$ in. can cause accidents, which is why most building codes allow a maximum variation of only $\frac{3}{16}$ in. in adjacent riser heights, and a maximum difference of $\frac{3}{8}$ in. between any two risers in the stairway (**Figure 195**)

General Stair Rules (Residential)

The rules for residential stairs vary widely throughout the country. Consult an architect or local code official before you finalize your design. The following standards are general rules that may or may not apply in your jurisdiction.

Landings and Maximum Rise—Limit the total rise - floor to floor height - in any straight run of stairs to 12 ft.

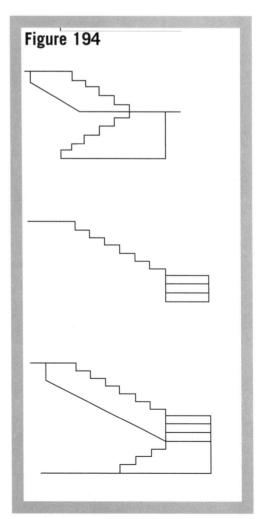

Figure 194

If the total rise is over 12 ft., provide a landing. Landings interrupt a fall, provide a rest stop, and should be at least as long as the stair is wide, up to 48 in. and not less than 44 in. Some building codes allow 36-in. landings in residential buildings.

Width—Service stairs - porch, basement, and attic stairs - should be at least 30 in. wide. Primary stairs should be at least 36 in. wide. Some building codes insist on a 36-in. wide minimum in all cases. Again, consult your local building official.

Headroom—The headroom should be at least 80 in., measured vertically from the tread nosing to the nearest ceiling. The psychological sense of clearance can be as important as the physical clearance. Accordingly, the

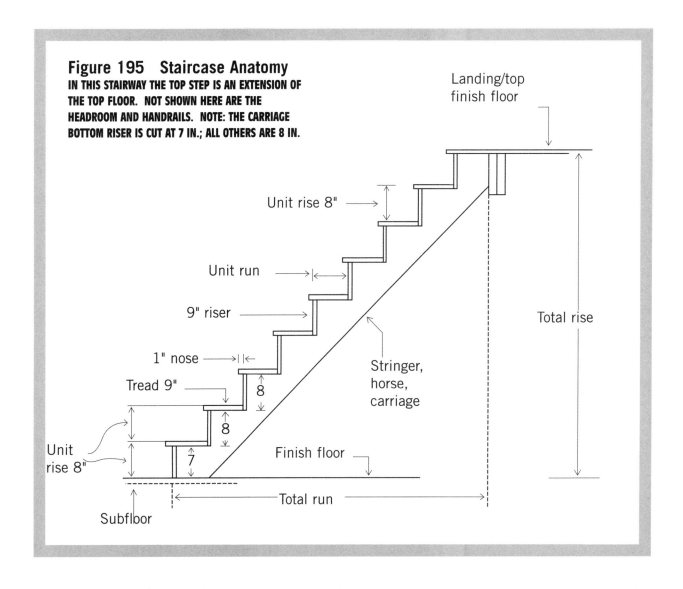

Figure 195   Staircase Anatomy
IN THIS STAIRWAY THE TOP STEP IS AN EXTENSION OF THE TOP FLOOR. NOT SHOWN HERE ARE THE HEADROOM AND HANDRAILS. NOTE: THE CARRIAGE BOTTOM RISER IS CUT AT 7 IN.; ALL OTHERS ARE 8 IN.

Landing/top finish floor

Unit rise 8"

Unit run

9" riser

1" nose

Tread 9"

Stringer, horse, carriage

Unit rise 8"

Finish floor

Total rise

Total run

Subfloor

clearance should be such that a person cannot reach up and touch the stair ceiling.

Handrails —Provide at least one handrail placed not less than 34 in. nor more than 38 in. above and parallel to the nosing of the treads. The handrail should accompany all steps and have no interruption at newel posts. A person's hand should be able to slide along the rail without interruption, and the ends of the handrail should be returned to, or end at a post. The easiest handrail profile to grasp is a round between $1\frac{1}{2}$ to 2 in. in diameter. Often, handrails are not required for stairways with less than three risers.

Risers and Treads—Risers should be 7 to 8 in. high, but not higher than 8 in. The treads should be 10 to 11 in. deep, not less than 9 in., exclusive of the nosing. The tread thickness should be $1\frac{1}{4}$ in. minimum, and the tread nosing should be 1 in. maximum. Stairs may have open or closed risers, although open risers are forbidden in some areas.

Rise-to-Tread Ratio—Builders use the following rules of thumb to figure the correct rise-to-tread ratio:

Rise plus tread = 17 to 18, the rise doubled plus tread = 24 to 25, or the rise times tread = 70 to 75.

Some builders consider the 7-11 staircase ideal—a 7-in. rise with an 11-in. tread. The 7-11 stair is universally approved and is a safe design. If the combination of rise and run is too great, the steps are tiring. If the combination is too small, the foot may kick the riser at each step. Narrow treads are more dangerous when descending a stair.

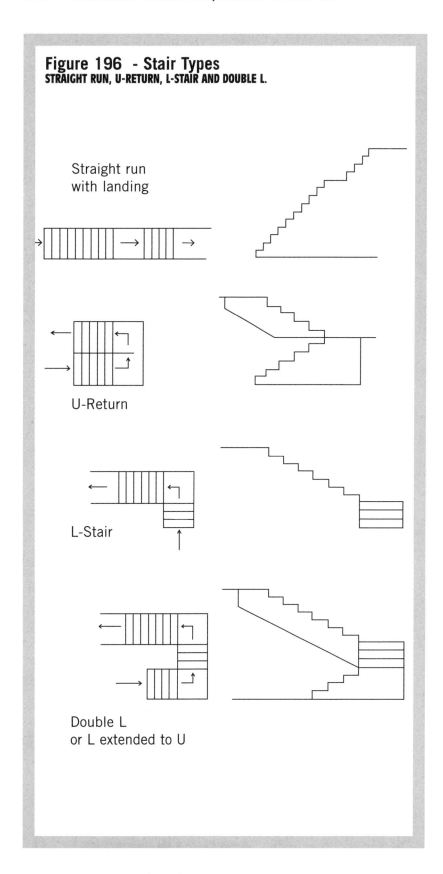

Figure 196 - Stair Types
STRAIGHT RUN, U-RETURN, L-STAIR AND DOUBLE L.

Straight run
with landing

U-Return

L-Stair

Double L
or L extended to U

Stairway Types

Straight—A straight stairway is limited to 12 ft. of total rise, at which a landing should be provided (**Figure 196**).

U Return—A stairway with a U-shaped return may occupy a square or rectangular area. Flights may be equal or unequal in total rise and run, but the best practice dictates that the risers and treads are of equal size on both runs. The landing depth should equal the stair width up to 48 in., with a 44-in. minimum width.

L Stair—An "L" stair may have equal legs, or one short and one long leg separated by a landing in the middle. The short leg may be at the top or bottom of the stairs. The landing length should equal stair width up to 48 in., with a 44-in. minimum width.

Double L Stair—The "L" stair may be extended to a U shape with a short flight between two corner landings.

Stairway With Winders—A turn can be made with radiating treads called winders (**Figure 197**). This type of staircase is less safe, so is not often used. At the inner corner where all the winders meet, there is very little, if any, tread to support one's foot. This is what makes winders rather dangerous. Turns can be accomplished much more safely with landings (**Figure 198**). Many areas, however, do allow winding stairways to be used in residential occupancies. When this type of stairway is used, the winder tread width must provide the minimum allowable tread length at a point 12 in. from the side of the stairs where the tread is narrowest, but in no case should any width of tread be less than 6 in.

Designing a Staircase
Run and Rise
On any flight of stairs there is always one less tread than riser. The total run can be determined once the unit rise, the unit run, and the number of risers are known.

Total Rise
Measure the distance from the bottom finish floor to the top finish floor. Adjust the distance if the measurement is to a subfloor and a finish floor is to be added later—usually $\frac{3}{4}$ in. for wood or $\frac{3}{8}$ in. for carpeting.

Number of Risers
To determine the number of risers, divide the total rise by an average unit rise. Use 7 in. for an average gradual assent, 8 in. for a steeper assent. Disregard fractions.

Unit Rise
This is the vertical distance

Figure 197   Stairway With Winders
THIS TYPE OF STAIRWAY IS LESS SAFE BECAUSE THERE IS VERY LITTLE TREAD AT THE INNER CORNER.

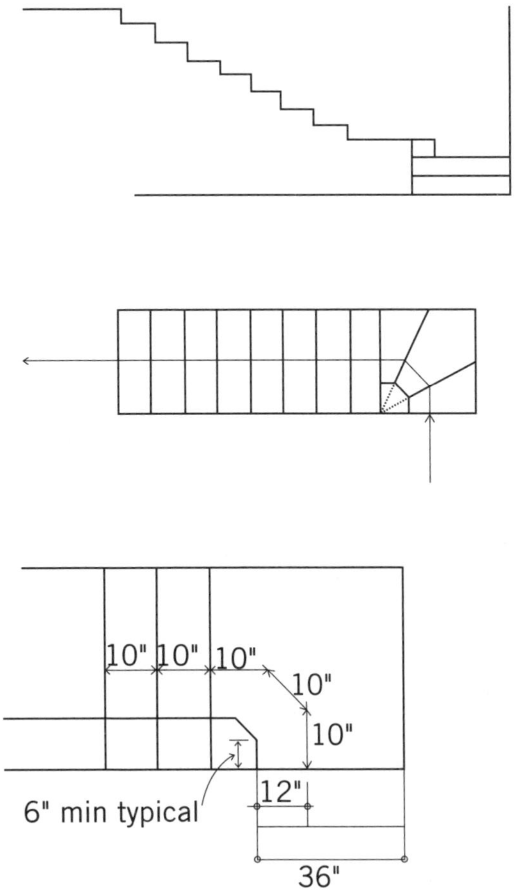

10" 10" 10" 10" 10" 12" 6" min typical 36"

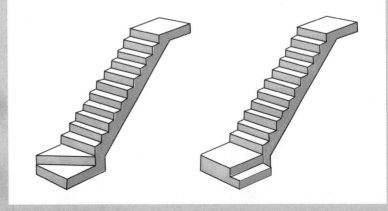

Figure 198 Winders Versus Landings
TURNS ARE SAFER WITH A PLATFORM LANDING.

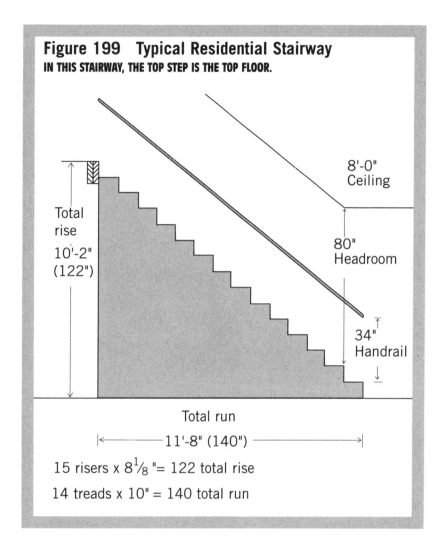

Figure 199 Typical Residential Stairway
IN THIS STAIRWAY, THE TOP STEP IS THE TOP FLOOR.

8'-0" Ceiling

80" Headroom

34" Handrail

Total rise 10'-2" (122")

Total run
|← 11'-8" (140") →|

15 risers x 8⅛ "= 122 total rise

14 treads x 10" = 140 total run

from the top of one step to the top of the adjacent step. The ideal rise is 7 in. To find the number of risers use 7 (or sometimes 8) as an average rise in order to find the exact rise. Divide the total rise by the number of risers.

Unit Run
The unit run is the same as the tread width (disregarding nosing) and depends somewhat on the unit rise. Use nine as a minimum for service stairs, 10

to 11 for others. This formula links an optimum tread width-to-riser height ratio.

Unit run + unit rise = 17½ in. or, Unit run = 17.5 - unit rise

Total Run
The total run is the number of treads times the unit run.

Residential Stairs
In **Figure 199**, the total rise is 10 ft. 2 in. We need to calculate

the total run and the size of the risers and treads. We want to use a tread length of 10 in. and a rise of approximately 8 in.

Total rise = 122 in. (10 ft. 2 in.)
Number of risers = 122 ÷ 8
= 15+ (disregard fractions)
Number of treads = 15 - 1 = 14
Exact riser height = 122 ÷ 15
= 8.133 in. (approx. 8⅛ in.)
Unit run = 10 in.
Total run = 14 x 10 in.
= 140 in. (11 ft. 8 in.)

Basement Stairs
Total rise = 8 ft. 2 in. = 98 in.
Unit rise = 8 in. (maximum allowable by many codes)
Unit run = 9 in. (minimum allowable by most codes)
Number of risers
= 98 ÷ 8 = 12+
Exact riser height = 98 ÷ 12
= 8.17 = 8 3/16 in.
Number of treads = 12 - 1 = 11
Total run = 11 x 9
= 99 in. (8 ft. 3 in.)

Check with your local building department to verify the maximum unit rise and minimum tread that they will allow (**Figure 200**).

Backyard Stairs
Building a Stairway From Ground to Deck
1. Measure the total rise (vertical height) from grade top to the top of the deck floor. Keep in mind that grade may be different at the point the

stair will rest than from the point immediately below the deck. **Figure 201**.

2. Divide the rise by 8 to give the number of risers. We're using 8-in. risers here as an average.

3. Multiply number of treads by 11.25 to give total run. We're using $11\frac{1}{4}$-in. treads here.

4. Cut two stringers to size from 2 x 10 material and fasten to deck frame.

5. Attach treads to stringer with wooden cleats or metal supports.

6. If there are more than three steps, install handrails on each side of the stairs.

7. Add deck railing if the deck is over 24 in. above the ground. Some codes require a railing only if the deck is 30 in. above the ground.

Summary:
Total rise = 53 in.
Number of risers = 53 ÷ 8
    = 6+ (including deck top)
Unit rise = 53 ÷ 6 = 8.83
    = $8\frac{7}{8}$ in.
Total run = 5 x $11\frac{1}{4}$ = $56\frac{1}{4}$ in.
Unit run = $11\frac{1}{4}$ in.
Number of treads = 6 - 1 = 5

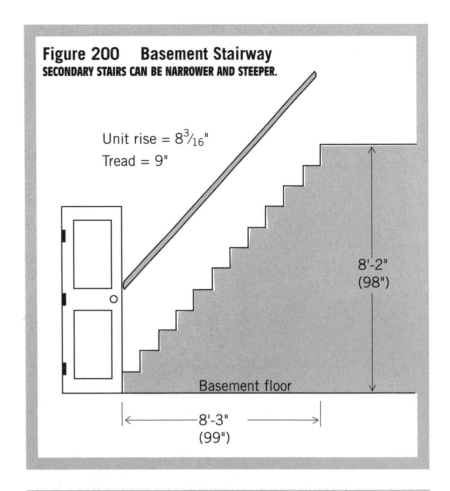

Figure 200   Basement Stairway
SECONDARY STAIRS CAN BE NARROWER AND STEEPER.

Unit rise = $8\frac{3}{16}$"
Tread = 9"

8'-2"
(98")

Basement floor

8'-3"
(99")

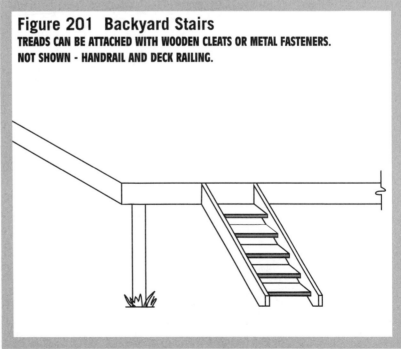

Figure 201 Backyard Stairs
TREADS CAN BE ATTACHED WITH WOODEN CLEATS OR METAL FASTENERS.
NOT SHOWN - HANDRAIL AND DECK RAILING.

Residential L-Shape Stairway

This stairway is more complicated (**Figure 202**). We've added a second story and have limited wall space for a stairway. We'll use a landing and an L-type stair design to rise 9 ft. 5 in. (113 in. total rise) over 10 ft. 5 in. (125 in. total run).

Total Run and Rise

Using the total rise and an approximate unit rise of 8 in., set the riser height.

$$113 \div 8 = 14.125$$
$$113 \div 14 = 8.07$$
$$= 8\frac{1}{16} \text{ in. (exact riser height)}$$

Therefore we need 14 risers, each $8\frac{1}{16}$ in. high.

Long Run and Rise

Find the long run for the stairway section from the first floor to the landing. Because the stairs are 44 in. wide, the landing must be 44 in. x 44 in.

Total distance available for the long run to landing:
$$129 - 44 = 85 \text{ in.}$$

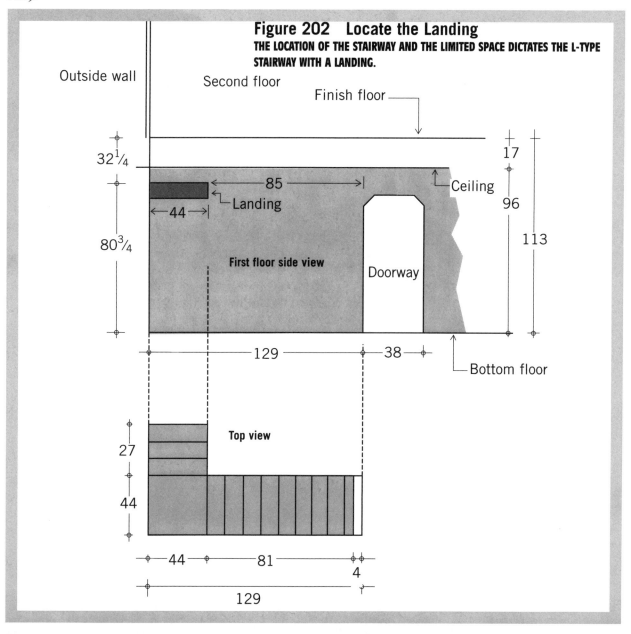

Figure 202   Locate the Landing
THE LOCATION OF THE STAIRWAY AND THE LIMITED SPACE DICTATES THE L-TYPE STAIRWAY WITH A LANDING.

The number of treads is:

$85 \div 9 = 9 + 4$ in. left over

This tells us we can have 9 treads in the distance between the landing and the doorway, starting 4 in. from the doorway.

Nine treads means 10 risers.

$10 \times 8.07 = 80.7 = 80\frac{3}{4}$ in. This is the total height for the long run from the floor to the top of the landing.

There will be 10 treads each 9 in. wide, and 11 risers $8\frac{1}{16}$ in. high. The landing will be 44 in. x 44 in. and constructed so the top will be $80\frac{3}{4}$ in. from the bottom finish floor. The landing is the 10th tread of the stairway. If the stairway is open, i.e., there are no physical risers, the distance from the top of one tread to the top of the next will be $8\frac{1}{16}$ in.

Short Run and Rise

Find the short run for the stairway section from the landing to the second floor.

$113 - 80\frac{3}{4} = 32\frac{1}{4}$ in.

The short rise is:

$32.25 \div 8.07 = 4$ risers

Use the unit run to find the total run:

4 risers - 1 = 3 treads

$3 \times 9 = 27$-in. total run

Summary:

Long Run

Total run = 125 in.,

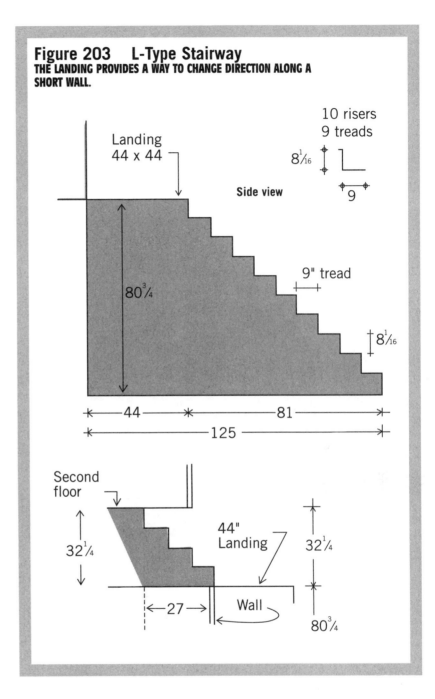

Figure 203   L-Type Stairway
THE LANDING PROVIDES A WAY TO CHANGE DIRECTION ALONG A SHORT WALL.

including 44-in. landing
Total rise = $80\frac{3}{4}$ in.
Unit run = 9 in.
Unit rise = $8\frac{1}{16}$ in.
Short Run
Total run = 27 in.,
    not including 44-in. landing

Total rise = $32\frac{1}{4}$ in.
Unit run = 9 in.
Unit rise = $8\frac{1}{16}$ in.

Fgure 203 shows the completed stairway.

KNOWING THE TOTAL RISE AND THE NUMBER OF RISERS, YOU CAN FIND THE RISER HEIGHT, TREAD WIDTH AND TOTAL RUN FOR STRAIGHT STAIRWAYS. MANY JURISDICTIONS REQUIRE A 7-11 STAIR FOR RESIDENTIAL APPLICATIONS

Figure 204   Straight Stairway Chart

Total Rise Flr to Flr Ht.	Num. Risers	Riser Height	Tread Width	Total Run (Inches)	Total Run (Feet)
8' 0" (96 in.)	12	8 in.	9 in.	99	8' 3"
	13	7 3/8	9 1/2	114	9' 6"
	13	7 3/8	10	120	10' 0"
	14	6 7/8	10 1/2	136.5	11' 4 1/2"
	14	6 7/8	11	143	11' 11"
8' 6" (102 in.)	13	7 7/8	9	108	9' 0"
	14	7 1/4	9 1/2	123.5	10' 3 1/2"
	14	7 1/4	10	130	10' 10"
	15	6 7/8	10 1/2	147	12' 3"
	15	6 7/8	11	154	12' 10"
9' 0" (108 in.)	14	7 3/4	9	117	9' 9"
	15	7 1/4	9 1/2	133	11' 1"
	15	7 1/4	10	140	11' 8"
	16	6 3/4	10 1/2	157.5	13' 1 1/2"
	16	6 3/4	11	165	13' 9"
9' 6" (114 in.)	15	7 5/8	9	126	10' 6"
	16	7 1/8	9 1/2	142.5	11' 10 1/2"
	16	7 1/8	10	150	12' 6"
	17	6 3/4	10 1/2	168	14'
	17	6 3/4	11	176	14' 8"

USE THE TOTAL RISE TO FIND THE NUMBER OF RISERS AND THE RUN LENGTH FOR THE TWO RUNS OF A STAIRWAY WITH A LANDING.

Figure 205   Stairway with Landing Chart

Total Total Rise Flr to Flr Ht.	Num. of Risers	Riser Ht. (Unit Rise)	Width of Tread (Unit Run)	Run #1 Num. of Risers	Run #1 Run Length (1)	Run #2 Num. of Risers	Run #2 Run Length
8'-0"	13	7 3/8"	10	11	8'-4"+WL	2	10"+WL
8'-6"	14	7 1/4"	10	12	9'-2"+WL	2	10"+WL
9'-0"	15	7 1/4"	10	13	10'-0"+WL	2	10"+WL
9'-6"	16	7 1/8"	10	14	10'-10"+WL	2	10"+WL

WL = Width of Landing
(1) Length Run #1 = Num Risers x Unit Run

Rule of Thumb

Use a framing square to cut the carriage (**Figure 206**).

1. Set unit run on the tongue of square.

2. Set unit rise on the body of the square.

3. Draw line A-B, the tread bottom.

Draw line B-C, the unit rise.

Make a ledger for the framing square (**Figure 207**). Take two short pieces of straight stock and fasten them together with short bolts and wing nuts. Adjust to the proper rise and run. Slide the square along the edge of the horse and mark.

The pitch board (**Figure 208**) is cut from $\frac{3}{4}$-in. plywood with one edge equal to the unit rise and another edge equal to the tread length. Use with or without the stair gauge.

Fig 206 Use a Framing Square to Lay Out a Carriage
USE TABS AS STOPS ON THE TONGUE AND BODY, WITH THUMBSCREWS TO KEEP THEM FROM MOVING.

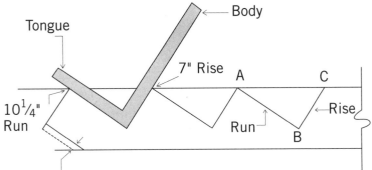

Tongue

Body

7" Rise

A   C

Rise

$10\frac{1}{4}$" Run

Run

B

Thickness of tread, or thickness of tread less thickness of finish floor ($\frac{3}{4}$" wood, $\frac{3}{8}$" carpet)

Figure 207   Run and Rise Jig
SLIDE THE JIG ALONG THE BOARD EDGE AND MARK RISE AND RUN.

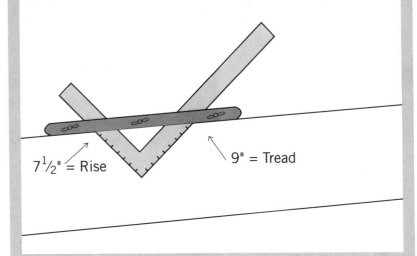

$7\frac{1}{2}$" = Rise

9" = Tread

Figure 208   Pitch Board and Stair Gauge
THE PITCH BOARD IS A HANDY TEMPLATE THAT CAN BE USED WITH OR WITHOUT THE STAIR GAUGE

Pitch Board

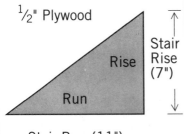

$\frac{1}{2}$" Plywood

Rise

Run

Stair Rise (7")

Stair Run (11")

Stair Gauge

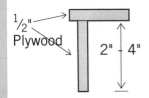

$\frac{1}{2}$" Plywood

2" - 4"

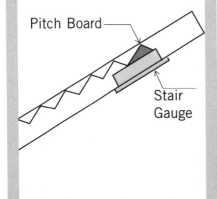

Pitch Board

Stair Gauge

CHAPTER 18

Shelf Loads

Every woodworker should know how to calculate beam loads - how much weight a piece of wood can carry without deflecting (sagging). It's one thing to design and build a nice looking bookshelf, but how disheartening to see shelves sag when put against the wall and loaded with books. In this chapter we'll learn what parts width, length, and thickness play in beam strength.

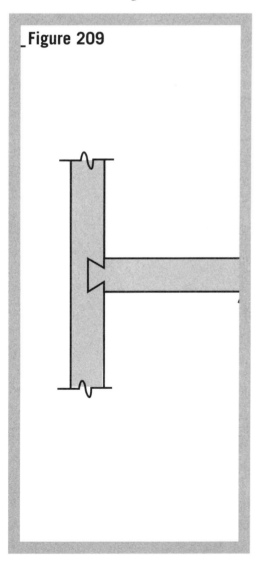

Figure 209

Two structural characteristics of wood must be considered when designing wooden shelves. The first is strength, i.e., the ability of the shelf to carry a load without breaking. The second is stiffness i.e., its ability to carry a load without deflecting excessively. In most cases, controlling the deflection is the more important consideration because while a shelf might sag, very seldom will it suddenly break.

To calculate the deflection of a wooden shelf, we need to examine four factors: the modulus of elasticity of the wood, the moment of inertia of the shelf under consideration, the span of the shelf, and the anticipated load. The modulus of elasticity depends on the type of wood used in constructing the shelf. The moment of inertia depends on the cross-sectional area of the piece. The span is the length of the shelf between supports, and the load is how much weight the shelf will carry.

Beam Strength

Beam strength, that is, the ability of the wood fibers to resist tension under load, is a function of the wood itself - species, quality, and cut. Other influencing factors include whether it is flat-sawn or quarter-sawn, straight-grained or burl, unflawed or full of knots. Once a woodworker has selected the type of wood to be used as a shelf - whether it is red oak, pine, or plywood - the most important factor from that point on is beam stiffness.

Beam Stiffness

Beam stiffness, or its resistance to bending, depends on four factors:

1. The **property of the wood to resist deformation** is known as the modulus of elasticity (MOE) and is usually denoted by "E". The E-value for various woods can be found in wood technology books (**Figure 210**), and varies from 1 to 2 million psi (pounds per square inch). Specifically, the modulus of elasticity is defined as stress divided by strain. In equations, the dimension of the E-value is millions of psi. In shorthand, modulus of elasticity is often abbreviated; 1,800,000 psi is written as E1.8. The higher the E-value of the wood, the more resistant it is to stress. White and red oak average about 1,650,000 psi, or E1.65, but this value varies by grade.

2. The **cross section** of the shelf. The moment of inertia (I) of a shelf depends on the cross-section. Because the cross-section of most shelves is rectangular, the I-value is the horizontal width times the vertical thickness cubed and divided by 12. Width and thickness are measured in inches.
I=(width x thickness^3)÷12

You can see that huge gains in I are achieved when we increase the thickness (vertical) number. This is why a 2x6 floor joist is so much stiffer on edge than when laid flat.

$$I = [1.75 \times (5.5)^3] \div 12$$
$$= (1.75 \times 166) \div 12 = 24.3$$

$$I = [5.5 \times (1.75)^3] \div 12$$
$$= (5.5 \times 5.36) \div 12 = 2.46$$

3. & 4. The **shelf length** or **span** (L) and the **load** (Wt.). Length is measured in inches, weight in pounds.

Shelving Type

For these discussions we'll examine four types of shelves which we will call Type A, B, C, and D. These are shown in **Figure 211** (next page).

A. Supported at both ends, evenly distributed load

B. Supported at both ends, centered load

C. Supported and pinned at both ends (fixed), evenly distributed load

D. Supported and pinned at both ends (fixed), centered load

To an engineer "supported and pinned" or "fixed' means no deflection or rotation at the ends. Because we are using engineering formulas, we will use the term "fixed" for the rest of the discussion.

STRESS FACTORS OF SOME COMMON HARDWOODS AND SOFTWOODS. THE E-VALUE CAN BE USED TO CALCULATE DEFLECTION.

Figure 210   E-Value Table

Hardwoods	E-Value*	Softwoods	E-Value*
Alder	1.38	Balsam Fir	1.23
Ash	1.77	Cedar	1.19
Beech	1.60	Doug Fir	1.95
Birch	1.80	Hemlock	1.40
Cherry	1.50	Pine	1.40
Chestnut	1.23	Redwood	1.34
Elm	1.40	(Old Growth)	
Locust	2.00	Spruce	1.40
Maple	1.70		
Oak	1.65		
Poplar	1.58		
Walnut	1.68		

* x 1,000,000 psi

Figure 211 Four Shelving Types

CALCULATE SHELF DEFLECTION BY USING ONE OF THESE FORMULAS. NOTE ALL FORMULAS ARE IDENTICAL EXCEPT FOR THE VARYING CONSTANT.

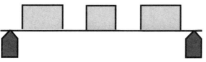

A. Supported at both ends, evenly distributed load

$$y = (5 \times Wt. \times L^3) \div (384\ EI)$$

Deflection factor
5 x standard

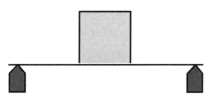

B. Supported at both ends, centered load

$$y = (Wt. \times L^3) \div (48\ EI)$$

Deflection factor
8 x standard

C. Supported and pinned at both ends (fixed), evenly distributed load

$$y = (Wt. \times L^3) \div (384\ EI)$$

Deflection factor
Standard

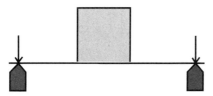

D. Supported and pinned at both ends (fixed), centered load

$$y = (Wt. \times L^3) \div (192\ EI)$$

Deflection factor
2 x standard

General formula

$$y = constant \times (Wt \times L^3) \div (E \times I)$$
where $I = (W \times T^3) \div (12)$

Deflection

Deflection (y)
$$= (5 \times Wt \times L^3) \div (384 \times E \times I)$$

Wt = weight of load in pounds.
L = board length in inches.
E = modulus of elasticity in PSI.
I = moment of inertia.
y = maximum deflection or sag
   at mid-span in inches.
384 = constant

We'll use a 1 in. x 8 in. x 6 ft. shelf, modulus of elasticity E1.5, and a 100 LB. weight. In all cases, inertia (I) will be the same.

Inertia
$$= (width \times thickness^3) \div 12$$
$I = (W \times T^3) \div 12$
$I = (8 \times 1^3) \div 12$
$I = 0.67$

Shelving Type A (supported both ends, even load):
$$y = (5 \times Wt. \times L^3) \div (384\ EI)$$
$y = (5 \times 100 \times 72^3)$
   $\div (384 \times 1.5 \times 10^6 \times 0.67)$
$y = (187 \times 10^6) \div (386 \times 10^6)$
$y = 187 \div 386 = 0.49$
   $\approx \frac{1}{2}$ in. deflection

Shelving Type B (supported both ends, load centered):
$$y = (Wt. \times L^3) \div (48\ EI)$$
$y = (100 \times 72^3)$
   $\div (48 \times 1.5 \times 10^6 \times 0.67)$
$y = (37 \times 10^6) \div (48 \times 10^6)$
$y = 37 \div 48 = 0.77$
   $\approx \frac{3}{4}$ in. deflection

Shelving Type C (supported and fixed both ends, even load):
$$y = (Wt. \times L^3) \div (384\ EI)$$
$y = (100 \times 72^3)$
   $\div (384 \times 1.5 \times 10^6 \times 0.67)$
$y = (37 \times 10^6) \div (386 \times 10^6)$
$y = 37 \div 386 = 0.10$
   $\approx \frac{1}{8}$ in. deflection

Shelving Type D (supported and fixed both ends, load centered):
$$y = (Wt. \times L^3) \div (192\ EI)$$
$y = (100 \times 72^3)$
   $\div (192 \times 1.5 \times 10^6 \times 0.67)$
$y = (37 \times 10^6) \div (193 \times 10^6)$
$y = 37 \div 193 = 0.19$
   $\approx \frac{1}{4}$ in. deflection

To summarize, deflection for the four types of shelving, using the same type and size of wood with equal loads and span:

Type A = 0.485 ≈ ½ in.
Type B = 0.771 ≈ ¾ in.
Type C = 0.096 ≈ ⅛ in.
Type D = 0.192 ≈ ¼ in.

This is theory, now for reality. In woodworking, when we support and pin a shelf we call it fixed. This could be a sliding dovetail, a dadoed shelf toe-nailed or pulled tight with screws from the outside. To a civil engineer, fixed means both ends of the beam are completely immobile. In their experiments, a 4-ft. piece of ¾-in. rebar with both ends embedded 12 in. into 2000-LB. blocks of concrete means fixed

—and even then there is some movement, however slight. The formulas for shelf types C and D in **Figure 211** are for engineers. As woodworkers, we cannot hope to affix a shelf end tight enough to use these formulas (**Figure 212**). It is, however, something to strive for. The tighter the ends of the shelf are held, the stiffer the shelf will be.

Relationship Between Shelving Types

The relationship between shelving types A, B, C, and D is 5:8:1:2. You can use these ratios or deflection factors (df) to find the approximate deflection for other shelf types, once you've calculated the deflection for any one.

If the deflection is 1½ in. for a Type A shelf, what will be the deflections for the other types?

Type A (df = 5)
   1.5 in. x 5/5 = 1½ in.

Type B (df = 8)
   1.5 in. x 8/5 = 2½ in.

Type C (df = 1)
   1.5 in. x 1/5 = ¼ in.

Type D (df = 2)
   1.5 in. x 2/5 = ½ in.

This shows by fixing both ends of the shelf (Type C) we would reduce sag from 1½ in. to ¼ in.

Shelf Thickness

Shelf thickness is cubed in the deflection formulas. Therefore, by halving the thickness of a shelf (dividing thickness by 2), we increase the deflection by eight times. Conversely, by doubling the thickness, sag is reduced eightfold.

To find the deflection of beams with thickness other than 1 in.,

use the following ratio factors:

1-in. material
= 1 x 1 x 1 = 1
(Standard in **Figures 213 & 214**)

$\frac{3}{4}$-in. material
= 0.75 x 0.75 x 0.75 = 0.42

$\frac{1}{2}$-in. material
= 0.5 x 0.5 x 0.5 = 0.13

$1\frac{1}{2}$-in. material

= 1.5 x 1.5 x 1.5 = 3.4

2-in. material
= 2 x 2 x 2 = 8.0

The deflection factor for shelf thickness other than 1 in. can be found by multiplying the 1-in. value by the cube of the new thickness. Find the deflection in one of the tables and multiply it by one of the factors above.

Example: How much weight can a 6 ft. 2x10 shelf carry before deflection exceeds $\frac{1}{8}$ in.? The ends are supported but not fixed, and the load is evenly distributed (Type A). The Type C chart (**Figure 213**) shows that, under these circumstances, a 6 ft. 1x10 shelf can carry a load of 160 LBS. A Type A shelf can carry 33 LBS. (160 ÷ 5). We know a 2-in. shelf is eight times stiffer than a 1-in. shelf. Thus a 2-in. shelf can carry 264 pounds.
   33 x 8 = 264 LBS.

If we made the same 6 ft. 1x10 shelf of $\frac{1}{2}$-in. material and wanted to leave it supported but unfixed at the ends (Type A, **Figure 214**), the calculations to find how much weight it could carry before deflection exceeded $\frac{1}{8}$ in. would be:
   33 ÷ 8 = 4 LBS.

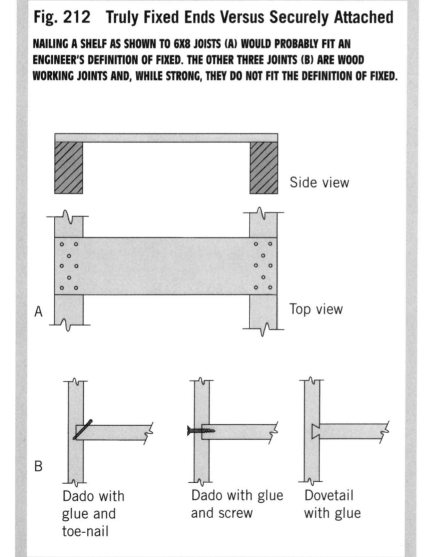

Fig. 212   Truly Fixed Ends Versus Securely Attached

NAILING A SHELF AS SHOWN TO 6X8 JOISTS (A) WOULD PROBABLY FIT AN ENGINEER'S DEFINITION OF FIXED. THE OTHER THREE JOINTS (B) ARE WOOD WORKING JOINTS AND, WHILE STRONG, THEY DO NOT FIT THE DEFINITION OF FIXED.

Side view

Top view

A

B

Dado with glue and toe-nail

Dado with glue and screw

Dovetail with glue

Shelf Width

Width plays a role in shelf stiffness, but is not as important as thickness. Other things being equal, a shelf twice as wide will carry twice the load. This means that its carrying capacity per square inch has remained the same. By doubling the width of the shelf, you've merely provided more square inches.

Shelf Length

Like thickness, the length of a shelf is important because this value is also cubed in the deflection equations. By doubling the shelf length, the deflection increases eight times. For example, if a 3-ft. shelf sags $\frac{1}{4}$ in., other things being equal, a 6-ft. shelf would sag 8 x $\frac{1}{4}$ = 2 in

.

Wood Types and Shelf Deflection

The type of wood is less important than the length or thickness of the beam. The following calculations use red oak (E1.65) and pine (E1.40) as examples; the E-values are from **Figure 210**. Each shelf is 1 in. x 6 in. x 6 ft., supported but not fixed at each end with a 100-lb. load, evenly distributed (Type A).

$I = (W \times T^3) \div 12$
$I = (6 \times 1^3) \div 12 = 0.5$
$\mathbf{y = (5 \times Wt. \times L^3) \div (384\ EI)}$

MULTIPLY ANY WEIGHT IN THIS TABLE BY 40% TO FIND DRESSED LUMBER LOAD VALUES, E.G. 3/4" X 3-1/2" X 4' WILL CARRY 40% THE WEIGHT THE 1" X 4" X 4' SHELF WILL. 215 X 0.40 = 85 LBS.

Figure 213   Weight Versus Deflection Fixed Ends (Type C)

Size	36" Long	48" Long	60" Long	72" Long
1 x 12	1,565*	654	333	193
1 x 10	1,300	570	290	160
1 x 8	1,050	440	225	130
1 x 6	780	330	165	97
1 x 4	515	215	110	64

* Pounds required to deflect shelf 1/8 In.

MULTIPLY ANY WEIGHT IN THIS TABLE BY 40% TO FIND DRESSED LUMBER LOAD VALUES, E.G., 3/4 IN. X 3-1/2 IN. X 4 FT. WILL CARRY 40% OF THE WEIGHT THAT THE 1 IN. X 4 IN. X 4 FT. SHELF WILL CARRY. 45 X 0.40 = 18 LBS.

Figure 214   Weight Versus Deflection Ends Not Fixed (Type A)

Size	36" Long	48" Long	60" Long	72" Long	I-Value**
1 x 12	320*	135	70	40	1.00
1 x 10	265	112	58	33	0.83
1 x 8	215	90	47	27	0.67
1 x 6	160	65	35	20	0.50
1 x 4	105	45	23	12	0.33

* Pounds required to deflect shelf $\frac{1}{8}$ In.

** $I = ($ width x thickness$^3) \div 12$

First, red oak (E1.65):
$y = (5 \times 100 \times 72^3)$
$\qquad \div 384 \times 1.65 \times 10^6 \times 0.5$
$y = (187 \times 10^6) \div 317 \times 10^6$
$y = 187 \div 317$
$y = 0.59$ in.
$\qquad \approx \frac{9}{16}$ in. deflection

Then pine (E1.40):
$y = (5 \times 100 \times 72^3)$
$\qquad \div 384 \times 1.40 \times 10^6 \times 0.5$
$y = (187 \times 10^6) \div 269 \times 10^6$
$y = 187 \div 269$
$y = 0.70$ in.
$\qquad \approx \frac{11}{16}$ in. deflection

The actual difference is 15% (0.59 ÷ 0.70 = 0.85), which also is the ratio of the E values:

E1.40 = pine
E1.65 = oak
1.40 ÷ 1.65 = 85%

Once you've calculated a deflection (sag) value for any type of wood you can compare it to another type by evaluating their respective E values. E-value, however, is highly dependent on the quality of the individual board. We could easily expect, for example, that a great piece of pine might outperform a poor piece of oak. Allowable unit stress tables for a single species, for example, Douglas fir, assign MOE values ranging from 1.3 to 1.9, depending on the size and commercial grade of the piece.

Even in the worst situation, unfixed shelving with the load centered (Type B), the difference between oak and pine is not significant. Compare the same size shelves, one of pine (E1.4) and the other of red oak (E1.65): 1 in. x 6 in. x 6 ft., 100-LB. weight.

Oak deflection = 0.93 ≈ $^{15}/_{16}$ in.
Pine deflection = 1.1 ≈ $^{17}/_{16}$ in.

Man-Made Materials

Man-made materials such as plywood and the fiberboards have E-values quite a bit lower than most natural woods (**Figure 215**). Use the E-value ratios to find deflection values. For example, if a piece of pine with E1.40 deflects $^1/_8$ in., then the same size MDF piece with E0.5 will deflect 2.8 times as much:

E1.40 ÷ E0.5 = 2.8
$^1/_8$ in. x 2.8 = 0.125 x 2.8
    = 0.35 ≈ $^3/_8$ in.

Pine deflection = $^1/_8$ in.
MDF deflection = $^3/_8$ in.

In the case of man-made materials like MDF, beam strength becomes important. While wood will deflect without breaking, fiberboards break easily when deflected.

How Much Weight Before A Shelf Sags?

When designing a bookcase, use the following formula to decide on the width and thickness of the shelf, and whether to fix the ends or not.

$$Wt = (y \times 384 \times EI) \div L^3$$
    and,
$$I = (W \times T^3) \div 12$$

Let's assume the shelf is 1 in. x 10 in. x 36 in. (T = 1, W = 10, L = 36), made of pine (E1.40), unfixed, resting on end supports, and the weight (unknown) will be evenly distributed (Type A). We will load the shelf until there is $^1/_8$-in. deflection (y = 0.125).

$$I = (W \times T^3) \div 12$$
$$I = (10 \times 1^3) \div 12$$
$$I = 0.83$$
$$Wt = (y \times 384 \times EI) \div 5 \times L^3$$
$$Wt = (0.125 \times 384 \times 1.4 \times 10^6 \times 0.83) \div 5 \times 36^3$$
$$Wt = 55.8 \times 10^6 \div 233 \times 10^3$$
$$Wt = 55800 \div 233 = 239 \text{ lbs.}$$

Earlier we found that fixed shelves (Type C) theoretically are five times as stiff as unfixed shelves (Type A).

USE THE E-VALUES TO CALCULATE THE AMOUNT OF DEFLECTION. FOR COMPARISON THE E-VALUES OF SOME COMMON METALS ARE ALSO LISTED.

Figure 215   E-Values for Metals and Man-Made Materials

	E-Value*
High Density Fiberboard (HDF)	0.6
Medium Density Fiberboard (MDF)	0.5
Low Density Fiberboard (LDF)	0.2
Tempered Hardboard	0.8
Plywood	0.6
Brass	9
Aluminum	10
Bronze	14
Iron	28
Steel	30

* x 1,000,000 psi

239 x 5 = 1195 lbs.

This theoretical shelf (Type C) would hold half a ton. In reality, you should expect more stiffness than the same shelf with ends that are not fixed but merely rest on end supports (Type A)—but certainly not five times as much.

General Rules

The stiffness of a shelf varies inversely with the cube of the length. If a shelf is twice as long, it is one-eighth as stiff, and deflection, or sag, will be eight times more. Shorten a shelf by half and it can carry eight times more weight for the same deflection.

The stiffness of a shelf varies with the cube of the thickness. A 1-in. thick shelf is eight times stiffer than a $\frac{1}{2}$-in. thick shelf. Divide the thickness by half and the shelf deflection will increase eightfold (**Figure 216**).

The end conditions are extremely important. An attached shelf (screwed to a cleat with screws, mortised, dadoed, or dovetailed) is stiffer than the same size shelf merely resting on end supports. Remember, it is almost impossible to create a fixed condition, but any type of end attachment will stiffen a shelf.

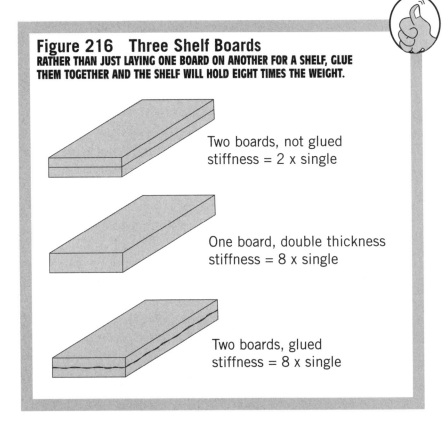

Figure 216   Three Shelf Boards
RATHER THAN JUST LAYING ONE BOARD ON ANOTHER FOR A SHELF, GLUE THEM TOGETHER AND THE SHELF WILL HOLD EIGHT TIMES THE WEIGHT.

Two boards, not glued
stiffness = 2 x single

One board, double thickness
stiffness = 8 x single

Two boards, glued
stiffness = 8 x single

Rules of Thumb

• Shorten the length by one-half and the shelf can carry eight times more weight.

• Double the shelf thickness and it can carry eight times more weight.

• Fix the shelf at both ends and, in theory, it can carry five times more weight. The actual increased strength is hard to figure, but the tighter the ends are fixed, the stiffer and the stronger the shelf.

• Slide a support under the shelf at mid-span and it can carry eight times more weight.

• Double the shelf width and it can carry two times the weight.

• Distribute the weight evenly along the length of the shelf. A concentrated weight at mid-span increases deflection 1.6 times.

• To compare deflection of different woods, use E-value ratios. The higher the E-value, the stiffer the wood.

• Put a facing on the shelf front, say, a $^3/_4$-in. x 2-in. nose on a $^3/_4$-in. shelf. The shelf will look more interesting and it will be stiffer. The exact amount of increased stiffness is difficult to figure.

• In addition to a front edging, or instead of it, glue a ledger beneath the back edge of the shelf (**Figure 217**). In some situations the back-edge ledger is even more functional when attached on top of the shelf—it creates a gallery that keeps your motorcycle parts from falling off behind. While the exact amount of increased stiffness is difficult to figure, ledgers fastened to the front and back edges of a shelf will solve almost any sagging problem.

• If the board has knots on one side only, place this weaker side up because the top side is under compression while the bottom must be stronger to resist tension.

References

E-Values of wood from: *Understanding Wood*, by R. Bruce Hoadley; The Taunton Press, 1980.

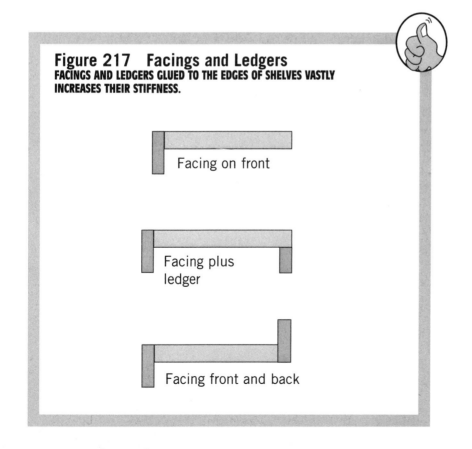

Figure 217   Facings and Ledgers
FACINGS AND LEDGERS GLUED TO THE EDGES OF SHELVES VASTLY INCREASES THEIR STIFFNESS.

Facing on front

Facing plus ledger

Facing front and back

CHAPTER 19

Bending Wood without Heat

Bending wood can be easy as a couple of Boy Scouts coaxing pieces of $\frac{1}{4}$-in. plywood around a few ribs to make a kayak. Or it can be as complicated as a skilled woodworker steaming an 8-ft. piece of ash and clamping it into complex forms to fashion the compound twists and turns of a Windsor chair.

Bending wood is really pretty simple—if it bends, bend it. If it doesn't bend—do something to make it bend. One of the easier ways to make wood pliable without heating is by lamination, i.e., cutting it into thin pieces. Almost any wood can be bent if it's cut thin enough. The other method is by kerfing, i.e., making cuts in the back side.

In this chapter, you'll also learn about springback, how to select and prepare stock, form preparation, and glues. Vacuum bags and tapered laminations are also discussed.

Thin Laminate Bending

Lamination is the building up of thin layers of firmly united materials to obtain a required thickness. Bent lamination is taking those layers and bending them before they are glued together. The resulting laminates are stronger than the original stock, and if done right, retain their curved shape with no springback. **Figure 227** shows why thin pieces bend easier that full dimension wood.

It's important to distinguish lamination from veneering. In a lamination, all the grains are oriented in the same direction and an even or odd number of layers can be used. In veneering and plywood, the grain directions alternate and an odd number of layers are used. An exception is bendable plywood, where the grain of all plies runs in the same direction. In lamination, the layers, when glued together, act like solid wood, expanding and contracting across the long grain (although somewhat

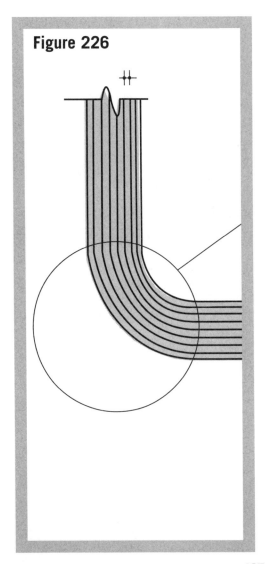

Figure 226

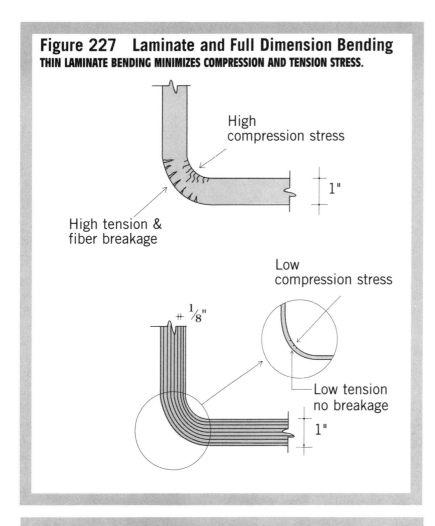

Figure 227 Laminate and Full Dimension Bending
THIN LAMINATE BENDING MINIMIZES COMPRESSION AND TENSION STRESS.

High compression stress

High tension & fiber breakage

1"

$\frac{1}{8}$"

Low compression stress

Low tension no breakage

1"

Figure 228 Lamination Makes Stronger Pieces and Saves Material
BY USING BENT LAMINATION, LESS WOOD IS USED TO MAKE A STRONGER PIECE.

Weak points

6"

Resaw

2"

No weak points

1"

restricted by the shear strength of the glue). In veneering, grain alternation stabilizes the unit and there is no movement either across or with the grain.

In thin lamination bending, the pieces are laid up in the same direction and in the same strict order as they were cut from the board, with the grains matched as precisely as possible. Bent lamination is an economical way of making curved furniture pieces. A chair leg can be thinner and will be stronger than a band-sawn piece because of the inherent weakness of short grain (**Figure 228**).

A general rule in bent lamination is to keep the layers at the maximum thickness to make the desired bend. This saves time in preparing the stock (less thin rips) and material (each thin strip that is cut generates another thin strip of sawdust). Thin layers (such as 1/28-in. veneer), risk surface unevenness from disparate clamp pressure or from telegraphing of unevenly cut stock or poorly spread glue. Thinner pieces will bend easier but will give stiffer, heavier laminations that will take longer to build up, require more glue, and take longer to dry in the forms. It's better to saw the stock to optimum thickness than to use many layers of thin veneer.

Springback

Springback is always a possibility. **Figure 230** shows that the amount of springback is inversely proportional to the number of laminations used.

Figure 229 shows that, given a 12-in. bend with five plies, you can expect 4% springback or about $\frac{1}{2}$ in. (12 x 0.04 = 0.48). Either adjust your forms accordingly or increase the number of thin lam pieces to achieve the springback you can tolerate.

Calculating Springback

As an example, we want to make a rocking chair and we need two 2-in. x 32-in. pieces bent up 4 in. at each end for the rockers. We'll use $\frac{3}{16}$-in. thick strips of red oak. Here's how to calculate the amount of springback.

Rocker height = 2 in.;
strip thickness = $\frac{3}{16}$ in.
$2 \div \frac{3}{16} = 2 \div 0.188 = 10.7$ plies
We'll use 11 thin strips.

Springback (in percent)
$= 1 \div (plies^2 - 1)$

Sb = 1 ÷ (11 x 11) - 1

Sb = 1 ÷ 120 = 0.0083 = 0.01%
4-in. bend x 0.01 = 0.04-in.
    ≈ $\frac{1}{32}$ in. springback

A $\frac{1}{32}$ in. springback will not be noticeable over the 32-in. length and is quite tolerable.

SPRINGBACK DECREASES AS THE NUMBER OF LAMINATIONS INCREASES.

Figure 229   Thin-Strip Laminate Springback

Number Of Plies	Percent Springback	Bending Inches & Inches Springback 6 In.	12 In.	18 In.
2	33	2	4	6
3	13	3/4	1 1/2	2 1/4
4	7	1/2	1	1 1/2
5	4	1/4	1/2	3/4
6	3	3/16	3/8	9/16
7	2	1/8	1/4	3/8
8	1 1/2	1/16	1/8	3/16
9	1 1/4	1/16	1/8	7/32
10	1		1/8	7/32
11	LT 1		3/32	5/32
12	LT 1		1/16	1/16

LT = Less Than

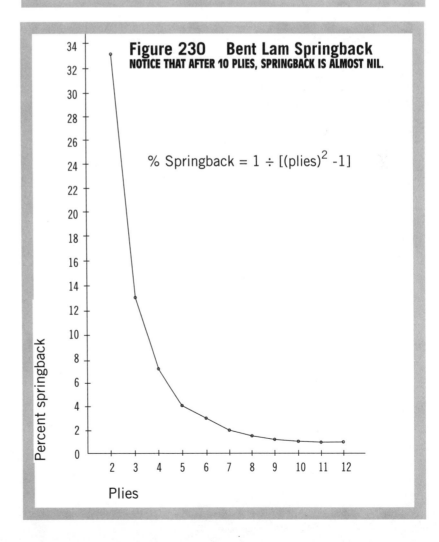

Figure 230   Bent Lam Springback
NOTICE THAT AFTER 10 PLIES, SPRINGBACK IS ALMOST NIL.

$$\% \text{ Springback} = 1 \div [(plies)^2 - 1]$$

Selecting Stock

For bending, look for straight grain stock with no knots or irregularities (**Figure 231**). Thin pieces of wood will all bend in a similar manner when cut from a homogeneous, straight grain plank. Laminations from boards with sections of curly, spiral, or wild grain will bend unpredictably.

You'll need stock 10-20% longer than the project asks for. Use kiln-dried stock—green wood or wood with high moisture content will bend easier but the springback is unpredictable. Obviously, the stock must be wide enough to accommodate both the multiple saw blade kerfs cut and the wood wasted. If the blade has a width of $\frac{3}{16}$ in. and you are cutting $\frac{1}{8}$-in. strips, multiply the sum of these widths times the number of strips needed, in this case, 12.

Stock Width
$$= \text{(Blade width + Strip Width) x Strips Needed}$$
Stock Width = $(\frac{1}{16} + \frac{1}{8})$ x 12
Stock Width = $(0.188 + 0.125)$ x 12
Stock Width = 0.313 x 12 = 3.75 in.

You should use at least a 4 in. wide board to cut 12 thin strips, each $\frac{1}{8}$ in. wide.

Figure 231 Selecting Stock for Bent Lamination

THIN STRIPS FROM QUARTER-SAWN LUMBER (A) WILL BEND WITHOUT BREAKING. THIN STRIPS CUT FROM PLAIN OR FLAT-SAWN LUMBER (B) WILL BREAK WHEN BENT. PLAIN-SAWN LUMBER CAN BE CUT IN A WAY THAT PRODUCES QUARTER-SAWN STRIPS (C).

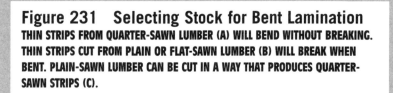

Strips from here will be short-grained and liable to break.

Strips from here will be long-grained and easy to bend

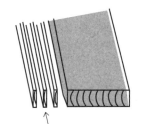

Cut thin strips from quarter-sawn lumber

A

These strips will bend without breaking

Strips from flat-sawn or plain-sawn lumber will break when bent

B

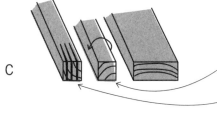

C

Rip plain-sawn lumber to width first. Then flip 90° and cut quarter-sawn strips for bending.

Preparing Stock

First, determine the thickness of the layer needed by testing the bend with a sample. A $\frac{3}{4}$ in. thick drawer front with a gentle curve might be made of two $\frac{3}{8}$ in. thick layers glued together. A curved $\frac{1}{4}$-in. side of a chest could be made of two $\frac{1}{8}$-in. pieces, with the outer layer cut from an expensive piece, sawn and book-matched to make a pleasing pattern.

Paint one end of the board with a red marker and cut the strips with a band saw. You could use a table saw with a thin kerf blade but you'll lose as much stock to sawdust as you gain in thin pieces. While a band saw cuts thinner kerfs, the table saw produces even, smooth, parallel strips ready to glue (**Figure 232**).

Different woods are easier to bend (**Figure 233**), although almost any straight-grained wood cut at $\frac{1}{8}$ in. will bend enough for cradle rockers, chair slats, or a settee back. Some of the springier woods will bend nicely at $\frac{1}{4}$ in. Keep the pieces in the same order they come off the saw. This will help to make the assembled piece nearly indiscernible from the original. **Figure 233** lists good, fair, and poor woods for bending.

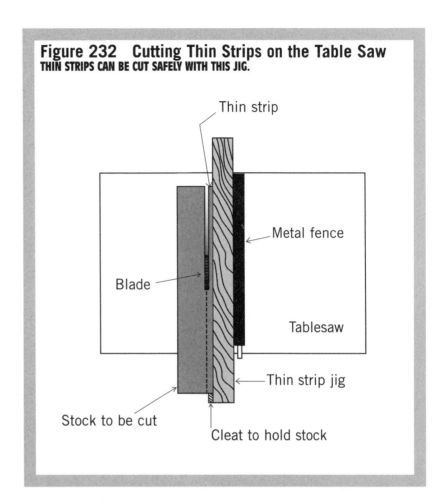

Figure 232   Cutting Thin Strips on the Table Saw
THIN STRIPS CAN BE CUT SAFELY WITH THIS JIG.

Thin strip

Metal fence

Blade

Tablesaw

Thin strip jig

Stock to be cut

Cleat to hold stock

WOODS THAT BEND EASILY
CAN BE SAWN INTO THICKER STRIPS

Figure 233   Relative Bending Comparison of Different Woods

Good	Fair	Poor
Ash	Birch	Mahogany
Beech	Cherry	Maple
Hickory	Elm	Pine
Oak	Doug Fir	Poplar
Walnut		Spruce
		Sycamore

Figure 234 Form for Laminating Curved Parts

GLUE UP LAYERS OF PLYWOOD, MDF, OR PARTICLE BOARD TO THE WIDTH OF THE STRIPS. BAND SAW OUT AND DISCARD A PORTION OF THE FORM EQUAL IN WIDTH TO THE THICKNESS OF THE DESIRED GLUE-LAM PART.

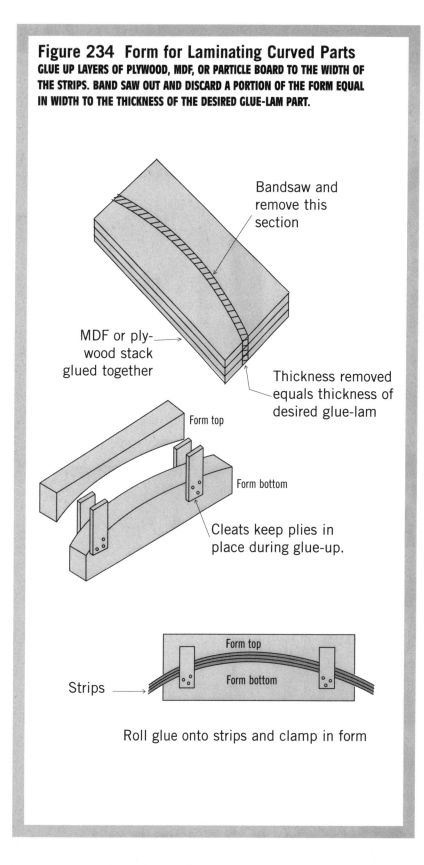

Bandsaw and remove this section

MDF or plywood stack glued together

Thickness removed equals thickness of desired glue-lam

Form top

Form bottom

Cleats keep plies in place during glue-up.

Form top

Form bottom

Strips

Roll glue onto strips and clamp in form

Forms

A form for bending the thin strips can be made by gluing up layers of MDF, plywood, or particle board to the width of the strips (**Figure 234**). Draw the outline of the final piece, and band saw out and discard the portion of the form equal in width to the thickness of the desired glue-lam part. Note that after removing the outlined portion, the top will not mate with the bottom. Screw alignment boards to both sides of the bottom to keep the press and the wood strips lined up. Wax the form so glue squeeze-out can be chipped off later.

Lay all the pieces onto the form and try clamping. If they don't fit during the dry run, they won't later when the laminations are slippery and glue is dripping from every piece. Time yourself and choose a glue with enough open and closed time to complete the assembly. See Glue Chart, **Figure 235.**

Glues for Thin Laminate

There are three factors to consider when choosing glue for a bent lamination job: open time, closed time, and resistance to creep. Open time is the time after the glue is spread on the pieces until they must be joined. Closed time is the amount of time after the pieces are placed in the form until the glue sets. Resistance to cold creep (shear strength) is how strong the bonding of glue and wood proves to be.

Open Time

Choose a glue so that the glue applied to the first strip isn't dry before all the pieces can be coated. The glue should have at least 10 minutes open time for a 10-12 strip laminating job.

Closed Time

The glue chosen must not set until all the pieces are positioned and clamped into the form. This closed time should be at least 10 minutes for the average job.

Resistance to Creep

The glue should have enough shear strength to hold the wood in the curved position after the piece has been removed from the form. Bent laminations are under constant stress, therefore they require a glue that greatly resists cold creep. Most adhesives are strong enough to hold the pieces in approximate position but even a small amount of movement will break glue joints and crack finishes. The bent lamination glue joint should be rock solid.

OPEN TIME IS HOW QUICKLY A GLUE BEGINS TO SET AFTER THE ADHESIVE IS SPREAD, IE, THE JOINT IS OPEN. CLOSED TIME IS HOW MUCH TIME THERE IS FOR REPOSITIONING ONCE THE PIECES HAVE BEEN PUT TOGETHER, IE, THE JOINT HAS BEEN CLOSED. SHEAR STRENGTH IS A MEASURE OF BONDING MUSCLE AND HOW WELL A GLUE RESISTS CREEP. WITH MORE LAMINATIONS OR THINNER STRIPS, CREEP RESISTANCE MATTERS LESS.

Figure 235   Glues for Bent Laminations

Glue Type	Open Time	Closed Time	Clamp Time(1)	Shear Strength	Water Resist.	Oily Woods
Hide						
Hot	1-5 min.	30-60 min.	8 hrs.	Good	Poor	Poor
Liquid	10-15 min.	30-60 min.	8 hrs.	Good	Poor	Poor
Polyurethane	10-20 min.	20-60 min.	24 hrs.	Good	Excellent	Excellent
Polyvinyl Acetate						
White	25 min.	15 min.	8 hrs.	Fair	Poor	Good (3)
Yellow	10 min.	10 min.	8 hrs.	Fair	Poor	Good (3)
Cross-Link	15 min.	45 min.	8 hrs.	Fair	Good	Good (3)
Epoxy (2)	30 min.	30 min.	15 min.	Excellent	Excellent	Poor
Resorcinol	30 min.	60 min.	12 hrs.	Excellent	Excellent	Good (3)
Urea-Formaldehyde	10-30 min.	30 min to 4 hrs. (4)	24 hrs.	Excellent	Good	Poor

(1) Special times given for laminations.
(2) Epoxy glues available with almost any open & closed time.
(3) On freshly cut surfaces or ones wiped with paint thinner.
(4) Depending on temperature.

The Glues

See **Figure 235**; check Chapter 28 "All About Glues" for more data.

Hide Glue

Historically, the traditional glue for bent laminations was hide glue. Use either hot hide glue made fresh from flakes or liquid hide glue purchased ready-to-use. Both glues give up to an hour of working time (closed time plus open time), have good strength, are easy to work with, and clean up with water. The

drawbacks: hide glue is not water or alcohol resistant and will not work on oily woods.

Polyurethane Glues

Another good choice for a bent lam job is polyurethane. These glues are very strong, water-proof, work well on end grain, will fill small gaps, and give you a long set-up time. They work well with wet, oily, and dense woods. They are, however, messy, and the foam is a pain to clean up.

Polyvinyl Acetate (PVA) Glues

The PVA glues (white, yellow, or cross-linking) are somewhat elastic and might allow the joint to creep. I've used yellow PVA glue on three bent wood, thin lamination cradles (red oak, maple, and hickory). I used twelve $\frac{1}{8}$-in. strips to make up the $1\frac{1}{2}$-in. stock and found no discernable creep and no springback.

$$12 \times \tfrac{1}{8}\text{-in.} = 1.5 \text{ in.}$$
$$\text{Springback} = (12 \times 12) - 1$$
$$= 0.007 = 0.7\%$$

If I had used fewer pieces or thicker strips, PVA glue would not have been a good choice. These glues have a short working time and the white and yellow formulations are not water resistant. The cross-linked PVA is waterproof and could be used if moisture will be a problem. Oily woods can be glued if the surfaces are fresh or if older surfaces are cleaned with paint thinner just prior to glue-up.

Epoxy Glues

A two-part epoxy with a long open time is a good choice for lamination. These glues set very hard, will bond almost anything to anything, and are waterproof. When strong bonding is needed, epoxy would provide protection against creep. One drawback—the glue joints are so hard they are not resistant to impact; a sharp blow could open a joint. Also, fresh squeeze-out must be cleaned up with lacquer thinner and the hardened glue must be scraped off.

Resorcinol Glues

These glues provide plenty of open and closed time to get the glue spread and the pieces placed into the forms. They create very strong joints and are waterproof. In fact, they are used in boat building. However, they have a dark glue-line which might be a problem with light woods, and they must be used above 70°F.

Urea Formaldehyde

These glues would be a good choice for bent lam work. They come in powder form and are mixed with water prior to use. They are water resistant but not waterproof. They have extremely long closed assembly times - from four hours at 70° to a half hour at 100°F. Some people are sensitive to formaldehyde and latex gloves should be worn during mixing and glue-up.

Glue and Clamp

Some glues give you lots of time for set up and repositioning. Others are water resistant or work well with oily woods like teak or the rosewoods. Use the chart to choose the right glue for your situation.

Spread glue on one surface of each ply and transfer them one at a time to the form. Keep the pieces in order, with all red ends together. Clamp by starting in the middle and working your way outward towards each end.

Allow the glue to cure; check the table to see how long to leave the project in clamps. The times listed in the table are only approximate. Cold shops, humid conditions, and forms wrapped in waxed paper all restrict water evaporation and slow curing of water-based glues. On the other hand, warm and dry conditions will facilitate faster glue set.

Remove the clamps and take the glue-lam from the form. You'll be surprised at how little springback there is—if you used enough thin strips, if your forms were designed right, and if you used the correct glue to hold it all together.

Clean up - here's where you'll be glad the plys were kept in order. Planing and scraping can be a bear when half the grain runs in one direction and half in the other. Also, keeping the plies in order will ensure that the color and grain are consistent in the final piece. You want the finished piece to look like the original, that is, a solid hunk of wood, except curved.

Vacuum Bending

Vacuum presses have been used for some time in flat veneer work. These same set-ups can also be used to hold bent laminations to a curved form until the glue sets. Vacuum presses work on the simple principle that, at sea level, atmospheric pressure applies over 2,000 pounds of pressure per square foot in all directions. By removing air from the bottom of the form, that is, putting it into a partial vacuum, all of that weight is distributed evenly onto the top of the work piece.

In the workshop, a curved form and thin plys are put into a tough vinyl bag. The bag is sealed and the air is evacuated using an industrial pump or an air compressor and a Venturi valve.

The benefits of vacuum bending are:

• The form design is greatly simplified because clamps and cauls are not required.

• Only one part of the bending form, the bottom, is needed. The plastic bag takes the place of the top caul and atmospheric pressure holds the thin layers firmly in place.

• The bending and gluing process are in plain view.

Initially, the pieces can be held in position by hand and the procedure can be stopped and the pieces repositioned, or the procedure stopped as the bag is being evacuated.

• Water-based glues set and cure quicker because the reduced pressure in the bag causes water to evaporate faster.

• The vacuum distributes the pressure uniformly across the work surface to eliminate bubbles, voids and to ensure even glue distribution.

Tapered Laminations

Tapered laminations (**Figure 236**) use layers that are not uniform thickness to make tapered pieces such as furniture legs. If the design requires cutting through the thickness of a layer of wood at any point, the whole part is weakened. The severed layers no longer contribute to the strength of the assembly, and the end grain now shows. The problem is avoided by gluing up tapered layers of wood, so the variation in thickness is built right into the lamination. Each layer should be made as thick as possible but still thin enough to follow the desired curve. Using tapered laminations allows you to make curved pieces whose width and

Figure 236   Tapered Laminations

A SIMPLE GLUED-UP LAMINATION (A) WHEN TAPERED ON A TABLESAW LEAVES THIN STRIPS, END GRAIN, AND UGLY GLUE LINES (B). USE A TAPERING JIG (D) TO MAKE TAPERED STRIPS AND A TAPERED LEG (C). THIS TECHNIQUE CAN ALSO BE USED FOR TAPERED BENT LAMINATION JOBS (E).

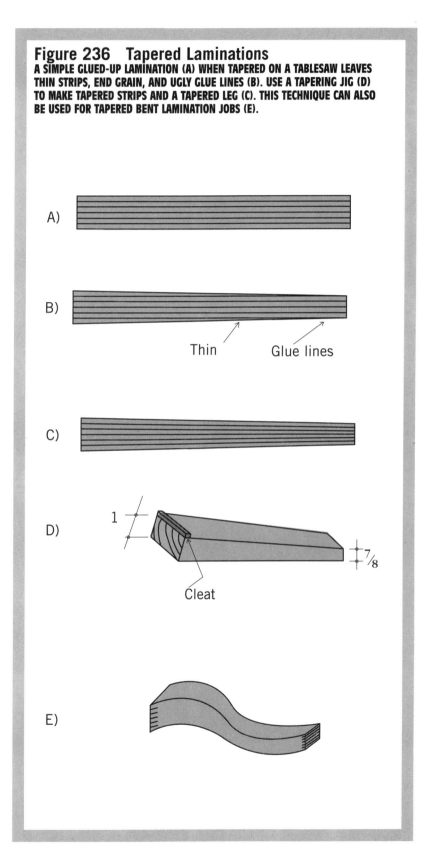

A)

B)

Thin   Glue lines

C)

1

D)

$\frac{7}{8}$

Cleat

E)

thickness vary, whereas a simple bent lamination can vary only in thickness.

Once you've decided on the dimensions of the curved, tapered part, you can figure the measurements of the layers. To calculate the slope on the tapering jig, you'll need the following information on the furniture part: the small thickness, the large thickness, and the length.

Large Thickness ÷ number of strips = strip maximum

Small Thickness ÷ number of strips = strip minimum

For example, we want to use eight thin strips to make a curved table leg 30 in. long with a top thickness of 2 in., and a bottom thickness of 1 in.

$2 \div 8 = \frac{1}{4}$ in.
$1 \div 8 = \frac{1}{8}$ in.

The jig should be made so it tapers $\frac{1}{8}$ in. over the 30-in. length.

A tapering jig can also be made for a thickness planer but putting $\frac{1}{4}$-in. to $\frac{1}{8}$-in. thick pieces through this machine is pretty scary. A tapering jig for the table saw or for a thickness sander makes more sense.

Kerf Bending

When a project requires a curved piece that can not be made of thin, glued-up pieces, radius kerfing might be the answer. In fact, it is a technique that in some cases might be the first method of choice. The material can be prepared faster, it does not require forms or clamps, and once in place there isn't much chance of springback.

Kerf bending utilizes a series of saw kerfs, cut side-by-side on one surface, making the material flexible enough to bend smoothly and gracefully. Saw cuts are made almost through the strip, leaving a thin layer of undisturbed wood beneath. When the panel is bent, the kerfs close and the thin, uncut surface is shaped into a smooth surface with a pattern of triangular voids, out of sight, on the back edge. It can be used on solid wood or plywood.

The first objective is to cut a sufficient number of kerfs so that when the piece is bent to the desired radius, the individual kerf edges close and can be glued together. This produces rigid stock and eliminates the need for backing support. However, the wider the saw kerfs are spaced, the more likely that the facets will be trans-ferred from back to front. This is especially noticeable when the surface is later polished to a high gloss.

Number of Kerfs

To determine the number of kerfs and the spacing required for a given bend (**Figure 237**), cut a single kerf on a board similar to the stock you will be bending and make a mark at a distance from the cut equal to the radius of the final bend. Clamp the piece to a flat surface and bend the one end up until the kerf closes. Measure distance 'h' from the surface to the radius mark.

Number of Kerfs

$$= (6.3 \text{ x radius}) \div 4 \text{ x h}$$

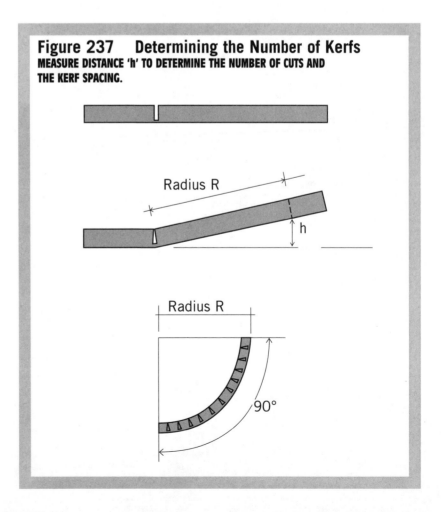

Figure 237   Determining the Number of Kerfs
MEASURE DISTANCE 'h' TO DETERMINE THE NUMBER OF CUTS AND THE KERF SPACING.

Radius R

h

Radius R

90°

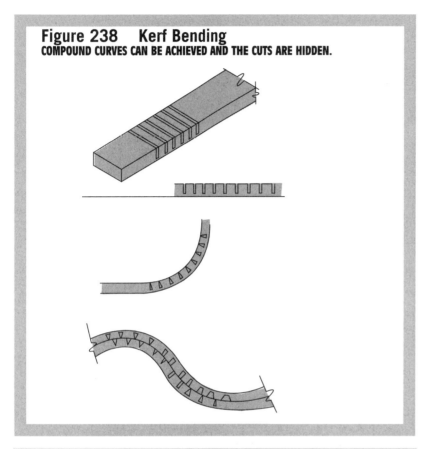

Figure 238　Kerf Bending
COMPOUND CURVES CAN BE ACHIEVED AND THE CUTS ARE HIDDEN.

Example: we want to bend a piece to a 12-in. radius and have determined that distance 'h' equals $1\frac{1}{2}$ in.

radius = 12 in., h = $1\frac{1}{2}$ in.
Number of Kerfs
　= (6.3 x radius) ÷ 4 x h
Number of Kerfs
　= (6.3 x 12) ÷ 4 x 1.5
Number of Kerfs
　= 75.6 ÷ 6 = 12.6

Kerf Spacing
The kerf spacing is distance 'h', therefore, cut 13 kerfs $1\frac{1}{2}$ in. apart.

Compound Bends
A compound bend, as shown in **Figure 238**, produces two finished sides and can be very strong. The two pieces can be bent and glued together at the same time. Conversely, each curve can be bent separately on a form and the kerfs filled with wedges and glue. Later the pieces can be glued together.

Kerf-Bent Picture Frame
In kerf bending, the multiple saw kerfs are usually made on the back of the project and hidden from view. In **Figure 239**, an interesting use of kerf bending was published (*Fine Woodworking*) where the kerfs were intentionally left visible and, in fact, were filled with a colored epoxy to emphasize them.

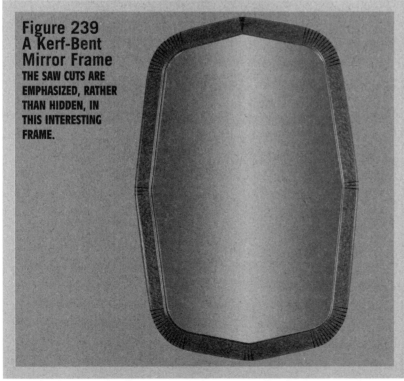

Figure 239
A Kerf-Bent Mirror Frame
THE SAW CUTS ARE EMPHASIZED, RATHER THAN HIDDEN, IN THIS INTERESTING FRAME.

Repairing Warped Woods

Warped woods can be rejuvenated using the kerf method (**Figure 240**): straightening a long piece of molding with twists and warps. Saw cuts are run from the back and the molding is bent and nailed in place. Alternately, after kerfing, wood spacers or wedges can be glued into the slots and the piece clamped to a flat surface. The resulting piece will be straight, strong, and ready to install.

In-the-Shop Summary of Kerf Bending

To determine the number of cuts and the spacing:

1. Use a scrap similar to the one you want to bend.

2. Cut a kerf from the back side to within $\frac{1}{8}$ in. of the good surface.

3. Wet the good side and bend the piece slowly. If it breaks or bends with difficulty, cut a deeper kerf.

4. Determine height ('h')—see **Figure 237**—and calculate the number of kerfs needed

Number of Kerfs = 6.3R ÷ 4h

5. Distance 'h' is also the spacing between kerfs.

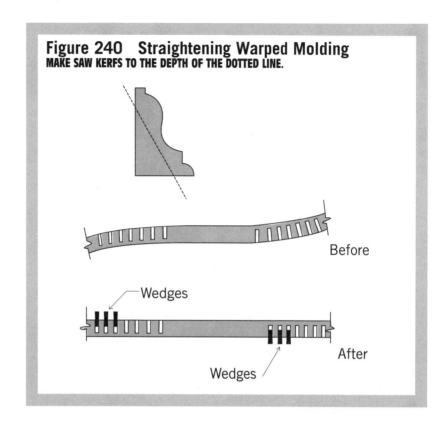

Figure 240   Straightening Warped Molding
MAKE SAW KERFS TO THE DEPTH OF THE DOTTED LINE.

Before

Wedges

Wedges

After

6. Cut a sample piece.

7. Wet the surface and bend.

8. If facets show on the good side, cut again using twice the number of kerfs.

Rule of Thumb

When bending $\frac{3}{4}$-in. plywood, space kerfs $\frac{3}{8}$ in. apart. Cut through from the back until the blade just touches the surface veneer. Wet the surface and suspend the plywood between two sawhorses or blocks, good side down. Adjust the block height, depending on the curve you want. Put a weight on the plywood and let it set. The wood fibers have to expand and stretch and they do this best slowly, with a steady weight. Check back in a half-hour and, if necessary, wet the surface again and add more weight. With this method, the board will bend nicely and facets will not telegraph from the back to the front.

References:
Fine Woodworking 94, 1992, p.73.

CHAPTER 20

Motors & 3-Phase Electricity

Purchasing the correct motor involves a lot of thought. How powerful does the motor need to be? 1/10 hp or 2 hp? Will it be used outside in the rain or in the shop? Does it need to be reversible, run on 120 or 240 volt electricity, AC or DC, run at 1725 or 3450 rpm or should it be variable speed? This chapter will answer these questions.

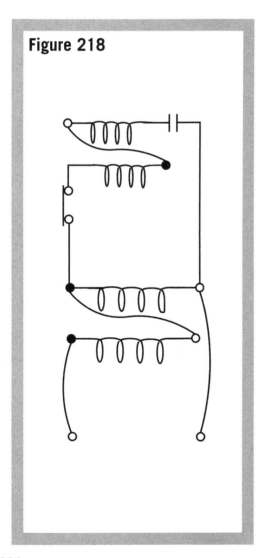

Figure 218

An electric motor is a device that converts electrical energy into motion. The amount of current (amps) that goes into the motor determines in part, how much horsepower (hp) the motor puts out. One amp under pressure of one volt equals 1/746 hp. Therefore:

Amps x volts ÷ 746 = horsepower

This is the theoretical case.

Power Factor and Efficiency

In real life, two additional factors affect the horsepower equation: the power factor (PF) and the efficiency (EFF) of the motor.

The **power factor** of a motor depends on the phase relationship between the voltage and the current in the AC circuit. When voltage and current get out of sync with each other, they create a weaker magnetic field. Because electric motors depend on strong magnetic fields to operate, this phase difference lessens the power of the motor. Power factor is a measure of the ratio of real power (watts) divided by apparent power (volts-amps). Power factor of a motor is given as a decimal; higher values mean stronger magnetic fields. Power factor is not to be confused with the efficiency of a motor.

The **efficiency** of a motor is a measure of how well the electrical energy input to a motor is converted into mechanical energy at the output shaft. Efficiency is given as a decimal derived from the output power divided by input power. The higher the efficiency, the better the energy conversion.

Both power factor and efficiency reduce the amount of power that a motor transmits and they are dependent on the motor type, how the motor was built, and how much of the electrical current goes directly into creating motion.

Power factor and efficiency are measured by the motor manufacturer. Ratings are sometimes found on a motor nameplate as PF and EFF, but most tool retailers do not publicize these measurements. A 20-30% energy loss due to power factor and a similar loss due to efficiency are pretty common. If you telephone them, the manufacturer's technical support will be able to supply these numbers. A power factor of 0.80 (PF80) combined with an efficiency of 0.85 (EFF85) reduces power output to 68%.

Energy = power factor x efficiency
Energy = 0.80 x 0.85 x 100 = 68%

Theoretical and Continuous or Real Horsepower
To calculate the theoretical horsepower of a motor, use amperage and voltage.
      Theoretical Horsepower = (amps x volts) ÷ 746
To calculate the real or continuous horsepower of a motor, use amperage, voltage, power factor, and efficiency.

Continuous horsepower = (amps x volts x power factor x efficiency) ÷ 746

In my shop I have a large motor that I took off a piece of farm machinery. The name plate shows: hp 3.0, amps 30, volts 110, EFF .85, PF .80.

The theoretical horsepower of this old motor is:
Theoretical Horsepower
    = (amps x volts) ÷ 746
Hp = (30 x 110) ÷ 746
Hp = 3300 ÷ 746 = 4.42

To calculate the real or continuous horsepower:
Continuous horsepower = (amps x volts x power factor x efficiency) ÷ 746

Continuous hp = (30 x 110 x 0.80 x 0.85) ÷ 746
Continuous hp
    = 2244 ÷ 746 = 3.0

Note that the theoretical horsepower of 4.42 is 47% higher than the real horse-power of 3.01.
    4.42 - 3.01 = 1.41
    1.41 ÷ 3.01 x 100 = 47%

Rule of Thumb

If you can't find the power factor and efficiency of a motor, it's a good rule to use this equation:

Estimated true horsepower = (amps x volts) ÷ 1000

Example: Amps =30
volts = 110
stated HP = 4.5
True horsepower = (30 x 110) ÷ 1000
True hp = 3300 ÷ 1000 = 3.3

This estimated 3.3 hp is a lot closer to the real 3.0 hp than the theoretical 4.4 hp (See Chapter 22, "Horse-power" for more.).

Another factor that affects the power output of a motor is the electrical line from the breaker box to the tool. The material the line is made of, the cross-section size of the wire, and length of the line all make a difference. Voltage drop starves a motor by reducing the amount of voltage it receives. (See Chapter 21 "Electricity" for more).

Types of Motors

There are three types of motors commonly used in the workshop: the **universal motor**, the **permanent magnet** motor, and the **induction motor**. The universal motor is commonly utilized in handheld power tools while the induction motor is normally found on stationary tools. Permanent magnet motors are found in battery-powered tools.

Universal Motors

Universal motors get their name from their ability to operate both on direct current (DC), and alternating current (AC). These motors run at a higher speed and are smaller and lighter in weight than induction motors of the same horse-power. Universal motors are used for hand drills, routers, saws, and other tools where high power output and small size is needed.

The speed of universal motors can be varied electronically, and convenient variable-speed controls are part of the appeal of hand tools with these motors. The high speed (5,000-20,000 rpm) combined with the large volume of air pulled through the motor by the cooling fan makes these tools noisier than induction motors. In a universal motor, speed drops rapidly as the load increases. Due in part to the high rpm, the brushes have a limited life, about 300 hours under normal conditions.

Permanent Magnet Motors

Permanent magnet motors are very similar to universal motors. The only real difference is that the field winding is a perma-nent magnet in lieu of an electrical coil. Permanent magnet motors enjoy efficiency even greater than the universal motor because no power is consumed by the field winding. The use of permanent magnets limits the maximum practical size. These motors operate on DC only, although some are operated on AC by passing the current through a full-wave rectifier to convert it to DC. Most are used on cordless tools and powered with battery packs.

Induction Motors

Induction motors are found mostly on stationary tools. They operate only on AC power and normally run at constant speeds of 1,725 or 3,450 rpm. Their operating speed is controlled by the line frequency, so if a 50-Hz induction motor is operated at 60 Hz it will operate 20% faster. Because the speed of an induction motor is regulated by the 50 or 60 Hz line frequency, the speed cannot be adjusted by one of the electronic speed controls commonly used on universal motors. Induction motors are designed to operate at either 120 or 240 volts. Often the wiring can be connected to accept either voltage, and to operate the motor in either direction.

There are several types of induction motors and they all share similar characteristics once they are at operating speed. But, they do differ in the system used to get them up to speed. These differences should be considered when selecting a motor for a specific application (**Figure 219**). Below I discuss some common types of induction motors.

Shaded Pole Induction Motors

These are available for 120 and 240 volt, AC, single-phase applications in sizes ranging from 1/400 to 1/60 hp. The starting torque ranges from 50 to 100% of the full-load torque. This means that this type of motor has relatively low starting power. It takes significantly more force to start a device rotating than it does to maintain running speed. This type of motor would be a good candidate for a tool that rotates freely, but not for a device that is under load at the start.

Shaded pole motors are designed with a winding that offsets the electrical phase. The winding gets the motor started

and remains connected during the normal operation of the motor. These small, low-cost motors with low starting and running torque find applications driving small fans and pumps. The inherent inefficiency of the motors normally requires them to be underwater or to have air flowing over them for cooling.

Split-Phase Induction Motors

These are available for 120 and 240 volt, AC, single-phase applications. They range from $\frac{1}{8}$ to 1 hp. Their starting torque ranges from 130 to 170% of the full load torque. These motors use a separate starting winding that offsets the electrical phase to start them turning. Once

COMPARING TYPES OF MOTORS FOR SHOP APPLICATIONS

Fig. 219 Induction Motor Types

Induction Motor Type	Starting Torque As Percent of Full Load Torque	Comparative Efficiency	Comparative Cost	Typical Uses
Shaded Pole	Very Low 50-100%	Low	Low	Small Direct-Drive Fans & Blowers
Permanent Split Capacitor (PSC)	Low 75-150%	Moderate	Low-Moderate	Direct-drive fans & blowers
Split-Phase	Moderate 130-170%	Moderate	Moderate	Belt-drive & direct drive fans & blowers, small tools, pumps & appliances.
Capacitor Start	Moderate-High 200-400%	Moderate-High	Moderate-High	Pumps, compressors, tools, conveyers, farm equipment & industrial ventilators.
Three-Phase	Moderate-High 200-300%	High	Moderate	Applications where 3-phase power is available.

they are at full speed, the starting winding turns off and they operate as an induction motor. They have moderate starting torque and tend to draw more current than other induction motors while the starting winding is engaged. They are useful for applications such as bench grinders and drill presses that don't require significant force to start rotation.

Capacitor Start Induction Motors

Available for 120 and 240 volt, AC, single-phase application in sizes ranging from $\frac{1}{4}$ to 5 hp. The starting torque ranges from 200 to 400% of the full load torque. Like the split-phase motors, these have a separate starting winding that starts rotation. A large capacitor improves the motor's power function during the starting phase.

When electric current flows through an inductor, the voltage and current are forced out of sync in one direction, which lessens the strength of the motor. A capacitor forces voltage and current out of sync in the opposite direction. This has a dramatic impact on the starting torque, allowing the motor to overcome the force required to rotate large, difficult-to-start items like compressors or conveyers.

Capacitor Start and Run Induction Motors

These motors are similar to the capacitor start motors except they employ a second capacitor in series with the running winding. This capacitor improves the motor's power factor during the running phase, allowing the motor to provide a higher output for a given frame size and input power. They also find application where a higher efficiency is desired. They are available in sizes ranging up to 10 hp.

Three-Phase Induction Motors

These are available for 240 to 480 volt, three-phase applications in sizes ranging from $\frac{1}{3}$ to 400 hp. Their starting torque ranges from 200 to 300% of the full load torque. These motors feature high operating efficiency with moderate initial cost and very low maintenance expense. They have no brushes, starting windings, centrifugal switches, or capacitors. Instead they have three identical windings, each wired to one of the three input power phases. Each of the windings increases in magnetic strength in sequence, causing the rotor to rotate at a speed governed by the frequency of the incoming power line. They are commonly available in the same speeds as other induction motors.

Switching any two leads can reverse three-phase motors, and most can be reversed while in operation. The one major disadvantage of the three-phase motor is that it requires three-phase electricity to operate. Three-phase power is not available in residential arcas, leaving the homeowner to choose between using one of the other types of motor, or using a single-to-three-phase converter.

Choosing the Right Motor

When you need a new motor you might be tempted to use the old, rusty quarter-horsepower motor that came off the washing machine you scrapped years ago. A better idea might be to make a list of what you need in a motor and buy one that fits your requirements.

Electricity

You can buy a motor that runs on alternating current (AC), direct current (DC), or a universal motor that will run on either AC or DC. The voltage supplied and the wire size used to connect your receptacle to the circuit breaker panel might limit the size of the motor that can be used. AC motors come as 120 volt, 240 volt or dual voltage (**Figure 220**). The higher the voltage, the lower the current (amps) required.

Speed

You can buy single-phase motors that operate at 1,140, 1,725 or 3,450 rpm; some motors have multiple speeds. Single-phase is the type of electricity supplied to homeowners.

Horsepower

To determine how much horsepower is needed, check the old motor you're replacing, or if this is a new application, check tool catalogs to see what

Fig 220 Dual-Voltage Motor (120 volt and 240 volt)
THERE ARE TWO IDENTICAL WINDINGS IN A DUAL-VOLTAGE MOTOR. THE STARTING WINDING IS DISENGAGED AFTER START-UP BY THE CENTRIFUGAL SWITCH.

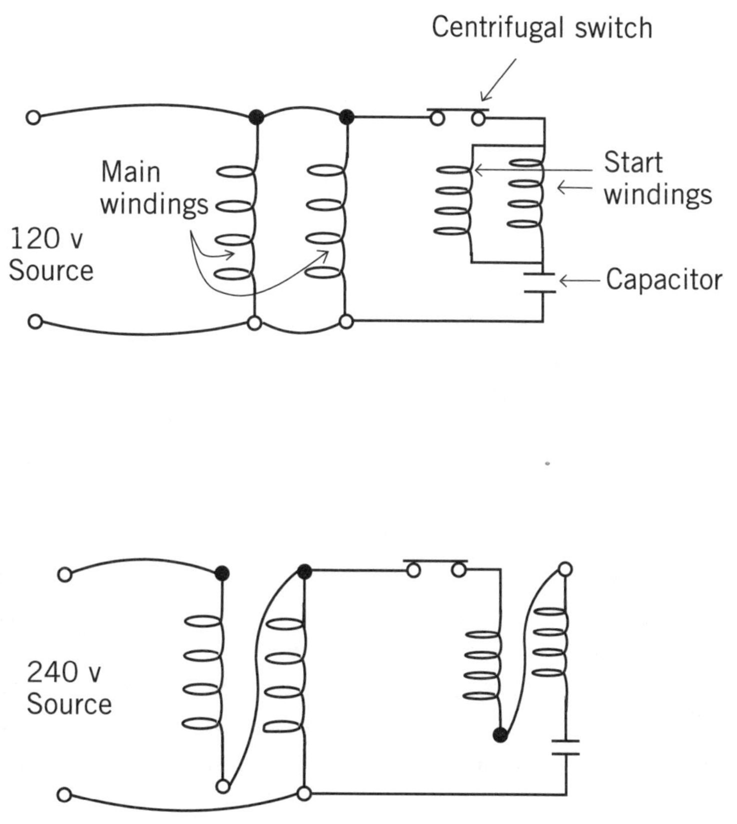

horsepower is required. Motors are rated according to their horsepower:

Power motor—1 hp and higher

Fractional motor—$\frac{1}{8}$ through $\frac{3}{4}$ hp

Micro motor—1/400 through 1/60 hp, for fans and clocks

Motor Enclosures

Motors are sold for different environments. Choose the one that fits your needs.

Open Drip-Proof (DP)

Open drip-proof motors are used in dry, clean areas with good ventilation, usually indoors. If installed outdoors, protect with a cover that does not restrict air flow.

Totally Enclosed (TE)

Use totally enclosed motors in wet, oily, or dirty conditions. There are no ventilation holes in the housing, but it is not airtight or waterproof.

Watertight

Watertight motors are used in submerged situations.

Totally Enclosed, Fan Cooled (TEFC)

TEFC motors include an external fan in a protective shroud to blow air over the motor.

Totally Enclosed, Non-Ventilated (TENV)

TENV motors are not equipped with an external cooling fan, but depend on moving air for cooling.

Totally Enclosed, Air-Over (TEAO)

In TEAO motors, cooling is provided from a driven or external device.

Hazardous Location (Explosion-Proof, EX-PRF)

Explosion-proof, totally enclosed motors have enclosures designed and constructed to withstand an explosion of a specified gas or vapor. The explosion may occur within the machine casing. These motors will withstand an internal explosion of specified gases or vapors, and not allow the internal flame or explosion to escape.

Other Enclosures

You can also buy motors with splash-proof, semi-enclosed, self-cooled, and fan-cooled enclosures.

Frequency

Sixty cycles per second of AC power (60 Hertz) is standard in the United States, and 50 cycles per second (50 Hertz) is standard in Europe and Mexico. Fifty hertz motors can operate on 60 Hz AC power but not visa versa.

Service factor

This is a measure of the reserve margin built into a motor. Rates over 1.0 SF have more than normal margin and are used where unusual conditions such as high voltage fluctuation, overloads, etc., are likely to occur.

Duty cycle

Continuous duty motors can be run for extremely long periods of time. Intermittent motors cost less and are used in most shops.

Horsepower and RPM

In general, both motor price and physical size increase as hp increases and rpm decreases.

Sleeve-bearing motors

Sleeve-bearing motors are used where moderate loads are encountered. They can usually be mounted in any position and are quieter and less expensive than ball-bearing motors.

Ball-bearing motors

Ball-bearing motors are recommended for powering devices that create heavy loads.

Rotation

Rotation is either clockwise (CW) or counter-clockwise (CCW). Some motors are reversible and are marked REV (CW/CCW); the rotation of these motors can be changed (**Figure 221**). The rotation usually is viewed facing the shaft end of the motor. On double shafted motors the rotation is viewed from the lead wire end.

Thermal protection

Motors with automatic reset thermal protection should not be used where the automatic or unexpected starting of a motor would be dangerous. Choose manual reset or thermal cut-off if a motor operates unattended, or where the operator may not detect a locked rotor. Where a hazard exists, use a manual-reset, thermally protected motor. Examples of hazardous restart are shop tools, compressors, conveyers, fans and blowers.

Speed control for induction motors usually is achieved by mechanical means with belts and pulleys. Maintenance is generally easy: blow out the sawdust and add a drop or two of oil. They are remarkably rugged. In woodshops all across the U.S., old motors are in use, salvaged after 20 years in the original household appliance. Induction motors are larger and heavier than universal motors. An induction motor is used on stationary tools because it lasts longer, has a fixed speed, and costs less.

Single-Phase and Three-Phase Motors

In the same electrical system, one, two, or three alternating currents can be generated. These currents, which reverse successively, are called phases. There is only one current supplied in a single-phase system; this is our normal household current. In a three-phase system there are three alternating currents of equal strength differing in phase by 1/3 cycle or 120°.

AC motors are manufactured to run on single-phase or three-phase electrical current (**Figure 222**). A three-phase motor does not require any special electrical components. It has three individual windings, each with its own phase voltage impressed across

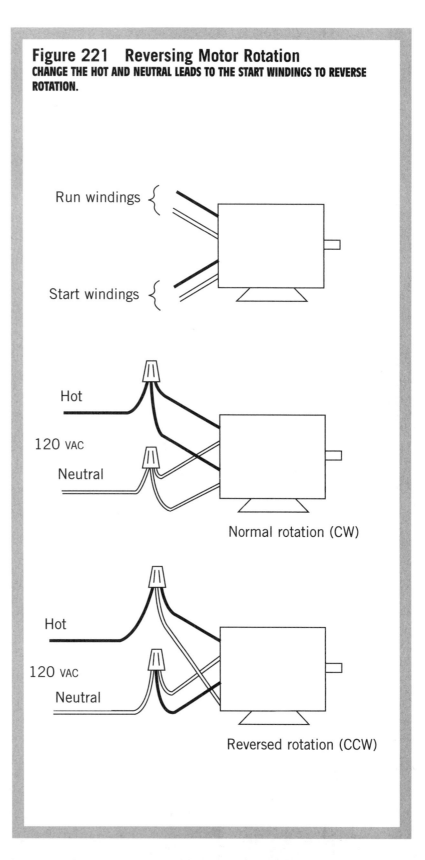

Figure 221   Reversing Motor Rotation
CHANGE THE HOT AND NEUTRAL LEADS TO THE START WINDINGS TO REVERSE ROTATION.

Run windings

Start windings

Hot

120 VAC

Neutral

Normal rotation (CW)

Hot

120 VAC

Neutral

Reversed rotation (CCW)

it. The currents start at different times in each winding as the voltages are introduced. This timing sequence creates a very strong starting torque.

Single-phase motors are practical to about 5 hp; above that they are only marginal, partly because of their great size. For example, a 5-hp motor will weigh 100 LBS., and a 10-hp motor 175 lbs. Also, even at 240 volts, a 5-hp motor draws nearly 21 amps during operation and perhaps 30 amps at start-up, even 60 amps if under load. A 10 hp single-phase motor would need over 40 amps in operation and perhaps 60-120 amps at start up. Most home workshops aren't equipped with 40 or 80 amp circuit breakers, or wired for such heavy electrical loads.

Three-phase motors have several well-known advantages over single-phase motors. They are smaller and simpler in construction than single-phase motors and so are less expensive, more efficient, and less likely to need repair. They have stronger starting torque and higher operating efficiency than single-phase motors of comparable size. They are available in voltages of 208 to 460 volts, therefore they draw less current and require smaller wires, fuses, and switches (for more on this, see *Chapter 21*, "Electricity."). Both types of motors are about the same price up to 1 hp, but after that three-phase motors cost substantially less than similar horsepower single-phase motors. Used three-phase motors and heavy duty industrial machinery are often available at bargain prices. By installing a forward-reverse switch on a three-phase motor, the direction of rotation can be instantly reversed. This is an

COMPARING CAPACITOR START, OPEN DRIP-PROOF SINGLE-PHASE AND THREE-PHASE MOTORS. OVER 2 HP, THE PRICE OF A THREE-PHASE MOTOR IS QUITE A BIT LESS THAN A SINGLE-PHASE MOTOR. SINGLE-PHASE MOTORS BECOME IMPRACTICAL AFTER 5 HP DUE TO PRICE, SIZE, AND HIGH CURRENT DRAW.

Figure 222   Single Phase & 3-Phase Motors *

Hp	Phase	RPM	Volts	Amps	Wt	Cost
1/3	1P	1,725	120/240	6.8/3.4	20 lbs.	$113
	3P	1,725	240/460	1.8/0.9	17	$110
1/2	1P	1,725	120/240	9.6/4.8	22	$129
	3P	1,725	240/460	2.0/1.2	21	$128
3/4	1P	1,725	120/240	11.2/5.6	27	$160
	3P	1,725	240/460	2.8/1.4	23	$143
1	1P	1,725	120/240	13.6/6.8	28	$175
	3P	1,725	220/440	3.4/1.7	26	$167
2	1P	1,725	120/240	22.4/11.2	36	$223
	3P	1,725	220/440	6.0/3.0	34	$175
5	1P	1,740	240	23	83	$298
	3P	1,750	220/440	14.6/7.3	65	$195
10	1P	1,740	240	42.2	144	$570
	3P	1,765	230/460	26.6/13.3	112	$340
20	1P	None				
	3P	1,770	230/460	51.0/25.6	230	$592
25	1P	None				
	3P	1,765	230/460	63.0/31.5	244	$717

*Grainger p.8

advantage, for example, on lathes, shapers, and sanders. This also provides greater flexibility if you build your own machinery, but the extra expense of installing three-phase lines or obtaining phase generators must be considered. Large motors over 5 hp almost always use three-phase power.

Three-Phase Power

There are two ways to get three-phase power: the power company can provide it directly to you, or you can convert single-phase current to produce a facsimile of three-phase power. The power company usually restricts three-phase service lines to industrial and farm locations, so most woodworkers use single-phase motors or convert single-phase current to three-phase with a phase converter. It is important to note that shop generated three-phase power is neither as powerful nor as efficient as that provided by the power company. Still, for many woodworkers, access to a whole world of inexpensive, well-built, powerful industrial motors and machinery is enough to warrant conversion.

Single-phase motors with the correct voltage can operate on a three-phase system when properly connected to any one of the three-phases. However, three-phase motors will not start by themselves on single-phase power unless they are mechanically rotated; more on this later in this chapter.

Static Versus Rotary Converters
Static Phase Converters

Static phase converters are small, lightweight electronic boxes that can be wall-mounted, and are used for only one, or at the most two, small three-phase motors. This type of converter generates a voltage whereby the motor thinks it sees three-phase current, and motors usually only operate at 70-85% of their rated horsepower. For small (up to $1\frac{1}{2}$ hp) three-phase motors that are not under heavy loads, a static converter will work fine. They cost about $100 for a $\frac{3}{4}$-hp box and $140 for a $1\frac{1}{2}$-hp converter. Some machine manufacturers will not warrant any of their motors over 3 hp if they are operated on static converted three-phase electricity.

Rotary Phase Converter

A rotary phase converter (**Figure 224**) is more accurately defined as a phase generator. It generates one voltage, which when paralleled with the two voltages from the single-phase line, produces three-phase power nearly like that supplied by the power company.

Rotary generators, unlike static generators, are large and heavy. A unit large enough to handle one 10-hp motor plus multiple smaller motors up to a total

COMPARING PHASE GENERATORS. MACHINES WITH MOTORS OVER 3 HP CAN ONLY USE ROTARY PHASE GENERATORS TO REMAIN UNDER WARRANTY.

Figure 223 Static and Rotary Phase Generators

Total Hp	Type	Efficiency	Number of 3-Phase Motors	Cost
1	Static	70%	1	$169
	Static	85%	2	$280
	Rotary	100%	3	$410
	Rotary	100%	6	$410
2	Static	70%	1	$179
	Static	85%	2	$335
	Rotary	100%	6	$496
5	Static	70%	1	$250
	Static	85%	2	$400
	Rotary	100%	3	$600
	Rotary	100%	6	$780
10	Static	70%	1	$315
	Static	85%	2	$520
	Rotary	100%	3	$950
	Rotary	100%	6	$1,330

capacity of 25 hp, measures 18 in. W x 21 in. L x 12 in. H and weighs 235 pounds. The multiple three-phase motors feeding off the generator may be operated in any sequence, simultaneously or individually, and stopped and restarted at will. This generator costs $2250.

Make Your Own

Rather than buying a three-phase converter, it is possible to make your own as described in The Workshop Book, where a dedicated three-phase motor is used as a generator (**Figure 224**). This slave motor must be at least as big as the biggest three-phase motor in the shop. Single-phase power is supplied to the slave on two hot wires with a separate ground. The slave is mechanically set in rotation either with a starter rope wrapped around the shaft or with a single-phase starter motor and a rubber wheel. I've even watched a friend start his slave by nudging the pulley a few times with his foot; it doesn't take much to get one started.

Once in motion, the starter motor (or rope or foot) is disengaged and the slave continues to operate on single-phase current because it is under no load. The rotation of the slave generates a third leg of electricity which is then directed to the other three-phase motor (or motors) in the shop.

In use, both the rotary phase generator and the homemade generator need safety switches, fuses, circuit breakers, junction boxes, and magnetic starter switches. Note that these were omitted from the drawings for simplicity (**Figure 225**).

Figure 224   Generating Three-Phase Electricity

SINGLE-PHASE, 240-VOLT AC CURRENT IS PROVIDED TO THE PHASE GENERATOR OR THE HOMEMADE DEVICE TO PRODUCE THREE-PHASE, 240-VOLT AC CURRENT FOR USE IN THE WORKSHOP.

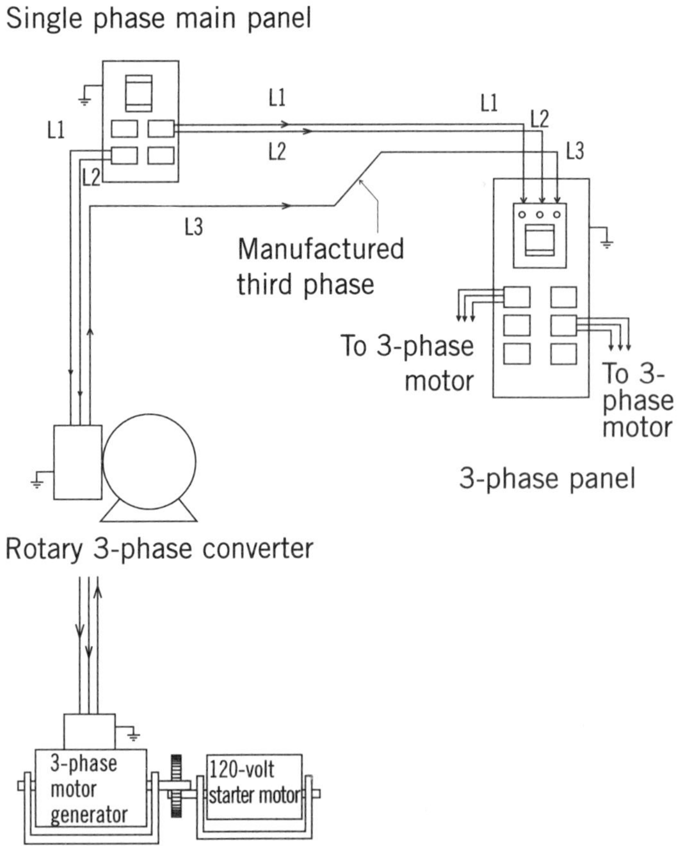

Variable Speed

Many tools can be purchased today with variable speeds—with both direct and alternating current motors.

Direct Current Motors

Solid state controllers create direct current (DC) from ordinary single-phase AC current. Tools with variable speed DC motors can thus be plugged into household current. This requires both a controller and a DC motor.

Alternating Current Motors

Because the speed of an induction-type AC motor is controlled by the cycle rate of the current (Hertz), slowing the cycle rate slows the speed of the motor. For variable-speed AC, a solid-state single-phase controller is attached to a standard three-phase motor. The controller takes normal single-phase 60-cycle (60 Hz) house current and delivers three-phase current at any cycle rate, usually between 4 and 60 cycles. Slowing the

cycle rate slows the motor speed.

References:

Grainger Industrial & Commercial Equipment (Motors)

J & L Industrial Supply (Phase Converters)

The Workshop Book, The Taunton Press, 1991, p.99 (Homemade Generator)

Figure 225   Three-Phase Converter Wiring Diagram
SINGLE-PHASE 240-VOLT AC CURRENT IS CONVERTED TO 240-VOLT THREE-PHASE CURRENT.

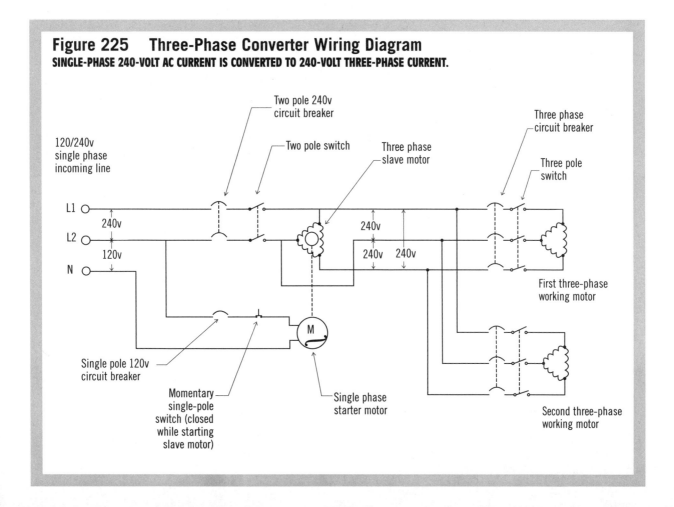

CHAPTER 21

Electricity & 120 volts vs 240 volts

Woodworkers use electricity every day without giving much thought to watts, amps, or volts. That is, until a table saw stalls due to a line voltage drop or the question of rewiring a 120-volt motor to enable it to use 240 volts comes up. Everyone should know the complex relationships of horsepower, voltage, and other components of electricity.

Electric Components

The four main components of electricity are:

Power (P)—measured in watts (W) (consumed energy)

Current (I)—measured in amps (flow)

Pressure (E)—measured in volts (stored energy)

Resistance (R)—measured in ohms (loss)

They are related thus:

Power (watts) = current (amps) x voltage (volts)

$$P = IE$$

Current (amps) = power (watts) ÷ voltage (volts)

$$I = P \div E$$

Voltage (volts) = power (watts) ÷ current (amps)

$$E = P \div I$$

Resistance (ohms) = voltage (volts) ÷ current (amps)

$$R = E \div I$$

AC and DC— Forms of Electric Energy

Electric energy is used as direct current (DC) or as alternating current (AC) and is almost always converted to heat, light, or magnetism. In a DC circuit, the electric current flows continuously in the same direction, and the electric pressure or voltage is applied in the same direction. All electric batteries provide direct current and electric generators may be built to produce direct current.

A few shop tools, like some wood lathes, have DC motors. One advantage of DC motors is that speed (RPM) can be moderated with an electronic control instead of mechanically changing pulleys and belts. Also, a DC motor can be reversed—a very nice feature, for example, on a lathe, where final sanding can be done while the turning spins in the opposite direction. Some DC motors can be plugged into the regular 120 volt AC outlets. See Chapter 19 for more on Motors.

Most homes and workshops are equipped with alternating current (AC), and most of our motors and appliances run on AC. In the AC circuit, the electric current, and thus the electric pressure, reverses periodically, usually 120 times per second. The number of double reversals, or cycles per second, is called the frequency. The standard in the United States is 120 volts AC and 60 cycles (60 hertz) per second.

In Europe and Mexico, the standard is 240 volts AC and a current frequency of 50 cycles (50 hertz) per second. A 50-hertz (hz) motor operated on 60-hz current will run cooler, about 20% faster and more efficiently. But trying to operate a 60-hz motor on 50-hz current will cause overheating and perhaps motor failure.

The voltage of AC circuits can be raised by transformers for transmission over a distance, then lowered for immediate use. AC circuits are more flexible in application and for this reason all large electric generating systems produce AC. Where DC is required, it is produced from AC by rotary transforming devices (converters or rectifiers).

To understand how electricity moves through a wire, imagine water flowing through a pipe. The energy causing the electric current to flow is measured in **volts**. The amount of current that flows through the wire is measured in **amps**. Electric power, the energy produced by the electrical current, is expressed in **watts**. For our purposes, the relationship among these units is represented by Watt's law:

Energy x Current = Power
      or
Volts x Amps = Watts

Using our water analogy, electrical voltage is equivalent to water pressure, and electrical current is equivalent to water flow. Both flowing water and moving electricity must overcome resistance—with water it's the pipe, with electricity it's the conductor. Both water and electricity follow the path of least resistance.

Resistance

All electric current that leaves a power source like a battery or generator, returns—none is lost. If one ampere flows out of the battery, one ampere flows through the circuit, and one ampere returns to the battery. When electricity flows through a wire, the wire has some resistance, and this resistance converts some electric energy into heat. The longer the wire, the more energy is lost for a given amount of current. The energy used in creating this heat causes a voltage drop in the wire, leaving less voltage to perform the work required. For example, 120 volts is supplied to your home. If you plug in a large, motor-driven device using a long extension cord, the voltage reaching the motor might only be 100 volts due to the energy consumed by the wire. As a result, the motor does not have the voltage it was designed for and lacks power.

Every material has some opposition to current flow, whether large or small, and this opposition is called resistance. Even the best conductors have some resistance that restricts the flow of electric current. The resistance of any object, such as a wire conductor, depends on four factors: the material the object is made with, its length, its cross-sectional area, and its temperature.

Material

Certain materials, usually metals, are said to be good conductors, i.e., they have low resistance. Other materials are poor conductors, for example, wood, rubber, and cloth. These materials are said to be insulators.

Figure 241 shows the relative electrical resistance of a few fairly common metals. The higher the resistance of the metal, the more power is consumed by the wire itself and the higher the voltage drop. As power is consumed by the wire, it heats up and the temperature rating of the insulation then becomes a factor. You can see that silver, copper, tungsten, and gold are the best conductors on this list. With equal lengths and cross-sectional areas of copper and aluminum wire, voltage drop due to resistance will be higher in the aluminum wire.

Length

The longer the length of a wire, the greater the resistance it will offer to electric current flow; the shorter the length, the lower the resistance. Doubling the length of a piece of copper wire doubles the resistance.

Cross-Sectional Area

Another factor affecting the resistance of a conductor is its cross-sectional area. The larger the cross-sectional area of a conductor, the lower the resistance. The smaller the cross-sectional area, the higher the resistance. Doubling the cross-sectional area allows current flow to double.

Temperature

The final factor affecting the resistance of a conductor is its temperature (**Figure 242**). For most materials, the hotter the material, the more resistance it offers to the flow of an electric current. The colder the

RESISTANCE MEASURED IN OHMS IN 14-GAUGE WIRE. THE HIGHER THE RESISTANCE, THE HIGHER THE VOLTAGE DROP.

Fig. 241 Resistance of Various Metals *

	Ohms Per 1000 Feet
Silver	2.39
Copper	2.53
Tungsten	3.07
Gold	3.57
Aluminum	4.14
Magnesium	6.74
Zinc	8.42
Brass	10.3
Nickel	11.4
Iron	14.6
Platinum	14.6
Steel **	15
Tin	16.8
Lead	32.2

* In 14-Ga wire
** Steel is an average

THOUGH NOT AS IMPORTANT AS LENGTH, AREA, AND MATERIAL, TEMPERATURE ALSO AFFECTS RESISTANCE.

Figure 242   Effect of Temperature on Resistance in 14-ga Copper Wire

Temp	32 deg F.	68 deg F.	122 deg F.	167 deg F.
Ohms per 1000 Ft.	2.33	2.53	2.82	3.07
Ohms per Foot	0.00233	0.00253	0.00282	0.00307

material, the less resistance it offers to the flow. The effect of temperature on resistance is the least important of the four factors controlling resistance—material, length, cross-sectional area and temperature—although resistance does increase by about 10% in a 14-ga copper wire going from 68° F. to 122° F.

2.53 ÷ 2.82 x 100 = 90%

There is little the average woodworker can do about the material a wire is made of (usually copper), or about the temperature.

Electric Components

The four main components of electricity (**Figure 243**) are:

Power (P)—measured in watts (W) (consumed energy)

Current (I)—measured in amps (flow)

Pressure (E)—measured in volts (stored energy)

Resistance (R)—measured in ohms (loss)

They are related thus:

Power (watts) = current (amps) x voltage (volts)

P = IE

Current (amps) = power (watts) ÷ voltage (volts)

I = P ÷ E

Voltage (volts) = power (watts) ÷ current (amps)

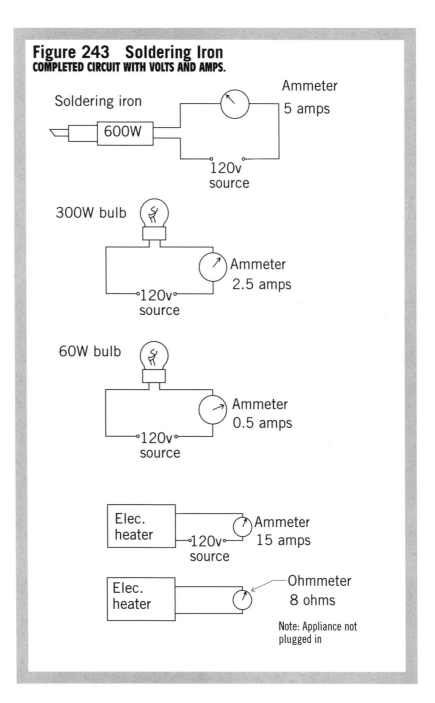

Figure 243   Soldering Iron
COMPLETED CIRCUIT WITH VOLTS AND AMPS.

Soldering iron — 600W — Ammeter 5 amps — 120v source

300W bulb — Ammeter 2.5 amps — 120v source

60W bulb — Ammeter 0.5 amps — 120v source

Elec. heater — Ammeter 15 amps — 120v source

Elec. heater — Ohmmeter 8 ohms

Note: Appliance not plugged in

E = P ÷ I

Resistance (ohms) = voltage (volts) ÷ current (amps)

R = E ÷ I

746 watts = 1 horsepower

Watts

Using the equations above, how much power is required to heat a soldering iron operating at 120 volts and drawing 5 amps?

Using Watt's law:
Power = current x voltage
Power = 5 amperes x 120 volts
= 600 watts

Amps

How much current (amps) does a 300-watt light bulb draw at 120 volts?

Current = power ÷ voltage
Current = 300 ÷ 120 = 2.5 amps

Volts

We put an ammeter, which measures current flow in amps, in line with a 60-watt light bulb. What is the voltage if the ammeter reads 0.5 amps?

Voltage = power ÷ current
Volts = 60 watts ÷ 0.5 amps

Volts = 120 volts

Resistance

An electric heater draws 15 amps at 120 volts. What is the line resistance?

Resistance = voltage ÷ current
Resistance = 120 volts ÷ 15 amps
Resistance = 8 ohms
Note: Resistance is measured with appliance unplugged.

Horsepower

A 120-volt motor draws 15 amps. What is the horsepower of the motor?

Power = 15 x 120 = 1800 watts
1 horsepower = 746 watts
Watts ÷ 746 = hp
1800 ÷ 746 = 2.41 hp

This is close to the listed 2.5 hp, assuming 100% efficiency, but because most motors achieve only 50-80% efficiency,

a more meaningful equation for horsepower is:

1 horsepower = 1000 watts
Watts ÷ 1000 = hp
1800 ÷ 1000 = 1.8 hp

This equation assumes 75% efficiency, and 1.8 hp is a little shy of the stated 2.5 hp. (See Chapter 22 on Horsepower for more on this).

120 Volts Versus 240 Volts

Some motors are designed to run on either 120 or 240 volts as shown in **Figure 244**. When the 1.5-hp motor is wired to run on 120 volts it needs three wires: one hot, one neutral, and, for safety, a ground. Wired at 240 volts, the same 1.5-hp motor also needs three wires: two hot, and a ground for safety. In each case only two wires are needed to carry current. The ground wires carry no current but are necessary to hold the frame of the motor at zero voltage in case of an electrical shortage or fault. To prevent shock, always use the ground wire on power tools.

At 120 volts, both the hot and neutral wires must be large enough to carry 16 amps. When wired at 240 volts, the two hot wires should be of sufficient size to carry 8 amps. You've probably heard of

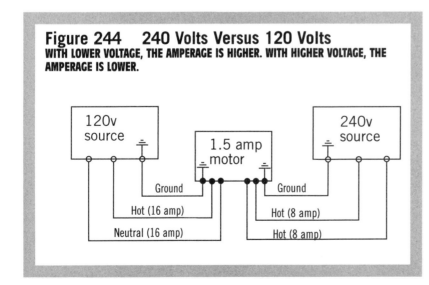

Figure 244   240 Volts Versus 120 Volts
WITH LOWER VOLTAGE, THE AMPERAGE IS HIGHER. WITH HIGHER VOLTAGE, THE AMPERAGE IS LOWER.

someone who rewired his shop so a dual voltage motor (120/240) could run on 240 volts instead of 120 volts, and the motor now runs cooler, has more power, costs less to operate, and is going to last longer. True? Maybe yes, maybe no. Let's look at the facts.

Power

The power is the same whether the motor runs on 120 or 240 volts. Power equals voltage times current, and a motor that draws 16 amps at 120 volts, draws only 8 amps at 240 volts.

Power (watts) = volts x current
Power = 120 volts x 16 amps = 1920 watts
Power = 240 volts x 8 amps = 1920 watts

Torque

The torque, or twisting force, produced is identical at 120 and 240 volts.

Speed

The motor speed is the same at 120 and 240 volts. If the motor runs at 1725 rpm on 120 volts, it will run at 1725 rpm on 240 volts.

Runs Cooler

A motor operating at 240 volts might run cooler than the same motor at 120 volts if the wire from the service panel were undersized. A motor will run hotter if it receives less than its full voltage as designated. Line voltage drop is dependent on amperage (voltage drop + amps x resistance) and a motor operating at 240 volts draws one-half the amperage that the same motor draws at 120 volts. An undersize wire affects the 120 volt motor more than the 240 volt motor in this respect.

Lasts Longer

The 240-volt motor might last longer because of the reduced amperage and less heat, but with motors lasting 15 to 20 years, you'll probably be ready to trade a machine off and move up before the motor wears out.

Costs Less to Operate

Utility companies charge by watts and kilowatts. Watts are figured by multiplying voltage times amperage. If a motor operating on 120 volt and 16 amps is rewired to operate on 240 volt and 8 amps, there is no difference in watts, thus no difference in operating cost.

There are, however, some differences between 120- and 240-volt circuits.

1) A 240-volt circuit can support a larger, more powerful motor.
Under normal circumstances a 16-amp, 120-volt circuit can serve a 2.5-hp motor.
Power = volts x current
Power = 120 x 16 = 1920 watts

A CIRCUIT WITH 14-GAUGE WIRE, COMMON INSULATION AND LIMITED TO 3 CONDUCTORS SHOULD BE PROTECTED WITH A 15-AMP BREAKER.

Figure 245
Allowable Capacity of Copper Wire

Gauge Size	Allowable Capacity of Copper Wire (1)
0	170 Amps
2	130
4	95
6	75
8	55
10	30
12	20
14	15

(1) Based on Common Insulation Rated at 90 Deg C./194 deg F. and number of Conducting Wires limited to 3.

746 watts = 1 hp (at 100% efficiency)
1920 watts ÷ 746 = 2.5 hp

By converting the circuit to 240 volts, the same 16-amp circuit can supply energy to a 5-hp motor.

Power = volts x current
Power = 240 x 16 = 3840 watts
746 watts = 1 hp (at 100% efficiency)
3840 watts ÷ 746 = 5.1 hp

Note: In this case, the current remains the same when we change from 120 to 240 volts, and from a 2.5 hp to a 5-hp motor. The wires from the source to the motor need not be changed because the current is the same even though the motor is twice as large.

2) The loss in line voltage (voltage drop) is less on a 240-volt circuit.
Because a 240-volt motor draws one-half the current, the circuit will have one-half the voltage drop that the same motor would have operating on 120 volts. The electrical line can also be twice the length for the 240-volt motor.

Voltage drop = current x resistance

3) Current starvation is less on a 240 volt circuit.
Because the current drawn by a 240-volt motor is one-half the current drawn at 120 volts, start-up or inrush current drop is also one-half. There will be fewer slow starts.

4) In a 240-volt line there is less chance of a circuit breaker tripping.
If a 120-volt motor stalls momentarily, the inrush current may trip the circuit breaker. Because the current drawn by a 240-volt motor is one-half that of the same motor operating on 120 volts, there is less chance of tripping the circuit breaker.

5) It costs less to wire for 240 volts.
The size of the wire from the electric service panel to the machine depends on current, not voltage. Less amperage means a cheaper and smaller diameter wire can be used.

In summary, an **example** might help clarify. If you have a receptacle that is connected to the circuit breaker panel with 100 ft. (200 ft., counting both wires) of 12-ga copper wire, then:

When wired for 120-volt service, the receptacle would normally be protected with a 20-ampere circuit breaker. If you connect a $1\frac{1}{2}$-hp motor to this circuit and run only that motor, the voltage on that circuit will measure 120 volts with the motor turned off. With the motor running under full load, it will draw 20 amperes. With 20 amperes flowing through the wires, a voltage drop of 6.6 volts will occur. This will reduce the voltage to the motor from 120 volts to 113 volts, a 5.5% reduction.

Voltage drop (VD)
= current x resistance
Resistance for 12 ga wire
= 1.65 ohms/1000 ft.
(see **Figure 246**)
VD = 20 amps
x [(1.65 x 200) ÷ 1000]
VD = 20 x .33 = 6.6 volts

If you used the same size wiring but rewired the receptacle for 240 volts, the same 1½-hp motor would draw 10 amperes under full load. With 10 amperes flowing through the wire, a voltage drop of 3.3 volts will occur. This would reduce the voltage to the motor from 240 volts to 237 volts, a 1.4% reduction. The motor operating from a 240-volt source and receiving 99% of its rated voltage will run cooler, have more reserve power, and last longer than the same motor operating from 120 volts and receiving just 95% of its rated voltage.

Whether the change is worth the cost will depend on a number of factors. These include: How well are the tools with large motors currently operating? Is the size of the wire in the circuit too small to adequately carry the current? How far are the tools from the

service entrance? And, how many tools are expected to be connected to the new 240-volt service? Probably the only valid reason to rewire a 120-volt motor to run on 240 volts and use the same wiring is if the motor is starved for voltage. The 240-volt line will use one-half the amperage and voltage drop will also be one-half. Note that you'll need an electrician to change the circuit from 120 volt to 240 volt in the main entrance panel.

Choosing motor voltage is mostly a matter of motor size. A rule of thumb is $^3/_4$ hp and smaller motors can easily be run on 120 volts. The convenience of being able to plug these tools into 120-volt plug outlets allows a lot of flexibility and most shops, garages, and homes have more standard 120-volt outlets.

Machines and tools with motors of 1½ hp and larger should be run on 240 volts because when run at 120 volts, the amperage of these larger motors is high and needs larger gauge wire than is normally run residentially.

One-hp motors can be wired to run either way—it comes down to a matter of preference and convenience.

Voltage Drop and Wire Size

Did you ever wonder why your circular saw lacks power when you're in the backyard working at the end of a 50-ft. extension cord? And why does the cord seem warm to the touch? Voltage drop starves a motor of power, and line resistance creates heat in the cord.

Resistance (Ohms) x Current (Amps) = Voltage Drop

All electrical conductors have resistance, therefore the voltage available at the working end of the wire is always less than at the source. Voltage drop depends on resistance, which is a function of the type of metal, cross-section, and the length of

DIFFERENT SIZE (GAUGE) COPPER WIRES OFFER DIFFERENT RESISTANCE TO ELECTRIC CURRENT.

Figure 246 Resistance of Copper Wire

Diameter in Inches	Gauge	Ohms per 1000 Ft. [1]
0.324	0	0.102
0.276	2	0.162
0.232	4	0.259
0.192	6	0.411
0.160	8	0.657
0.128	10	1.036
0.104	12	1.650
0.080	14	2.621
0.064	16	4.174
0.048	18	6.636

(1) Measured at 70 deg. F.

the wire. Most homes and shops use copper wire, therefore we need concern ourselves only with the other two variables: wire size and length. **Figure 246** shows the resistance of different gauges (sizes) of copper wire.

Note that the larger the wire, the less the resistance, and thus the greater the conductivity. Using the data from this table we can calculate the voltage drop and determine what gauge wire to use.

Most appliances and tools are designed for a +/- 10% variation in voltage. This means a 120-volt unit can operate safely when the voltage is between 90% and 110% of the rated voltage.

120 volts x 0.9
= 108 volts (minimum voltage)
120 volts x 1.1
= 132 volts (maximum voltage)

However, when designing an electrical circuit or buying wire for an extension cord, you should choose a wire gauge that keeps the voltage drop to 5% or less.

120 volts x 0.95
= 114 volts (Minimum Voltage)
120 volts x 1.05
= 126 volts (Maximum Voltage)

Power companies supply power to homeowners varying between 114 and 126 volts.

Recently, with power shortages, power suppliers have suggested lowering voltage to 110 to save energy.

Example: We need to run a 3-wire line (hot, neutral, and ground) 125 ft. to serve a 20 amp, 120-volt motor. We also want to keep the voltage drop to 5% (6 volts) or less.

First calculate the amount of line resistance that such a circuit can tolerate.

Resistance
Resistance
  = (voltage drop ÷ current)
Resistance = 6 ÷ 20 = 0.3 ohms

In the circuit we will have to limit the resistance to 0.3 ohms over 250 ft.—125 ft. there and 125 ft. back. The chart in Figure 6 lists resistance in ohms per 1000 ft. To convert ohms/250 ft. to ohms/1000 ft., multiply by 1000/250:

0.3 ohms x 1000 ÷ 250
    = 0.3 x 4 = 1.2 ohms/1000 ft.

Figure 246 shows 10-ga copper wire has 1.036 ohms/1000 ft; 12-ga wire is listed at 1.650 ohms/1000 ft. Choose 10-ga copper wire for the circuit. This will limit the voltage drop in our line to 6 volts.

Resistance with Maximum Voltage Drop

A general formula for finding resistance in a copper wire and limiting the voltage drop is:

Resistance = (voltage drop ÷ current) x (1000 ÷ distance x 2)

The answer is in ohms/1000 feet. Find the proper gauge copper wire by consulting **Figure 246**.

A general formula for finding resistance in a copper wire where the voltage drop is limited to 5% of a 120-volt circuit is:

Resistance = 3000 ÷ (current x distance)

3000 is a combined constant which converts the distance (from outlet to motor and back) into feet of wire. It also converts ohms to ohms-per-1000 ft. and incorporates the 5% voltage drop. Find the proper gauge copper wire by consulting **Figure 246**.

Now, back to the problem. Given: Amps = 20, volts = 120, voltage drop = 6, distance = 125 ft.

> **Resistance = 3000 ÷ (current x distance)**
> Resistance = 3000 ÷ (20 x 125)
> Resistance = 3000 ÷ 2500 = 1.2 ohms/1000 ft.

Therefore we would use 10-ga copper wire.

Some experts recommend building in a 150% safety factor for current surges during start-up (inrush) or heavy loads. This can be done by multiplying the current by 150% and doing the calculations.

In the previous problem we needed to run a circuit 125 ft. to serve a 20-amp, 120-volt motor. We also wanted to keep the voltage drop to 5% (6 volts) or less. Now we want to build in a 150% safety factor to handle heavy current surges.

Resistance with Maximum Voltage Drop and 150% Safety Factor

Resistance = [voltage drop ÷ (current x safety factor)] x (1000 ÷ distance x 2)

Given: Amps = 20, safety factor = 1.5, volts = 120, voltage drop = 6, distance = 125 ft.
Resistance = 6 ÷ (20 x 1.5) x [1000 ÷ (125 x 2)]
Resistance = 0.20 x 4 = 0.8 ohms/1000 ft.

Figure 246 shows 10-ga wire at 1.04 ohms/1000 ft., which is too small. An 8-ga wire is listed at 0.66 ohms/1000 ft. Choose 8-ga copper wire for the circuit. This will limit the voltage drop to 6 volts and provide a 150% safety factor for current surges.

The following equations will also do the calculations:

For a 120-Volt Circuit:
    Resistance = 2000 ÷ (Distance x Current)

2000 is a combined constant that converts the distance (from outlet to motor and back) into feet of wire. It also converts ohms to ohms-per-1000 ft., incorporates the maximum 6-volt line drop, and incorporates a 150% current surge protection.

Problem 2

A 15-in. planer rated at 15.5 amps needs to be hard wired. It is 75 ft. from the 120-volt source. We want a maximum 5% voltage drop and 150% current surge protection.

Answer 2

Resistance = voltage drop ÷ (current x 1.5) x [1000 ÷ (distance x 2)]
Resistance = 120 x 0.05 ÷ (15.5 x 1.5) x (1000 ÷ 75 x 2)
Resistance = (6 ÷ 23.25) x 6.67 = 1.72 ohms

Figure 246 shows that a 12-ga wire rated at 1.65 ohms/1000 ft. would suffice.

For a 240-Volt Circuit
Resistance = 4000 ÷ (distance x current)

Problem 3

A 240-volt, 5-hp motor is 75 ft. from the electrical source. What size wire is needed if we want to maintain a 5% or less voltage drop and have a 150% current surge safety factor?

Answer 3

1 hp = 1000 watts

5-hp motor = 5 x 1000
         = 5000 watts

Current = watts ÷ volts

Current = 5000 ÷ 240
        = 20.8 amps

Note: If the current (amps) is

listed on the motor nameplate, this is a more reliable value than calculating it from horsepower. Using hp = 1000 watts instead of the theoretical 746 watts recognizes that no motor is 100% efficient.

Resistance =
    4000 ÷ (distance x current)
Resistance =
    4000 ÷ (75 x 20.8)=2.56 ohms

Figure 246 shows a 12-ga wire rated at 1.65 ohms/1000 ft. is needed.

FIND THE DISTANCE AND THE AMPERAGE DRAWN TO CHOOSE THE CORRECT WIRE SIZE.

Figure 247 Copper Wire Gauge (120 Volt Circuits)

Amps	125 ft.	100 ft.	75 ft.	50 ft.	25 ft.	15 ft.
0.1 — 2.0	18	18	18	18	18	18
2.1 — 3.5	16	18	18	18	18	18
3.6 — 5.0	14	16	16	18	18	18
5.1 — 7.0	12	14	14	16	16	16
7.1—10	12	12	14	16	16	16
10.1—13	10	10	12	14	14	14
13.1—16	8	10	12	12	12	12
16.1—20.	8	10	10	12	12	12

Built in: 150% Safety Factor (amps x 1.5)
Built in: Double Wire distance (To and From)
Built in: 5% maximum voltage drop (6v.)

R = 2000 / Distance x current

Figures 247 & 248 show the minimum size copper wire to use on 120- or 240-volt systems based on current (amperage) drawn and distance (feet). The smaller the wire size (gauge), the greater the resistance. This chart is calculated with a safety factor of 150% of the amps and limits line voltage drop to 5%.

Example: We want to paint the back fence using an air compressor that draws 15 amps at 120 volts. The distance is 70 feet. What gauge wire should be used in the extension cord?

FIND THE DISTANCE AND THE AMPERAGE DRAWN TO CHOOSE THE CORRECT WIRE SIZE.

Figure 248 Copper Wire Gauge (240 Volt Circuits)

Amps	125 Ft.	100 Ft.	75 Ft.	50 Ft.	25 Ft.	15 Ft.
0.1 — 2.0	18	18	18	18	18	18
2.1 — 3.5	18	18	18	18	18	18
3.6 — 5.0	18	18	18	18	18	18
5.1 — 7.0	16	16	16	16	16	16
7.1—10	14	16	16	16	16	16
10.1—13	14	14	14	14	14	14
13.1—16	12	14	14	14	14	14
16.1—20	12	12	12	12	14	14

Built in: 150% Safety Factor (amps x 1.5)
Built in: Double Wire distance (To and From)
Built in: 5% maximum voltage drop (12 v.)

R = 2000 / Distance x current

Figure 247 shows a 12-ga wire should be used.

Example: A 240-volt air compressor draws 15 amps. We need a 100-ft. cord. What size wire should be used?

Figure 248 shows 14 ga.

Electrical Shock and Safety

Leakage Current

Everyone, at one time or another, has experienced a tingle from an electrical tool. Although not painful, it could be an indication that the device is defective and should be repaired or replaced.

Under normal circumstances, electric power goes in one wire and out the other and is kept within proper bounds with insulation around all the current-carrying parts. When the insulation becomes defective, the electricity is free to seek another direction. At this point, an operator may feel only a slight tickle until a grounded object is touched. The current now has found a new path and part of the electricity will travel through the operator to ground. The amount of shock received depends on how defective the tool is and how well grounded the user is. The current that flows from the defective tool is called leakage current.

The skin offers a barrier to the flow of leakage current and a hazard doesn't exist until the voltage exceeds about 24 volts. At 120 volts—normal house voltage—current can easily pass through the skin. Once it starts to flow, the skin's resistance decreases, allowing even more electricity to pass through the body.

Threshold of Perception

One milliampere (1/1000 of an amp) will be felt as a slight tingling sensation to a person standing on a dry wooden floor. Not bothered by it, he may continue to use the defective tool until he happens to touch a grounded object. Now, he has completed the circuit to ground and a much larger current will flow through his body.

Shock Hazard

If only 5 milliamps (1/42 of the current required to light a 25-watt lamp) flow through his body, there will be a violent muscle reaction, throwing him away from the equipment, probably with some injury. Some 30,000 people in the U.S. are hurt each year like this.

Dangerous Shock Hazard

If the current is much above 10 milliamps, the person will not be able to release his grip on the electrical tool. While the heart usually continues to function, fatigue sets in, followed by death when no help is available.

Lethal Shock Hazard

At about 100 milliamps (less than half that used by a 25-watt lamp) ventricular fibrillation occurs, the muscle fibers lose control, and the heart is no longer able to pump blood. The levels of current for

Rule of Thumb

As discussed in Motors, *Chapter 20*, internal out-of-phase voltage and current (the power factor) reduces the power output from an induction motor. You can't do much about this, but you can avoid adding to the problem. A coiled wire also forces the passing voltage and current out-of-phase, so when you're using a long extension cord, uncoil it. By leaving it in the reel, you reduce the motor's power.

perception, let-go, and ventricular fibrillation vary widely from person to person. The above figures are based on the standard reactions of normal, healthy individuals. The effect of electrical shocks to children, the sick, or elderly is more severe. Even small shocks can startle a person causing him to spill hot liquid, fall from a ladder, or jump back into a greater hazard. Underwriter's Laboratory recommends maximum leakage current of 0.5 milliamps.

Rule of Thumb

For your own safety, **ALWAYS** disconnect the electricity before you change cutters or do any work inside any shop machine. Don't rely on someone else to turn off the power— make sure of your own safety by pulling the plug or throwing the cricuit breaker for yourself.

Making Sure the Tool is Safe
Use a Three-wire, Grounded Outlet.

The three-wire, grounded outlet has two wires to carry electricity, with one wire connected to ground. The third wire in a tool cord is connected directly to the tool housing (the part you hold in your hand) and then to ground through the grounded outlet. If there is a short circuit in the tool, the leakage current drains to ground through the third wire and not through the operator. This is because the third wire is a better conductor than you are—unless you're standing there naked, dripping wet, and in a pool of water.

The ground wire normally provides a safe drain for the leakage current. If the ground wire becomes defective, or is not connected because of an adapter plug, or because the third prong of the tool plug has been cut off, this leakage will pass through anyone coming in contact with the tool and a grounded metal object.

All metal stationary shop tools should be considered grounded. If the motor on a floor tool shorts, the third wire conducts the leakage current safely to ground. This same safety feature on the floor tool can be lethal if a hand tool shorts and you touch the metal floor tool.

Use Double-Insulated Tools

Double-insulated tools are those designed with normal insulation around the internal wires plus a second insulation outside. The internal workings are encased in a heavy plastic enclosure to provide a second or double insulation. In drills, even the chuck is insulated with plastic around the shaft. Such insulation provides excellent protection from leakage current. Unfortunately, higher cost limits the number of double-insulated tools available to the woodworker. You can distinguish the double-insulated tools because they have plastic housings and two-prong plugs.

When a Shock Occurs

When you feel that little tingle, what do you do? Immediately lay the tool down and unplug it. Now, write "SHORT" on a piece of masking tape and wrap it around the plug so anyone trying to use the tool will see the warning. If the tool is old and you were about to replace it anyway, toss it. If it's worth fixing or it's still under warranty, return the tool to the dealer. A normal shop volt meter isn't sensitive enough to measure small amounts of current leakage. You can check for a major short with the tool unplugged. Use an ohm meter to test for continuity between each of the prongs (not the grounded one) and the body of the tool. If the insulation is still good, there should be no electrical connection between the metal body of the tool and the inside wiring.

References
Electrical Shock and Safety, Fred Sotcher.

CHAPTER 22

Horsepower—Real & Imagined

Horsepower measurements by manufacturers are confusing to woodworkers. A small, 5-gallon shop vacuum is advertised as having a 5 hp-motor. How can this be? Learn to figure horsepower yourself using voltage and amperage and bypass the advertising hype.

The best way to compare the power of electric tools or motors is horsepower. One horsepower is the force required to lift a 550-lb. weight one foot in one second. Motors are usually rated by amperage, voltage, and, sometimes, horsepower. The U.S. government specifies that the true voltage and current must be listed for electric motors, but does not specify how horsepower will be measured and not all tool manufacturers measure horsepower the same way.

Power (watts) = volts x current (amps)
1000 watts = 1 horsepower (assuming 75% efficiency)

Using these formulas it is obvious that a shop vacuum rated at 6 amps and 120 volts cannot have a 5-hp motor as the manufacturer claims.

Power = 120 volts x 6 amps = 720 watts
720 watts ÷ 1000 = 0.72 hp

How does the $\frac{3}{4}$-hp motor somehow become 5-hp in the interval between manufacturing and advertising? Let's review some pertinent history first.

The Scottish inventor James Watt (1736-1819), patented an improved version of the steam engine in 1769, and together with partner, Matthew Boulton, started a manufacturing plant near Birmingham, England in 1775. Humans and horses provided most of the mechanical work in England

Definitions of Horsepower

Power = Work over a period of Time

1 Horsepower = 33,000 ft. lbs/min.

1 Horsepower = 550 ft. lbs/sec.

1 Horsepower = 746 watts

1 Horsepower = 0.746 kilowatts

1 Horsepower = 2545 Btu/hr.

1 Horsepower = 42.4 Btu/min.

1 Horsepower = 0.71 Btu/sec.

1 Horsepower = 2.64 lbs. water evaporated/hr. at 212° F.

1 Horsepower = 22.8 lbs. water heated/hr. from 62° to 212° F.

1 Horsepower = 550 lbs. water falling 1 ft. in 1 sec.

1 Horsepower = 32,998 lbs. water falling 1 ft. in 1 min.

1 Horsepower = 8.81 cu. ft. water falling 1 ft. in 1 sec.

1 Horsepower = 528.6 cu. ft. water falling 1 ft. in 1 min.

1 Horsepower = 2.64 lbs. water evaporated/hr. at 212° F.

1 Horsepower = 178 calories/sec.

1 Horsepower = 10,700 calories/min.

1 Horsepower = 642,000 calories/hr.

at the time, so in 1783, Watt and Boulton devised a way to compare the power of their engine to the power of a horse.

Various tales exist as to how the value of horsepower was derived. In one story, Watt and Boulton had a horse draw a large, loaded scuttle of known weight up from the depths of a coal pit. They measured the distance the horse traveled in one minute and used the following formula:

Work
= Force x Distance Traveled

They found that one horse-power of work equaled 33,000 ft. pounds per minute. The experiment might have gone like this:

A large bucket at the bottom of a mine shaft is loaded with 200 lbs. of coal. A rope is attached to the bucket and led up and over a pulley. The rope is attached to an average-size horse, which at a signal is led off at a good pace. After 60 seconds, the distance traveled is marked and is found to be 165 ft.

Horsepower
= Force x Distance Traveled

Horsepower = 200 lbs. x 165 ft.
  = 33,000 ft. lbs. in 1 minute
Thus 33,000 ft. lbs/min.
  = 1 Horsepower (hp)
33,000 ÷ 60 = 550 ft. lbs/sec.
  = 1 hp

A second story has Watt timing the speed with which a horse plodded around a circular track. The horse was tethered to a long pole attached to the millstone in a grist mill. This experiment might have gone like this:

The force necessary to move the lever was determined to be 175 lbs. The lever was 15 ft. long and the horse made two laps around the circuit in one minute.

Horsepower
= Force x Distance Traveled
Distance traveled = 2πd
  = 2 x 3.14 x 30 = 188.4 ft/min.
Horsepower = 175 lbs. x 188.4 ft.
Horsepower
  = 32,970 ≈ 33,000 ft. lbs/min.

This experiment too, determined that 1 hp equaled 33,000 ft. lbs. per minute.

The third story has Watt and Boulton timing horses as they pulled boats up a canal. In one account Watt theorized that the horses were not working at full capacity, so arbitrarily raised the value of the horses' work by 150%. Later, researchers indicated that 33,000 ft. lbs. were actually about three-quarters of the actual power of a horse.

Whatever experiments Watt

devised, horsepower was now defined and became a part of our lexicon as a convenient unit for measuring and defining power. We still use horsepower to measure work, even though most of us who use the term have never seen a horse work and have no idea how much power a real horse has. Horsepower is defined in other ways (**box page 233**) too.

We can use the first formula to calculate the horsepower of a motor.

Horsepower = ft. lbs. per
min. ÷ 33,000

Example:
A motor raises a 1500-lb. weight 100 ft. in 1 minute. What is the demonstrated horsepower?
Hp = ft. lbs. per min. ÷ 33,000
Hp = 100 ft. x 1500 lbs. ÷ 33,000
Hp = 150,000 ÷ 33,000 = 4.5 hp

In this instance we've determined the motor does actual work of 4.5 demonstrated horsepower. We do not know, or perhaps care, what the theoretical hp is.

The shaft, or brake horsepower (bhp), is used to indicate the practical power of an engine. Bhp is the theoretical or indicated hp (Ihp) minus power lost through friction, compression, cooling fans, etc. With an automobile, approximately 25% of the Ihp is delivered to the wheels (bhp). With an electric motor, 50-80% of the power is transmitted from shaft to the desired output.

Current x volts ÷ 760
    = indicated hp (Ihp)
Current x volts ÷ 1000
    = brake hp (bhp)

Phony Horsepower

The Prony Brake is a machine that loads a motor in order to determine the amount of hp actually transmitted from the motor to machinery. As an induction motor experiences drag, it draws more electrical current in an effort to maintain constant speed.

Now back to the "5-hp" shop vacuum. In an effort to beat competitors, the manufacturer of the shop vac used a dynamometer, similar to the Prony Brake, not to simulate friction and drag, but to measure peak amps and from this to calculate peak horse-power. This peak horsepower is arrived at by the following process:

An ammeter is attached to a motor, and an external braking device is attached to the shaft. The motor is switched on and after attaining full speed the ammeter registers running current, 6 amps in this case.

The brake is then fully activated and the rotation stops dead. Naturally, the motor smokes, sparks, and finally fails. Just as the motor gasps and is in its death throes, the current shoots up to 31 amps, five times normal, and is measured using the ammeter. This unrealistic, unusable amperage from a totally ruined motor is now used to calculate peak horsepower, which is then put into catalogs and used in advertisements. Tool buyers around the world, such as you and me, are now asked to purchase this "magnificent, high-horsepower motor."

Peak horsepower
    = destructive amps
    x voltage ÷ 746

In the case of the "5-hp" shop vacuum, the math would have looked like this:

Peak horsepower = destructive amps x voltage ÷ 746
Peak horsepower
    = 31 destructive amps
    x 120 volts ÷ 746
Peak horsepower
= 3720 Watts ÷ 746 = 4.99 Hp

Using 746 watts/hp also assumes the current and voltage convert 100% to power. One-hundred percent efficiency of energy from input to output is something from a fairy tale, and until someone invents a perpetual motion machine, it just doesn't happen.

And can you plug this "31-amp" shop vacuum into your 15-amp home circuit without blowing the breaker? Of course you can. No problem. Because the true current is only 6 amps, not 31. The 31 amps are present only in the advertising

---

Rule of Thumb

For 120-volt motors, divide amps by 8 to get horsepower
    Hp = amps ÷ 8

Example: Motor listed at 4 amps and 120 volts
    $4 ÷ 8 = \frac{1}{2}$ hp

Example: Motor listed at 6 amps and 120 volts
    $6 ÷ 8 = \frac{3}{4}$ hp

For 240-volt motors, divide amps by 4 to get horsepower
    Hp = amps ÷ 4

Example: Motor listed at 4 amps and 240 volts
    $4 ÷ 4 = 1$ hp

Example: Motor listed at 12 amps and 240 volts
    $12 ÷ 4 = 3$ hp

literature of the manufacturer, and measured just before total destruction of the motor.

Imagine what it would be like to duplicate the manufacturer's experiment on a 10-in. table saw.

You'd need a large piece of oak 2x4, and a fire extinguisher. You'd turn on the switch. When the motor reached full speed, you would jam the 2x4 into the blade and hold firm until the blade stopped and the motor stalled. When the motor started crackling and smoking and just as the thermal overload clicked (if you were lucky) or the

circuit breaker tripped, you would have achieved peak horsepower, as defined by some manufacturers.

If you survived this experiment, you could then phone the manufacturer and ask, now that you had achieved the same peak hp that they advertised and now that the motor was ruined, if they were ready to replace the motor.

So now that you know how NOT to compare motors, how DO you compare them?

As a general rule, as long as the voltage is the same, the power of a motor is directly proportional to the rated current (amps).

Power = current x voltage

Aware of this horsepower hype, one woodworking magazine chose not to list manufacturer's published horsepower in their story rating 120-volt woodworking machinery. They listed amps

instead (**Figure 250**).

By listing only amps, the magazine was able to convey relative hp. And by not listing peak hp, they also were fair to their readers.

In another publication, a review of 10 in. to $18\frac{1}{2}$ in. 120-volt thickness planers, continuous hp between $1\frac{3}{4}$ and 5 was listed for 18 of the motors. Six of the planers were listed with amps only instead of hp (**Figure 249**). This indicates those machines could not possibly have the listed hp, given the amps and voltage. To their credit, the magazine chose to publish the amps and voltage and let the consumer do his own hp calculation instead of publishing peak hp as supplied by the manufacturer.

These six machines (**Figure 249**) all were less than 2 hp (average hp = 1.7) with average selling price $465. The other 18 thickness planers in the review ranged from 1.75 to 5 hp and averaged 3.0 hp. The cost of the 18 more powerful machines averaged $1130. The less powerful machines cost less and will fit some woodworkers' budgets and needs. The more powerful machines with the correspondingly higher prices will fit other woodworkers' budgets and needs. But in either case, the consumer should be

Figure 249 Calculate Usable HP from Amps

Size	Amps	Calc. Hp*	Cost
12"	16	1.92	$385
12"	15	1.80	$400
12"	15	1.80	$620
12"	14	1.68	$500
10"	13	1.56	$380
12"	12	1.44	$510

*Our calculations - Multiply volts times amps and divide by 1000 to find usable horsepower.

Figure 250 Some Published Horsepower Is Phony

Machine	Amps	Hp Calc*	Price	Their Comments
1	6.0	0.72	$231	Powerful Motor
2	5.1	0.61	$549	No Comment on Motor
3	5.0	0.60	$242	No Comment on Motor
4	4.0	0.48	$200	Motor Stalls
5	2.3	0.28	$150	Underpowered Motor

*Our calculations - Multiply volts times amps and divide by 1000 to find usable horsepower.

able to make that decision based on honest data.

One magazine commented that machines imported from Asia frequently had power specifications on the motor nameplate that were "optimistic."

Problem 1

Two motors are to be compared. On the manufacturer's ID plate of motor #1, we find "120v, 12A." Motor #2 lists "120v, 8A." In advertisements, both motors claim to be $1\frac{1}{2}$ hp. Which is the more powerful? And, equally as important, which manufacturer is telling the truth?

Answer 1

Use this formula:

Volts x amps ÷ 1000 = usable horsepower

Motor #1:

120 x 12 ÷ 1000
  = 1440 ÷ 1000 = 1.44 hp

Motor #2:

120 x 8 ÷ 1000
  = 960 ÷ 1000 = 0.96 hp

Motor #1 is $1\frac{7}{16}$ hp, while Motor #2 is just under 1 hp. Motor #1 is the more powerful and we could have determined this by just comparing the amps listed for each.

Rule of Thumb

As long as they all run on the same voltage, the motor with the most amps listed usually will be the most powerful (**Figure 251**).

Problem 1:

Using the chart, what is the available hp of a 120-volt, 13-amp motor?
Answer 1:

From the chart, read $1\frac{1}{2}$ hp.

Problem 2:

The description plate of a 240-volt motor lists 18 amps. What is the available hp?
Answer 2:

From the chart, read $4\frac{1}{4}$ hp.

Problem 3:

If a 120 volt motor draws 12.5 amps, what is the hp?
Answer 3:

The chart shows 12 amps = $1\frac{7}{16}$ hp, and 13 amps = $1\frac{1}{2}$ hp, so the motor in question could be rated at $1\frac{1}{2}$ hp.

Figure 251 Amperage to Horsepower
THE LISTED AMPERAGE IS DIRECTLY PROPORTIONAL TO AVAILABLE HP. THIS IS RUNNING CURRENT, NOT START-UP OR FULL LOAD CURRENT.

Amps	120v Hp	240V Hp
1	1/8	1/4
2	1/4	1/2
3	3/8	3/4
4	1/2	1
5	5/8	1-1/4
6	3/4	1-1/2
7	7/8	1-3/4
8	1	2
9	1-1/8	2-1/4
10	1-1/4	2-1/2
11	1-3/8	2-3/4
12	1-7/16	2-7/8
13	1-1/2	3
14	1-5/8	3-1/4
15	1-3/4	3-1/2
16	1-7/8	3-3/4
17	2	4
18	2-1/8	4-1/4
19	2-1/4	4-1/2
20	2-3/8	4-3/4
21	2-1/2	5
22	2-5/8	5-1/4
23	2-3/4	5-1/2
24	2-7/8	5-3/4
25	3	6
26	3-1/8	6-1/4
27	3-1/4	6-1/2
28	3-3/8	6-3/4
29	3-1/2	7
30	3-5/8	7-1/4
31	3-3/4	7-1/2
32	3-7/8	7-3/4
33	4	8
34	4-1/8	8-1/4
35	4-1/4	8-1/2
36	4-3/8	8-3/4
37	4-1/2	9
38	4-5/8	9-1/4
39	4-3/4	9-1/2
40	4-7/8	9-3/4
41	5	10

CHAPTER 23

Pulleys & Speed

Most stationary shop tools use a system of pulleys and belts to transmit power from the motor to the business end. By altering the size of the pulleys, the speed at the business end can be made faster or slower. The rules are pretty simple.

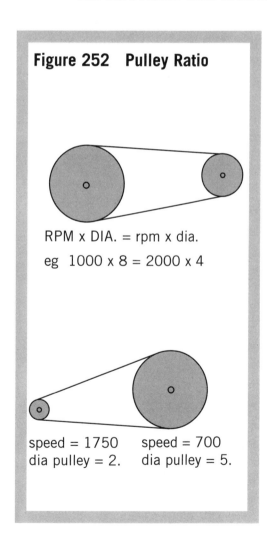

Figure 252   Pulley Ratio

RPM x DIA. = rpm x dia.

eg   1000 x 8 = 2000 x 4

speed = 1750   speed = 700
dia pulley = 2.   dia pulley = 5.

Two Pulley System

When a motor is used to drive a shop tool and power is transmitted with a series of pulleys and belts, the motor pulley is called the *driver* pulley and the pulley to which the power is transmitted is called the *driven* pulley. To change the speed of the *driven* shaft, it is necessary to make the diameter of the driver pulley different from the diameter of the driven pulley.

Figure 252, it doesn't matter whether power originates from the small or the large pulley, the ratio works either way.

The basic formula for transmitting power and speed from one source to another via belts and pulleys is:

Speed of driver (S) x driver pulley diameter (P)
    equals
Speed of driven (s) x driven pulley diameter (p)
    S x P = s x p

Example: A lathe has a $\frac{1}{2}$-hp motor with a speed of 1725 rpm (S). We want to rough turn bowl blanks with a speed of about 600-800 rpm (s). If the motor has a 2-in. pulley (P), what size pulley (p) should the lathe have?

    S x P = s x p
Where S = 1725, P = 2, s ≈ 700, p = unknown
    p = (S x P) ÷ s
    p = (1725 x 2) ÷ 700
    p = 5 in.

Example: We have a $\frac{1}{2}$-hp motor with speed of 3450 rpm (S) and a 3-in. pulley (P). If this driver is hooked up to a 4-in. pulley (p) on a jack-shaft, what is the resulting speed (s)?

$$S \times P = s \times p$$
$$s = (S \times P) \div p$$
$$s = (3450 \times 3) \div 4$$
$$= 0.75 \times 3450 = 2588 \text{ rpm.}$$

Stepped Pulleys

A simple way to determine the spindle speeds is by ratio. As an example (**Figure 253**), let's look at some step pulleys which usually are used in pairs. In the example, the motor has a speed of 1725 rpm with the motor

pulley and the spindle pulley having equal step diameters but inverted placement.

We will assume the 4-speed pulleys have step diameters of 2 in., 3 in., 4 in., and 5 in. Follow this process to find the spindle speeds:

1. Divide the diameter of each driver (motor) step pulley by the corresponding step size of the pulley mounted on the spindle (driven), i.e., its opposite.

$$2 \div 5 = 0.4$$
$$3 \div 4 = 0.75$$
$$4 \div 3 = 1.33$$
$$5 \div 2 = 2.5$$

2. Multiply the motor speed by the results of the above calculations to get the spindle speed at each pulley step.

1725 x 0.4
 = 690 rpm (2 in. to 5 in.)
1725 x 0.75
 = 1294 rpm (3 in. to 4 in.)
1725 x 1.33
 = 2294 rpm (4 in. to 3 in.)
1725 x 2.5
 = 4312 rpm (5 in. to 2 in.)

If a motor with a different speed is used, the ratios of the step pulley system remain the same. Multiply the new motor speed by the ratios to find the new spindle speeds.

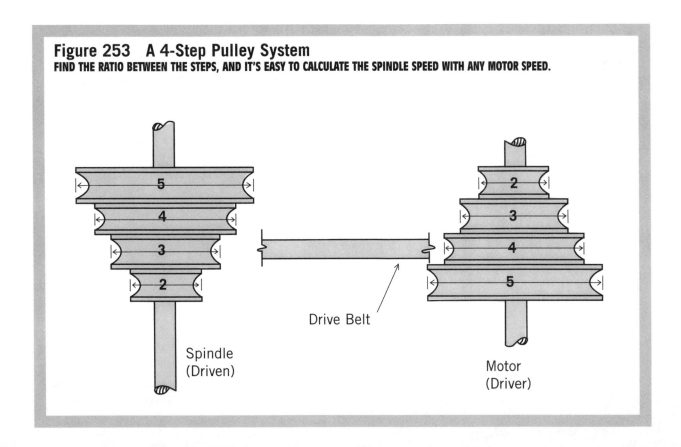

Figure 253   A 4-Step Pulley System
FIND THE RATIO BETWEEN THE STEPS, AND IT'S EASY TO CALCULATE THE SPINDLE SPEED WITH ANY MOTOR SPEED.

Spindle
(Driven)

Drive Belt

Motor
(Driver)

Figure 254   Driver, Idler, and Driven
THE THREE PULLEY SYSTEM GIVES A WIDE RANGE OF SPEEDS.

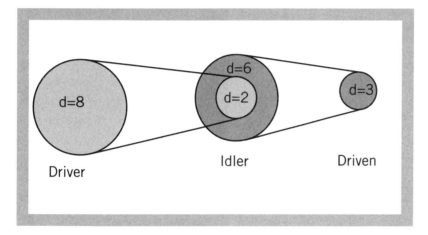

Driver   Idler   Driven

Rule of Thumb

Small pulley to large pulley—SLOW DOWN Large pulley to small pulley—SPEED UP

How can we reduce the speed of a bench grinder from 1725 to about 1400 rpm? From the above rule of thumb, we know that in order to slow down, we need to go from a small pulley to a large pulley.

$1400 \div 1725 = 0.8$
Choose pulleys with this ratio:

5 in. x 0.8 = 4 in.

Put a 4-in. pulley on the motor and a 5-in. pulley on the grinder.

Three Pulley System

A more complicated system, such as one found on a large boring machine, might have a three pulley system, with an idler pulley joining the driver and the driven pulleys (**Figure 254**). This setup gives a wide range of boring speeds.

To find the speeds, break the three pulley system down into two parts:

Part 1:
$S \times P = s \times p$ (for driver to idler)
and
Part 2:
$S \times P = s \times p$ (for idler to driven)

Part 1:
Motor driver speed = 1725, driver pulley = 8 in.
Idler speed = unknown, idler pulley = 2 in.
$S \times P = s \times p$
$1725 \times 8 = s \times 2$

$s = (1725 \times 8) \div 2$
$= 6900$ rpm (idler speed)

Part 2:
Idler driver speed = 6900 rpm, idler driver pulley = 6 in.
Driven speed = unknown, driven pulley = 3 in.
$S \times P = s \times p$
$6900 \times 6 = s \times 3$
$s = (6900 \times 6) \div 3$
$= 13,800$ rpm

The problem can also be solved by grouping all drivers together and all followers together. The speed of the first driver times the diameter of all driver pulleys equals the speed of the last follower times the diameter of all followers.

$$S \times P_1 \times P_2 = s \times p_1 \times p_2$$

$1725 \times 8 \times 6$
= speed of last follower x 2 x 3
Speed of last follower
$= (1725 \times 8 \times 6) \div 2 \times 3$
Speed of last follower
$= 82,800 \div 6 = 13,800$ rpm

This equation works for any number of pulleys in a system.

Figure 255 shows a typical three pulley system as might be found on a drill press. Belts can only be attached to pulleys on the same horizontal plane. The slowest speed would be A-4, where the smallest pulley on the driver (A), would be attached to the largest pulley on the idler, then the smallest pulley on the idler would be

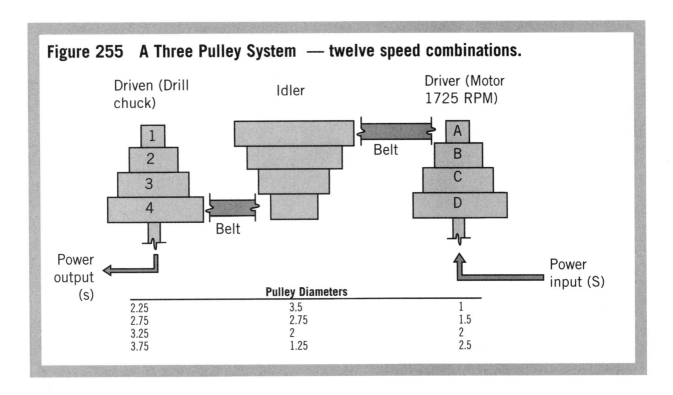

Figure 255   A Three Pulley System — twelve speed combinations.

Driven (Drill chuck)

Idler

Driver (Motor 1725 RPM)

Belt

Belt

Power output (s)

Power input (S)

Pulley Diameters		
2.25	3.5	1
2.75	2.75	1.5
3.25	2	2
3.75	1.25	2.5

attached to the largest pulley on the driven set (4).

The motor speed is listed as 1720 rpm and speed to the chuck would be calculated thus:

$$S \times P_1 \times P_2 = s \times p_1 \times p_2$$
$$s = (S \times P_1 \times P_2) \div (p_1 \times p_2)$$
$$s = (1720 \times 1 \times 1.25) \div (3.5 \times 3.75)$$
$$s = 2150 \div 13.13$$
$$s = 164 \text{ rpm}$$

The fastest speed with this machine would be D-1, where the largest pulley on the driver (D) would be attached to the smallest pulley on the idler. Then the largest pulley on the idler would be attached to the smallest pulley on the driven set (1).

Speed would be calculated thus:

$$S \times P_1 \times P_2 = s \times p_1 \times p_2$$
$$s = (S \times P_1 \times P_2) \div (p_1 \times p_2)$$
$$s = (1720 \times 2.5 \times 3.5) \div (1.25 \times 2.25)$$
$$s = 15050 \div 2.81$$
$$s = 5356 \text{ rpm}$$

Variable-Width Pulleys

Some manufacturers are now providing variable speed machines by installing variable-width pulley sets (**Figure 256**). A mechanical control adjusts the width of the driver pulley that changes the pulley diameter and thus the speed. Moving the two halves of the pulley apart decreases the diameter and decreases the speed. Moving the two halves closer together increases the speed.

On one lathe system, a mating driven pulley on the head stock is similarly split but is spring-loaded so the changing tension on the v-belt makes it automatically adjust to the state of the driver pulley. Within the alterable limits of the pulleys, this setup gives a wide range of variable speeds.

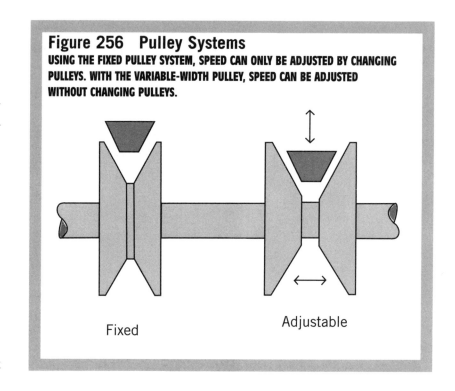

Figure 256 Pulley Systems
USING THE FIXED PULLEY SYSTEM, SPEED CAN ONLY BE ADJUSTED BY CHANGING PULLEYS. WITH THE VARIABLE-WIDTH PULLEY, SPEED CAN BE ADJUSTED WITHOUT CHANGING PULLEYS.

Fixed

Adjustable

CHAPTER 24

RPM & Speed

We measure the speed of a motor in revolutions per minute. Rpm, however, does not tell us how fast the rim of a saw blade or the outer edge of a piece of work on the lathe is actually moving. For example, the speed-past-surface at the center of a 10-in. saw blade, at 2 in. from center, and at the rim of the blade are all different. A lathe running at a demure 840 rpm seems quite safe, yet the outer rim of a 12-in. platter is moving past the tool rest at a frightening speed.

Rim speed is a measure of how fast a piece is moving relative to the surface and is usually stated in inches per minute (ipm) or feet per minute (fpm). Rim speed (or cutting speed) is used in industry to regulate tool speed while machining different materials.

The formula for calculating rim or perimeter speed is:

Rim speed (ipm) = rpm x pi x diameter (in.)

If the diameter is measured in inches, this formula calculates the rim speed in inches per minute. Dividing the answer by 12 converts it to feet per minute. Thus:

Rim speed (fpm) = rpm x pi x diameter (in.) ÷ 12

Example: What is the rim speed of a 12-in. platter on a lathe turning at 840 rpm?
Rim speed (ipm) = rpm x pi x diameter (in.)
Rim speed = 840 x 3.14 x 12
Rim speed = 31,651 ipm
Rim speed = 31,651 ÷ 12 = 2638 fpm

Example: By reducing the lathe speed to 600 rpm, we would reduce the rim speed:

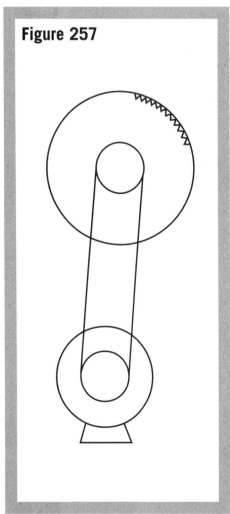

Figure 257

Figure 258 Table Saw Blade
A 10-IN. SAW BLADE HAS RIM SPEED OF OVER 9,000 FPM.

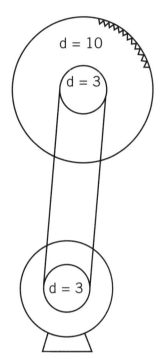

Rim speed = 9028 fpm

Blade speed = 3450 RPM

Motor speed = 3450 RPM

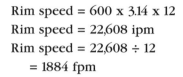

Rule of Thumb

Use this simple formula to find **rim speed in feet per minute**.

Round off the value of pi from 3.14 to 3, then...

divide the diameter by 4 and multiply the result by rpm.

Rim speed = rpm x (diameter ÷ 4)

In the above instance where the lathe is turning at 840 rpm, what is the speed at the rim of a 12-in. platter?

Rim speed = 840 x (12 ÷ 4)
    = 840 x 3 ≈ 2500 fpm

Rim speed = 600 x 3.14 x 12
Rim speed = 22,608 ipm
Rim speed = 22,608 ÷ 12
    = 1884 fpm

Ratio rpm: 600/840 = 0.71
Ratio rim speeds:
    22608/31651 = 0.71

From this we see the rim speed is directly proportional to rpm.

Example: What would be the rim speed if we were turning a 36-in. diameter bowl and the lathe was turning at 1000 rpm?

Rim speed
    = (1000 x 36 x 3.14 ÷ 12)
Rim speed
    = 113,040 ÷ 12 = 9420 fpm

There are 5,280 feet in a mile and 60 seconds in a minute; this translates to miles per hour thus:
9420 x (60 / 5280) = 107 mph

Example: What is the rim speed in mph. of a 10-in. circular saw blade turning at 3,450 rpm (**Figure 258**)?
Note: 60 / 5280= 0.01136.

Rim speed = (motor speed
    x diameter x pi) ÷ 12
Rim Speed =
    (3,450 x 10 x 3.14 ÷ 12)
    = 9028 fpm
9028 x 0.01136 = 103
Rim speed = 103 mph

No wonder accidents happen so fast on this machine!

CHAPTER 25

Taps & Threads

The chart that comes with a tap and die set lists only one drill size to use with each tap, e.g., for a $\frac{1}{4}$"-20 tap you use a $\frac{13}{64}$-in. drill. This will give 72% thread depth, that is, when the screw is inserted into this tapped hole, the screw thread will engage 72% with the tapped threads. This might be fine in a hard metal like steel, but the same tap used with other drill sizes will produce threads that will engage the screw 96, 79, 75, 72, and 48%. It's important that woodworkers know these options and be able to select the best size drill for their purposes.

Taps and dies are used to cut threads in metals, plastics, wood, and sometimes in hard rubber (**Figure 259**).

Dies are used to cut external threads for bolts and screws. A solid die is basically a nut in which flutes have been machined at right angles to the threads. The die is hardened to provide cutting edges. There are adjustable split dies and adjustable two-piece dies.

A tap, which is used to cut internal threads in holes already drilled, is basically a screw in which longitudinal channels or flutes have been ground. The flutes allow chips to escape and lubricants to reach the cutting area and threaded material. Most of the threads that woodworkers cut are right-handed, that is, the tap or die is turned clockwise and the bolt, screw, or nut also is turned in a clockwise manner to engage or tighten. If a thread runs counter-clockwise it is a left-handed thread.

The United States has been using the American National thread system since 1933. This system is based on a 60° thread angle with flat crests and roots. The system is divided into NC (National Coarse) and NF (National Fine) thread series (**Figures 261 and 262**).

Rule of Thumb

Use the charts in **Figures 261 and 262.** (American National Coarse Threads and American National Fine Threads) to find tap drill sizes for different screws and bolts. In hard metals, pick the drill that gives lower thread engagement, for example, 50-60%. With soft metals or plastics, use the bit that gives higher thread engagement, 70-80%. In each table the Percent Full Thread Depth (PC FTD) was calculated by using the formula:

Percent Full Thread Depth
  = Threads per Inch
  ÷ 1.3 x (Screw outside
  Diameter – Drill Diameter).

PC FTD
  = TPI/1.3 x (Screw OD
  – Drill Diameter).

Figure 259 Taps and Dies
TAPS ARE USED TO CUT INTERNAL THREADS AND DIES ARE USED TO CUT EXTERNAL THREADS.

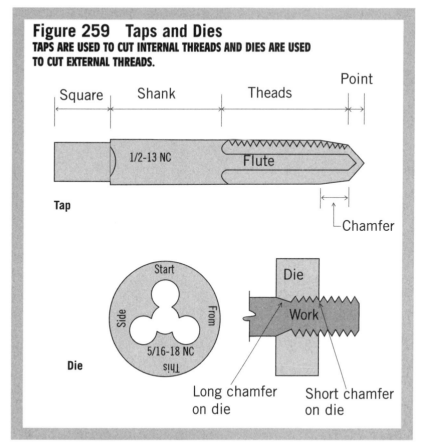

Figure 260 Threads
AMERICAN NATIONAL COARSE OR AMERICAN NATIONAL FINE THREAD.

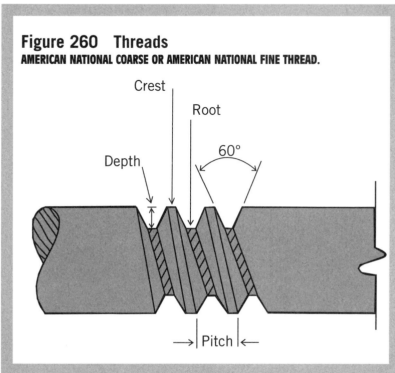

When cutting internal threads, the size of the drilled hole should not be smaller than is necessary to give adequate strength to the thread. The size of a tap is the outside diameter of its threads (**Figure 259**). Theoretically, the hole drilled for tapping could be smaller than the tap by twice the depth of the thread if a full thread is cut. Usually, however, only about 75% of the threads are engaged, so a drilled hole should be of sufficient diameter to produce a thread depth of approximately 75%. A common mistake is trying to cut threads in holes that are too small for the tap. Even a hole that is just slightly undersized increases the torque required for tapping and often results in broken taps.

This 75% thread engagement is only an average and may vary from 50 to 85%. The best thread depth will vary according to the diameter of the hole, the kind of material being tapped, the depth of the tapped hole, and the pitch of the threads.

Diameter of the Hole and Pitch of the Threads
The larger the hole, the farther apart are the threads (coarser the pitch) and the greater the thread depth. Large holes have big, deep threads.

IN MATERIAL WHOSE THICKNESS IS 1.5 TIMES THE BOLT OD, 50% THREAD DEPTH MAY BE USED.

Figure 261 American National Coarse Threads

Tap Size	Bolt or Screw O. D.	Drill Size	Drill Diam. Inches	% Full Thread Depth	Tap Size	Bolt or Screw O. D.	Drill Size	Drill Diam. Inches	% Full Thread Depth
1-64	0.074 in.	1.45 mm	0.0571	78	5/16" - 18	0.313 in.	1/4 in.	0.2500	87
		1.50 mm	0.0591	68			F	0.2570	77
		#53	0.0595	66			G	0.2610	71
		1.55 mm	0.0610	59			17/64 in.	0.2656	65
		1/16 in.	0.0625	58					
					3/8" - 16	0.375 in.	5/16"	0.3125	77
2-56	0.086 in.	#51	0.0670	82			O	0.3160	73
		#50	0.0700	69			P	0.3260	64
		#49	0.0730	56			21/64 in.	0.3281	58
					7/16" - 14	0.438	23/64 in.	0.3594	84
3-48	0.099 in.	5/64 in.	0.0781	77			U	0.3680	75
		#47	0.0785	75			3/8"	0.3750	67
		#46	0.0810	66					
		2.1 mm	0.0827	60	1/2" - 13	0.500	27/64 in.	0.4219	78
4-40	0.112 in.	#44	0.0860	80			11.0 mm	0.4331	67
		#43	0.0890	71			7/16 in.	0.4375	62
		2.3 mm	0.0906	66					
		3/32 in.	0.0938	56	9/16" - 12	0.563	31/64 in.	0.4844	72
							12.5 mm	0.4921	65
5-40	0.125 in.	#39	0.0995	79					
		#38	0.1015	72	5/8" - 11	0.625	17/32 in.	0.5313	79
		2.60 mm	0.1024	70			13.5 mm	0.5315	79
		#37	0.1040	65			35/64 in.	0.5469	66
6-32	0.138 in.	#36	0.1065	78	3/4" - 10	0.750	41/64 in.	0.6406	84
		7/64 in.	0.1094	70			16.5 mm	0.6496	77
		#33	0.1130	62			21/32 in.	0.6563	72
		1/8 in.	0.1250	56			17.0 mm	0.6693	62
8-32	0.164 in.	3.40 mm	0.1339	74	7/8" - 9	0.875	49/64 in.	0.7656	76
		#29	0.1360	69			19.5 mm	0.7677	74
		3.50 mm	0.1378	65			25/32 in.	0.7813	65
10-24	0.185 in.	9/64 in.	0.1406	82	1" - 8	1.000	22 mm	0.8661	82
		#26	0.1470	79			7/8 in.	0.8750	77
		#24	0.1520	70			57/64 in.	0.8906	67
		#23	0.1540	67					
		5/32 in.	0.1563	66	1-1/8" - 7	1.125	25 mm	0.9842	76
							63/64 in.	0.9844	76
12-24	0.241 in.	11/64 in.	0.1719	80			1.0 in.	1.0000	67
		#17	0.1730	79					
		#16	0.1770	72	1-1/4" - 7	1.250	28.0 mm	1.1024	80
		#15	0.1800	67			1 7/64 in.	1.1094	76
							28.5 mm	1.1220	67
1/4" - 20	0.250 in.	3/16 in.	0.1875	96					
		#8	0.1990	79	1-3/8" - 6	1.375	30.5 mm	1.2008	80
		#7	0.2010	75			1 13/64 in.	1.2031	79
		13/64 in.	0.2031	72			1 7/32 in.	1.2188	73
		7/32 in.	0.2188	48					
					1-1/2" - 6	1.500	1 21/64 in.	1.3281	79
							1 11/32 in.	1.3438	72
							1 23/64 in.	1.3594	65

IN MATERIAL WHOSE THICKNESS IS 1.5 TIMES THE BOLT OD, 50% THREAD DEPTH MAY BE USED.

Figure 262
American National Fine Threads

Tap	Bolt or Screw	Drill	Drill Diam.	% Full Thread	Tap Size	Bolt or Screw O.D.	Drill Size	Drill Diam. Inches	% Full Thread Depth
0-80	0.060	3/64 in.	0.0469	81	3/8" - 24	0.375	21/64 in.	0.3281	87
		1.2 mm	0.0472	79			Q	0.3320	79
		1.25 mm	0.0492	67			R	0.3390	67
1-72	0.073	1.50 mm	0.0591	77	7/16" - 20	0.438	W	0.3860	79
		#53	0.0595	75			25/64 in.	0.3906	72
		1.55 mm	0.0610	67			X	0.3970	62
		1/16 in.	0.0625	58			13/32 in.	0.4063	48
2-64	0.086	#50	0.0700	79	1/2" - 20	0.500	29/64 in.	0.4531	72
		#49	0.0730	64			15/32 in.	0.4688	48
3-56	0.099	5/64 in.	0.0781	90	9/16" - 18	0.563	1/2 in.	0.5000	87
		#46	0.0810	78			13.0 mm	0.5118	70
		2.10 mm	0.0827	70			23/64 in.	0.5156	65
		#44	0.0860	56	5/8" - 18	0.625	9/16 in.	0.5625	87
4-48	0.112	2.30 mm	0.0906	79			14.5 mm	0.5709	75
		#42	0.0935	68			37/64 in.	0.5781	65
		3/32 in.	0.0938	68	3/4" - 16	0.750	11/16 in.	0.6875	77
		#41	0.0960	59			17.5 mm	0.6890	75
5-44	0.125	2.60 mm	0.1024	77			45/64 in.	0.7031	58
		#37	0.1040	71	7/8" - 14	0.875	51/64 in.	0.7969	84
		#36	0.1065	63			20.5 mm	0.8071	73
		7/64 in.	0.1094	53			13/16 in.	0.8125	67
6-40	0.138	7/64 in.	0.1094	88			53/64 in.	0.8281	51
		#33	0.1130	77	1" - 12	1.000	29/32 in.	0.9063	87
		#32	0.1160	68			59/64 in.	0.9219	72
8-36	0.164	3.40 mm	0.1339	83	1" - 14	1.000	59/64 in.	0.9219	84
		#29	0.1360	78			23.5 mm	0.8252	81
		3.50 mm	0.1378	73			15/16 in.	0.9375	67
		9/64 in.	0.1406	65	1-1/8" - 12	1.000	26.5 mm	1.0433	75
10-32	0.190	5/32 in.	0.1563	83			1 3/64 in.	1.0469	72
		#21	0.1590	76	1-1/4" - 12	1.250	29.5 mm	1.1614	82
		#20	0.1610	71			1 11/64 in.	1.1719	72
		#19	0.1660	59			30.0 mm	1.1811	64
12-28	0.216	#15	0.1800	78	1-3/8" - 12	1.375	1 9/32	1.2813	87
		#13	0.1850	67			1 19/64 in.	1.2969	72
		3/16 in.	0.1875	61	1-1/2" - 12	1.500	36 mm	1.4173	76
1/4" - 28	0.250	#3	0.2130	80			1 27/64 in.	1.4219	72
		5.5 mm	0.2165	72					
		7/32 in.	0.2188	67					
5/16" - 24	0.313	17/64 in.	0.2656	87					
		I	0.2720	75					
		J	0.2770	66					

The Kind of Material Being Tapped

Soft metals such as copper and aluminum tap easily, and a thread depth of 80% can easily be achieved. In hard materials, sometimes a 70% thread depth is the most that can be cut, so use the largest drill possible to achieve 50-60% thread depth. Even a nut with only 50% thread engagement will break the bolt before it strips the threads.

The Depth of the Tapped Hole

When the drilled hole is deeper than 1.5 times the tap diameter, thread depths of 50-60% may be used with little chance of stripping. Thus a $\frac{1}{4}$-in. hole in $\frac{3}{8}$-in. material may safely use 50-60% thread depth.

Calculate Drill Size

Use the formula below to calculate the size of the drill bit to use in conjunction with a tap. The formula assumes a 75% thread engagement, i.e., that the threads of the screw will engage 75% of the threads in the hole. The 75% figure is usual, but if you are threading into a soft metal such as aluminum, you might try using 85% thread engagement first. If the screw won't go in, recalculate the initial hole size at 70-75%, drill this slightly larger hole and, using the same tap, make new threads. Going

from 75% thread engagement to 100% only adds 5% to the holding strength.

Tap drill diameter
= screw outside diameter
- (fractional thread engagement x 1.3 ÷ threads per inch

TDD = SOD - (TE x 1.3 ÷ TPI)

Example: Find the drill bit size to use for tapping a $\frac{5}{16}$ in. 18-tpi hole in hard steel.

$\frac{5}{16}$ in. = 0.313
TDD = SOD - (TE x 1.3 ÷ TPI)
TDD = 0.313 - (0.75 x 1.3 ÷ 18)
TDD = 0.313 - (0.9750 ÷ 18)
TDD = 0.313 - 0.0542
TDD = 0.259 in.

Because there is no drill bit with this diameter (0.259 in.), we can calculate the percent thread engagement for bits nearly the same size.

$\frac{17}{64}$-in. bit = 0.266 in.
$\frac{1}{4}$-in. bit = 0.250 in.

Calculate Thread Depth

Thread engagement =
threads per inch ÷ 1.3
x (Screw OD - drill dia)
**TE = TPI ÷ 1.3
x (screw OD - drill dia.)**

Example:
For the $\frac{17}{64}$-in. bit:
TE = 18 ÷ 1.3 x ($\frac{5}{16}$ - $\frac{17}{64}$)
TE = 13.8462 x (0.3125 - 0.2656)

TE = 13.8462 x 0.0469 = 0.649
Thread engagement = 65%.
Example:
For the $\frac{1}{4}$-in. bit:
TE = 18 ÷ 1.3 x ($\frac{5}{16}$ - $\frac{1}{4}$)
TE = 13.8462 x (0.3125 - 0.250)
TE = 13.8462 x 0.0625 = 0.865
Thread engagement = 87%.

With softer metals, the $\frac{1}{4}$-in. bit (0.25) would probably be appropriate but it might prove impossible to tap 87% threads in the 0.250 in. hole in hard material. With hard steel, the best choice would be the $\frac{17}{64}$-in. drill bit (0.266) and 65% thread engagement.

Rule of Thumb

To find the tap drill diameter in inches, subtract from the outside diameter of the tap the reciprocal of the threads per inch.
**Tap drill size
= tap diameter - (1 ÷ TPI)**
TDS = TD - (1 ÷ TPI)

What size drill should be used to tap a $\frac{1}{4}$-in., 20-tpi hole?
TDS = TD - (1 ÷ TPI)
TDS = 0.25 - (1 ÷ 20)
TDS = 0.25 - 0.05
TDS = 0.20
0.20 ≈ $\frac{13}{64}$ in.

This Rule of Thumb gives threads with approximately 75% thread engagement.

CHAPTER 26

Dust Collection Systems

Woodworkers should be able to determine what size dust collection system they need based on the type and number of dust and chip producing machines in their shop, the size and length of the ducting, and how many machines will be operating at one time. Once the system is designed on paper, manufacturers' catalogs can be consulted to choose the appropriate system. And what about the danger of fire from static electricity in PVC pipes? Well, that may be a fairy tale perpetuated by ill-informed "experts" over the years.

Rules of Thumb

1. Locate the dust collector close to the machines that produce the most sawdust.

2. Keep the main line short.

3. Use 'Y' joints instead of 'T' joints.

4. Use a minimum of flexible pipe.

5. Close each branch with a blast gate at the machine.

Dust collectors move large volumes of air, 350 to 1800 cubic feet per minute (CFM), from woodshop machines through 4 to 6-in. diameter pipes. The velocity of movement is sufficient to keep dust and other particulates suspended until they reach the filter bag. These collectors move, filter, and bag large amounts of shavings and dust that would clog a shop vacuum. To do this, they require much larger blowers and are usually driven by totally enclosed, fan-cooled, continuous duty induction motors rated from $1/2$ hp to 3 hp or more. To efficiently filter such a large volume of exhaust, dust collectors have one or more huge external filter bags or, in the case of two-stage collectors, a barrel and filter bag. A few years back these big collectors were available only to commercial and industrial shops. Now the weekend woodworker can buy and install one himself.

Why would you change from your old shop vacuum to a complicated, expensive dust collection system? By efficiently capturing dust as it is being produced, your shop motors will last longer, less dust will creep into the house, furnace filters will need to be changed less frequently, and your shop will be cleaner. The floor will need less sweeping and the shop will be safer; you won't slip and slide in the saw dust. Also, and here's a biggie, the central dust collector is quieter - that annoying, high whine is eliminated. All convincing arguments, but the overriding reason might be your health. I don't mean to dwell too much on this point, but fine dust can cause eye and skin irritation. When it lodges in the lungs and throat, it can cause respiratory illnesses such as asthma and bronchitis, and aggravate other existing throat and lung conditions.

Theory

Shop vacuums and dust collectors operate on the same principle—both use a blower or impeller to move a volume of air to remove and store dust and debris. The exhaust volumetric flow rate is measured in cubic feet per minute (CFM). We generally speak of air or dust being sucked into the vacuum system but technically this is not correct. The blower reduces pressure (creates a differential or a partial vacuum) within the collector; at a higher pressure, the outside atmospheric air pushes the dust into the collector.

To design an effective central dust collection system you need to consider three variables associated with air movement: volume, velocity, and friction. The larger the pipe, the greater the volume of air, but the smaller the velocity for a given motor. Conversely, the smaller the pipe, the greater the velocity but the smaller the air volume.

THE MINIMUM CFM OF AIR NEEDED TO EXHAUST DUST AND CHIPS FROM TOOLS AND MACHINES IN THE HOME SHOP, WITH SUGGESTED DIAMETER OF THE EXHAUST PIPES.

Figure 263
Minimum Air Movement for Machines

Machine	Size	Volume CFM	Diam. Of Exhaust Ducts
Band Saw	3-Wheel	300	4 In.
	12-16 in.	400	4
	18-24 in.	450	5
Belt Sander	1-2 in. Wide Belt	300	3
	8 in. Wide Belt	450	4
	9-12 in. Wide Belt	650	5
Chop Saw	8-12 in.	400	4
Disc Sander	To 6 in. Wide	300	4
	To 12 in. Wide	350	5
Drill Press	All	400	4
Drum Sander	12-24 in.	500	4
	24 in. and Larger	650	5
Floor Sweep	All	450	5
Jointer	6-8 in.	350	4
	9-12 in.	450	5
Lathe	All	500	5
Planer	10-15 in.	450	5
	16-20 in.	600	6
	24-30 in.	600	7
Portable Hand Tools	All	300	3-4
Radial Arm Saw	8-10 in.	400	4
	12-14 in.	450	5
Sanding Table	Up To 3 Sq. Ft.	450	4
Scroll Saw	All	350	4
Shaper	1/4 - 1/2 in. Spindle	350	4
	1 in. Spindle	550	5
Spindle Sander	All	400	4
Table Saw	8 in.	300	4
	10-12 in.	400	4
	14-16 in.	500	5

Rule of Thumb

In the home shop, figure 350 CFM is needed for a machine that makes dust, and 450 CFM for a machine that produces chips.

Figure 264   Measuring Static Pressure

A MANOMETER IS USED TO MEASURE THE DIFFERENCE IN AIR PRESSURE OUTSIDE AND INSIDE THE PIPE. THE UNITS OF MEASUREMENT ARE IN INCHES OF WATER.

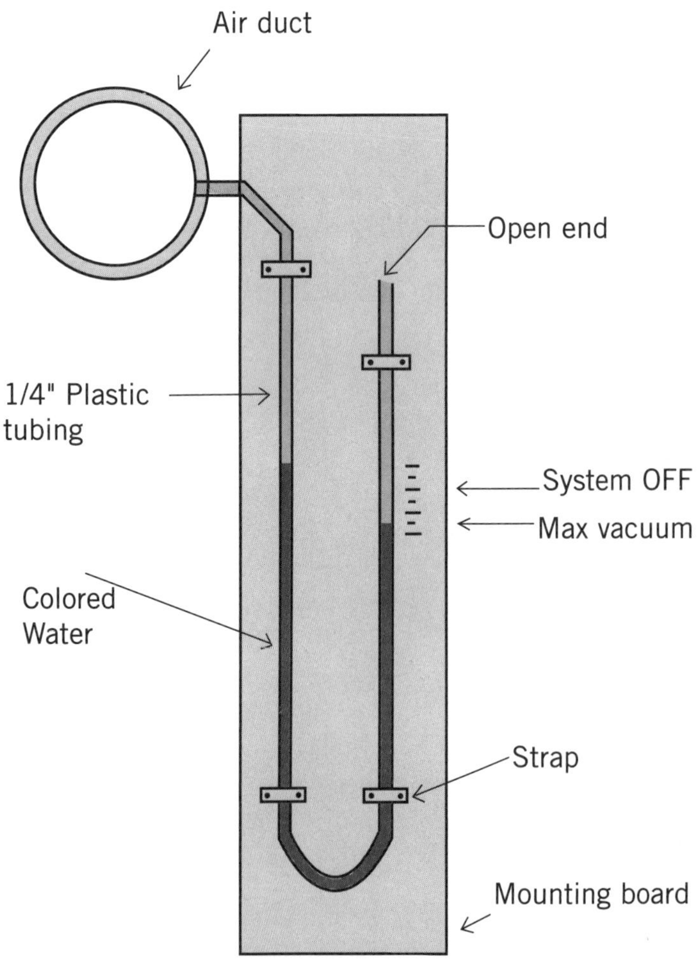

Friction affects both velocity and volume.

Air Volume

Air volume is measured in cubic feet per minute (CFM). Each machine in your shop requires a minimum volume of air to remove chips and dust. **Figure 263** lists machines and the minimum volume of air required to move dust.

Air Velocity

Air velocity is measured in feet per minute (FPM). The air in the main pipes of your dust collection system should move at a velocity of at least 3500 FPM to keep wood debris suspended. The type of ducting, number of air leaks, kinds of couplings, number of joints, and presence of flexible pipe all contribute to friction that slows air velocity.

Air Friction

Friction slows air velocity and thus decreases volume moving through the duct. Friction in the ducts is increased by turbulence due to changes in air direction necessitated by the joints and fittings, and by physical restrictions such as clogged filter bags and flexible pipes. Friction loss due to air movement contributes to static pressure loss (SP).

Static Pressure

Static pressure for a dust collector is measured with a

manometer (**Figure 264**), and the units of measurement are inches of water. In **Figure 264**, the left leg is plugged into the ducting while the right leg remains open to the air. At rest, the liquid levels in the tubes are equal. When the system is working, reduced pressure in the ducting causes the atmospheric pressure to raise the water level in the left leg while lowering it in the right.

Dust Collector Types

Shop Vacuums

Shop vacuums have small, universal (brush type) motors that drive small blowers at very high speeds, thus the whine (**Figure 265**). They move only about 80-150 CFM of air at high velocities through relatively small $1^1/_4$-in. to $2^1/_2$-in. diameter hoses. The debris is deposited in a tank and the air is then passed through a filter element or bag before being exhausted through a port. Because both the filter and the tank are small, shop vacuums must be emptied and the filters cleaned frequently.

Single-Stage Collectors

Single-stage collectors (**Figure 266**) create negative air pressure with an in-line impeller or fan. Dust and wood chips are drawn from the dust-producing machines, through the ducting, into collection and filter bags after passing through the impeller blades. With this type of collector, objects that are too large to pass through the fan blades should not be introduced into the system. Fortunately, most shop machines produce small debris. However, a floor sweep can pick up nails and larger pieces of wood that can dent or damage the fan blades. A screen or size restrictor on the floor sweep will prevent this.

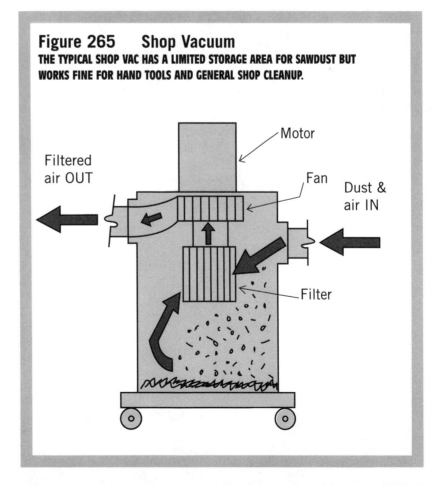

Figure 265   Shop Vacuum
THE TYPICAL SHOP VAC HAS A LIMITED STORAGE AREA FOR SAWDUST BUT WORKS FINE FOR HAND TOOLS AND GENERAL SHOP CLEANUP.

Motor

Filtered air OUT

Fan

Dust & air IN

Filter

Figure 266   Single-Stage Dust Collector
DUST AND CHIPS ARE PUSHED THROUGH THE FAN BLADES. HEAVY MATERIAL FALLS INTO THE LOWER FILTER BAG WHILE THE LIGHTER DUST IS FILTERED OUT IN THE TOP BAG

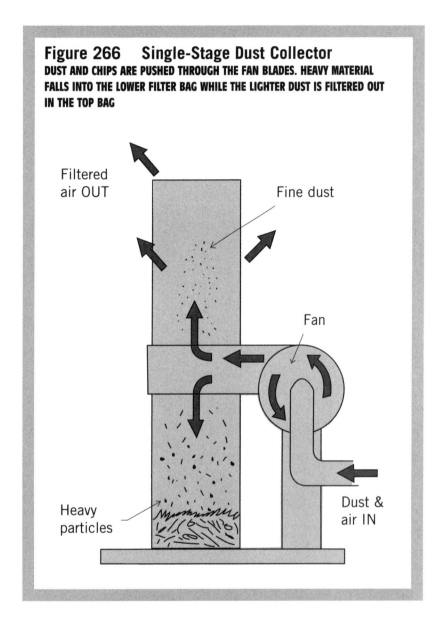

Filtered air OUT

Fine dust

Fan

Heavy particles

Dust & air IN

essence, a two-stage collector is a single-stage collector with a collection can placed before the impeller.

Dust Collection Separators

If you find that chips and debris are causing trouble in your single-stage system, or that distinctive ping when a nail hits the blades sends chills up your spine, you can add a pre-separator to remedy the problem. Dust collection pre-separators (**Figure 268**) increase the holding volume and filtering capacity of one-stage systems by removing larger chips from the air flow before they reach the collector. You can buy plastic separator tops that attach to 10- or 30-gallon garbage cans and convert a single-stage system into a two-stage collection system.

If you decide to make your own pre-separator (**Figure 269**), perhaps by altering the lid of a plastic garbage can, remember that a baffle between the in-take and out-take ports helps to slow the air enough to cause the chips to drop to the bottom of the can. In another homemade design, the input port is turned so the chips and debris are started in a circular motion around the inside of the can. This creates a cyclonic action which causes heavier particles to settle before the airflow carries smaller dust

Two-Stage Collectors

Two-stage collectors (**Figure 267**) also create negative pressure with an impeller, but heavier chips drop into a first-stage collection container before encountering the impeller. The finer dust then passes through the fan blades and is collected in a second-stage filter bag or bags. In

Figure 267   Two-Stage Dust Collector

THE SEPARATOR, PLACED IN-LINE BETWEEN THE SHOP MACHINES AND THE FAN, COLLECTS LARGER DEBRIS BEFORE IT GETS TO THE FAN BLADES. CYCLONIC AIR FLOW CAUSES CHIPS TO DROP INTO THE TANK WHILE LIGHTER DUST AND PARTICLES PASS THROUGH THE FAN AND ARE CAPTURED IN FILTER BAGS.

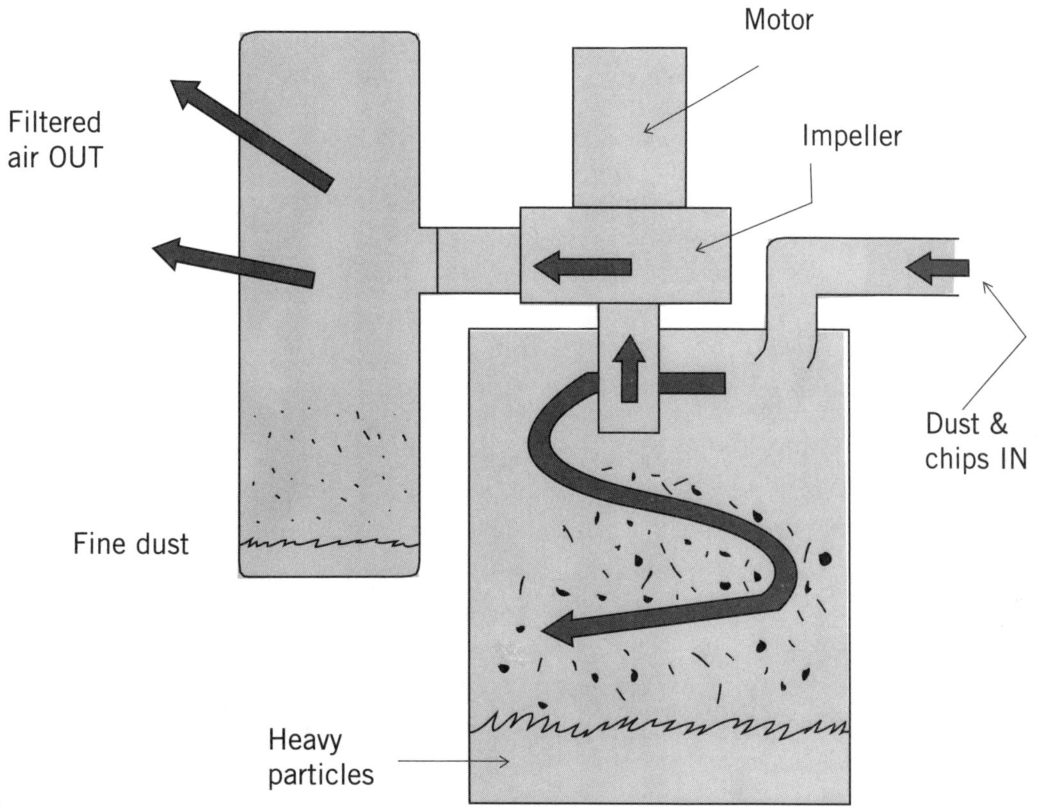

through the fan. Both separators reduce the potential for fire hazard by removing metal objects before they hit the impeller. Some dust collectors have plastic or aluminum fan blades that also reduce the chance of sparking.

Designing a System

Before you choose a dust collection system you should decide first what you want to accomplish in terms of moving and collecting wood debris. Do you want to connect every machine in your shop, or only hook up the table saw and the

Figure 268   Separator

THE SEPARATOR, PLACED IN-LINE BETWEEN THE SHOP MACHINES AND THE FAN, COLLECTS LARGER DEBRIS BEFORE IT GETS TO THE FAN BLADES. THE LID FITS HARDWARE STORE TRASH CANS.

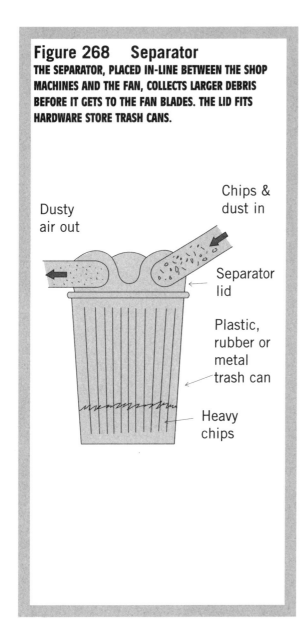

Figure 269
Homemade Pre-separator Containers

WITH BAFFLE (A) AND WITH CYCLONIC ACTION (B).

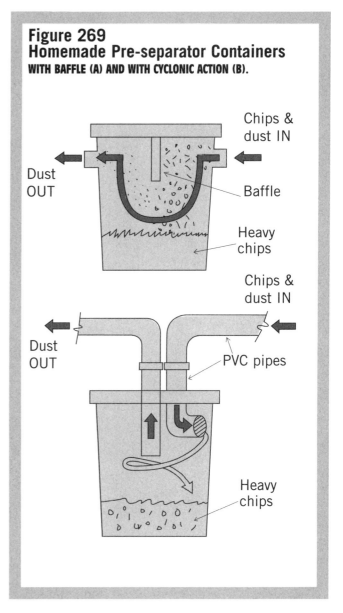

jointer and use your shop vacuum for the drill press and the oscillating sander?

Next, you need to design the most efficient main duct system possible because this is the heart of the system, i.e., where the dust moves from machine to collector. As the diameter of a pipe decreases, static pressure increases. If the main duct is too small, friction will restrict air volume until chips are not removed from the shop machine. On the other hand, if the main duct is too large, air velocity will be reduced and the chips will settle out in the ducts.

Design Your Collection System

1. Draw a floor plan of your shop area (**Figure 270**).

2. Determine the size of each branch line.

3. Determine the size of the main line.

4. Figure the static pressure loss for the system.

5. Select a dust collector.

1. Draw a Floor Plan of Your Shop Area

Locate the following items:
a. The dust collector.
b. Each dust producing machine.
c. The main line.
d. The branch lines.

If some of your tools are portable and you share your shop with the family car, locate ducts near the ceiling and plan on using flex hose when you move a machine out to the center of the shop.

2. Determine the Size of Each Branch Line

a. If a machine has a factory-installed port, use this size for the pipe to the main duct. However, if the machine outlet is smaller than 3-in. diameter, use an enlargement coupler with a 3-in. branch line to the

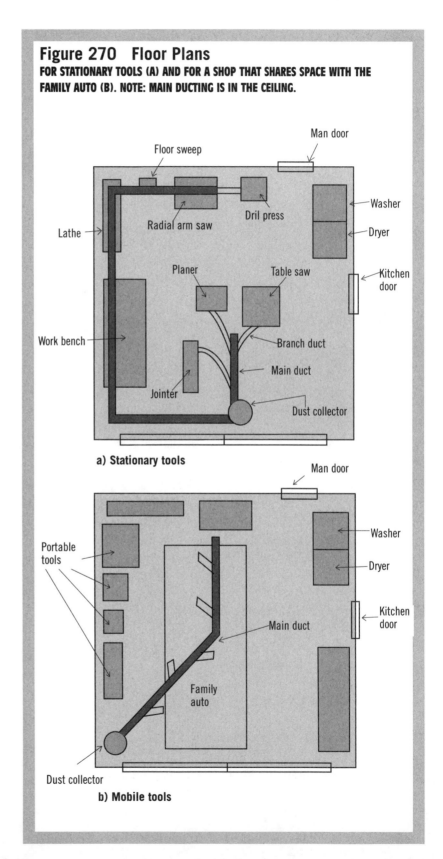

Figure 270   Floor Plans
FOR STATIONARY TOOLS (A) AND FOR A SHOP THAT SHARES SPACE WITH THE FAMILY AUTO (B). NOTE: MAIN DUCTING IS IN THE CEILING.

a) Stationary tools

b) Mobile tools

main. A 3-in. diameter should be the minimum duct size in your system.

b. If the outlet is square or rectangular, calculate the area and use the equivalent round diameter pipe. See the chart in **Figure 271** to convert square port areas to circular areas.

c. For suggested sizes of pipes to carry dust from a machine to the main ducting, see **Figure 263**.

3. Determine the Size of the Main Line

a. Use the machines that produce the most dust and the machines that are the greatest distance from the collector to calculate the size of the main line.

b. Run that size pipe from the collector to this main machine.

FOR RECTANGULAR OR SQUARE PORTS, FIND THE AREA IN SQUARE INCHES AND THEN CONVERT TO PIPE DIAMETER.

Figure 271
Pipe Diameter to Area

Diameter Inches	Sq. In.	Sq. Ft.
3	7.07	0.05
4	12.57	0.09
5	19.63	0.14
6	28.27	0.20
7	38.48	0.27
8	50.26	0.35
9	63.61	0.44
10	78.54	0.55
11	95.03	0.66
12	113.09	0.79

Rules of Thumb

1. Locate the dust collector close to the machines that produce the most sawdust.

2. Keep the main line short.

3. Use 'Y' joints instead of 'T' joints.

4. Use a minimum of flexible pipe.

5. Close each branch with a blast gate at the machine.

If there are two main machines, run that size pipe to both.

The main duct should be large enough to move the volume of air required to exhaust the debris from the main machine, but if it is too large, the air velocity will be slowcd and the chips will settle out without being moved all the way to the collector.

Duct Size (ft^2)
= Largest Machine Volume $(ft^3/min.$ or CFM)
÷ Main Duct Velocity (ft/min.)

Example: The main machine is a 12-in. surface planer. Engineers have determined that a velocity of 3500 FPM is required to keep sawdust suspended. **Figure 263** shows the planer needs 450 CFM.

Duct size = 450 ÷ 3500 = 0.13 ft^2
Now convert 0.13 ft^2 to the diameter of a round pipe.
$$1 ft^2 = 144 in^2$$
$$0.13 ft^2 \times 144 in^2/ft^2 = 18.7 in^2$$
Area circle = $\pi r^2 = \pi \times (d/2)^2$
And d = 2 $\sqrt{[area/\pi]}$
d = 2 $\sqrt{[18.7 / 3.14]}$
= 4.9-in. diameter

Therefore, use a 5-in. diameter pipe for the line from the main machine (12-in. planer) to the dust collector. **Figure 271** also shows duct size 0.13 ft^2 will need 5-in. diameter pipe. You can also use the chart in **Figure**

272 to find the appropriate main line size.

If the radial arm saw and the band saw are going to be used at the same time, the CFM of each is added, for example: 400 plus 400 equals 800 CFM. The ducting size should be calculated using the 800 number. The chart (**Figure 272**) shows 6-in. main line size.

4. Figure the Static Pressure Loss for the System

Figure the SP loss by using the run from the main machine to the dust collector. List all of the components and assign them equivalent length values, using the **Work Table** on the next page. Equivalent length means assigning each type of fitting that has more air flow resistance than straight duct a value equal to a certain length of straight pipe. Make a blank table like the one shown. It isn't necessary to include all the components in the system. As long as the system is designed so blast gates or plugs shut other branches off and only one machine is running at a time, the other lines will not be participating.

Static Pressure Loss (inches water gauge)

= [Length of pipe (feet) x Velocity^2 (ft/sec.)]

÷ [25,000 x pipe diameter (in.) x 0.58]

$$SP = (L \times V^2)$$
$$\div (25,000 \times d \times 0.58)$$

Example: We are building a dust collection system with the following requirements: the velocity in the main line is to be 3,500 ft/min. (58 ft/sec.); the ducting diameter is 5 in.; and the main line will be 65-ft. long.

The 0.58 figure is a constant used to convert the answer to inches of water where 1 in. water = 0.577 oz/in^2.

$$SP = (65 \times 58^2)$$
$$\div (25,000 \times 5 \times 0.58)$$
$$SP = 218,660 \div 72,500$$
$$= 3.02 \text{ in. water gauge}$$

You also can read the SP values from the table in **Figure 273**. In Column 1, find 5-in. pipe diameter. In column 2, read 0.0472 SP per foot. Then 0.0472 x 65 equivalent feet = SP 3.07.

Three inches water gauge is the static pressure loss in the pipes from the main machine to the collector. Some experts add another 1 in. for leaks and another 2 in. for back pressure due to dirty filter bags. Doing this we have a total of 6-in. static pressure. We will look for a dust collection system that is big enough to overcome 6-in. static pressure while still maintaining at least 450 CFM, the volume needed by our main machine, the 12-in. planer. If a separator container is used, add another 2-in. SP to the total.

Figure 272   Machine CFM and Main Duct Size
THE CFM (FOR EXAMPLE, 450) FOR THE MACHINE IN QUESTION (A 12-IN. PLANER) AND THE VELOCITY (3,500) GIVE THE REQUIRED DIAMETER OF THE MAIN DUCT (4.9 IN.).

Machine Volume CFM	Main Duct Diameter At 3500 FPM (Decimal)	Main Duct Diameter At 3500 FPM (Nearest In.)	Main Duct Diameter At 4000 FPM (Decimal)	Main Duct Diameter At 4000 FPM (Nearest In.)
300	4.0 Inch	4 Inch	3.7 Inch	4 Inch
350	4.3	4	4.0	4
400	4.6	4	4.3	4
450	4.9	5	4.5	4
500	5.1	5	4.8	5
550	5.4	5	5.0	5
600	5.6	5	5.2	5
650	5.8	6	5.5	5
700	6.1	6	5.7	6
750	6.3	6	5.9	6
800	6.5	6	6.1	6

Diam. = 2 x Sq Rt (Vol x 144 / Vel x 3.14)

Work Table

Straight Pipe   _____ ft. x 1.0 = _____ ft.

Flexible Pipe   _____ ft. x 3.0 = _____ ft.

90° Joints (No.)   _____ x _____*   = _____ ft.

       * 3 in. = 5 ft., 4 in. = 6 ft., 5 in. = 9 ft., 6 in. = 12 ft.

45° Joints (No.)   _____ x _____**.   = _____ ft.

       ** 3 in. = 2.5 ft., 4 in. = 3 ft., 5 in. = 4.5 ft., 6 in. = 6 ft.

Total Equivalent Straight Pipe After Conversion _____ ft.

Work Table

Straight Pipe   ___34___ ft. x 1.0 = ___34___ ft.

Flexible Pipe   ___3___ ft. x 3.0 = ___9___ ft.

90° Joints (No.)   _2_ x _9_*   = ___18___ ft.

45° Joints (No.)   _1_ x _4_**   = ___4___ ft.

Total Equivalent Straight Pipe After Conversion ___65___ ft.

LOCATE THE PIPE DIAMETER AND VELOCITY OF AIR IN THE MAIN DUCT. THE FRICTION/STATIC PRESSURE LOSS CAN BE READ.

Figure 273   Static Pressure Loss

Pipe Dia. In Inches	3500 fpm SP per ft.	3500 fpm SP per 100 ft.	4000 fpm SP per ft.	4000 fpm SP per 100 ft.	4500 fpm SP per ft.	4500 fpm SP per 100 ft.
1	0.2358	23.58	0.3081	30.81	0.3899	38.99
2	0.1179	11.79	0.1541	15.41	0.1950	19.50
3	0.0786	7.86	0.1027	10.27	0.1300	13.00
4	0.0590	5.90	0.0770	7.70	0.0975	9.75
5	0.0472	4.72	0.0616	6.16	0.0780	7.80
6	0.0393	3.93	0.0514	5.14	0.0650	6.50
7	0.0337	3.37	0.0440	4.40	0.0557	5.57
8	0.0295	2.95	0.0385	3.85	0.0487	4.87
9	0.0262	2.62	0.0342	3.42	0.0433	4.33
10	0.0236	2.36	0.0308	3.08	0.0390	3.90
11	0.0214	2.14	0.0280	2.80	0.0354	3.54
12	0.0197	1.97	0.0257	2.57	0.0325	3.25

Note: Static pressure values in inches of water
$$SP = LV^2 / 25000\,d$$

But what if you already have duct work installed? You installed 4-in. PVC before calculating that you needed 5-in. pipe? Here are the figures:

Length = 65 ft., planer = 450 CFM, duct diameter = 4-in.,
duct area = $\pi r^2 \div 144$
   = 0.0873 sq ft.
Vel = Vol ÷ Area
Vel = 450 ÷ 0.0873 = 5,155 FPM

More velocity than we need, but it should work.

$$SP = (L \times V^2)$$
$$\div (25,000 \times d \times 0.58)$$

The formula uses velocity (V) in ft/sec.
5155 ft/min. ÷ 60 = 85.9 ft/sec.

$$SP = [65 \times (85.9)^2$$
$$\div (25,000 \times 4 \times 0.58)]$$
SP = 479,809 ÷ 58,000
SP = 8.3 @ 4-in. plus 3-in. for dirty bags and leaks
   = SP 11.3 @ 4 in.

5. Select a Dust Collector

Finally, this is what the figuring and calculating was all about. We now know what we need in a dust collection system - volume of at least 450 CFM and SP 6 with 5-in. ducts, or 450 CFM and SP 11.3 with the 4-in. ducting. But now it really gets complicated. Rick Peters, author of a 128-page book on dust collecting wrote: "I've yet to come across a tool as confusing to buy as a dust collector."

Ideally, manufacturers should rate their dust collectors by volume of air moved (CFM) at a given static pressure (SP). This would allow woodworkers to purchase the smallest system that would handle their needs. As you look through catalogs, some manufacturers provide this data (CFM and SP) and some don't. In the chart (**Figure 274**) I've listed a few dust collectors from catalogs.

Note that no manufacturer lists 450 CFM, 6 SP @ 5 in. (our system requirement). Because the same dust collector hooked up to 4, 5, 6, or 7-in. pipes will have different static pressures we have to convert the SP figures in the catalog. Static pressure rises as the size of the pipe gets smaller. Use **Figure 275** to convert catalog sizes to your size.

Looking at the catalog list of dust collectors:
Eliminate machines 2, 4, & 6—Don't want a 3-phase motor.

Eliminate machines 1, 2, 3 & 4—Don't want a two-stage system.

Eliminate machines 5, 6 & 15—No Static Pressure Loss listed.

Eliminate machines 5, 10, 13 & 16—CFM too small.

This leaves six machines. Use **Figure 275** to convert SP as listed to SP at 5 in.

#7 SP 7.0 @ 4 in.   7.0 ÷ 1.25 = SP 5.6 @ 5 in.

#8 SP 9.5 @ 5 in.   9.5 ÷ 1.00 = SP 9.5 @ 5 in.

#9 SP 10.2 @ 4 in.   10.2 ÷ 1.25 = SP 8.16 @ 5 in.

#11 SP 16.7 @ 6 in. 16.7 ÷ 0.83 = SP 20.1 @ 5 in.

#12 SP 10.5 @ 9 in. 10.5 ÷ 0.56 = SP 18.8 @ 5 in.

#14 SP 8.9 @ 6 in.   8.9 ÷ 0.83 = SP 10.7 @ 5 in.

Now we can compare apples to apples (**Figure 276**). Note that machine #7 seemed large enough with SP 7.0 @ 4 in., but when converted was SP 5.6 @ 5 in. and probably would be underpowered. Machines #11 and #12 are larger than we need while machines #8, #9, and #14 fit our criteria and warrant further consideration. Now that we know these three

Rule of Thumb

If you decide this is all too complicated, here is a typical system that probably will suit 90% of the wood working shops in the USA. If you have a 20 x 20-ft. shop and only plan to use one machine at a time, pick a dust collector that has a suction capacity of 600 CFM or more and has at least the following static pressure readings:

SP	at Inches	
6.0	@	4
4.8	@	5
4.0	@	6
3.4	@	7
3.0	@	8
2.7	@	9
2.4	@	10

This Rule of Thumb assumes that this is a single-stage collector with no pre-separator can, that only one woodworking machine operates at a time, that 600 CFM volume will handle the largest machine, that there are 4-in. diameter main lines, 3 to 4-in. branch lines, and that there are approximately 60 ft. of equivalent straight pipe. Use this guideline and you'll solve your dust collection problems.

MANUFACTURERS VARY IN THE AMOUNT OF DATA THEY PROVIDE. A MACHINE
WITH NO LISTING OF CFM OR SP SHOULD BE ELIMINATED FROM CONSIDERATION
WHEN SHOPPING FOR A DUST COLLECTOR.

Figure 274 Sixteen Dust Collection Systems

Dust Collector	Hp / Phase	Volts	Stage	CFM	SP	Velocity FPM	Cost
1	3.0 / 1	220	Two	1800	9.0 @ 8"		$1,700
2	3.0 / 3	230/460	Two	1800	9.0 @ 8"		$1,500
3	5.0 / 1	220	Two	2100	11.0 @ 8 "		$2,000
4	7.5 / 3	230/460	Two	2400	14.8 @ 8"		$2,300
5	0.5 / 1	120/240	Single	450		5100	$450
6	2.0 / 3	220/440	Single	1100		5600	$740
7	1.0 / 1	120	Single	650	7.0 @ 4"		$275
8	2.0 / 1	120	Single	1200	9.5 @ 5"		$450
9	3.0 / 1	120	Single	1900	10.2 @ 4"		$750
10	1.0 / 1	120	Single	450	2.76 @ 4"		$150
11	3.0 / 1	120/240	Single	2300	16.7 @ 6"		$450
12	2.5 / 1	120/240	Single	2900	10.5 @ 9"		$900
13	0.75 / 1	120	Single	260	6.2 @ 6"		$425
14	2.0 /1	120	Single	690	8.9 @ 6"		$300
15	1.5 / 1	120	Single				$660
16 - P	1.0 / 1	120	Single	450	2.76 @ 4"		$170

P=Portable

TO CONVERT SP FROM ONE SIZE PIPE TO ANOTHER, DIVIDE BY THE PROPER NUMBER,
FOR EXAMPLE, SP 4.9 @ 7 IN. CONVERTS TO SP 6.9 @ 5 IN. (4.9 ÷ 0.71 = 6.9).

THREE OF THESE MACHINES (#8, 9 AND
14) MEET OUR CRITERIA AND WARRANT
FURTHER CONSIDERATION.

Figure 275   Static Pressure Conversion

To change Static Pressure at this dia.	To static Pressure at 8" dia. Divide By	To static Pressure at 7" dia. Divide By	To static Pressure at 6" dia. Divide By	To static Pressure at 5" dia. Divide By	To static Pressure at 4" dia. Divide By
3	2.67	2.33	2.00	1.67	1.33
4	2.00	1.75	1.50	1.25	1.00
5	1.60	1.40	1.20	1.00	0.80
6	1.33	1.17	1.00	0.83	0.67
7	1.14	1.00	0.86	0.71	0.57
8	1.00	0.88	0.75	0.63	0.50
9	0.89	0.78	0.67	0.56	0.44
10	0.80	0.70	0.60	0.50	0.40
11	0.73	0.64	0.55	0.45	0.36
12	0.67	0.58	0.50	0.42	0.33

Figure 276 Six Dust Collectors

Dust Collector	CFM	SP@5"	Cost
7	650	5.6	$275
8	1200	9.5	$450
9	1900	8.2	$750
11	2300	20.1	$450
12	2900	18.8	$900
14	690	10.7	$300

machines will do the job, we can consider price, footprint size, and other data before making our choice.

PVC and Static Electricity

For years, woodworkers have been bombarded by books, articles, and advertisements about the dangers of static electricity when PVC ducting is used in dust collection systems. A typical warning is: "If you elect to use plastic pipe or flex-hose, your hose must be grounded to safely discharge static electrical build-up." An ad for dust collectors and all the paraphernalia for grounding PVC pipe screamed: "Warning: There is a fire or explosion hazard if all duct work is not properly grounded."

Elaborate instructions follow these warnings on how to string copper wire down the middle of each pipe, or how to wrap wire around the outside of the pipe, how to install pop-rivets or screws every foot or yard, and how to connect these all together. As writers attempt to correct other writers, the literature has become so full of "facts" that it has become confusing and ridiculous.

In an attempt to clear the air, Dr. Rod Cole, a mathematician at the Lincoln Labs at MIT, along with a friend, who is a professor at MIT and an expert in the physics of lightning, made the following points (*Fine Woodworking* and online).

1. In lab-sized experiments, no one has been able to get electrostatic discharge ignition of even highly combustible dusts in remotely realistic situations.

2. There has never been a documented case of an explosion problem with PVC in a home shop, or a case of an explosion in a filter bag.

3. It is impossible to ground an insulator. Plastic pipe is an insulator and cannot be grounded.

Dr. Cole, who is a woodworker himself, points out that there are distinct dust-related hazards in the small shop. He mentions specifically sawdust in a pile under a tool and dust in a filter bag.

1. The Dust Pile - A saw blade or sander can hit a piece of metal and the spark can land in a dust pile. This spark might go out or smolder for hours before a fire erupts. Fires have been reported that have started in a floor sander bag left emptied, and in a dust pile under a table saw.

2. The Filter Bags - The same spark that could land in the dust pile can also be sucked up and land in a dust collection bag. Also, metal that is swept up with dust from the floor could hit the impeller blade and cause a spark. A pinched saw blade can cause hot embers.

References
(1) Dr. Rod Cole, *Fine Woodworking* – "Tools & Shop," Winter 2001, p.48. (PVC Pipe Dangers Debunked).

(2) Dr. Rod Cole, Online gis.net/~dheaton/woodworking/woodworking .shtml, (Grounding PVC and Other Dust Collection Myths)

CHAPTER 27

Clamps, Pressure & Joints

If two pieces of board could be made to fit together perfectly, so that a thin, even glue line could be produced by merely snuggling the pieces together, and further, that we could be assured that nothing would disturb the joint before the glue set, clamps would not be required. From a practical standpoint, such a joint is not possible. A certain amount of pressure must be used, because machining of stock is never perfect.

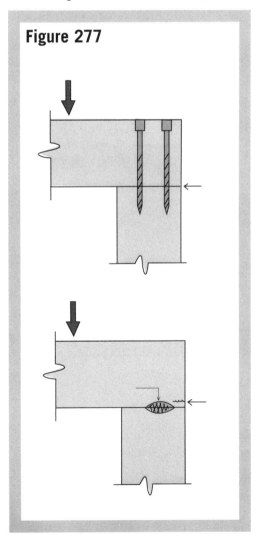

Figure 277

In gluing, the role of clamps is to provide this pressure and thus force the edges of the stock close together. This helps spread the glue evenly across the joint and holds the wood tight until the glue penetrates and sets. On a microscopic level, which is where the glue-to-wood bonding develops, a seemingly smooth wood surface is really quite uneven. Pressure pushes glue into the little crevices and also forces air from the surface of the wood. There should be just enough force applied to assure that the joint surfaces are touching each other. Excessive pressure will crush the fibers of the wood, strain the clamp, bow the material, and weaken the joint by forcing glue out. The joint loses strength when the glue line is too thick, but on the other hand, the joint also loses strength if the glue line is too thin because of glue squeeze-out. It is more important that the pressure be uniform than that there is a lot of it. Uneven pressure puts unnatural strains on the wood and results in part of the joint having a thick glue line and another part perhaps having none at all.

Pressure Distribution

Tradition has it that in edge-to-edge gluing there should be one clamp 2 in. from each end of the panel and then one clamp every 8 to 10 in. along the glue line. Actually, determining the pressure needed for a good joint is more complicated. The number of clamps necessary is in direct proportion to the width of the pieces being joined, the thickness of the stock used, and the rigidity of the wood.

Width

In edge-to-edge joints, the pressure from a clamp fans out at 45 degrees in each direction. This is the key when choosing how many clamps to use when you glue up panels. In **Figure 278** we see how force radiates and is transmitted to the joint in the direct pressure area, that is, the area within the 90-degree sweep. The wider the boards being glued, the wider is the spread of the direct pressure area, and the fewer clamps that are needed.

In **Figure 279**, note that by using a stiff clamping pad, the direct pressure area is widened because the effective clamping edge is enlarged. Narrow boards should be placed in the center of the panel and not on the edge.

Direct Pressure Area (DPA)
  = 2 x board width
  + pad width

a) Board width = 2, clamp width = 1, pad width = 4
DPA = 2 x 2 + 1 = 5 in.
DPA = 2 x 2 + 4
    = 8 in. (with pad)

b) Board width = 4, clamp width = 1, pad width = 4
DPA = 2 x 4 + 1 = 9 in.
DPA = 2 x 4 + 4
    = 12 in. (with pad)

c) Board width = 6, clamp width = 1, pad width = 4
DPA = 2 x 6 + 1 = 13 in.
DPA = 2 x 6 + 4
    = 16 in. (with pad)

Hardness

The hardness of a board affects how many clamps are used and the pressure needed to bring the joint surfaces together in two ways. In the case of a poorly-made joint, the more rigid the boards are, the more clamps and pressure are needed to bring the two into

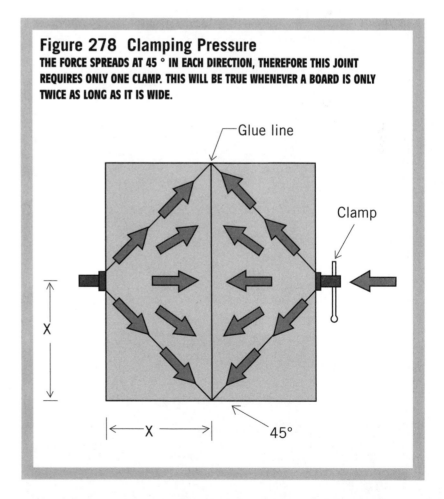

Figure 278 Clamping Pressure
THE FORCE SPREADS AT 45° IN EACH DIRECTION, THEREFORE THIS JOINT REQUIRES ONLY ONE CLAMP. THIS WILL BE TRUE WHENEVER A BOARD IS ONLY TWICE AS LONG AS IT IS WIDE.

Glue line
Clamp
X
X
45°

line. On the other hand, because of this same rigidity, if the joint is well-prepared and straight, less clamps are needed to bring the two pieces together because rigid boards transmit pressure better than less dense boards.

Hardwoods transmit pressure better than softwoods, a case which argues for fewer clamps.

Conversely, because of this rigidity, they are also harder to pull into position if the joint is poorly made, which argues for more clamps. Because of these two diametrically opposed properties, the density of wood probably should be ignored when determining how many clamps to use.

Softwoods can be removed from clamps earlier than hardwoods because with their lesser strength and rigidity, there will be a reduced amount of stress on the glued joint when the boards are unclamped. After clamp pressure is removed, both hard and softwoods should be allowed to cure until all moisture has left the glue line area.

Wood can be divided into categories of hardness, **Figure 280**.

Hard—Beech, hickory, hard maple, oak, purpleheart, rosewoods.
Medium hard—Elm, soft maple, teak, walnut.

Soft—Basswood, birch, cedar, cherry, Douglas fir, lauan, mahogany, pine.

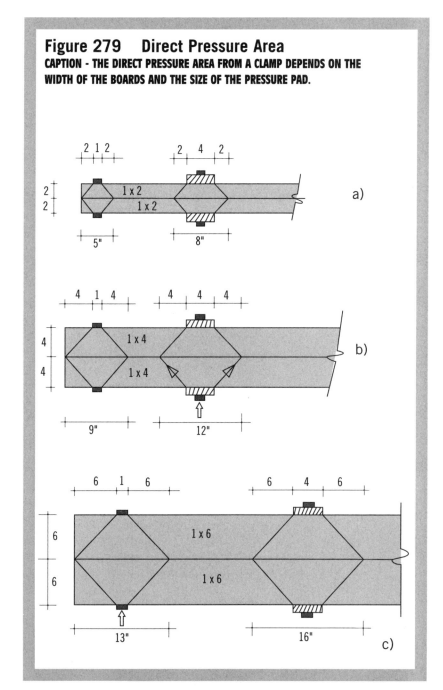

Figure 279   Direct Pressure Area
CAPTION - THE DIRECT PRESSURE AREA FROM A CLAMP DEPENDS ON THE WIDTH OF THE BOARDS AND THE SIZE OF THE PRESSURE PAD.

Thickness

On a poor joint, the thicker the stock, the more pressure is needed to force and hold the edges together, however, if the joint is straight and well-prepared, thicker stock will require fewer clamps because it transfers pressure better.

Joints and Strength

What joint is the strongest? Until now we've been talking about edge-to-edge glue joints where a lot of experts feel that the only reason for using dowels is to keep the pieces aligned while the glue dries. But what about end-grain to end-grain or end-grain to long-grain joints? We use these joints in attaching chair rails to legs, table aprons to legs, and door rails to stiles. These are the types of unions where we utilize aids to add strength to the joint. Are dowels stronger than mortise and tenons? Should we use metal screws? Do any of these lend strength or are they only useful to align wood and keep the pieces from slipping while the glue sets? For years, cabinetmakers and woodworkers have used the big three: mortise and fixed tenon, mortise and floating tenon, and dowels. Recently, a newcomer, the biscuit, has appeared. So how do they compare?

A woodworking magazine

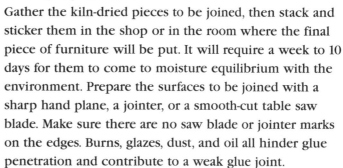

Rule of Thumb
Gluing Up a Panel

Gather the kiln-dried pieces to be joined, then stack and sticker them in the shop or in the room where the final piece of furniture will be put. It will require a week to 10 days for them to come to moisture equilibrium with the environment. Prepare the surfaces to be joined with a sharp hand plane, a jointer, or a smooth-cut table saw blade. Make sure there are no saw blade or jointer marks on the edges. Burns, glazes, dust, and oil all hinder glue penetration and contribute to a weak glue joint.

Apply just enough glue to put a thin film along the edges of both pieces, rub the surfaces together, and allow the pieces to stand for about five minutes before being clamped. This closed time gives the glue enough time to penetrate into the wood before the clamps squeeze the excess out. For edge gluing, use 4-in. clamping pads to spread the pressure and protect the wood. A good rule of thumb is to space the clamps at intervals about twice the width of the adjacent board. This means two 5-in. boards should be clamped every 10 in.

Apply moderate clamping pressure and stop when you have a thin, uniform squeeze-out line of glue. A well-made edge-to-edge joint should require very little clamp pressure. Let the panel stand for an hour then remove the clamps and scrape off the squeeze-out. Lean the panel upright and let it cure overnight before working it further.

Figure 280   Wood Hardness
SOFTWOODS REQUIRE LESS CLAMPING PRESURE.

Hard	Medium Hard	Soft
Beech	Elm	Basswood
Hickory	Soft Maple	Birch
Hard Maple	Teak	Cedar
Oak	Walnut	Cherry
Purpleheart		Douglas Fir
Rosewoods		Lauan
		Mahogany
		Pine

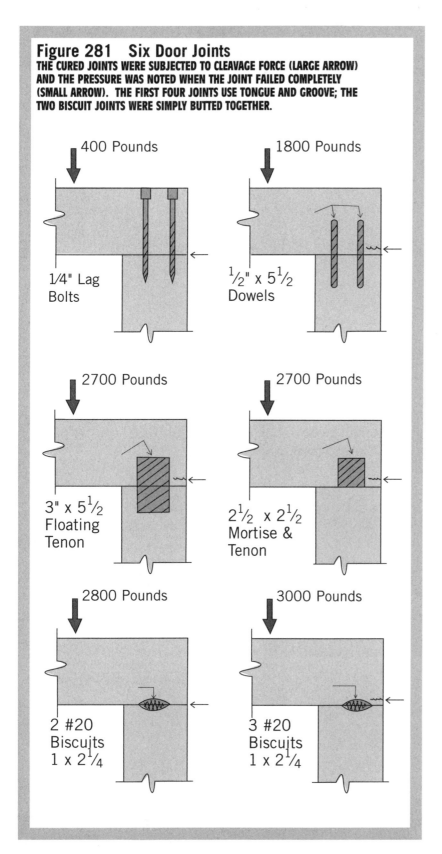

Figure 281   Six Door Joints
THE CURED JOINTS WERE SUBJECTED TO CLEAVAGE FORCE (LARGE ARROW) AND THE PRESSURE WAS NOTED WHEN THE JOINT FAILED COMPLETELY (SMALL ARROW). THE FIRST FOUR JOINTS USE TONGUE AND GROOVE; THE TWO BISCUIT JOINTS WERE SIMPLY BUTTED TOGETHER.

400 Pounds

1/4" Lag Bolts

1800 Pounds

$\frac{1}{2}$" x $5\frac{1}{2}$ Dowels

2700 Pounds

3" x $5\frac{1}{2}$ Floating Tenon

2700 Pounds

$2\frac{1}{2}$ x $2\frac{1}{2}$ Mortise & Tenon

2800 Pounds

2 #20 Biscuits 1 x $2\frac{1}{4}$

3000 Pounds

3 #20 Biscuits 1 x $2\frac{1}{4}$

published results of tests on a rail and stile joint as used in a wooden door frame (**Figure 281**). They first tested a simple tongue and groove joint, glued, which failed at 1,300 pounds.. Then they tested tongue and groove plus dowels, mortise and tenons, and finally lag bolts. Biscuit joinery was tested with simple butt joints plus two biscuits, then three biscuits. Elmer's yellow glue was used and the joints were allowed to cure for two weeks.

The joint with no glue and two $\frac{1}{4}$ x 5-in. lag bolts failed after only 400 pounds, demonstrating how little holding power threads have in end grain. The joint with just tongue and groove plus glue failed at 1300 pounds. The joint with two $\frac{1}{2}$ x 5 $\frac{1}{2}$-in. dowels failed at 1800 pounds. Surprisingly, the old carpenter's favorite, the mortise and tenon, was not the strongest. Fixed tenon ($2\frac{1}{2}$ x $2\frac{1}{2}$ in.) or loose tenon (3 x 5 in.), it made no difference, both failed at 2700 pounds. The butt joint using two #20 biscuits (each approx. 1 x $2\frac{1}{4}$ in.) failed at 2800 pounds. The three-biscuit butt joint was a bit stronger and failed at 3000 pounds. Both biscuit joints were quite a bit stronger than dowels, and out-performed the mortise and tenon joints too (or at least performed just as well). In all cases where glue was used, the wood split before the joint failed.

CHAPTER 28

All About Glues

At the start of every project, usually during the planning stage, the woodworker has to decide on the joinery - mortise and tenon, dowels, splines, biscuits, or maybe half laps. Hand in hand with joinery, he must also decide which adhesives to use. When I first started woodworking in the 1950's, we didn't have a choice of glues. The first one who arrived in the high school manual training class would plug in the glue pot. The dark brown hide glue was rock hard, with the brush stuck upright in the pot. By the time we had our wood and tools laid out and the instructor had made his rounds, the glue was hot, liquid, and ready to use - and whatever the project, whatever the wood or type of joinery, we used it, as had craftsmen for centuries before us. Today, we have many choices. In fact, it isn't unusual to use two or three types of glue on different parts of the same project.

When I first came to California in 1963, I met an old German cabinetmaker. I asked him what the biggest changes were that he had seen in 40 years of woodworking. Without hesitation he said, "glues and stains." He went on to say that when he started working with wood in Germany in the 1920's, he had to make all his own stains. He used tobacco, tea, coffee, and the leaves of different trees. He boiled, strained, combined, mixed, and finally applied the concoction to the wood. The result was uncertain and seldom reproducible. He was amazed at the stains he could buy now.

The other big difference was glue. His only adhesive in the old country was hide glue. You had to heat it up; too hot and it was ruined, not hot enough and it set before the two boards could be brought together. Then you'd clamp the boards for 24 hours. Hide glue joints weren't waterproof, so the piece couldn't be used outdoors or even indoors in conditions of high humidity. He said the old hide glues also seemed to have a definite lifetime. After 20 to 25 years the joints started coming apart and the hide glue became a brown powder.

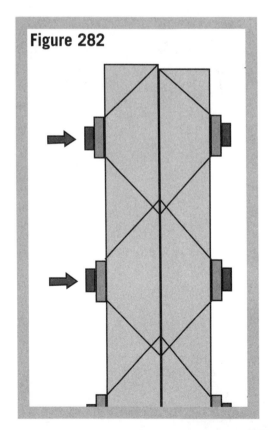

Figure 282

The old cabinetmaker told me he was constructing wooden rain gutters for his house. He planned on gluing them together with an epoxy that was completely waterproof, would not expand or contract with heat changes, and was readily available from the local hardware store.

Glue or Adhesive?

Glue is a natural substance that absorbs water to form a viscous suspension with strong adhesion properties. Examples are hide, casein, fish, rice, and blood protein glues. An adhesive is any substance that provides steady or firm attachment, for example, natural glues but also synthetic products like urea, phenol, resorcinol, polyvinyl acetate, cyanoacrylate, epoxy, and acrylic resin adhesives.

Types of Adhesives

In general terms, there are only two types of adhesives - thermoplastic and chemically reactive. These differ by the process in which they achieve a set.

Thermoplastic

These types of adhesives form a bond by physical change. When heated, they melt and are applied to the pieces where they bond, cool, and become solid again. Examples are: hot-melt glues, roofing tars, caulking resins, and sealing wax.

Some adhesives, such as polyvinyl acetates (PVA) and hide glues, can be reactivated by heat after their initial set. This is useful in veneering, where panels can be coated with glue, then allowed to dry. In use, the veneers are positioned and the glue is reactivated with heat to form strong bonds. Bubbles can be also be repaired. White PVA glue can be reactivated over a longer time than the yellow and the cross-link formulations.

Chemically Reactive

These adhesives react

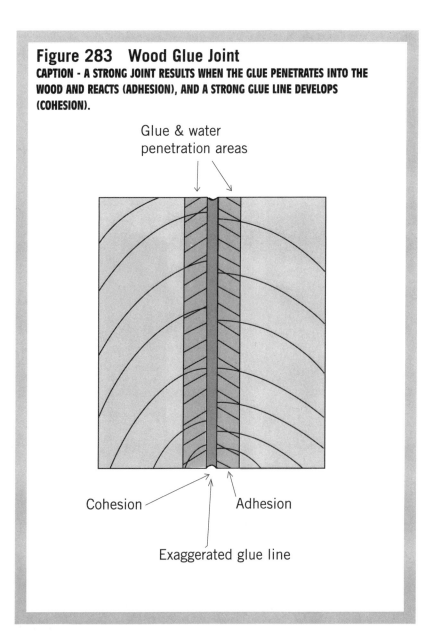

Figure 283   Wood Glue Joint

CAPTION - A STRONG JOINT RESULTS WHEN THE GLUE PENETRATES INTO THE WOOD AND REACTS (ADHESION), AND A STRONG GLUE LINE DEVELOPS (COHESION).

Glue & water penetration areas

Cohesion

Adhesion

Exaggerated glue line

chemically to form strong bonds when glue molecules come into contact with cellulose molecules in the wood. The chemical reaction begins automatically, or can be started by radiation, heat, light, or a catalyst.

How Does Glue Work?

In a nutshell: penetration, reaction, evaporation (**Figure 283**). For an adhesive to work, it must penetrate into the pores of the wood and react chemically within the wood cells. This reaction is dependent upon the evaporation of the solvent, usually water.

About 95% of a board consists of cellulose, lignin, and hemicellulose, which form the structural matrix of wood and give it strength, rigidity, and elasticity. The remaining 5% of dry wood is resins, tannins, oils, gums, coloring agents, and sugars.

Once in the wood, glue molecules are attracted to and react with cellulose molecules. This is called adherence. The glue remaining on the surface of one board bonds with glue on the surface of the other board. This is called cohesion. Both adhesion - glue bonded to wood - and cohesion - glue bonded to glue - must be present for a good joint. The

speed of set, assembly time, and depth of glue penetration depend on evaporation of the water.

Adhesives that are not water-based diffuse into the wood and react without loss of solvent. In both cases, the strength of the joint, i.e., the resistance to stress, water, solvents, and heat depends on the nature of the glue.

Most adhesives produce bonds that are stronger than the wood itself, so claims of extremely high bonding strength aren't meaningful to a woodworker. Of more concern is the setting rate, viscosity, water resistance, color, flexibility, ease of sanding, and gap-filling properties.

5 Keys to Success

The success of any glue joint depends on five things - the properties of the glue, the properties of the wood, the condition of the wood, the gluing process and the environment in which the operation is carried out.

1. The Properties of the Glue

There are three properties of adhesives that are necessary for the formation of a strong bond: penetration, reaction, and cure.

Figure 284 Grain Orientation
MOST GLUES WORK BEST ON SIDE GRAIN-TO-SIDE GRAIN JOINTS.

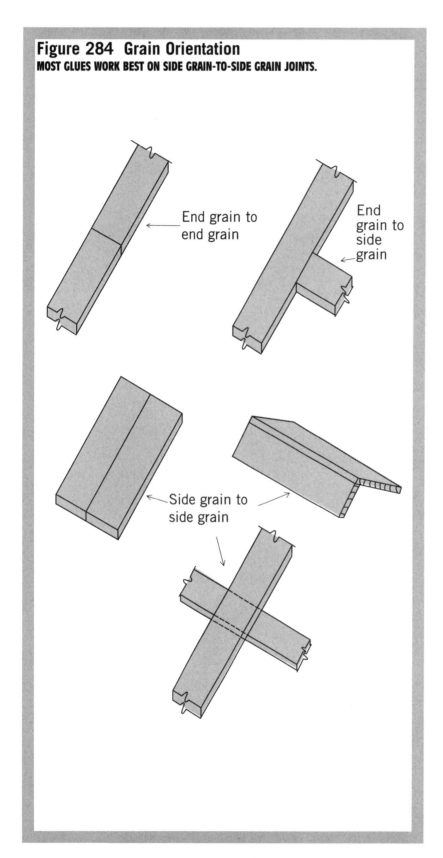

End grain to end grain

End grain to side grain

Side grain to side grain

The ability of the glue to penetrate into the wood depends, in large part, on the properties and condition of the wood. Once glue has penetrated, the ability of the glue to react with the wood molecules is not in doubt. Modern adhesives are formulated so they do react with cellulose molecules.

Release of the solvent to permit curing of the glue-cellulose bonds depends on the properties of the wood, the gluing process, and the environment. With the slower setting water-based glues, the strength of the joint develops slowly. As the first bit of water leaves the glue film by wicking into the dry wood, the glue begins to bond with wood molecules. After this quick initial set, water in the adjacent wood evaporates and the molecular reaction continues, finally giving complete bond strength.

2. Properties of the Wood

The properties of wood that affect the bond are density, grain orientation, and the presence of saps or oils.

Water carries glue into the wood, then, as it evaporates, reaction and cure begin. Because this reaction depends on water evaporation, and there is less water-glue penetration into hardwoods, set time in the denser woods is faster.

The strongest bonds are made with long grain joints (**Figure 284**). End grains pose a problem because they are like a bundle of straws where the open ends offer only a small solid area for bonding. Porous surfaces, like end grain, absorb the adhesive and leave little on the surface for cohesion. Polyurethane glue and the epoxies can bond end grains because they have good gap-filling ability, that is, they are not absorbed deeply into the end grain. Polyvinyl acetate glues will give stronger joints on end grain or miters by pre-sealing. This is done by diluting the glue 25-50% with water, coating the surface, and allowing the glue to dry, then proceeding in the normal fashion with full strength glue. Another method of sealing end grain is to butter the surface with a thin coat of full strength glue, allow it to stand 5 to 10 minutes, then re-coat and clamp in the usual way.

Difficult-to-glue, oily woods (such as teak and cocobolo) can be bonded by using special glues (cyanoacrylate, resorcinol, polyurethane), or by cleaning both bonding surfaces with acetone, lacquer thinner, or paint thinner first. This removes oil from the surface and allows glue to penetrate into the wood. Some glues work well on oily woods if the surfaces are freshly machined, but work poorly on older joints. In general, water-based glues do not work well on oily woods.

3. Condition of the Wood

The condition of the wood is largely up to the woodworker. Joints should be free of saw and jointer marks and should be straight, sound, and square. Burned, glazed, or burnished edges should be reworked because these conditions prevent glue penetration. It is usually easier to make a straight and square edge in the first place than to try and pull poorly jointed pieces together with clamps. When possible, joints should be prepared and glued the same day.

In the past, it was thought that smooth wood surfaces did not bond together well and that good glue joints resulted only when surface irregularities interlocked. Old timers used to advocate "toothing" a joint to let the fibers interlock. This was done by roughening the surfaces with a special toothing plane, a rasp, or with coarse sandpaper. Today we know that roughing up a surface is not a good practice as this introduces small pockets of air and wood dust. By keeping the two wood surfaces farther apart, toothing produces a thick, weaker glue line. Oil, wax, dirt, or sawdust on the surface of the joint hinders penetration, also making a joint weak.

When parts with dissimilar moisture contents are joined, the moister part moves more than the drier one. This also might happen if a flat-sawn plank were joined to a quarter-sawn piece. Even if the two pieces were kiln dried to the same moisture content, each will move at different rates. Before working wood, make sure it has a chance to acclimate or reach equilibrium with the humidity in your shop.

Green wood won't allow glue to penetrate, and an over-dry board will soak up glue and leave the joint dry. Moisture content of 6 to 10% is considered ideal for gluing.

4. The Gluing Process

In home shops a plastic squeeze bottle is the usual glue applicator. Casein, polyvinyl acetate, and some of the two- or three-part resin glues should not be mixed in metal containers because some chemicals in the adhesives react with iron, and then react with certain woods (oak, cherry, walnut, and mahogany) to form a black stain. Apply the glue in a thin, even coat on both surfaces (except in the case of the polyurethane adhesives, where glue is applied to one surface and

water to the other) and let the glue penetrate for a few minutes. Rub the boards together and if the glue requires pressure, apply clamps. Denser woods require higher clamping pressure than do softer, lighter woods. (See the discussion in Chapter 27 on clamping pressure.) Strive for a small line of extruded glue. Too much squeeze-out means more clean up and possible swelling of fibers. If no glue is squeezed out, you've either added just the right amount (unlikely) or you've applied too little and are now looking at a starved joint. In the later case, the joint should be pulled apart and more glue applied. Check the properties of the glue to see how long to keep the project under pressure.

Good joinery is necessarily a large part of good glue bonding. The best joint uses side grain, gives maximum bonding surfaces, makes use of the natural strength of the wood, and avoids concentrating stress over a small area. The pieces should be cut accurately with sharp tools and the joint should fit snugly when assembled. Glue should not be expected to act as a gap filler. Read a good joinery book and become familiar with all types of joints. Joints often fail because of wood movement. Remember that wood moves across the grain width-wise on

a board. Any joint that does not take wood movement into consideration is a joint that is suspect and likely to fail.

Joint aids such as dowels, mortise and tenon, panel and groove, dovetails, corner blocks, miters, and butterfly inlays are often used in gluing end-grain joints. If wooden aids are used, put an even coat of glue on the sides of the hole and on the inserts themselves. Dowels should be 1/32 to 1/64 in. smaller than the diameter of the hole so that all of the glue is not scraped off or pushed to the bottom of the hole. A dowel that has to be hammered into place is too tight. Dowels with grooves along their length help with this problem. Because biscuits are designed to swell in the presence of moisture, once you apply a water-based glue, the joint should be assembled quickly. I've found that white and yellow PVA glues give 1 to 3 minutes adjustment times while polyurethane glue gives 15 minutes, and hide glue gives 30 to 45 minutes.

Clamp time is dependent on the adhesive used, the wood type, the moisture content of the wood, and the environmental conditions (**Figure 285**). High humidity in the shop will slow down the set of water-based glues because the rate of cure is dependent on water evaporation.

After the minimum clamping period, the glued-up piece will have enough strength to be removed from the clamps and the glue scraped off. Removing excess squeeze-out will help evaporation and cure. The condition of the glue outside the joint is no indication of the set of the joint. The squeeze-out will be much softer than the glue inside the joint. An overnight cure is recommended prior to further machining. A curing period of three to four days may be required to eliminate swollen spots caused by residual moisture in the glue line.

Sunken spots in the final piece can occur with water-based glues if you are not patient (**Figure 286**). with the glue drying process. Wood in the vicinity of the glue line tends to swell, leaving a small hump or ridge along the glue joint. Sanding or machining across this area before it is fully dry makes it flush, but once the glue dries and the moisture in the wood equalizes, the leveled area shrinks, leaving a depression. Sunken joints occur along a glue line or where biscuits or dowels are placed. Swelling can be avoided by using less adhesive or by warming the joints prior to gluing. Once swelling occurs it can only be corrected by waiting until the glue dries and the boards have all come to moisture equilibrium.

WHEN CONSIDERING ENVIRONMENTAL CONDITIONS FOR WATER-BASED GLUING, THINK OF WATER AND EVAPORATION.

Figure 285   Shop Conditions

Shop Environment	Open Joint Time	Closed Joint Time	Clamping Time
Warm or Hot	Less	Less	Less
Chilly or Cold	More	More	More
Dry	Less	Less	Less
Damp	More	More	More
Airy or Breezy	Less	Less	Less
No Breeze	More	More	More
Warm, Dry Wood	Less	Less	Less
Cold, Damp Wood	More	More	More

Figure 286   A Sunken Joint
MOISTURE FROM THE GLUE OR FROM CLEAN-UP CAUSES THE FIBERS NEAR THE JOINT TO SWELL. MACHINING BEFORE THE FIBERS HAVE DRIED AND SHRUNK CAUSES A SUNKEN JOINT.

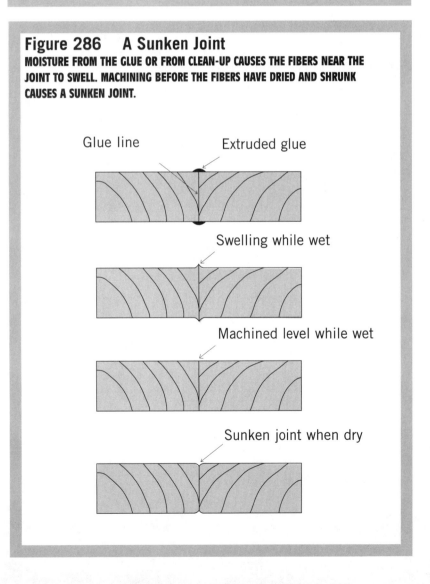

Glue line   Extruded glue

Swelling while wet

Machined level while wet

Sunken joint when dry

5. The Gluing Environment

Check the label for the working temperature range of the glue; most glues work well from 70 to 150°. PVA adhesives cure faster in hot weather but also have less open joint time. Moisture in kiln-dried woods will rise in high humidity conditions and slow down the rate of cure for PVA adhesives. On the other hand, polyurethane glues will cure more rapidly in warm and humid weather. Because speed of set is directly related to the drying time of the glue in the joint, dried wood with fast water absorbency will set faster than wet or high moisture content wood. Wood with high moisture content will need longer clamp time.

Testing

If you prepare the wood pieces properly, use the correct glue and apply it properly, any failures will occur in the wood, not in the glue joint. A good glue joint will actually be stronger than the wood surrounding the glue line. You can test joints yourself to choose the correct adhesive for your project. There are four strength tests usually performed on wood joints: tensile, shear, cleavage, and peel (**Figure 287**).

If you decide to test a few glues for strength, pick the type of joint in your project where failure is most likely to occur – end grain and high stress areas like chair-leg to seat-rail joints. Prepare two or three identical joints with similar pieces of wood using different glues. The test needn't be elaborate; secure one part in a vise and rap the other with a hammer. Not a very sophisticated experiment, but if two of the test joints break at the glue line, and the third splits the wood and leaves the glue line intact, you've answered your question. The same for a shear test: squeeze the pieces in a vise one by one and see if any fail at the glue joint.

I have a friend who checks water resistance in glues by putting test pieces into a dishwasher. He runs them through multiple washes and inspects the joints. Again, not sophisticated, but effective.

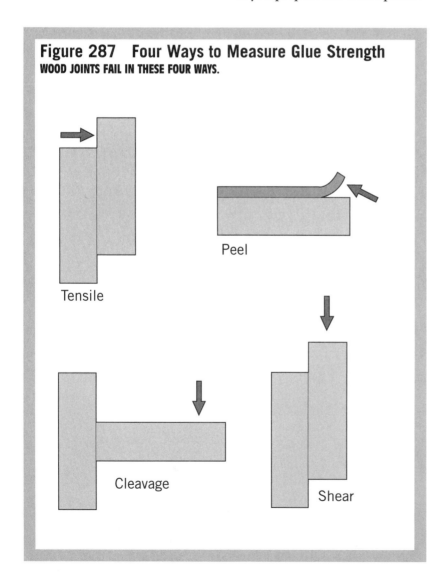

Figure 287   Four Ways to Measure Glue Strength
WOOD JOINTS FAIL IN THESE FOUR WAYS.

Tensile

Peel

Cleavage

Shear

CHAPTER 28: All About Glues

Types of Glues

In the last chapter we learned how to apply pressure and whether dowels or biscuits are stronger. We know how adhesives work so it's time to look at the different types of glue (**Figure 288**).

In the following discussions the terms "open time" and "closed time" are defined thus:
Open time is the time after the glue is spread on the joint until the pieces must be joined.
Closed time is the time after the pieces are joined side by side until the glue sets.
In other words, open time is how fast you must get the pieces together, closed time is how long you have to reposition and play with the assembly before the glue sets.

Hot Melt

These glues form fairly weak bonds. Hot melt glue has only about one tenth the shear strength of yellow carpenter's glue but it still can withstand 400 psi of pressure before failing.

Hot melt glues depend on mechanical bonding rather than chemical reaction for strength. These glues are cheap, easy to apply, and set up instantly. They have good gap filling properties and low toxicity. The glues cure by cooling and develop most of their strength by the time they

are back at room temperature. The glue penetrates poorly and remains somewhat flexible so the joints are prone to creep. They are available as pellets, sticks, chunks, or in sheet form, which can be activated with a household iron for veneering.

The types sold in the form of a solid stick are dispensed from electrically heated glue guns at about 350°F. They set and cool in 15-20 seconds. This is the only glue type where the applicator can injure you - the gun is hot. The adhesive can be released by heating with a paint stripper gun and the rubbery residue can be easily scraped from wood. In the workshop, hot melts are used for mock-ups, one-time jigs, and temporary attachments.

Because they contain no water, no volatiles, little, if any, solvent, and are easy to apply, hot melt glues are used extensively in manufacturing furniture, shoes, and clothing, in book binding, packaging, and pressure-sensitive adhesives. Hot melts are used to mount glass mirrors, slate, and wall paneling.

Recently, polyurethane adhesives have been introduced for hot melt application. This is not a true example of a hot melt adhesive.

Contact

Contact cements are made from synthetic rubber and are unique in that they are applied in one or more coats to both pieces and allowed to dry for 30 minutes to 2 hours before the surfaces are mated. Both surfaces should be clean and dry before an even coat is spread. The cement bonds without clamping although pressure should be applied after joining to insure close contact of both surfaces.

The solvent-based formulations are volatile, flammable, and highly toxic if ingested and moderately toxic with skin contact or by inhalation. The new water-based formulations are non-toxic and non-flammable but slower drying - they need 30 minutes to 1 hour to dry to the touch before assembly, and three days to cure completely.

In marquetry, contact glue will sometimes fail - not because of the contact adhesive itself, but because of the finish that is ultimately applied over the veneer. For example, if lacquer or shellac dissolved in methyl alcohol is used as a finish, the solvent can penetrate through the pores of the wood veneer or between the pieces of marquetry and soften the adhesive bond causing checking, splitting, and delamination. Think of the reason you use lacquer thinner to clean up dried contact glue - because it dissolves the rubber and resin. A better choice for veneer work is the water-based contact glues which are very solvent resistant once cured (72 hours after bonding).

Contact glues are heat and water resistant and are thus widely used for plastic laminates. They bond plastics, veneer, rubber, metal, and canvas with tenacity, but extreme care must be used in glue ups; parts cannot be shifted once contact is made. They are used in many industries, including auto making, shoe manufacture, and in construction. In the workshop, contact glues are used in veneering, inlay, and in any job where dissimilar substances are to be joined and shear strength isn't needed.

Cyanoacrylate (CA)

These glues are quite expensive but will bond most common plastics, hard PVC, rubber, glass, metals, wood, porcelain, ceramics, and skin - to itself and to each other. They set up in 5 to 10 seconds and have tensile strengths of 5,000 psi in metal-to-metal bonds. They are usually sold in thin, medium, thick, and gel formulations and can be mixed to achieve any viscosity desired. They are fast setting and can be used for a variety of different joints. The thin formulation will penetrate wood quickly, and the thicker gel works great on end grains. They are usually applied to one surface, then spread by rubbing the pieces together. The cure time is very short - sometimes seconds. With slower reacting CA glues, the glue is spread on one surface and an accelerator spread on the other, then the two are mated and bonding is immediate. Smooth, hard surfaces will bond more rapidly than rough, porous ones. The pieces can be machined immediately although maximum strength is not reached for 8 to 48 hours.

CA glues cure by excluding air (anaerobic). When cured, they have good water resistance, low heat resistance, and are resistant to most solvents. Turners use CA glues extensively to harden punky woods, repair cracks, and for inlays, for example, to glue turquoise chips into voids in a cocobolo bowl.

CA glue is not recommended for cloth, paper, polyethylene, or teflon. Ca glues are sold in polypropylene bottles, which is one more plastic it isn't recommended for. Most manufacturers recommend storing CA glues in a cool, dark place.

CHOOSE THE RIGHT GLUE TYPE FOR YOUR PROJECT USING THIS CHART. BECAUSE THERE ARE HUNDREDS
OF GLUE FORMULATIONS, THE DATA IS GENERAL. CHECK MANUFACTURER'S LABEL FOR SPECIFICS.

Figure288   Selecting the Right Adhesive

Glue Type	Form	Clamp Time Hard Woods	Clamp Time Soft Woods	Open Time (2)	Closed Time (3)	Water Resist	Water Proof	Oily Woods	End Grain	Shear Strength	Gap Filling
Polyvinyl Acetate White, Yellow or Aliphatic	Ready To Use	2 hrs.	1 hr.	10-15 min.	30-45 min.	Fair	No	Yes (4)	Fair (6)	3,600 psi	Fair
Hi-Performance, Cross-linked	Ready To Use	2 hrs.	1 hr.	3-5 min.	2-15 min.	Good	Yes	Yes (4)	Fair (6)	3,600 psi	Fair
Natural Hide	Ready To Use	4 hrs.	2 hrs.	10 min.	30 min.	Poor	No	No	Poor	3,800 psi	Fair
Casein	Mix with Water	3 hrs.	2 hrs.	15-20 min.		Good	No	No	Poor		
Fish	Ready to use	6 hrs.	10 hrs.	1 min.	1 hr.	Good	No			3,200 psi	Fair
Blood Protein	Mix with water					Fair	No				
Rice	Mix with Water	12 hrs.	12 hrs.			Fair	No			High	
Rabbit Skin	Mix with Water					Fair	No			High	
Resorcinol Phenol-Resorcinol	2 part mix	15 hrs.	15 hrs.	30 min.	30 min. to 4 hrs.	Good	Yes	Yes (4)		2,800 psi	Good
Hot Melt	Solid	none	none	10-60 sec.	10 sec.	Good	Yes	No	Good	400 psi	Good (1)
Cyanoacrylate CA	Ready to use	1 min.	1 min.	10-25 sec.	3-5 sec.	Good	Yes	Yes	Good(6)	5,000 (5) psi	Good
Contact	Ready to use	none	none	30 min. to 3 days	none	Good	No			500 psi	Poor
Urea Formaldehyde Plastic resin	2 Part mix with water	4-6 hrs.	4-6 hrs	10-30 min	30 min. to 4 hrs.	Good	No	No		2,800 psi	Fair
Epoxy	2 Part mix	1 min.	1 min.	5 min to 1 hr	none	Good	Yes	No	Good	15,000 psi	Good
Polyurethane	Ready to use	1-4 hrs.	1-4 hrs.	10-20 min.	20-60 min.	Good	Yes	Yes	Good	3,500 psi	Good (1)

(1) But no strength
(2) Open time is after glue applied until pieces put together.
(3) Closed time is wiggle time after pieces mated
(4) Works well on freshy machined or wiped joints.
(5) Tensil strength metal to metal.
(6) With buttering.

copyright Ken Horner 2001

Epoxy

The epoxies are expensive but bond almost anything to anything. They are sold as a two-part, cold liquid mix (resin and hardener), and cure by exothermic polymerization rather than by solvent evaporation. When an epoxy cures, nothing is given off during the reaction except heat. The heat generated when the components are mixed raises the temperature of the joints making it ideal for cold weather work. It is extremely strong, absolutely waterproof, and capable of setting at temperatures as low as 50°, with little or no clamping. Moreover, the glue is a good gap filler and has a clear, inconspicuous glue line. This glue doesn't work well with wet or oily woods. Squeeze-out is difficult to remove after it has dried but it can be cleaned with water before the mixture hardens. After the glue sets up, use lacquer thinner, alcohol, or acetone for clean-up. A fully cured glue line must be chipped off.

Unlike most glues that set under pressure, epoxy needs only contact to cure. Spring clamps, rubber bands, even staples can be used to hold the pieces together. The bonds are resistant to creep, impervious to water, don't shrink while curing, and machine easily.

These are not general woodworking adhesives but are good for bonding dissimilar materials such as wood to glass or metal. They can be used in humid or thermally variable environments and have high strength. Some formulations have greatly extended open assembly time.

The permanence of the bond is, paradoxically, a limitation - the bond is so hard that it is not resistant to impact and joints can break if the piece is dropped. Some formulations cure in minutes even under water.

Many epoxy hardeners are fairly strong caustics and can cause burns on the skin, so wear disposable gloves. Cleaning epoxy off the hands with a solvent will dissolve and possibly carry chemicals into the skin. The vapors from epoxy in the liquid state are toxic and you should use a respirator or have adequate ventilation. Some woodworkers have developed sensitivity to epoxies in general and can't even be in the shop when one is being used without developing a rash.

Epoxy resins can be used with several types of fabrics to increase the strength of very light laminated structures such as wood-strip canoes, glider wings, or surf boards.

Polyvinyl Acetate, Aliphatic Resin, White, Yellow, and Cross-linking Glues

These are the old faithful, ready-to-use, general purpose glues that we all have in our shop: white (polyvinyl), yellow carpenter's (aliphatic), and the cross-linking (waterproof). All PVA glues contain the same polymer, polyvinyl acetate. Different colors (white, yellow) and names (polyvinyl, aliphatic, water-proof, cross-linking) are used by manufacturers to differentiate their formulations.

All of the PVA glues are water-based, have no odor, and are non-flammable. They cure by water evaporation and only the cross-linking PVA is waterproof. You generally have 5 to 15 minutes open time. Closed time is about 20 minutes. Open time is how fast you have to get the pieces together; closed time is how long you have to reposition and play with the assembly before the glue sets. Clamp time is 2 hours with soft woods and 1 hour with hard woods. Because there are so many brands on the market, read the label to get the exact set and clamp times.

PVA glues are fair in gap filling, and work with oily woods if the edge is wiped with a solvent first. They will spoil if frozen and have poor creep resistance, i.e., they will slowly stretch under stress.

In general the differences between the white, yellow, and cross-linking glues are:

White

It has no water resistance and the open assembly time is up to 15 minutes. White glue can be reactivated by heat (approximately 180°F.) indefinitely.

Yellow

Yellow glue has better sandability but a shorter open assembly time (5 to 10 minutes). It develops tack faster than the white, forms a harder glue line, is less prone to creep, and has better resistance to water. Yellow glue can be reactivated by heat (about 250°F.) for about 10 days after initial set.

Cross-linking

This formulation is waterproof, has better initial tack, and a shorter open assembly time (about 5 minutes). It, too, can be reactivated by heat (about 350°F.) for a few days after initial set.

None of the PVA glues will cure in wood wetter than 12%. They do not require heavy clamping, give strong joints, are easy to use, set fast, and clean up easily. Because of the tendency to creep and because the glue line is semi-hard, PVA glues should not be used for table tops or laminations subject to stress (see Chapter 19 on Bent Lamination). All PVA glues clog sandpaper and do not accept a stain, although they can be dyed prior to use.

The PVA glues have a tendency to thicken during storage. This is not due to polymerization but is because of water loss by diffusion through the walls of the plastic container. In this case, you can rejuvenate the glue by adding a little water to replace what's been lost. Hardening or gelling of the glue is due to a chemical reaction where the vinyl acetate has been hydrolyzed. One of the products is acetic acid, which produces a vinegar-like odor. In this case, the glue has deteriorated and it should be tossed. PVA glues are so inexpensive and so much rides on a good, strong glue joint, it makes sense to buy a new bottle.

Different manufacturers make hundreds of special formulations such as non-drip, waterproof, multiple colors, gap filling, and non-bleed for veneer work. PVA glue is available with a fluorescent additive so, after clean up, any missed glue shows up under a UV light.

The PVA glues can be colored with water-based aniline dyes, with ordinary food coloring

Rule of Thumb

If a glue joint fails when the clamps are removed or soon after:

1. You used the wrong glue.

2. There was too much moisture in one or the other piece of wood.

3. The temperature was too high or too low.

4. The surface was dirty, oily, or rough.

5. Two- or three-part adhesives were mixed incorrectly.

6. Poor clamping or poor joinery.

7. The glue was too old.

If a glue joint fails later:

1. Wood movement— You used green wood or wood with moisture content not matched to the environment.

2. You used the wrong joint.

3. There was no mechanical backup to the joint.

4. You used the wrong glue.

from the kitchen, or with fabric dyes you can buy at the grocery store. Just a few drops are enough to change a clear or yellow glue line to a color - just make sure the dye is water soluble.

Iron contamination will cause PVA glues to react with tannins in wood to produce a dark stain. When gluing up a panel with pipe clamps, contact between the iron and fresh glue results in the stains. Use a piece of waxed paper between the pipe and the glue line or change your iron pipes for aluminum ones. Aluminum does not react with the glue the way iron does.

Sawdust is often mixed with glue and used as a filler. Make sure the sawdust is free of iron filings or fibers of steel wool when making a light-colored filler. If the sawdust was obtained from floor sweepings it's almost certain to contain trace amounts of iron and only a few parts per million can discolor light-colored sawdust like maple, ash, or pine. Use only fresh, clean sawdust for the filler mixture.

Either white or yellow glue can be used for veneering. White has a longer open time. Clamp overnight and use cardboard instead of waxed paper to insulate the press from the veneer because water-based

adhesives won't cure until the water evaporates. Bubbles resulting from poor contact can be reheated and pressed into place.

Because PVA glues can be rejuvenated with heat, they are used extensively in veneer work. PVA glue is applied to both substrate and veneer, then allowed to dry. The veneer is placed in position and ironed on. The heat from the iron melts the glue and the two surfaces bond.

In furniture manufacturing, bent laminations are done with PVA glues. The pieces are hydraulically pressed at 20,000 lbs. Curing is done with a radio frequency modulator, sending 5,000 megahertz signals through the wood. This enables a manufacturer to get absolute consistency from one bend to another. In home shops, PVA glues are generally not used for complex bent laminations because of their tendency to creep.

The PVA glues can be used on wood, leather, canvas, cork, cardboard, paper, particle board, veneers, and fabrics. PVA emulsions are used in paints, textiles, paper, drywall joint compound, coatings, pressure sensitive adhesives, and glues that can be remoistened.

Urea Formaldehyde, Plastic Resin Glues

These glues are sold as pre-catalyzed, water-activated powders made up of a mixture of dry resins and hardeners that, if kept dry, have an indefinite storage life. The urea formaldehyde glues are very strong and have no creep. They are highly water resistant but not completely waterproof. They are also economical and once mixed are easily spread. The glue is put on one edge only, and open assembly time is 10 to 30 minutes. Closed assembly time is from 4 hours at 70° to $1/2$ hour at 100°F. Urea formaldehyde glues require closely mated edges for effective bonding. Clamp time can vary from 4 to 14 hours. The extremely long assembly time makes it great for gluing up complicated projects.

They are perhaps the best all-around glue for applying veneer (paper-back or standard) to any surface (particle-board, plywood, regular wood). They don't bleed through, they allow plenty of time for positioning, and they don't allow veneers to creep. The dried glue is also impervious to paint thinner and alcohol – two solvents used in marquetry finishes.

Plastic resin glue is used to make particle board, plywood,

fiberboard, and laminates. In the woodshop it is used for joinery and veneering.

Resorcinol Glues

Resorcinol glue was used in World War II to assemble wooden naval vessels. It is still called "waterproof glue," and is very strong and durable. In use, a liquid resin is mixed with a powdered hardener to produce a red paste. Open assembly time is 30 minutes, including mix time, and closed assembly time is 1 hour. They make excellent gap fillers when mixed with various solids. Resorcinol glue is applied to both surfaces and clamped while the glue is wet. It requires overnight clamping to fully set up. On dense or non-porous materials, the glue should be allowed to set for 5 to 10 minutes before joining. This type of glue is good for outdoor projects in or near the water and is excellent for poorly fitted joints.

Resorcinol glue is used when no creep is wanted and water resistance is needed. It has a very dark glue line and might be unsuitable for light woods like maple. Once mixed, it must be used within an hour or two and requires a minimum setting temperature of 70°F. It sets within 8 hours, though it doesn't reach full bond strength for several days. Acidic hardwoods such as oak may require 100° to 110°F temperatures for maximum bonding.

It is used for waterproof plywood, laminated beams and outdoor construction.

Polyurethane Glues

These glues come ready-to-use and consist of an isocyanate resin that cures by reacting with moisture in the wood. Polyurethane glue is spread on one surface and works best if moisture content is 10 to 25%. If the moisture in the wood is below 10%, the other surface should be moistened. In dense hardwoods like oak and maple, both surfaces should be dampened. It is non-toxic, waterproof, and can fill gaps - though the fill has no structural strength. It has an open assembly time of 10 to 20 minutes and a closed assembly time of 20 to 60 minutes. It works well on wet, oily, and dense woods. Resistance to creep is excellent and it can bond end-grain joints. It attains 90% strength in 4 hours and 100% strength in 24 hours. It should be clamped overnight. Cleanup is easy - a chisel or knife cuts the extruded foam. Very little glue gets into the pores near the glue line, so this really isn't a problem with staining or finishing.

The polyurethane glues allow lots of working time with excellent resistance to water,

making them ideal for exterior projects. They do, however, have one annoying side effect - they stain your hands dark brown. Apparently, it is not toxic but will be unsightly for about a week. You might want to wear latex gloves during glue ups. Recently, polyurethane glue has been introduced in cartridges for application using hot melt guns. The glue from these cartridges sets in 30 to 60 seconds.

Polyurethane glues work well on metal, plastic, ceramic, and stone. On wood joints it has shear strength equivalent to PVA glues. Once opened, the bottle life is about 6 months, so because it is somewhat expensive, buy only enough for the job at hand. Polyurethane foam in aerosol cans is used as an expanding insulator around light fixtures, doors, and windows.

Natural Protein Glues

Glues from natural sources have been used by woodworkers for centuries. Today, except for hide glues, most have been replaced by the easier-to-use polyvinyl acetate (PVA) glues.

Hide Glue

There are two principal types of hide glue, one derived from hides, the other from bone - and contrary to all you've heard, hide glue is not made from horns, muscle, tendons, or

hooves. The main ingredient in hide glue is gelatin, a complex combination of protein chains. Traditional hide glue is sold in a dry state as pearls or flakes that must be mixed with water and heated in a glue pot to 130° to 140°F before use.

Hide glue is the only strong, general purpose glue that is reversible after the joint has completely set; the application of heat will soften a hide glue line and injection of water or steam makes disassembly possible. It is a good choice for general furniture work but not for outdoor projects. It is easy to use, very strong, and inexpensive. It provides some strength even when the joints are poorly fitted. The bonding strength of hide glue is on a par with polyurethane and PVA glues, and it will bond glass to wood. It does not work on oily woods and is only fair at gap filling.

Hide glue doesn't creep like PVA, will stand temperatures up to 400°F, and is so strong that a film of diluted glue applied to a pane of glass will dry, shrink, and chip the surface away to produce frosted glass. Full-strength hide glue would be too strong, taking giant chips out of the glass.

The glue cures in two stages. First, a quick-set gel results from the rapid temperature loss immediately after application;

this gives the traditional hide glue a short open time (1 to 5 minutes). This is an advantage in rubbed joints and some veneering where strong initial tack is desirable. The second stage develops over a longer period as water evaporates and the protein-cellulose bonds form to give a hard glue line. The joint remains water- and alcohol-soluble but other solvents won't affect it.

Today, hide glue is manufactured using mostly the trimmings from cattle and horse hides - the parts not worth turning into leather. They are washed, soaked in lime, and then heated to separate the gelatin—a protein made of 19 different amino acids. The resulting adhesive material is filtered and evaporated, and the dry solids are ground up and packaged. To use, the powder is soaked in water until it swells, then heated and used hot. A good test of whether the glue is ready to use is to put a drop between your finger and thumb, press for a moment, then pull apart. Hide glue that is ready to use has a very strong tack.

Hide glue works best if the wood is at room temperature. Open time is about 10 minutes and closed time is about one-half hour. Clamp time is about 2 hours for hardwoods and 4 hours for softwoods. Glycerin can be added to hide glue to increase flexibility. Urea can be added to increase the open time, and the cure time also can be extended by seconds or minutes.

There are a few differences between the hot hide glue made from flakes and the liquid hide glue purchased ready-to-use. Traditional hot hide glue made from flakes has a stronger initial tack, a quicker set, can be made up in various strengths, and has an indefinite shelf life. Once it is mixed with water, it should be used within two or three days.

Liquid hide glue has two big advantages - convenience and a long open time. Liquid hide glue contains an anti-gelling agent, like urea, to prevent it from solidifying in the bottle. Liquid hide glue cures through moisture loss alone, rather than with cooling, and has a longer open time (10 to 15 min). Liquid hide glue has a shelf life of up to one year.

If you restore or reproduce old furniture, hide glue flakes should be on your shelf. Luthiers use traditional, cooked, hot hide glue made fresh each day from flakes. A hard joint is necessary for vibration in violins and other wooden musical instruments. A soft glue line would muffle the sound and act like a damper. Some antique restorers contend that the same chemicals that keep the liquid hide glue in liquid form in the bottle, keep it from forming a truly hard joint. Because liquid hide glues contain a fungicide, some believe this might also stain the wood. Fine woodworkers still use hide glue for violins, pianos, and other fine instruments.

To take a hide glue joint apart, remove as much of the dried glue as possible. This might require several washings with warm water. Allow the joint to sit a few minutes before rewashing with more warm water. Repeat this process until no more color comes out. A toothbrush is good for applying the wash if the joint is accessible, but a bamboo splinter or a stainless steel blade will also work. Any other metal besides stainless steel may leave a stain when it contacts the glue. For troublesome joints, try warm vinegar or a solution of meat tenderizer and water. For reassembly, reglue one joint at a time with traditional cooked hide glue.

To soften old hide glue when removing veneer, use a solution of half vinegar and half water. Apply moist heat with a wet bath towel and a steam iron. Once the glue is softened, lift the veneer off with a wooden wedge or putty knife.

Any of the lower aliphatic class of alcohols - methyl (wood alcohol), ethyl (denatured or grain alcohol), or isopropyl (rubbing alcohol with 10% water) - will cause a hide glue joint to fracture and weaken. This is not the same as dissolving with water, because the joints weaken but don't fall apart. Pressure must be applied to separate the pieces. Find a small crack in an edge-to-edge joint and insert alcohol with a syringe. Then force a wedge such as a screwdriver into the crack and pop the joint apart. For mortise and tenon joints, introduce the alcohol and tap the joints apart with a leather mallet. Once the alcohol has evaporated, the hide glue in the joint can be rehydrated with hot water or more hot hide glue.

Hide glues are used on match heads, gaskets, and in paper manufacturing. They are used for making sandpaper, sealing tapes, gummed tape, wallpaper sizing, and cork. Hide glue is used by the U.S. Mint to coat paper currency.

Rabbit Skin Glue
This type of glue gives a beautifully clear joint with incredible strength. It is sold as a quick-mixing powder at large art supply stores, and is still used by Luthiers and musical instrument craftsmen. In one report, after PVA glues failed,

rabbit skin glue was used to attach a harpsichord rail with 120 pins, each holding a string pulling with 20 pounds of force.

Rice Glue
This glue is still used in Japan, much as hide glue is used in the United States. It is reversible, cleans up with water, will not show splotches under stains and finishes, and is easy to scrape or plane off after the joint has set. It dries transparent and doesn't discolor with age. While rice glued joints in softwoods are strong enough to sustain normal use, they can't stand shock, so a broken shoji screen can be easily knocked apart for repair.

Traditional Japanese woodworkers make rice glue fresh each day. Short grain rice is washed in cold water and rinsed until the water runs clear. It is then drained and kept damp overnight. In the morning, one part rice and one part water are boiled for 20 minutes in a heavy lidded pot, then taken off the burner and allowed to sit for 10 minutes.

A bowl of the tight, but not mushy, rice kernels is taken to the shop. A ball of the boiled rice is transferred to a smooth board and mashed with a wooden paddle until the mixture is smooth and pasty. Any hulls or debris are removed, and the glue is ready for use. If the paste is too thick to spread, a little cool water is added. A thin coat of glue is spread on each edge and the piece is clamped lightly. Squeeze-out can be cleaned up with a damp cloth. The joint requires about 12 hours of clamp time and another 12 hours before machining. Whatever rice is left in the bowl after gluing can be eaten for lunch.

Casein Glue

At one time casein glue was derived from soured milk. Today, a synthetic powder is mixed with water, allowed to stand for 15 minutes, and is ready for use. It is not waterproof but has good moisture resistance. It can be used in cold weather and on woods containing up to 15% moisture. The open assembly time is 15 to 20 minutes before set. Clamp time is 2 hours on hardwoods, 4 hours on softwoods. Full cure takes 8 hours. It is good for oily woods like teak, lemon wood, yew, and the rosewoods, and it is fair as a gap filler. Casein glues are alkaline (pH greater than 7) and should not come into contact with metal. It reacts with iron and the resultant contaminant then reacts with oak, walnut, cherry, or mahogany to form a dark stain.

Fish Glue

Fish glue is made from the water-soluble proteins in fish skins, mainly cod. It is used in two ways, dictated by the manner in which it sets. First, both pieces can be coated with glue, clamped, and the glue sets as the water is drawn away. The second method is to coat both pieces and let the glue dry. At assembly time, one piece is moistened and the parts pressed together. Fish glue is sold ready-to-use and can be applied over a wide temperature range (40° to 400°F.). It is very strong and can bond unlike materials such as rubber, paper, steel, plywood, wood, cloth, hardboard, particle board, and leather. It is fair at gap filling and has good creep resistance. Like hide glue, fish glue is reversible with water.

In use, you have about 1 minute after the glue is spread before the parts must be joined. Closed time or wiggle room is 1 hour and clamp time is 6 to 10 hours.

Fish glue is used widely to attach paper labels to bottles and as an additive to white PVA glues to improve initial tack.

Blood Protein Glue

This adhesive is mixed with water before use. It has fair water resistance but is not waterproof. It is seldom used today.

Rule of Thumb
A Glue Project

Perhaps the most difficult glue job is joining a dozen or so boards together edge-to-edge for the top of a dining table. The finished panel will be long and flat and everyone who walks into the room will check it for flatness, color, wood grain, and finish. The completed top must be smooth and the glue lines should be invisible. The stain must be consistent, so squeeze-out will have to be cleaned up completely. Over the years, through temperature and humidity changes, the glue joints must be stable and strong. In large part, all of these requirements depend on the glue chosen.

For the project, we'll use kiln-dried red oak with water content 6 to 10 percent. The boards will be glued edge-to-edge. Start with straight, flat, sound stock, and cut each board 4 to 6 in. wide and about 6 in. longer than the final table width - the extra 6 in. is to take care of possible snipes. If the pieces are not the same thickness, then put them through a thickness planer.

Lay the pieces out side by side and match the grain and color. When you have a pleasing pattern, draw a large triangle on the panel with chalk to position each board, then joint the pieces to get the edges square, even, and smooth. Inspect the edges - if there are saw or knife marks, burns or glazing - do it again. Hold mating boards together and look for light through the joint. When all joints are perfect, figure out which glue to use.

For the tabletop we should choose a glue that is strong so the joints won't part or creep, otherwise, with time, the varnish might crack at the joints. We need a glue that will give us an open assembly time of at least 10 minutes to smear the glue on all the edges and dowels, and a closed time of at least 15 minutes as we position each board and get the clamps tightened. We want water resistance but don't necessarily need a waterproof glue. We don't plan on disassembling the top so reversibility isn't important.

With these criteria in mind we can eliminate these adhesives immediately:

Hot melt - Not strong enough, not a construction adhesive.

Cyanoacrylate - Too expensive, sets too fast, not a construction adhesive.

Contact - Not strong enough, no open and closed assembly time.

Epoxy - Too expensive, messy to mix and use, hard to clean up, not enough open or closed assembly time.

These glues come close, but:

polyvinyl acetate, PVA - It is strong, ready to use, easy to apply and cheap. The high performance PVA has enough open and closed assembly time, and it's right there on my shelf. The downside is that it gives a semi-hard glue line, and the joints have a tendency to creep, which might produce cracks in the finish later. It also soaks into the grain near the joint, and causes problems later when it's time to stain and finish.

Hide - It is very strong, easy to clean up, has long open and closed assembly time, and is cheap. However, it may get brittle with age, and is not resistant to water or alcohol.

Resorcinol - Produces very strong joints with no creep, has long open and closed assembly time, and is fairly cheap. The downside is that it has to be mixed, is toxic (should be applied with gloves in good ventilation), is difficult to clean up, and has a dark glue line.

The glues that would work:
Urea formaldehyde - Urea

formaldehyde is strong, water resistant, and has no creep. It has a 10 to 30 minutes open, and up to 4 hours closed assembly time. It also gives a glue line that can be sanded. On the other hand, it is fairly expensive, has to be mixed, and can't be applied below 70°F.

Polyurethane - Polyurethane is ready to use, has long open and closed assembly times, is strong, works great with open grains, isn't absorbed into the wood near the joints (good for later staining), squeeze-out can be removed with a chisel or scraper, and works on oily woods. It is waterproof and impervious to alcohol.

For this project it's a toss up, but for red oak I would choose urea formaldehyde. If the top was to be teak or some other oily wood I'd choose polyurethane. I don't think either glue would be a bad choice.

Now, mix the glue and apply a thin coat to each edge. Apply pressure with clamps and 4-in. pressure pads. (See Chapter 27 on Pressure and Clamps.)

Direct Pressure Area (DPA) = 2 x board width + pad width
DPA = 2 x width + pad width
DPA = 2 x 6 + 4 = 16 in.

For the 46-in. panel of 6-in. boards, we would use three clamps with 4-in. pressure pads (**Figure 289**). Place one clamp in the middle and the other two 6 in. from each end. Apply pressure as soon as possible until the joints are snug and a thin, even glue line appears. Leave the clamps on for at least 8 hours or overnight. Remove the panel from the clamps and scrape off the squeeze-out. Prop the panel upright and examine for swelling at the glue lines. If there is no swelling, continue with machining. If swelling is present, let the panel dry until the joint area is flat.

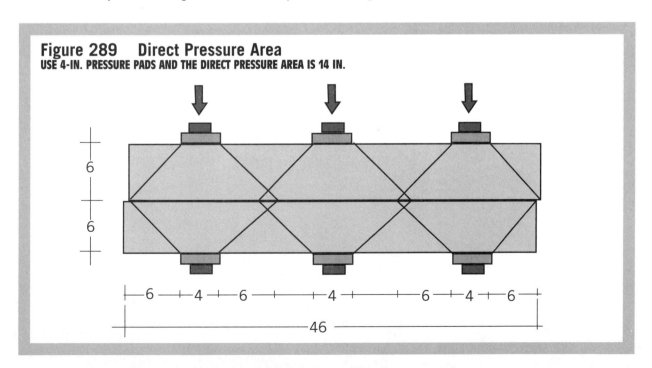

Figure 289   Direct Pressure Area
USE 4-IN. PRESSURE PADS AND THE DIRECT PRESSURE AREA IS 14 IN.

6
6

6   4   6   4   6   4   6
46

CHAPTER 29

Miters, Bevels & Crown Molding

Shadow box picture frames look great, and once you know the technique they're pretty easy to cut. The trick in cutting the corners, a combination miter cut and bevel cut, is in knowing how far to tilt the blade and how much to angle the miter gauge. Like most wood workers, I think I know the difference between a miter and a bevel but I have trouble putting it into words. Think of a miter as a cut made with the miter gauge on a table saw at a setting other than 90° or the tracking arm on a radial arm saw at some setting other than 0°. Then think of bevels as cuts made with the blade tilted.

On a table saw, a simple miter is cut with the blade at 90° and the miter gauge set at any angle except 90°. A simple bevel is cut with the blade tilted at any angle except 90°. The bevel can be across the board (flat bevel) or lengthwise (rip bevel) (**Figure 290**).

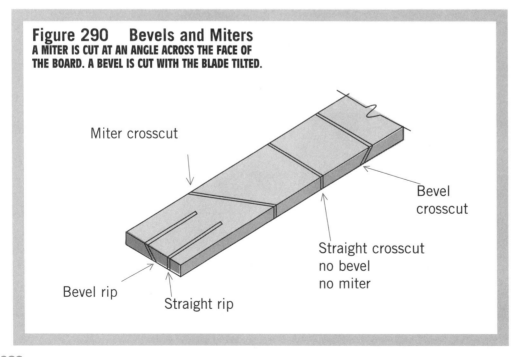

Figure 290   Bevels and Miters
A MITER IS CUT AT AN ANGLE ACROSS THE FACE OF
THE BOARD. A BEVEL IS CUT WITH THE BLADE TILTED.

Miter crosscut

Bevel crosscut

Straight crosscut
no bevel
no miter

Bevel rip

Straight rip

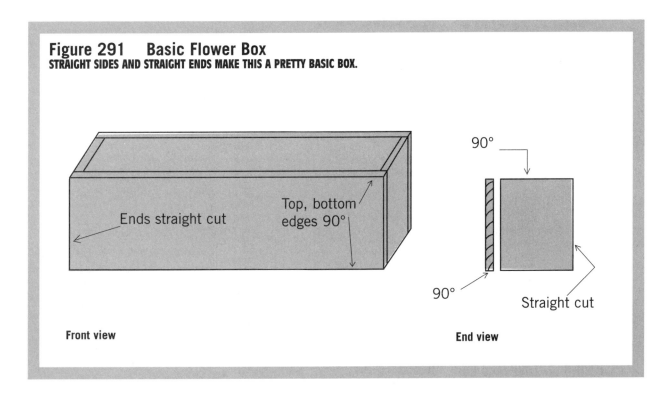

Figure 291   Basic Flower Box
STRAIGHT SIDES AND STRAIGHT ENDS MAKE THIS A PRETTY BASIC BOX.

Ends straight cut

Top, bottom edges 90°

Front view

90°

90°

Straight cut

End view

Ninety Degree Joints

Perhaps the best way to explain miters and bevels is with an example (**Figure 291**). Assume we are building a planter box with four sides. In the simplest version, the sides and the ends are all square with no slope. Pretty simple. Take a 1x6 and cross-cut two 6-in. long pieces and two 24-in. long pieces. Nail them together—no miters and no bevels—a pretty basic box.

Simple Miters and Bevels

Now, let's get a little fancy and make a box with sloped sides. The ends will have to be mitered, that is, cut at an angle

across the face, while the sides will be cut as before (**Figure 292**). To figure the miter angle we'll use high school geometry. Any of the following will give you the answer.

sin = opposite ÷ hypotenuse
tan = opposite ÷ adjacent
cos = adjacent ÷ hypotenuse

To find the correct angle:
    tan = opposite ÷ adjacent
    tan = 1.5 ÷ 6 = 0.25
    arctan = 14.0°
Note: See Chapter 9 for more on using a calculator for this type of problem.

Whether you use a table saw or a radial arm saw (**Figure 293**), a degree is a degree. But, because of the difference in the

way the radial arm saw's tracking arm and table saw's miter gauge are marked, you must be careful to use 0° or 90° as the starting reference point. **Figure 293** shows the basic difference in the two saws. The starting point for a miter gauge is 90°, and the starting point for a tracking arm is 0°. For example, if we were to cut a 14° miter on the table saw using the miter gauge, we would set it at 76° (90°—14° = 76°). If we were to cut the very same angle on a radial arm saw we would set the tracking arm miter at 14° (0° + 14° = 14°). Keep in mind that in both cases the angle we want is 14° from the normal setting.

Figure 292   Simple Miters
USE GEOMETRY TO FIND THE CORRECT MITER SETTING.

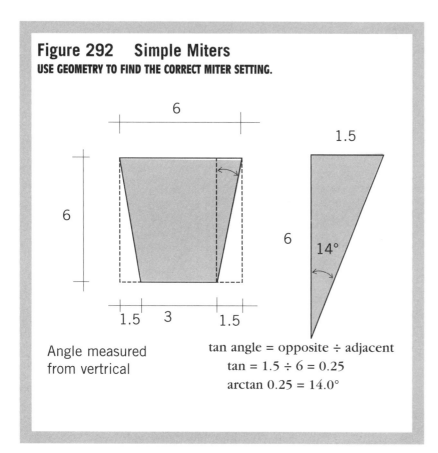

Angle measured
from vertrical

tan angle = opposite ÷ adjacent
$$\tan = 1.5 \div 6 = 0.25$$
$$\arctan 0.25 = 14.0°$$

Set the table saw miter gauge at 76° (90°—14°) and cut the two end pieces from ¾-in. x 6½-in. stock. When the sides are cut and placed against the ends, you can see that this kind of joint would be fine if we were making a pig trough. However, for our flower box (**Figure 294**), the top edge of the sides should also be cut at an angle, beveled at 14°. Tilt the blade to 14° and rip the top and bottom edges of the sides. We can now construct the box with mitered ends and beveled sides.

Compound Miters and Bevels

Now let's get really wild and slope both the sides and the ends (**Figure 295**). Making

Fig 293   Different Settings for Table Saw and Radial Arm Saw
ON A TABLE SAW, THE MITER GAUGE REGISTERS 90° WHEN A CUT IS MADE AT 90° TO THE BLADE. ON A RADIAL ARM SAW, THE TRACK ARM MITER REGISTERS 0° WHEN A CUT OF 90° IS MADE.

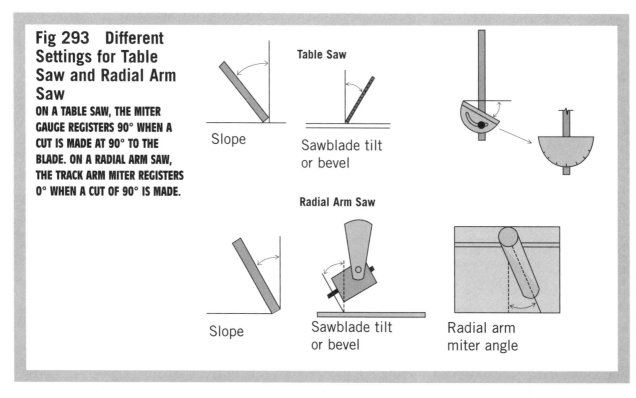

Table Saw

Slope

Sawblade tilt
or bevel

Radial Arm Saw

Slope

Sawblade tilt
or bevel

Radial arm
miter angle

Figure 294   Improved Flower Box With Mitered Ends and Edges

BY MITERING THE ENDS AND BEVELING THE EDGES OF THE SIDES, THE BASIC BOX BECOMES MORE INTERESTING.

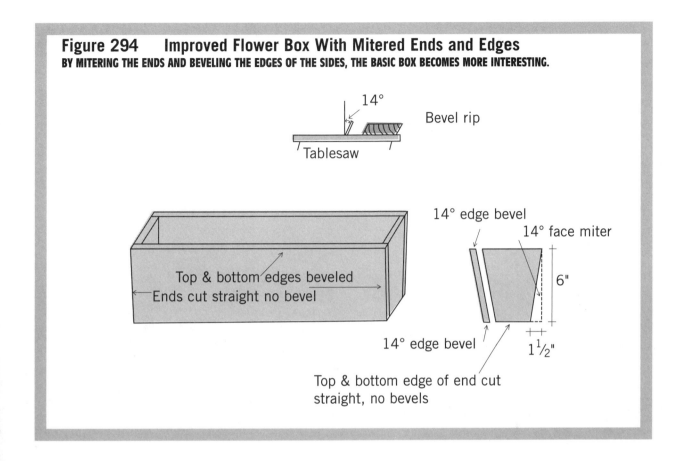

compound miters—a miter joint that is both mitered and beveled—is a special technique that most woodworkers don't use that often. It's a neat joint and the finished project is intriguing because, when done correctly, all the slopes and bevels merge. Once you learn the technique you'll find lots of uses – shadow box picture frames, patio plant holders, pedestals, and wooden buckets.

When cutting a compound miter you have to set the miter angle (use the miter gauge on the table saw and the tracking arm on the radial arm saw) and the bevel angle (tilt the saw blade)—and each angle depends on the other. The miter and bevel angles also depend on how many sides the box has and the slope of the sides. For our purposes, the slope should be measured from vertical with the frame resting on a flat surface.

Boxes and Picture Frames

A slope-sided butter churn and a shadow box picture frame both have compound mitered joints. The difference between the two is their height, that is, the length of the bevel.

Compound miters can be made using a table saw, providing that the wooden pieces fit between the miter gauge and the saw blade—like the 4-in. picture frame or a 6-in. high planter box. Edge bevels for a 24-in. high churn are cut with a taper jig, and the bevel is ripped with the grain; length is somewhat immaterial. In this chapter, we are concerning ourselves with the small, cross-cut bevels.

For every frame and slope, there is only one pair of angles and these must be precise or the miter joints will gap. The math is a little complicated but

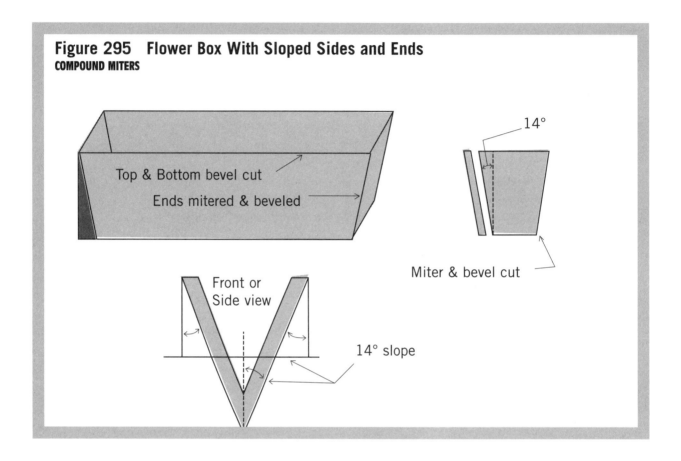

Figure 295 Flower Box With Sloped Sides and Ends
COMPOUND MITERS

Top & Bottom bevel cut

Ends mitered & beveled

14°

Miter & bevel cut

Front or Side view

14° slope

to make it easier, charts are included for the radial arm saw (**Figure 296**) and the table saw (**Figure 297**). Note the values in the two tables are different because on one the baseline vertical is 90° and in the other it is 0°.

For box slopes that are not in the table, use the following equation where:

BA = Bevel angle or blade tilt
MA = Miter angle
N = Number of sides in box
S = Slope of sides measured from vertical

For example, in a wooden bucket with six sides (N = 6) and a slope of 10° off vertical (S = 10), we can figure the saw settings.

Table Saw Settings
**Miter Angle (for table saw):
arctan MA**
$$= 1 \div [\sin S \times \tan (180 \div N)]$$
$$= 1 \div [\sin 10 \times \tan (180 \div 6)]$$
$$= 1 \div (\sin 10 \times \tan 30)$$
$$= 1 \div (0.17 \times 0.58)$$
$$= 1 \div 0.099 = 10.1$$
arctan 10.1
Miter Angle = 84.3°

The miter angle to be set on the table saw miter gauge is

THE FIGURES IN THE TABLE ARE TO THE NEAREST 1/10-DEGREE AND ARE TO SET THE RADIAL ARM SAW TRACK ARM AND THE BLADE TILT. A FOUR-SIDED BOX WITH A SLOPE OF 20° MEASURED FROM VERTICAL REQUIRES THE BLADE TO BE SET AT 41.6° AND THE ARM SWUNG TO 18.9°.

Figure 296   Compound Miter Chart for the Radial-Arm Saw

Side Slope *	3 Sides Trk Arm Setting	3 Sides Blade Angle	4 Sides Trk Arm Setting	4 Sides Blade Angle	5 Sides Trk Arm Setting	5 Sides Blade Angle	6 Sides Trk Arm Setting	6 Sides Blade Angle	7 Sides Trk Arm Setting	7 Sides Blade Angle	8 Sides Trk Arm Setting	8 Sides Blade Angle	Side Slope *
0	0	60	0	45	0	36	0	30	0	25.7	0	22.5	0
5	8.6	59.6	5	44.8	3.6	35.7	2.9	29.9	2.4	25.6	2.1	22.4	5
10	16.7	58.5	9.8	44.1	7.2	35.4	5.7	29.5	4.8	25.3	4.1	22.1	10
15	24.1	56.8	14.5	43.1	10.6	34.6	8.5	28.9	7.1	24.8	6.1	21.7	15
20	30.6	54.5	18.9	41.6	14	33.5	11.2	28	9.3	24.1	8.1	21.1	20
25	36.2	51.7	22.9	39.9	17.1	32.2	13.7	26.9	11.5	23.2	9.9	20.3	25
30	40.9	48.6	26.6	37.8	20	30.6	16.1	25.7	13.5	22.1	11.7	19.4	30
35	44.8	45.2	29.8	35.4	22.6	28.8	18.3	24.2	15.4	20.8	13.4	18.3	35
40	48.1	41.6	32.7	32.8	25	26.8	20.4	22.5	17.2	19.4	14.9	17.1	40
45	50.8	37.8	35.3	30	27.2	24.6	22.2	20.7	18.8	17.9	16.3	15.7	45
50	53	33.8	37.4	27	29.1	22.2	23.9	18.8	20.3	16.2	17.6	14.2	50
55	54.8	29.8	39.3	23.9	30.8	19.7	25.3	16.7	21.5	14.4	18.7	12.7	55
60	56.3	25.7	40.9	20.7	32.2	17.1	26.6	14.5	22.6	12.5	19.7	11	60
65	57.5	21.5	42.2	17.4	33.4	14.4	27.6	12.2	23.6	10.6	20.6	9.3	65
70	58.4	17.2	43.2	14	34.3	11.6	28.5	9.9	24.3	8.5	21.3	7.5	70
75	59.1	13	44	10.5	35.1	8.8	29.1	7.4	24.9	6.5	21.8	5.7	75
80	59.6	8.6	44.6	7.1	35.6	5.9	29.6	5	25.4	4.3	22.2	3.8	80
85	59.9	4.3	44.9	3.5	35.9	2.9	29.9	2.5	25.6	2.2	22.4	1.9	85
90	60	0	45	0	36	0	30	0	25.7	0	22.5	0	90

* Measured from vertical

Miter Angle: MA =[90 - arctan 1 ÷ [sin Slope x tan (180 ÷ Sides)]]

Blade Angle: arctan BA = arctan [(cos Miter Angle x cos Slope x tan (180 ÷ Sides)]

84.3°. Always figure the miter angle first because you need it to figure the bevel angle.

Bevel Angle (for table saw):
arctan BA
   = [(sin MA x cos Slope
      x tan (180 ÷ sides)]
   = sin 84.3 x cos 10
      x tan (180 ÷ 6)]
   = 0.99 x 0.98 x 0.58
Arctan 0.56
Bevel Angle = 29.4°
We now know that to cut a six-sided bucket with sides sloping at 10°, we need the following table saw settings:
   Miter gauge = 84.3°
   Blade tilt = 29.4°

Radial Arm Saw Setting

Remember that the radial arm saw will have different settings because the miter gauge (tracking arm) is set at 90° when the blade is at 90° to the wood. On a table saw, the miter gauge reads 0° when the blade is at 90° to the wood.

Miter Angle (for radial arm saw):

MA = 90 - arctan [1 ÷ [sin S x tan (180 ÷ N)]]
   = 90 - arctan
   [1 ÷[sin 10 x tan (180÷6)]]
   = 90 - arctan [1 ÷ (sin 10 x tan 30)]
   = 90 - arctan [1 ÷ (0.17 x 0.58)]
   = 90 - arctan (1 ÷ 0.099)
   = 90 - arctan 10.14
   arctan 10.14 = 84.3°
Miter Angle = 90 - 84.3 = 5.7°

THE FIGURES IN THE TABLE ARE TO THE NEARESTS 1/10 DEGREE AND ARE TO SET THE MITER GAUGE AND BLADE TILT. A FOUR-SIDED BOX WITH A SLOPE OF 20° MEASURED FROM THE VERTICAL REQUIRES THE BLADE TO BE SET AT 41.6° AND THE MITER GAUGE SET AT 71.1°.

Figure 297 Compound Miter Chart for the Table Saw

Side Slope *	3 Sides Miter Angle	3 Sides Blade Angle	4 Sides Miter Angle	4 Sides Blade Angle	5 Sides Miter Angle	5 Sides Blade Angle	6 Sides Miter Angle	6 Sides Blade Angle	7 Sides Miter Angle	7 Sides Blade Angle	8 Sides Miter Angle	8 Sides Blade Angle	Side Slope *
0	90.0	60.0	90.0	45.0	90.0	36.0	90.0	30.0	90.0	25.7	90.0	22.5	0
5	81.4	59.6	85.0	44.8	86.4	35.7	87.1	29.9	87.6	25.6	87.9	22.4	5
10	73.3	58.5	80.2	44.1	82.8	35.4	84.3	29.5	85.2	25.3	85.9	22.1	10
15	65.9	56.8	75.5	43.1	79.4	34.6	81.5	28.9	82.9	24.8	83.9	21.7	15
20	59.4	54.5	71.1	41.6	76.0	33.5	78.8	28.0	80.7	24.1	81.9	21.1	20
25	53.8	51.7	67.1	39.9	72.9	32.2	76.3	26.9	78.5	23.2	80.1	20.3	25
30	49.1	48.6	63.4	37.8	70.0	30.6	73.9	25.7	76.5	22.1	78.3	19.4	30
35	45.2	45.2	60.2	35.4	67.4	28.8	71.7	24.2	74.6	20.8	76.6	18.3	35
40	41.9	41.6	57.3	32.8	65.0	26.8	69.6	22.5	72.8	19.4	75.1	17.1	40
45	39.2	37.8	54.7	30.0	62.8	24.6	67.8	20.7	71.2	17.9	73.7	15.7	45
50	37.0	33.8	52.6	27.0	60.9	22.2	66.1	18.8	69.7	16.2	72.4	14.2	50
55	35.2	29.8	50.7	23.9	59.2	19.7	64.7	16.7	68.5	14.4	71.3	12.7	55
60	33.7	25.7	49.1	20.7	57.8	17.1	63.4	14.5	67.4	12.5	70.3	11.0	60
65	32.5	21.5	47.8	17.4	56.6	14.4	62.4	12.2	66.4	10.6	69.4	9.3	65
70	31.6	17.2	46.8	14.0	55.7	11.6	61.5	9.9	65.7	8.5	68.7	7.5	70
75	30.9	13.0	46.0	10.5	54.9	8.8	60.9	7.4	65.1	6.5	68.2	5.7	75
80	30.4	8.6	45.4	7.1	54.4	5.9	60.4	5.0	64.6	4.3	67.8	3.8	80
85	30.1	4.3	45.1	3.5	54.1	2.9	60.1	2.5	64.4	2.2	67.6	1.9	85
90	30.0	0.0	45.0	0.0	54.0	0.0	60.0	0.0	64.3	0.0	67.5	0.0	90

* Measured from vertical
Miter Angle: arctan MA = 1 ÷ [sin Slope x tan (180 ÷ Sides)]
Blade Angle: arctan BA = [(sin Miter Angle x cos Slope x tan (180 ÷ Sides)]

Bevel Angle (for radial arm saw):

arctan BA = [(cos MA
    x cos Slope
    x tan (180 ÷ sides)]
= sin 84.3 x cos 10
    x tan (180 ÷ 6)]
= 0.99 x 0.98 x 0.58
arctan 0.56
Bevel Angle = 29.3°

The settings for the radial arm saw are 5.7° on the tracking arm and blade tilt at 29.3°.

For a chop saw setting, use either the table for radial arm saw or table saw, depending on whether the miter setting of your saw, when making a 90° cut, is set at 0° (radial arm saw table) or at 90° (table saw table).

Using a Calculator

Buy an inexpensive scientific calculator and the math will go a lot faster (**Figure 298**). If you own a personal computer you can use a calculator on Microsoft Windows under Program/Accessories. Make sure the calculator has buttons for TAN, SIN, and COS. You'll also need the inverse values - these keys are sometimes listed as INVTAN, INVSIN, INVCOS, or ATAN, ASIN and ACOS.

Example: Let's make a five-sided box with a slope of 9° off vertical. We'll use a calculator to find the miter and bevel angles for a table saw. Here is the step-by-step procedure:

Miter Angle (for table saw):
arctan MA
= 1 ÷ [sin S x tan (180 ÷ N)]
where slope S = 9 and the number of sides N = 5.
= 1 ÷ (sin 9 x tan 36)
= 1 ÷ (0.1564 x 0.7265)
= 1 ÷ 0.1136 = 8.800
    arctan 8.800
Miter Angle = 83.52°

The miter angle to be set on the table saw miter gauge is 83.5°. Always figure the miter angle first because you need this angle to figure the bevel angle.

Bevel Angle (for table saw):
arctan BA

= [(sin MA x cos Slope
    x tan (180 ÷ sides)]
    = sin 83.52 x cos 9 x tan 36
    = 0.9936 x 0.9877 x 0.7265
    arctan 0.7130
Bevel Angle = 35.49°

We now know that to cut a five-sided box with sides sloping at 9°, we need the following table saw settings:

Miter gauge = 83.5°
blade tilt = 35.5°

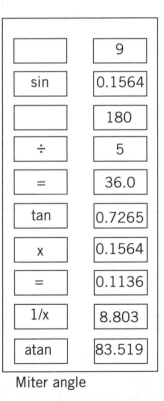

Figure 298   Using a Calculator for Compound Miters
MAKE SURE YOUR CALCULATOR HAS BUTTONS FOR SIN, COS, TAN AND INV OR ASIN, ACOS AND ATAN.

	9			83.519
sin	0.1564		sin	0.9936
	180			9
÷	5		cos	0.9877
=	36.0			36
tan	0.7265		tan	0.7265
x	0.1564		x	0.9936
=	0.1136		x	0.9877
1/x	8.803		=	0.7130
atan	83.519		atan	35.49

Miter angle   Blade angle

Figure 299   No-Math Slope-Sided Box
STARTING WITH A SKETCH, SET THE BEVEL AND THE MITER ANGLE FOR A COMPOUND MITER JOINT.

1.

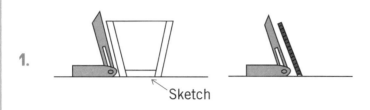

Sketch

2.

3.

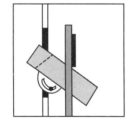

4.

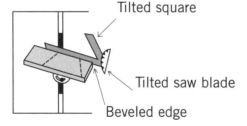

Tilted square

Tilted saw blade

Beveled edge

5.

6.

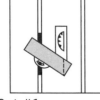
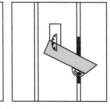

Cut #1   Cut #2

Rule of Thumb

It is possible to make a slope-sided box without ever calculating an angle. Here is a method for transcribing angles from a plan, laying the pieces out, setting the table saw, and cutting the elusive angles involved (**Figure 299**).

1. Draw the plan and transfer the slope angle to the table saw.

2. Rip the front width on both top and bottom edges.

3. Transfer the same angle to the face of the board.

4. With a long, straight edge, set the miter gauge so the end-cut line is parallel to the blade.

5. Place a framer's square flat against the beveled edge of the board and crank the blade over until it lies tightly against the arm of the square.

6. Lower the blade and cut the first end. Move the board to the other side of the blade, turn the work over and cut the other end.

Compound Miters on a Table Saw

Here's a compound miter technique for a table saw (**Figure 300**). First, bevel both top and bottom edges of the board at the slope angle. Attach a long, high extension board to the face of the miter gauge, extending at least 12 in. to the right and left of the blade. Angle the miter gauge and tilt the saw blade.

Make the first cut, with the board to the right of the blade, the inside face of the frame up, and the short edge against the fence.

Set a stop on the fence to insure all sides are cut the same length, and make the second cut with the board to the left of the blade, outside face up and long edge against the fence. Both the blade tilt and the miter setting remain the same for both cuts.

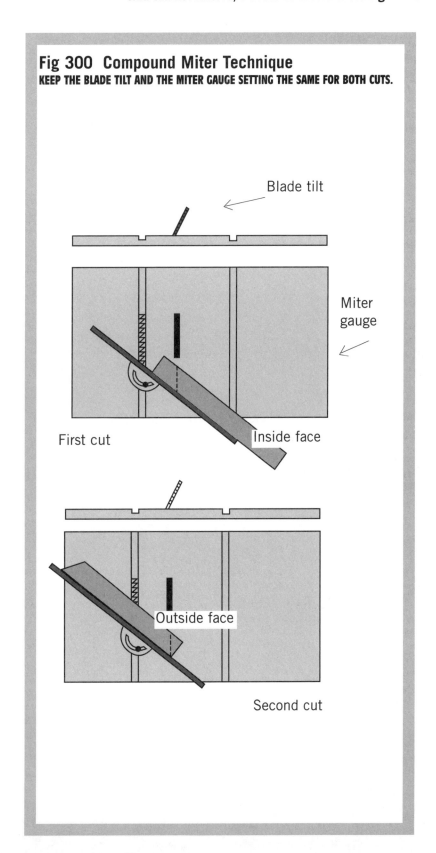

Fig 300 Compound Miter Technique
KEEP THE BLADE TILT AND THE MITER GAUGE SETTING THE SAME FOR BOTH CUTS.

Blade tilt

Miter gauge

First cut

Inside face

Outside face

Second cut

Compound Miters on a Radial Arm Saw

Let's try a six-sided bucket on the radial arm saw with its sides pitched at 30° (**Figure 301**).

Using the look-up table (**Figure 296**) for radial arm saws, find the miter and bevel settings. The miter angle is 16.1° and the blade tilt is 25.7°. First, make a board of sufficient length with its (soon to be) top and bottom edges beveled at 30°, with these beveled faces opposite (each facing the opposite side of the board from each other).

Both the miters and the bevels of the two opposite sides of each piece have to be cut at reverse angles, however, you can avoid resetting your tool with the following: Set the tracking arm at 16.1° miter and set the power unit (tilt the blade) for a 25.7° bevel. If the sides are to slope outward at the top, the usual configuration, then the top edges will be longer than the bottom edges. Place the first piece on the work table with the longer (top) edge against the fence and with the bevel at that edge facing down. Now cut the first compound miter at the left side of the piece (using a left-handed pull-through stroke).

Now flip the piece over, top-over-bottom, so the opposite face is up and the opposite (bottom) edge is against the fence. The bevel at the fence edge will again be down. Now cut the other compound miter at the (now) right side, using a right-handed pull-through stroke. Do the remaining five pieces in the same manner.

Adjusting the Angles

It's a good idea to make some test cuts first on scrap wood to check the setup. Use masking tape or hot melt glue to assemble the box. If the joints gap at the inside of the frame, the bevel angle is too large. If the gap is on the outside of the frame, increase the bevel, i.e., the blade tilt.

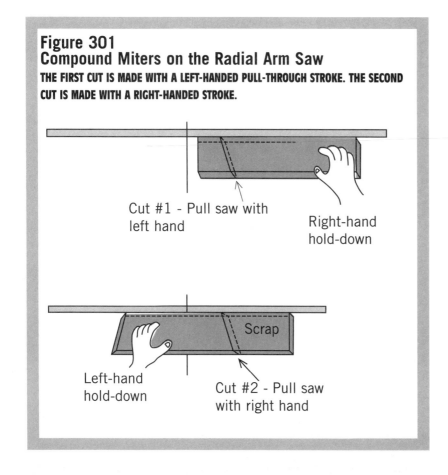

Figure 301
Compound Miters on the Radial Arm Saw
THE FIRST CUT IS MADE WITH A LEFT-HANDED PULL-THROUGH STROKE. THE SECOND CUT IS MADE WITH A RIGHT-HANDED STROKE.

Cut #1 - Pull saw with left hand

Right-hand hold-down

Left-hand hold-down

Scrap

Cut #2 - Pull saw with right hand

Crown Molding

Crown molding is cut at each end with compound miters as if the molding were the sides of a large shadow box. Because of the long lengths, cutting crown molding on a table saw is really not feasible and is unwieldy on a radial arm saw. The 12 to 20-ft. lengths are usually cut right in the room where they are to be installed, either by hand, using a miter box and back saw, or with a chop saw. The following procedure is particularly suited to long pieces, like crown molding, but can also be used for small boxes and picture frames.

Miter Box

If the molding is 4 in. wide or less, you can use this method. Prepare a miter box big enough so the molding can tilt against the back wall and there's enough height left over to guide the handsaw blade (**Figure 302**). Attach a guide strip to the bottom of the box so that the molding is at the same angle in the box as it will be when it's nailed up in the room.

Place the molding in the box so that the bottom edge of the molding - the edge that will go against the wall of the room - rests against the back wall of the box. This will put the top edge of the molding - the edge that will go against the ceiling - on the bottom of the miter box.

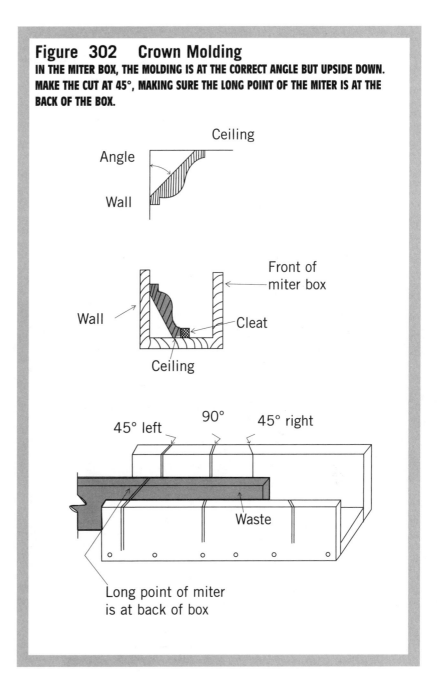

Figure 302   Crown Molding

IN THE MITER BOX, THE MOLDING IS AT THE CORRECT ANGLE BUT UPSIDE DOWN. MAKE THE CUT AT 45°, MAKING SURE THE LONG POINT OF THE MITER IS AT THE BACK OF THE BOX.

Ceiling

Angle

Wall

Front of miter box

Wall

Cleat

Ceiling

45° left   90°   45° right

Waste

Long point of miter is at back of box

By holding the molding in the box at the same angle it will be when attached to the wall - except upside down - we have taken care of the bevel. All we have to do now is cut the 45° miter. For a left-side corner of the room, swing the saw left or use the left 45° slot in the miter box. Be sure the long point of the miter is at the back of the box.

For a right-side corner of the room, swing the saw right or use the right 45° slot in the miter box. Again, be sure the long point of the miter is at the back of the box.

Miter Saw or Chop Saw

If it's so easy to cut crown molding with a hand saw and miter box or by tilting the molding against the fence and cutting it with a chop saw, then why go to the trouble of calculating compound miters? The reason is size. Most back saws have at the most 5 to 6-in. blades and thus can only cut molding up to maybe 4 in. wide. A 10-in. chop saw can cut molding up to about $4\frac{1}{2}$ in. wide. Crown molding comes in widths of $6\frac{1}{2}$ in., and even $8\frac{1}{2}$ in., so these require the molding be cut flat instead of tilted upright.

To calculate the miter and bevel angles of any crown molding (**Figure 303**), hold the molding to the inside of a framing square and measure distances 'A' and 'B' to the nearest $\frac{1}{16}$ in. In the figure, A = $2\frac{3}{8}$ (2.375) and B = $1\frac{13}{16}$ (1.8125).

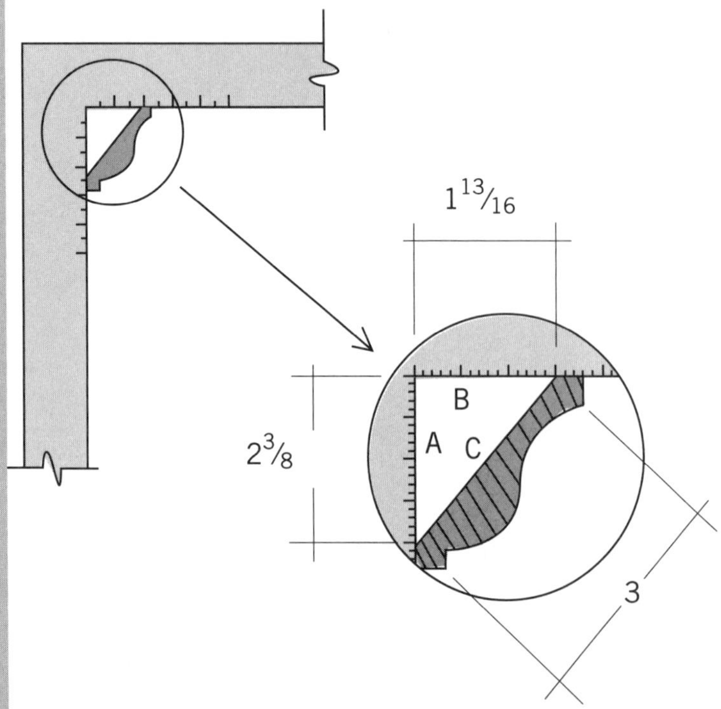

Line 'C' can be measured or calculated.

$C = \sqrt{[A^2 + B^2]}$
$C = \sqrt{(2.375)^2 + (1.8125)^2}$
$C = \sqrt{[5.6406 + 3.2852]}$
$C = \sqrt{8.9258} = 2.9876 \approx 3.0$ in.

Miter Angle

Arctan = (B ÷ C)
$= (1.8125 \div 3.0)$
$= 0.6042$
arctan 0.6042 = 31.1
Miter Angle = 31.1°

Bevel Angle

Arcsin = A ÷ (1.41 x C)
$= 2.375 \div (1.41 \times 3.0)$
$= 2.375 \div 4.23$
arcsin 0.5615 = 34.2
Bevel Angle = 34.2°

The chop saw should be set at 31.1° miter and 34.2° bevel. As long as you use molding with the same dimensions, the saw settings will work in any four-cornered room. Because the miters and bevels are so difficult to envision, I would recommend you make some "golden examples," i.e., left- and right-side pieces for both inside and outside corners. Label these 12-in. sections of molding clearly – "left inside" with edges marked "ceiling," "wall," etc. Guard these pieces with your life until the job is over. Ruining a 20-ft. piece of molding because of a wrong cut means another trip to the lumber yard and, at a cost of $10 to $20 per foot, a lot of money wasted.

Figure 303 Finding the Angles for Crown Molding
HOLD THE MOLDING TO A SQUARE AND MEASURE DISTANCES 'A' AND 'B'. DISTANCE 'C' CAN BE MEASURED OR CALCULATED.

CHAPTER 30

Furniture Dimensions

Once you decide on the piece of furniture you're going to make, figuring out how big it should be is the next order of business. This chapter will help you in this regard - the drawings and chart can be used as a general guide to furniture sizes. Some of the dimensions are an average and some are given as a range.

A few years ago the average person in the United States was 68.8 inches tall (5'10") and 172 pounds for men and 63.6 inches (5'-3$\frac{1}{2}$") and 145 pounds for women. The charts and drawings in this chapter are based on these sizes.

Furniture made for general sale must stay within narrow dimension limits, i.e. stay close to the national sizes. You are under no such restrictions. Scale your furniture project up or down depending on the size of the person you're building it for. Some questions you should consider.

• Who is the furniture for? Is the piece for a tall, heavy man, for a short woman, or for a child?

• Where will it go? A piece for a teenager's rec room will be built heavier than a piece for Aunt Eva's parlor.

Fig. 304 Standard Furniture Dimensions (in.)

TABLES	Height	Width	Length
Bedside	26	15	19
Buffet	34-38	24	60
Card	30	36	36
Coffee	19	18	36 - 48
Conference	30	36	96
Dining	29	40	64
End	20	17	28
Hall	27	15	55
Kitchen	29	36	60
Picnic	28	36	72
Poker	29	48	48
Printer	26	22	26
Sofa	26	14	72
Typewriter	25	18	30
Workstation	26	30	48

MATTRESSES	Height	Width	Length
Double	8	54	75
Queen	8	60	80
King (Calif)	10	72	84
King (East)	10	80	80
Twin Regular	6	39	75
Twin Long	6	39	80

CHESTS	Height	Width	Depth
Lowboy (incl 7" leg)	36	36	18
Tall chest (incl. 6" leg)	54	36	18
Bookcase (paperbacks)	38	36	7
Bookcase (clothbound)	50	36	10
Blanket	24	36	19
Cedar	20	40	19
Buffet	34	50	20

CHAIRS	Seat Width	Seat Depth	Seat Height	Back Height
Barstool	17	17	30	42
Dining, Side	19	19	18	36
Dining, Arm	24	18	18	36
Easy	25	26	17	31
Kitchen	19	19	19	34
Kitchen Stool	12	12	27	
Rocker	20	26	16	42
Upholstered	30	26	16	40

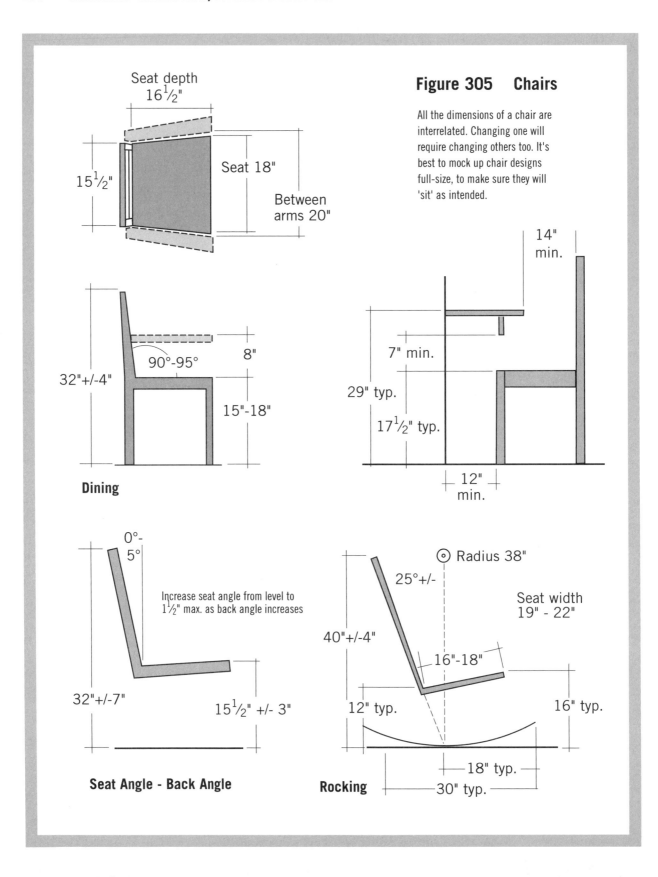

Seat depth
16 1/2"

Seat 18"

15 1/2"

Between
arms 20"

Figure 305   Chairs

All the dimensions of a chair are
interrelated. Changing one will
require changing others too. It's
best to mock up chair designs
full-size, to make sure they will
'sit' as intended.

14"
min.

90°-95°

8"

32"+/-4"

15"-18"

Dining

7" min.

29" typ.

17 1/2" typ.

12"
min.

0°-
5°

Increase seat angle from level to
1 1/2" max. as back angle increases

32"+/-7"

15 1/2" +/- 3"

Seat Angle - Back Angle

Radius 38"

25°+/-

Seat width
19" - 22"

40"+/-4"

16"-18"

12" typ.

16" typ.

18" typ.

30" typ.

Rocking

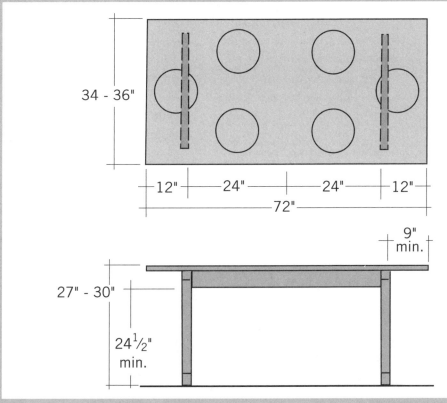

Figure 306
Dining Table

Table height and seating closeness both affect the dining atmosphere. A high table (30") with extra elbow room feels formal. A low table (27") with snug seating feels intimate. For comfortable seating, allow 24" per person. For chairs with arms, allow 26" to 28". For snug seating, allow 21" per person.

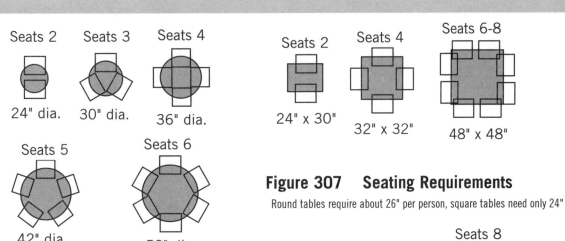

Figure 307   Seating Requirements

Round tables require about 26" per person, square tables need only 24"

• What other furniture is in the room? A petite Chippendale end table in mahogany might look out of place next to a white oak Arts-and Crafts arm chair. Tailor the piece to your own specifics.

• What is the function of the piece? Ian Kirby once suggested one should try to fuse "the functional, spiritual, structural and detail design aspects into a harmonious whole." Size is an integral part of each of these aspects.

Chair Anatomy

All the dimensions of a chair are interrelated. Changing one dimension will require

changing others too. **Figure 305** shows how the various parts of a chair relate to each other. If you increase the back tilt, you'll also have to tilt and lower the seat. Arm chairs that slide up to and under a dining table must have clearance under the table apron; chairs may later be fitted with glides and floor protection pads under the legs, and a close tolerance may change to no clearance.

Tables and Chairs

It is most important that tables are made big enough so that diners have enough room. A round table conserves space more efficiently than a square

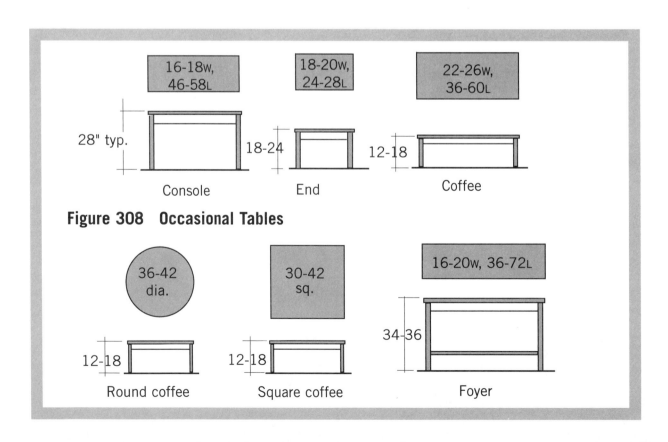

Figure 308   Occasional Tables

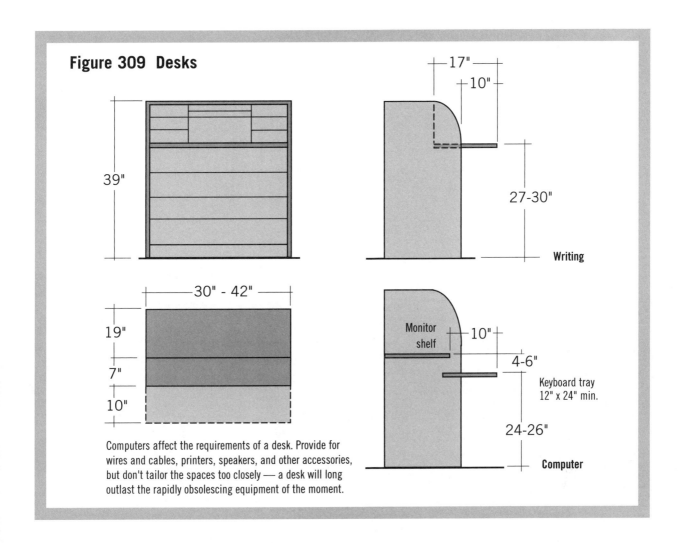

Figure 309 Desks

39"

30" - 42"

19"

7"

10"

17"

10"

27-30"

Writing

Monitor shelf

10"

4-6"

Keyboard tray
12" x 24" min.

24-26"

Computer

Computers affect the requirements of a desk. Provide for wires and cables, printers, speakers, and other accessories, but don't tailor the spaces too closely — a desk will long outlast the rapidly obsolescing equipment of the moment.

or rectangle (**Figure 306**). At a round table all persons have equal space while at square and rectangle tables the corners interfere.

The placement of the table legs also affects how easy it is to pull a chair up. Tables with pedestals and legs moved towards the center facilitate chair placement.

Dining Tables

Table height and seating closeness both affect the dining atmosphere. When figuring out how much room to allow for chairs, allow 24 in. per person for regular chairs and 26 to 28 in. for arm chairs (**Figure 306**). There should be 7 in. thigh space between the seat of a chair and the table apron. Dining table height varies from 27" to 30", and has a tremendous impact on how the table feels. High tables and chairs feel formal, while lower ones encourage relaxation and conviviality.

Desks

A desk for a student's bedroom will be smaller than a desk for an office. In the likely event that the desk will be used for a computer, remember to provide holes for cables and wires in the rear. **Figure 309** shows a desk to be used for writing with an added keyboard tray.

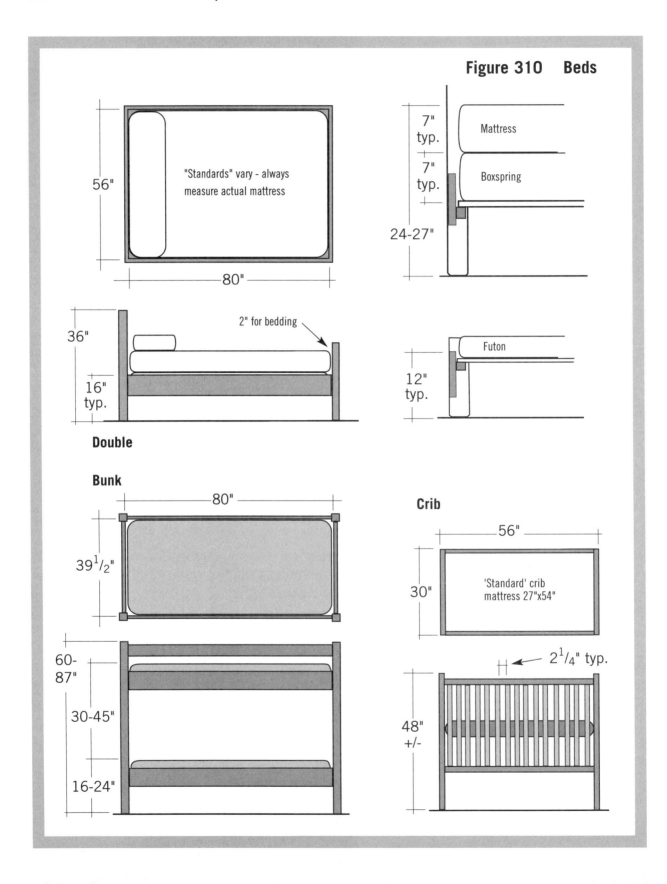

Figure 310   Beds

"Standards" vary - always measure actual mattress

56"

80"

7" typ.   Mattress

7" typ.   Boxspring

24-27"

36"

2" for bedding

16" typ.

Double

12" typ.   Futon

Bunk

80"

39 1/2"

60-87"

30-45"

16-24"

Crib

56"

30"   'Standard' crib mattress 27"x54"

2 1/4" typ.

48" +/-

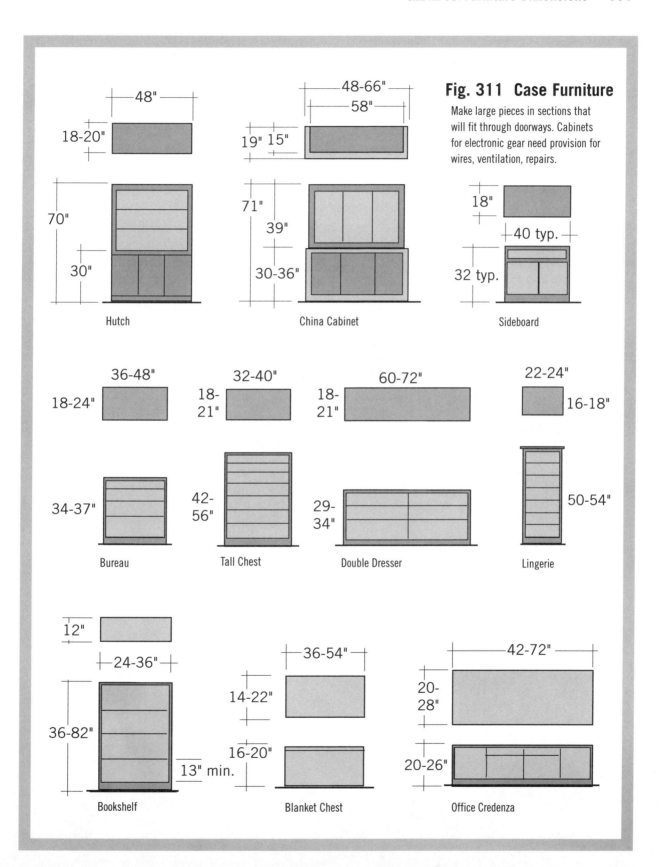

Fig. 311 Case Furniture

Make large pieces in sections that will fit through doorways. Cabinets for electronic gear need provision for wires, ventilation, repairs.

48"
18-20"
70"
30"
Hutch

48-66"
58"
19" 15"
71"
39"
30-36"
China Cabinet

18"
40 typ.
32 typ.
Sideboard

36-48"
18-24"
34-37"
Bureau

32-40"
18-21"
42-56"
Tall Chest

60-72"
18-21"
29-34"
Double Dresser

22-24"
16-18"
50-54"
Lingerie

12"
24-36"
36-82"
13" min.
Bookshelf

36-54"
14-22"
16-20"
Blanket Chest

42-72"
20-28"
20-26"
Office Credenza

Beds

Beds are usually made for a box spring and mattress. Whether the box spring is hidden within the side rails or is fully visible (**Figure 310**), the sleeping elevation should be 24 to 27 inches. Not only are mattresses made in various sizes, **Figure 310,** but also mattresses of the same size may differ in depth. It's best to have the mattresses on hand before you begin your design.

In children's cribs, the spacing between slats must not exceed $2^1/_4$ inch by federal safety law. The crib design should also provide a means whereby the mattress can be progressively lowered as the child grows and becomes able to stand up in the bed.

Case Furniture

Case furniture such as bookcases, credenzas, dressers and chests are large pieces that usually can be made in sections that will fit through doorways and are easier for the woodworker to manage in the shop. **Figure 311** shows typical sizes. Bookcases that fit the books closely leave less space for dust to collect; 13 inches is a good general shelf interval that will fit most hardcover books.

Upholstered Furniture

The dimensions of upholstered furniture are quite variable. Seat and armrest heights of sofas should be considered together so the armrest won't be too high above the seat. If the chair or sofa is being designed for a small person, reduce the typical seat depth of 21 to 22 inches to 19 to 20 inches so the front edge won't hit the back of the leg at the knee, which otherwise forces short people to slide forward. Upholstered seats generally slope 1 inch from front to back. A word with the upholsterer will determine how big to make the underlying skeleton.

Children's Furniture

The dimensions in **Figure 312** should be used as a guide only — a five-year-old will require a much smaller chair and table than a sixth grader, even though the proportions remain about the same. Rounded, smoothed edges and a washable, crayon-proof finish are important.

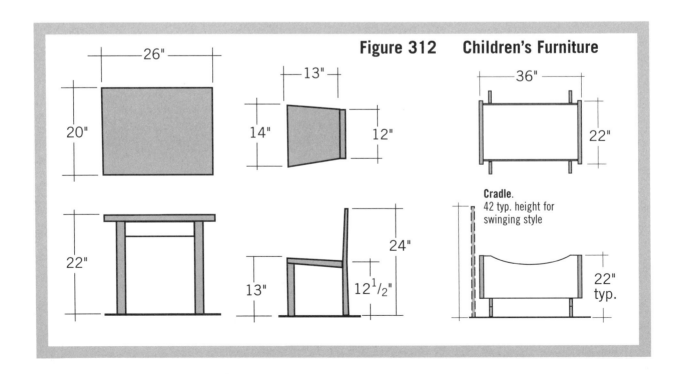

Figure 312   **Children's Furniture**

Cradle. 42 typ. height for swinging style

Useful Tables

Every project of this complexity ends with a left-over pile of short ends — information that didn't quite fit anywhere. In order to make this book as complete as possible, it's included here.

Figure 313
General Conversions

To Convert	To	Multiply By
Cubic Centimeters	Cubic Inches	14.5
Cubic Feet	Cubic Meters	0.0283
Cubic Feet	Liters	28.317
Cubic Feet	Cubic Inches	1728
Cubic Feet/Min	Pounds Air/Hour	4.5
Cubic Inches	Cubic Millimeters	16,387
Cubic Inches	Liters	0.01639
Cubic Inches	Cubic Feet	0.0006
Cubic Meters	Cubic Feet	35.31
Feet	Centimeters	30.48
Feet	Meters	0.3048
Feet	Millimeters	304.8
Gallons	Liters	3.785
Inches of Mercury	Pounds/sq in	0.4912
Inches of Water	Pounds/sq in	0.03613
Pounds/sq in	Inches of Water	27.7
Square Feet	Square Inches	144
Square Inches	Square Feet	0.0069
Ounces/Inch	Pounds/Inch	0.0625
Ounces/Sq In	Pounds/Sq In	0.0039
Miles	Feet	5280
Acres	Sq Feet	43,560
Square Yard	Sq Feet	9
Inch	Centimeters	2.54
Meter	Inches	39.37
Cubic Yard	Cubic Feet	27

Fig. 314 Specific Gravity and Weights of Woods

Wood (Seasoned)	Specific Gravity	Weight (lbs per cu ft)
Apple	0.66 - 0.84	41 - 52
Ash	0.65 - 0.85	40 - 53
Balsa	0.11 - 0.14	7 - 9
Basswood	0.32 - 0.39	20 - 37
Beech	0.70 - 0.90	43 - 56
Birch	0.51 - 0.77	32 - 48
Blue Gum	1	62
Box	0.95 - 1.16	59 - 72
Butternut	0.38	24
Ebony	1.11 - 1.33	69 - 83
Greenheart	1.06 - 1.23	66 - 77
Hickory	0.60 - 0.93	37 - 58
Ironwood	1.08	67
Lignum Vitae	1.17 - 1.33	73 - 83
Mahogany, Honduran	0.66	41
Mahogany, Spanish	0.85	53
Maple	0.62 - 0.75	39 - 47
Oak	0.60 - 0.90	37 - 56
Pine, Pitch	0.83 - 0.85	52 - 53
Pine, White	0.35 - 0.50	22 - 31
Pine, Yellow	0.37 - 0.60	23 - 37
Redwood	0.44	27
Satinwood	0.95	59
Spruce	0.48 - 0.70	30 - 44
Teak, African	0.98	61
Teak, Indian	0.66 - 0.88	41 - 55
Walnut	0.64 - 0.70	40 - 43
Willow	0.40 - 0.60	24 - 37

Figure 315   English System Units to Metric Metric Units to English System

To Convert From	Multiply By	To Get	To Convert From	Multiply By	To Get
Inches	25.4	Millimeters	Millimeters	0.0394	Inches
Inches	2.54	Centimeters	Centimeters	0.3937	Inches
Feet	30.48	Centimeters	Centimeters	0.0328	Feet
Feet	0.3048	Meters	Meters	3.2808	Feet
Yards	0.9144	Meters	Meters	1.0936	Yards
Miles	1.6093	Kilometers	Kilometers	0.6214	Miles
Square Inches	6.4516	Square Centimeters	Square Centimeters	0.155	Square Inches
Square Feet	0.0929	Square Meters	Square Meters	10.764	Square Feet
Square Yards	0.8361	Square Meters	Square Meters	1.196	Square Yards
Acres	0.4047	Hectares	Hectares	2.4711	Acres
Square Miles	2.5899	Square Kilometers	Square Kilometers	0.3861	Square Miles
Cubic Inches	16.387	Cubic Centimeters	Cubic Centimeters	0.061	Cubic Inches
Cubic Feet	0.0283	Cubic Meters	Cubic Meters	35.315	Cubic Feet
Cubic Feet	28.316	Liters	Liters	0.0353	Cubic Feet
Cubic Yards	0.7646	Cubic Meters	Cubic Meters	1.3079	Cubic Yards
Cubic Yards	764.55	Liters	Liters	0.0013	Cubic Yards
Fluid Ounces	29.574	Milliliters	Milliliters	0.0338	Fluid Ounces
Cups	0.2366	Liters	Liters	4.2268	Cups
Pints	0.4732	Liters	Liters	2.1134	Pints
Quarts	0.9464	Liters	Liters	1.0567	Quarts
Gallons	3.7854	Liters	Liters	0.2642	Gallons
Pints	0.5506	Liters	Liters	1.8162	Pints
Quarts	1.1012	Liters	Liters	0.9081	Quarts
Pecks	8.8098	Liters	Liters	0.1135	Pecks
Bushels	35.239	Liters	Liters	0.0284	Bushels
Bushels	3.5239	Dekaliters	Dekaliters	0.2838	Bushels
Drams	1.7718	Grams	Grams	0.5644	Drams
Ounces	28.35	Grams	Grams	0.0353	Ounces
Pounds	0.4536	Kilograms	Kilograms	2.2046	Pounds
Fahrenheit	-32 X 5/9	Centigrade	Centigrade	x 9/5 + 32	Fahrenheit

Figure 316   Decimal and Millimeter Equivalents

4ths	8ths	16ths	32nds	64ths	dec.	Milli-meters	4ths	8ths	16ths	32nds	64ths	dec.	Milli-meters
				1/64	0.016	0.397					33/64	0.516	13.097
			1/32		0.031	0.794				17/32		0.531	13.494
				3/64	0.047	1.191					35/64	0.547	13.891
		1/16			0.063	1.588			9/16			0.563	14.288
				5/64	0.078	1.984					37/64	0.578	14.684
			3/32		0.094	2.381				19/32		0.594	15.081
				7/64	0.109	2.778					39/64	0.609	15.478
	1/8				0.125	3.175		5/8				0.625	15.875
				9/64	0.141	3.572					41/64	0.641	16.272
			5/32		0.156	3.969				21/32		0.656	16.669
				11/64	0.172	4.366					43/64	0.672	17.066
	3/16				0.188	4.763			11/16			0.688	17.463
				13/64	0.203	5.159					45/64	0.703	17.859
			7/32		0.219	5.556				23/32		0.719	18.256
				15/64	0.234	5.953					47/64	0.734	18.653
1/4					0.250	6.350	3/4					0.750	19.050
				17/64	0.266	6.747					49/64	0.766	19.447
			9/32		0.281	7.144				25/32		0.781	19.844
				19/64	0.297	7.541					51/64	0.797	20.241
		5/16			0.313	7.938			13/16			0.813	20.638
				21/64	0.328	8.334					53/64	0.828	21.034
			11/32		0.344	8.731				27/32		0.844	21.431
				23/64	0.359	9.128					55/64	0.859	21.828
	3/8				0.375	9.525		7/8				0.875	22.225
				25/64	0.391	9.922					57/64	0.891	22.622
			13/32		0.406	10.319				29/32		0.906	23.019
				27/64	0.422	10.716					59/64	0.922	23.416
		7/16			0.438	11.113			15/16			0.938	23.813
				29/64	0.453	11.509					61/64	0.953	24.209
			15/32		0.469	11.906				31/32		0.969	24.606
				31/64	0.484	12.303					63/64	0.984	25.003
1/2					0.500	12.700	1					1.000	25.400

Figure 317
Common Nails

Size	Length (Inches)	Nails per Lb
2d	1	900
3d	1-1/4	615
4d	1-1/2	322
5d	1-3/4	254
6d	2	200
7d	2-1/4	154
8d	2-1/2	106
9d	2-3/4	85
10d	3	74
12d	3-1/4	57
16d	3-1/2	46
20d	4	29
30d	4-1/2	24
40d	5	18
50d	5-1/2	14
60d	6	11

Figure 318
Finishing Nails

Size	Length (Inches)	Nails per Lb
2d	1	1,350
3d	1-1/4	807
4d	1-1/2	585
5d	1-3/4	500
6d	2	310
8d	2-1/2	190
10d	3	120
18d	3-1/2	90
20d	4	60

Casing Nails

Size	Length (Inches)	Nails per Lb
4d	1-1/2	490
6d	2	250
8d	2-1/2	140
10d	3	100
16d	3-1/2	75

Figure 319   Wood Screws

Gauge No.	2.	4	5	6	7	8	9	10	12	14
Body Dia.	0.086	0.112	0.125	0.138	0.151	0.164	0.177	0.190	0.216	0.242
Pilot Hole (Soft Wood)	3/64	1/16	5/64	5/64	3/32	3/32	7/64	7/64	1/8	9/64

Figure 320   Coated Abrasives

Super Fine	Extra Fine	Very Fine	Fine	Medium	Coarse	Very Coarse
600 (12/0)	320 (9/0)	220 (6/0)	150 (4/0)	80 (1/0)	50 (1)	30 (2-1/2)
400 (10/0)	280 (8/0)	180 (5/0)	120 (3/0)	60 (1/2)	40 (1-1/2)	24 (3)
	240 (7/0)		100 (2/0)		36 (2)	20 (3-1/2)
						16 (4)
						12 (4-1/2)

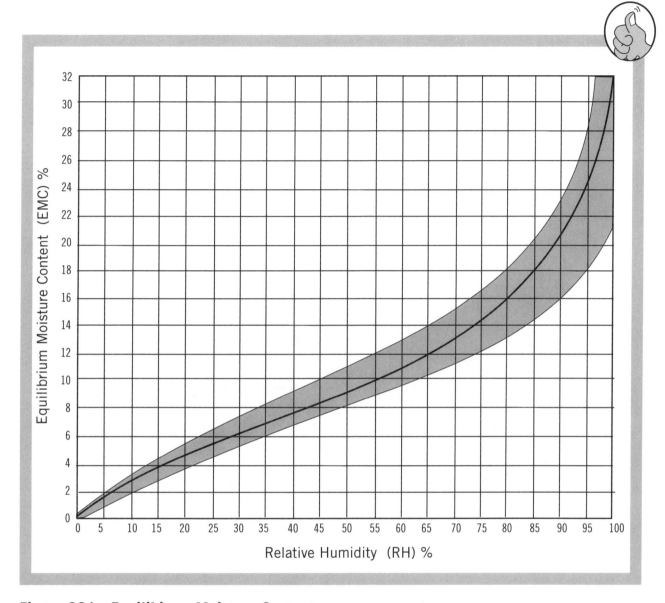

Figure 321   Equilibirum Moisture Content

IF YOU KNOW THE RELATIVE HUMIDITY OF THE ATMOSPHERE, YOU CAN ESTIMATE THE MOIS-
TURE CONTENT OF SEASONED WOOD. THE HEAVY LINE REPRESENTS WHITE SPRUCE; MOST
DOMESTIC SOFTWOODS AND HARDWOODS FALL INTO THE GREY BAND. FOR STABLE CABINET-
MAKING, WOOD THAT HAS BEEN DRIED TO THE 6% TO 8% RANGE SHOULD BE STORED AT
HUMIDITY LOWER THAN 50%. WHEN THE HUMIDITY RISES, THE WOOD WILL SLOWLY ABSORB
MOISTURE, AND ITS DIMENSIONS WILL INCREASE. THIS CHART IS ADAPTED FROM BRUCE
HOADLEY'S CLASSIC BOOK UNDERSTANDING WOOD.

Index

Published by Cambium Press, Bethel CT USA

Publisher & Editor: John Kelsey
Copy editor: Janet Jemmott
Design: Peggy Bloomer
Illustrations: Ken Horner with Bran Chapman and John Kelsey

Text font: Garamond Book
Caption font: Antique Olive, Trade Gothic

Printer: Phoenix Color
Paper: Tradebook antique white

CAMBIUM PRESS

PO Box 909   Bethel, CT 06801
phone 800-238-7724   fax 203-778 2785   www.cambiumpress.com

APPEARANCE & REALITY:
A Visual Handbook for Artists, Designers, and Makers
Stephen Hogbin

This new design handbook goes beyond tired Modernism. Hogbin examines the fundamentals of line, form, color, and pattern, then moves on to investigate such broader issues as context, gender, community, region, the enviornment, and cultural diversity - which together govern the meaning conveyed by the made object. Essential for students and important for mature designers.

list price $29.95
192 pgs, 8.5 x 10, color, paperback, ISBN 1-892836-05-X

NATURE AND AESTHETICS OF DESIGN

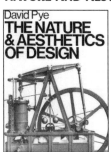

David Pye

Prof. Pye establishes a basic theory of design, in a lucid style and in jargon-free language. This book is of special importance to crafts artists, for Pye himself was an architect, industrial designer, and woodworker. He illuminates the issues confronting every thoughtful maker.

list price $22.95
160 pgs, 8.5x11, b&w, pbk, ISBN 0-9643999-1-1

NATURE AND ART OF WORKMANSHIP

David Pye

In a mechanized age, does it make any sense to work with hand tools when machines can do the same job? Cutting through a century of fuzzy thinking, Prof. Pye proposes a new theory based on the concepts of "workmanship of risk", and "workmanship of certainty."

list price $22.95
160 pgs, 8.5x11, b&w, pbk, ISBN 0-9643999-0-3

CABINETMAKING PROCEDURES FOR THE SMALL SHOP

Kevin Fristad & John Ward

Here's an updated rundown on how commercial cabinetshops work, with advice for the ameteur as well as for the professional. Emphasizes practical standards, smart planning, accurate measurements, and organized workflow.

list price $21.95
128 pgs., 8x10, b&w, paperback, ISBN 1-892836-11-4

SHOP DRAWINGS FOR CRAFTSMAN FURNITURE
27 Stickley Designs for Every Room in the Home
list price $22.95
144 pp, 8.5 x 11, b&w, pbk.
ISBN 1-892836-12-2

MORE SHOP DRAWINGS FOR CRAFTSMAN FURNITURE
30 Stickley Designs for Every Room in the Home
list price $22.95
144 pp, 8.5 x 11, b&w, pbk.
SBN 1-892836-14-9

Robert W.Lang

Here, at last, are accurate shop drawings of Stickley Craftsman furniture. Woodworker Bob Lang has sought authentic Craftsman antiques for measuring. Each project is complete with dimensioned orthographic views, details and sections, plus a cutting list. Projects include tables, chairs, bureaus, armoires, bookcases, desks, and plant stands. Technical introduction.

WITH WAKENED HANDS:
Furniture by James Krenov and Students
James Krenov

Krenov has been silent for the past 15 years, quietly working and teaching at the College of the Redwoods in Fort Bragg, CA. Now he is ready to share photos of his own recent work, alongside that of his students, with his thoughts about it.

136 pages, 8.5 x 11, 225 color photographs
paperback list price $29.95 ISBN 1-892836-06-8
hardcover list price $39.95 ISBN 1-892836-07-6

TRADITION IN CONTEMPORARY FURNITURE
[Furniture Studio Two]

Great furniture speaks in many ways. Materials and colors and textures, form and function - great furniture enriches daily life, contributing ease, order and visual harmony to the contemporary interior. The essays in this volume link current work to the grand furniture traditions. Includes gallery of best new work by Furniture Society members.

list price $30.00
144 pgs, 9x12, color, paperback with flaps ISBN 0-9671004-1-0